A Stream of Windows

A Stream of Windows

Unsettling Reflections on Trade, Immigration, and Democracy

Jagdish Bhagwati

The MIT Press
Cambridge, Massachusetts
London, England

This book was set in Palatino on the Monotype "Prism Plus" PostScript Imagesetter by Asco Trade Typesetting Ltd., Hong Kong.

Printed and bound in the United States of America.

Library of Congress Cataloging-in-Publication Data

Bhagwati, Jagdish N., 1934–
  A stream of windows : unsettling reflections on trade,
  immigration, and democracy / Jagdish Bhagwati.
     p.   cm.
  Includes bibliographical references and index.
  ISBN 0-262-02440-3 (hc : alk. paper)
  1. Free trade. 2. Protectionism. 3. United States—Emigration
and immigration. 4. United States—Foreign economic relations—
Japan. 5. Japan—Foreign economic relations—United States.
6. Democracy. I. Title.
HF1713.B472   1998
337.73—dc21   97-35314
                                                           CIP

Contents

Preface

I have run up a debt to many friends, especially editors and columnists at the *New York Times*, the *New Republic*, the *Economist*, and the *Financial Times*, who have encouraged me over the years to write in the public domain. It would, however, be invidious to cite and titillate a few when many can be identified with ease by the reader.

My greatest debt is to my wife, Padma Desai. She runs an excruciatingly busy career. As the Gladys and Roland Harriman Professor of Comparative Economics at Columbia, she teaches through the year while steadily producing scholarly research on the Soviet and now Russian economy. She also maintains a public persona in the leading print and television media on Russia's economic misfortunes. She has nonetheless found the energy to manage the household and the patience to put up with my manifold activities. It is small recompense, but a measure of my love and gratitude, for me to dedicate this book to her. I also dedicate it to our daughter, Anuradha Kristina, who is majoring in English literature at Yale and is doubtless amused, given her far greater gift for writing, by her parents' heroic attempts at making the dismal science palatable to the wider public.

I should add a word on the title I have chosen. It comes from a poem by James Schuyler. "A stream of windows" is a fetching metaphor. A stream, suggesting fluidity in contrast to a pool in place, conveys the essence of the writings collected here: they challenge, probe, and question. Schuyler's lovely phrase evokes yet another apt and reinforcing image: I have sought, in what I have written, to throw the windows open to let in fresh air, even gusts of gale.

Introduction

The essays, op-eds, reviews, and letters to the editor in this volume have been selected from my policy writings during the past ten years. They share in common a passion and a temperament, a strategy to access and influence public policy, and an agenda to advance.

The Passion: Active Advocacy

The passion reflects my conviction that, in a social science such as economics, those who work at the frontiers of the science should also get down into the trenches of public policy in the only way they can: through advocacy. The best economists have always done this, and some have even distinguished themselves with a pen touched by wit and elegance.

John Maynard Keynes remains the twentieth century's compelling example. Our superstars also fit the mold: Nobel laureates Paul Samuelson, Robert Solow, Milton Friedman, and James Tobin are among the economists whom most literate readers of our newspapers and magazines will have no difficulty recognizing as engaged and engaging gladiators in the arena when the great policy debates reck Washington.

In fact, nineteenth-century Britain, which produced several important economists such as David Ricardo, John Stuart Mill, and

Robert Torrens who developed vigorously the discipline that Adam Smith had founded, was witness to an astonishing sym- biosis between the great economists of the time and the policy- makers. My Columbia student, Douglas Irwin of the University of Chicago, a gifted young historian of the vicissitudes of the doc- trine of free trade, has reminded us that the Hansard, the record of British parliamentary debates, reveals an extraordinary input by economists into those debates, with the latest writings on the principles of political economy—closely tied to the policy issues of the day—finding their way immediately into the members' speeches on these questions.[1] In consequence, prime ministers such as Peel and Disraeli were impressively better informed on economics than modern politicians, including even such policy aficionados as President Clinton.

The Temperament: Being Contrary and Probing Deep

The temperament that informs the writings here is one of con- trariness. Ever since I turned to economics as an undergraduate in Cambridge, England, in the mid-1950s, I have felt that an aca- demic scholar can best advance the public good by becoming a public nuisance.

Few others can do that without being heroic. Politicians must play to their constituencies. Bureaucrats cannot forget the politi- cians. Think tanks must seek funds to survive. All must mind their manners, trim their sails, and bend to the wind. Only pro- fessors have tenure, protecting them from the retribution that the indulgence of independence may bring. Indeed, that alone makes it an obligation, not just a luxury, for the academic scholars to break ranks, to cut through the fog of obfuscations that attends the politics of policymaking, to call a spade a spade, to say "oh, bunk!" when necessary, and to propose policies and advance agendas that reflection and analysis lead one to believe to be good and beneficial, even when they appear outlandish now and will bring one neglect, at best, and opprobrium, at worst.

The contrariness also requires in my view an ability and a willingness to probe systematically and patiently: a habit of mind that is best cultivated in the academe. One's public writings in pursuit of better policy must be informed by deep scholarship. The op-ed must be the tip of an iceberg sculpted by reflection and analysis. Therefore, I have not built a wall between my research and my policy writing, between my academic and my public persona. Nearly all my scientific work has been on the theory of policy, much of it again on the theory of trade policy. It has informed, and in turn been stimulated by, my policy interests and writings. Indeed, while I select here only my public writings, they form a seamless tapestry with my scientific work: as was the case most remarkably with utilitarians James and John Stuart Mill, whose important writings in political economy and in related fields of inquiry such as logic informed their public writings advancing reform in England's body politic, while their impassioned efforts at reform prompted in turn the deeper reflections that they are better known for today.

Thus, op-eds on issues such as managed trade and aggressive unilateralism, where I castigate the Clinton administration and its allies, reflect deeper research on the subject, available in articles in professional journals and volumes written for my professional peers. Again, the writings on fair trade owe much to the ideas developed in my two-volume publication *Fair Trade and Harmonization: Prerequisites for Free Trade?* (MIT Press, 1996) and the result of a research project involving several international economists and lawyers of different political persuasions over three years that Professor Robert Hudec of the Minnesota Law School and I directed.

It is not arrogance, but an overriding sense of despair at the state of public policy writing by economists who are quick on the draw but have not bothered to think deeply and carefully about a burning issue of the day—captured in my *American Enterprise* essay (chapter 48)—which makes me point the finger at times at those who may be soldiers in the battles on my side but whose ammunition embarrasses me. I am afraid that I have no patience with economists whose conclusions are more obvious than their arguments. They corrupt the policy discourse when the crying need is to improve it. As I argue in Part Nine, Democracy and Its Contents, you weaken the sinews of democracy when you do this.

Take one example. Did we really need the economist allies of the North American Free Trade Agreement to claim speciously, when economic analysis tells you that trade could not generally speaking affect (total) employment, that employment would increase thanks to NAFTA? Either they were incompetent, which is a charge hard to maintain since the error is elementary, or they were unwittingly or wittingly playing political games. Scholarship will clearly not guarantee that such a travesty will be avoided; but scholarship should minimize the travesty's occurrence if for no other reason than that scholars would have more to lose from public displays of illogic and folly and that the standards of scrutiny they face in their work are fairly stringent.

The Strategy: Multiple Assaults

But the passion to advance an agenda, especially one that leans to contrariness, will not suffice. It must be matched by an ability to take today's multiplicity of media and sources of influence on public policy and exploit them successfully to influence the shape of events. That is, of course, an extraordinarily difficult task.

The Swedes tell how, when television arrived, Bertil Ohlin, who then headed the Liberal Party, was expected to make a clean sweep: he was a man of great good looks—a reflective rather than romantic Robert Redford—and a great economist who would later win the Nobel Prize. But his presence on TV turned out to be somewhat wooden, a trifle too intellectual, costing him when the world thought he would collect.

In my own pursuit of policy, I have tried to work with virtually all the instrumentalities that would help shape policy. I confess, I work better in the print media, where I am able to develop a sustained argument with necessary nuances in my own language, than on television, where it is generally harder to do so. But I am convinced that everything helps. Here I differ reluctantly from my remarkable MIT pupil, Paul Krugman, who has written, in the preface to his essays in *Pop Internationalism* (MIT Press, 1996) of his writing for magazines such as *Foreign Affairs*, at some length, as a novel and the only effective way to influence policy.

So, to give a glimpse of the vast landscape on which one can operate today in propagating one's ideas, I shall risk being charged with self-indulgence and sketch now the various ways in which I have pursued my policy agendas. In so doing, I seek to give the reader both a closer glimpse of the way intellectuals today must advance policy agendas and a coherent view of the contents of this volume.

In television, I have occasionally appeared in snippets that allow only soundbites. True, these are more exhilarating to your mother and your friends than they are useful aids in advancing your agenda. But often, you can give a huge audience a small glimpse of a contrary viewpoint in a story that is otherwise heavily slanted in favor of the policy you deplore. It is not a chance you want to sneeze at. Thus, right after the car dispute between Japan and the United States had been settled in Geneva and U.S. Trade Representative Mickey Kantor had fully retreated in an ignominious defeat (as forecast in the op-eds reprinted here as chapters 19 and 20 and as demonstrated bluntly in the long essay in chapter 21), the disinformation apparatchiks of the Clinton administration, whose ceaseless activities make you think of the famous purgative ad, "It works while you sleep," had begun their new assignment in earnest in Washington. When CNN gave me a spot to talk briefly about the agreement right after, I could quickly insert the truth of the matter into the program and even say that, while the Japanese firmness and the resulting U.S. failure greatly pleased me as an economist, I was unhappy as an American: the defeat, brought about by incompetent bureaucrats and hard-driving lobbyists pursuing manifestly foolish tactics hand in hand, was humiliating.

But television also has programs that enable you to develop a viewpoint more systematically. Here, CNN and the *MacNeil-Lehrer News Hour* have given me occasional opportunities, which I have always found it useful to accept.

This is true also of radio, which I myself do not hear any more, as I no longer keep a car and therefore do not need to sit in commuter traffic with the radio on. The reason, of course, is that since 1980 I have been teaching at Columbia and living in Manhattan, where keeping a car is foolhardy and unnecessary. I now realize the full force of the story that sociologist Daniel Bell told me about how he too used to live on Claremont Avenue as we do, in a university apartment, and walk or take cabs or the subway. Once, an aunt, very competitive with Dan's side of the family, was visiting him when Dan decided to go out, saying he would take a cab from around the corner at Broadway. "You mean you do not own a car?" asked the aunt. "No," said Dan. "Ah," came the cry of accusatory joy from the aunt, "you do not live in a house; you do not have a car either. I always knew that you were not a professor at Columbia University!" Yes, I have had some fine, extended debates and interviews on National Public Radio, in particular; NPR is indeed a national treasure.

But the print media offer the best choices, and a rich menu of possibilities, that I have fully exploited in advancing my policy agendas, as indeed the selections in this volume suggest.

I have used op-eds in several newspapers, chiefly the *New York Times*, the *Wall Street Journal*, and the *Financial Times*, but also in the *Economist*, the *Christian Science Monitor*, and the *Boston Globe*. Frequently, I have also written, where specific foreign audiences were critical to an issue, in newspapers and magazines such as the *Far Eastern Economic Review, Nikkei* (Japan's *Wall Street Journal*), and *India Today* (India's *Time*). While the space allowed varies across those outlets, all enable one to develop a sustained argument in support of a well-defined policy.

The short book reviews, like the ones reprinted here of Ross Perot's anti-NAFTA book in the *Wall Street Journal*, of Pat Choate's anti-Japan book in the *Detroit News*, and of George Soros's pro-Soros *Alchemy of Finance* in the *New Republic*, offer a similar, short format where one can skillfully hang one's thoughts on someone else's peg, while occasionally hanging the author himself, as I did in those instances.

Indeed, it is more satisfying when one can go to greater lengths with one's reviews. The *New Republic*, under the exceptional literary leadership of Leon Wieseltier, offers precisely this room to roam. There, I have published some of my best-known pieces, including a deconstruction of Laura Tyson's book (chapter 8) on confronting Japan and embracing industrial policy that got her the attention of Silicon Valley–indebted president-elect Clinton and subsequently the chairmanship of the Council of Economic Advisers.

Then there are the short articles that are reproduced here from magazines such as *Foreign Policy, Scientific American, Foreign Affairs, Challenge,* and the *American Enterprise*. They offer greater scope for more nuanced development of one's thoughts. But there are also truly long articles in magazines such as Chatham House's *International Affairs*, also reprinted here, where I published a full-scale post mortem of the U.S.-Japan car dispute and of its causes and consequences that I had only fleetingly touched upon in the op-eds that I had written as the dispute progressed to its denouement.

A forum that I have followed to advantage and that permits virtually limitless access—unlike op-eds that have an upper cap of three a year in many newspapers unless you are a regular columnist—is the Letters to the Editor column. Exploited with great success by influential economists in the nineteenthth century, for example, by John Stuart Mill, whose earliest public writings at the age of sixteen included letters to the *Traveller*, this form of writing has fallen into relative neglect today (though, I recall seeing my Cambridge teacher, Lord Kaldor, often in the Letters to the Editor columns in the *Times* of London and my Columbia colleague, the late Nobel laureate William Vickrey, with great frequency in the *New York Times*, both economists of great scientific distinction and influential in informing public policy as well).[2]

Letters are not merely an important, if constrained, way of making an incisive point that can illuminate and transform a policy debate. They are also a marvelous outlet for one's frustration at what one reads in the morning when one is fresh from a night's sleep and words flood a rested mind to readily match one's outrage. I have published many and select here only a few of those letters from newspapers such as the *New York Times* and the *Financial Times* and magazines such as the *Economist* and the *New Republic*. They put on the mat, chastising gently, our best journalists, such as James Fallows and Thomas Friedman, whom I much admire and whose policy transgressions, chiefly on trade with Japan, I therefore find yet more deserving of censure. They also expose the half-truths spread by celebrated lobbyists such as Jack Valenti in the cause of their clients, while coming down firmly on mistaken arguments by influential policy figures such as Fred Bergsten.

When it comes to the media, there are yet other ways in which one can access public opinion. Interviews and question and answer columns become an important outlet for one's views once one has crossed a threshold and is recognized. I have done many, in *Forbes*, in the *New York Times*, in *Newsweek*, in the *International Herald Tribune*, and in business magazines and newspapers in Europe, India, and the Far East. Here, I have included only one substantial interview from the U.S. magazine *Audacity* that ranges over a variety of trade policy issues of the day.

But one also gets one's views across if the leading economics columnists today decide to give one's ideas some play. I have had the good fortune to have interest taken in my policy and scientific writings by Leonard Silk and Peter Passell of the *New York Times*, Hobart Rowen of the *Washington Post*, Martin Wolf and Sam Brittan of the *Financial Times*, Clive Crook of the *Economist*, Bob Davis of the *Wall Street Journal*, and David Warsh of the *Boston Globe*, who must rank among the best and the brightest in the profession today. They have written on my work, some devoting whole columns to it at times—to my great delight.

Of course, there are the innumerable times these and lesser journalists call you up to discuss ideas with you and then cite your views. With the explosive growth of business pages in most newspapers today, this is a growing outlet. I do talk, like many others of my profession, to several journalists in that way; while they sometimes get you wrong, mostly they do not. The economists who blame the journalists for distorting their views are, in my experience, mostly scapegoating them for the errors of their own imprecise statements. On balance, this is a good use of your time if you want to canvass your views.

Since I get cited to my heart's content on things I do know, the only discipline I exercise is to say no when I am asked to comment on something that I do not know. Of course, I know many things as a consumer of economics; but I know only a few things as a producer of it. I believe that economists should talk only about the latter, since that is what the public expects when you are cited. When economists talk about matters they are not experts on, just to see their names in the newspapers, instead of telling the journalists whom instead to contact, they perpetrate a fraud on the public. Thus, I must confess I cringe, and even get mightily upset, when I see for instance a macroeconomist expressing shallow opinions on international trade in the media: this is for me the equivalent of dropping one's pants to attract attention. This is not "credentialism"; rather, it is a matter of discipline and obligation.

I should add that matters are wholly different, however, when one reviews books: nothing requires that the reviewer be as expert on a subject as the author. In fact, the talents required of a reviewer, in style and sensibility, are altogether different from those that make for an author. While some such as T. S. Eliot have given us both great poetry and glorious literary criticism, most reviewers and critics of distinction have not themselves created works in the genre where they practice their craft. And that is perfectly proper. As it happens, many of my longer reviews in the *New Republic*, as also the shorter ones in newspapers and magazines, are within a shouting distance of my expertise; but many others are not. And my most successful ones are not exclusively in the former group.

When one's policy writings are the tip of an iceberg of scholarship, as I seek to make them, one also has the advantage that public platforms will be provided through invitations to lectures that virtually guarantee large elite audiences. These can have an extraordinary influence in getting an idea into the public domain. Here, I reproduce two particularly apt examples of such writing. The Rajiv Gandhi Golden Jubilee Memorial Lecture (chapter 40) was one of four that were organized in New Delhi on the occasion of the late prime minister's fiftieth anniversary. I had been the third invited lecturer. The first two were Mrs. Thatcher and Mr. Gorbachev, so—since I had long campaigned for Indian reforms and hence was considered in India to be "on the right" by professional leftists—my favorite crack was that I was the most radical of them all! Unfortunately, the fourth lecture was then assigned to John Kenneth Galbraith, who had been ambassador to India under President Kennedy, so I lost both my cachet and my witticism. This lecture provided me with an apt occasion to talk about democracy and development. After all, India has been the most remarkable example of a functioning democracy—huge, multiethnic, and multireligious; and the economic issues relating to India's democratic ways had made me, and others, think about the subject matter since the early 1960s—nearly four decades ago.

The other is the Raul Prebisch Lecture (chapter 2) that I gave in Johannesburg. It had in the audience numerous ministers of trade and ambassadors to the international agencies in Geneva, the World Trade Organization, and the United Nations Conference on Trade and Development, because the lecture was under the auspices of UNCTAD at its ninth quadrennial conference. I could thus use the occasion to address some of the most compelling issues before the world trading system, in time for the WTO's important, first ministerial meeting in Singapore a few months later in December 1996.

I have turned yet other lectures into short, accessible policy-oriented books with a measure of success. Thus, my Bertil Ohlin Lectures in Stockholm turned into the small book *Protectionism* (MIT Press, 1988), now in eleven languages. I expanded the Harry Johnson Lecture in London into *The World Trading System at Risk* (Princeton University Press, 1991). On Indian reforms, writing furiously about which in the mid-1960s was my first act of contrariness since the scene was rife then with doctrinaire socialism, I turned my Radhakrishnan Lectures at Oxford into *India in Transition* (Clarendon Press, 1993).

For the economist who seeks to influence policy, however, there are also other outlets. Testifying before Congress is an obvious one. I have done this rarely, for the simple reason that congressmen mostly invite testimony that is agreeable to their views. In consequence, given my views on U.S. trade policy that have become yet more critical in the Clinton years on many fronts, I have not had the pleasure of testifying before Congress on these matters, where my skills are the greatest any my scholarly credentials are difficult to doubt.

I might recall the time when I did testify, along with James Fallows, before Congressman Robert Garcia of New York on the pending immigration bill, opposing employer sanctions and proposals for an ID card to identify the illegals. Evidently, Fallows and I were chosen as the only witnesses, because we had both, in different ways, written about immigration in ways supportive of what Congressman Garcia wanted to hear. For me, the funny thing was that Congressman Garcia, who came from a constituency where there were Indians such as myself and who was worried sick about the discrimination against Hispanics that the ID card would entail, could not see the irony in the fact that the could not pronounce my name and kept calling me "doctor"! Since this was my first performance in the U.S. Congress, I was not sure that I could puckishly tease Congressman Garcia about this and prudently held back.

Years later, however, when I debated Senator Carl Levin of Detroit on the U.S.-Japan auto trade, I was not playing on the senator's turf. So, when he too could not pronounce my name and kept calling me "professor," a perfectly agreeable epithet in my book, I kept calling him "senator," though "Levin" is not beyond my oriental grasp. Also, noting mischievously that he was arguing that the U.S. auto market was open, whereas the Japanese market was closed, I pointed out that he must be forgetting that it was the United States that had imposed voluntary export restraints since 1981 on auto imports from Japan, whereas Japan had done nothing of the kind. And I could not help prefacing that observation with the remark: "Senator, having come from India to the United States, I can tell you that I feel perfectly at home. For, I have come from one self-righteous country to another."

Then, for sure, one can access the highest policymaking levels directly. This is, in fact, the least likely thing to happen to you if you play the public nuisance. At the same time, I agree wholly with MIT linguist Noam Chomsky that this embrace from the top is a sure-fire way to lose one's independence: it is hard to bite the hand today that one has shaken the day before. And so I must count my blessings that I have not found my way to the White House, which has not been spared, especially in the Clinton years, the chastisement that bad trade policy gets from my writings.

In fact, I have not merely written extensively against that administration's embrace of aggressive unilateralism, its infatuation with reciprocity, its mindless pursuit of preferential trade agreements as if they were free trade, and its obsession with Japan as a wickedly unfair trader-all of those making that administration among the worst in our postwar history of leadership on world trade policy. I have also led the fight by writing open letters and organizing signature campaigns by economists against such policies.

For instance, I organized and released a statement on our trade policy on April 10, 1989, when U.S. trade policy under President Bush was beginning to lean in the directions that the Clintonites later tried to set in cement. U.S. Trade Representative Carla Hills disagreed with what my fellow signatories and I had to say but took it in good spirits: I was even invited once to talk to the USTR on the issues, with Carla Hills graciously coming in for a few minutes but firmly telling me in her office that I was wrong in my views. I afforded the Clinton administration the same treatment by releasing, just before the Clinton-Hosokawa summit in Washington in 1994, an open letter to President Clinton and Prime Minister Hosokawa. The letter carried as many signatures as could be gathered in less than a week, urging that the two statesmen back off from the demands for import targets that the United States was principally demanding and refocus their attention on other things: it was a combination of firm *no*s and clear *yes*es. The summit happened to to fail dramatically as Prime Minister Hosokawa took the cue from our letter and from the first-ever letter organized by numerous Japanese economists that was prompted by ours. The U.S. demands were rejected altogether.

The Clinton administration's response to our letter was one of fury, with the rapid-response and disinformation machines going into fast forward. While I myself had an exchange of letters on the substance of Japan's trade with a prominent economist within the administration, no effort was made to bring in the eminent trade economists who had signed the letter to discuss the issues with Ambassador Mickey Kantor or his advisers, even though most of the signatories were Democrats. Instead, some of the Nobel laureates who had signed were hassled. And their natural embarrassments were played up in a congressional hearing, where Senator Max Baucus of Montana dutifully asked about the letter and the Noble laureates, and Roger Altman, then deputy secretary of the Treasury, translated those embarrassments into self-serving and misleading assertions that the Nobel laureates had had second thoughts! Wonders will never cease.

On the other hand, precisely because my writings signified a spirited defense of the General Agreement on Tariffs and Trade–centered, open multilateral trading regime, I had the good luck to be invited by Arthur Dunkel, director general of the GATT, to be his economic policy adviser during the critical years, 1991–1993, when the Uruguay Round of multilateral trade negotiations was in peril and was successfully protected by Dunkel from collapse, making it possible for his successor, Peter Sutherland, to stand on Dunkel's mighty shoulders and secure the prize: the conclusion of the Uruguay Round and the creation of the World Trade Organization.

I recall that, right after I had accepted Dunkel's invitation, Ambassador Gottlieb of Canada, who had served in Washington, a diplomat with considerable knowledge of trade issues, came to me when I had given an after-dinner speech in Toronto and expressed his regrets that I would no longer be writing in the newspapers on trade matters. A fine if excessively kind compliment, it was. But I reassured him that, while I could not openly and undiplomatically take member governments to task, I had Dunkel's agreement that I could continue writing firmly and pointedly on trade issues just as if I was not his adviser, provided I made it clear that I was writing from New York as a Columbia University professor. Yes, I did at times get some governments expressing outrage to Dunkel over what I had written; but whenever that happened, Dunkel stood by me. But the fact remains that one is not so free to play the role of an independent academic, writing with fierce independence, once one gets entangled in actual policy advising.

I might add, however, that matters are far worse when we allow ourselves to take money from corporations to testify on their behalf, or to sit on their boards, or worse to write leaflets on public policy to advance policy agendas of benefit to them with our names prominently on them. Of course, we can be independent and we will generally not be "bought." Though, this reminds me of the story that the Nobel Laureate, Princeton University economist Arthur Lewis, regaled his friends with. Once he found himself invited by the president of Princeton to a fundraising luncheon for the Iranian ambassador in Washington, a man known to those who read the Style sections of the newspapers because he used the sudden oil wealth of his nation to entertain flamboyantly the likes of Elizabeth Taylor. So Lewis was minding his manners and quietly getting through the lunch when he was suddenly startled to hear the president promising the ambassador "Professor Lewis's help to Iran on development." As he walked back morose from the luncheon, he ran into sociologist Marion Levy, a man of some wit, who asked him what the matter was. When Lewis told him, Levy said, "Arthur, you should have told the president that professors may be bought but cannot be sold."

But though we cannot be sold, the independence of the best of us can be unwittingly corroded nonetheless. English cartoonist David Low told Lord Beaverbrook, who wanted to hire Low for his newspaper, that he could not accept because he would not be free to caricature him any longer. Told by Beaverbrook that he would be free to ridicule him as tartly as he wished, Low said, "Ah, but since I would be working for you, I would not be able to bring myself to do so." In fact, when Eastman Kodak, Corning, Intel, and other corporations seek our academics as board members, what they are buying is not their expertise, which is available from their public writings, but rather their ear. For instance, by getting them to hear anti-Japan lobbying rubbish at one board meeting after another, corporations can hope to get these influential economists progressively to change their views and to corrode their earlier benign positions toward Japan that undercut the corporations' ability to increase profits by getting politicians to go along with complaints against Japanese rivals.

Consultancies are equally dangerous to an academic economist's health. Large fees, amounting to significant fractions of academic salaries, are typically paid for such consultancies today; and typically again your name is then used in the public domain, in professional-looking pamphlets and documents, to support policy positions that just happen to coincide with the corporation's interests. Indeed, the use of your good name is the name of the game. And, while the tough-minded among us will retain our independence nonetheless, it would be too optimistic to think that some will not see profit in prudence if those rewarding consultancies are to be obtained again.

The process of "corruption" is extremely subtle; and I have no doubt that the corporations know this well. I believe therefore that an economist is likely to serve the cause of public policy better by refraining from such lucrative opportunities, no matter how independent in spirit he is. I, as indeed many economists of my generation, have chosen to act in accord with this belief. We do so not because we feel we are morally superior but because we know that we are not and think instead that we are fallible. For this reason, the reader will not find here anything that I wrote for corporations: unlike Ralph Nader, I believe that they do much good but, like him, I also believe that we should not lie in the same bed, even if we plan to remain virtuous.

Tenacity and the Uses of Repetition

So, the economist who seeks to advance his agenda must tenaciously work at the task, using the myriad ways in which public opinion, and hence policy, can be influenced and shaped. As is evident from the pieces I select here, as also the larger menu of my writings, the task requires passion and engagement.

Indeed, toward that end, I have repeated important policy ideas again and again, through writing on different occasions, in diverse contexts, in varying language, and with changing nuances. Nothing explains my lifestyle better than Alexander Herzen's remark, citing Proudhon:[3]

I have said this a dozen times, but it is impossible to avoid repetitions. Persons of experience know this. I once spoke to Proudhon of the fact that there often appeared in his journal articles which were almost identical, with only slight variations.

"And do you imagine," Proudhon answered, "that once a thing has been said, it is enough? That a new idea will be accepted straight off? You are mistaken. It has to be dinned into people, it has to be repeated, repeated over and over again, in order that the mind may no longer be surprised by it, that it may be not merely understood, but assimilated, and obtain real rights of citizenship in the brain."

Indeed, in economics as in art, different nuances and contexts within which the same essential truth is set will, in skilled hands, only please, adding value. Who among the economists does not appreciate the endless painting by Monet of the *Rouen Cathedral* or the *Morning on the Seine*, at different hours, in different seasons, and not think of his own craft in a similar vein?

The Agenda: An Open Economy and a Good Society

One cannot succeed, however, in seizing the public ground just because one has passion and the ability to navigate. One also has to have an agenda—indeed, a vision of the good society in which good economic policy must be set. As it happens, the agenda that I set for myself fairly early on has served me well. In overall conception, and in several specific instances within it, my economics and my sensibilities have triumphed, though I am well aware of the swing of the policy pendulum that no triumphalist must forget.

Democracy

The broad view that I have long held is that a society is best organized when its economics embraces openness, in particular in its trade and immigration, and when its politics is democratic, not just for the elite few but in the effective participation of the many, including women and the ethnic and religious minorities. Besides, democratic politics works best when civil discourse is maintained, eschewing the ready resort to the accusatory finger of "special interests" or "ah, you are tainted by the financial support you got" and turning wholly instead to the content of the debate at hand. It also benefits, as Orwell reminded us long ago, when the participants in the policy debates set themselves the highest standards of linguistic and conceptual clarity. I have also come to believe for quite some time that democracy, when combined with markets and openness, offers the best prospect, in turn, of achieving an efficient economy.

It is perhaps not remarkable that, coming from India, which held on to its post-Independence democracy with a tenacity that nearly all other underdeveloped countries failed to display, I first thought precisely about such matters as I returned from Oxford in 1961 to work at India's Planning Commission on the problem of ensuring for the poor of India what we then called a "minimum income."

And so would be many of my later thoughts, as is evident from the subject matter of several pieces in Part Nine. The Rajiv Gandhi Lecture (chapter 40) is in part an intellectual history and in part current economic and political analysis. The lecture advances the thesis that democracy may not be inimical to economic development but may even promote it and considers at length the problem of the "quality of democracy" as reflected in the participation of the peripheral groups in the political process. The participation of women, and the economic and social importance of such participation, has interested me from the earliest times: the bias against girls in education and in nutrition was at the heart of an article I published on the issue in the Oxford journal, *World Development*, in 1973. Of course, the reaction to the article in India, as elsewhere, was that this was not really economics: bright young "development" economists such as myself were supposed to work instead on more conventional "planning" problems critically related to the notion that capital accumulation was the key source of growth and development.

That reaction reminded me then of what I had heard from an economist friend in the United States in 1966, when I published my first book, *The Economics of Underdeveloped Countries*. This was a splendidly edited, beautifully illustrated, and dejargonized book that was simultaneously published in six European languages as part of a first set of commissioned books by Weidenfeld and Nicholson in their newly launched World University Library series and reached worldwide sales in excess of 150,000 before it expired unrevised. My friend had overheard a colleague say: "Bhagwati has gone bananas. He has just published a book with a picture of a starving child in it."[4]

In 1975 I wrote a joint paper with Padma Desai entitled "Women in Indian Elections," examining how many women candidates were fielded by different parties in three different elections. It helped shrink further my circle of leftist friends, who were not happy at the fact that I had already parted company with them with a major book *India* (again coauthored with Padma Desai and published by Oxford University Press), which devastated the Indian planners' pretensions to socialism by demonstrating at length that all we had was an excessively regulated, inefficient "bureaucratic socialism" that was best dismantled. For, it turned out that the right-wing parties had fielded a higher proportion of female candidates, despite the progressive talk on the left-wing side of the political spectrum.[5]

With that early and long-standing interest in gender questions, at a time when these issues were not on center stage of either public policy or economic analysis, I must say that I was distressed to see the fine *Financial Times* political columnist, Edward Mortimer, be misled by the non sequitur that, just because poverty and famines can arise despite lack of population pressure (a proposition that is perfectly obvious since no serious observer of famines or food insufficiency can have failed to know that the world has generally had enough food to go around if only we divided it up on a per capita basis), the 1994 Population Conference in Cairo *therefore* should not worry about the possibility of explosive population growth and its downside implications for both poverty and gender issues. Besides, if a sense of crisis around such an explosive possibility attended the conference, I argued in my letter to the editor on Mortimer's column on Cairo (chapter 44), the women's groups in Cairo were more likely to secure a focus on their just causes, including their right to plan their families with methods they chose.

The issue of accommodating religious and ethnic diversity in an agreeable and inclusive way, a question of increased importance today as these differences around the world are pulling nations apart and even unleashing brutalities, has also interested me from the beginning as it is critical to a good society. Both India and the United States have multireligious societies; the question is how their societies should accommodate this fact. This is not yet an issue that has been confronted as fully in the United States as it has been in India. Interestingly, while India has been pejoratively called a Hindu nation by American reporters who would not dream of calling the United States a Christian nation, both nations share in common the social reality that the population is overwhelmingly of one faith. India, however, has directly confronted the issues raised by such dominance of a single religion. India has struggled from her independence in 1947 with the question of how to ensure minorities not just formal tolerance but also equality in the public domain. That is not yet true of the United States.

The United States, while predominantly of Christian faith, has minorities of whom only a few have gained significant public recognition: chiefly the Jewish faith and then, thanks to the black community's substantial conversion, increasingly Islam. But the nation has considerable diversity, embracing Zoroastrians, Hindus, Buddhists, and many others. Yet, for example, few public ceremonies, whether in politics or in the academe, nod to them: these faiths are tolerated but not recognized. For the most part, only ministers, bishops, and now occasionally rabbis grace these occasions with their benedictions, as if the ethnicity and religiosity of our population had remained unchanged. Here, India has something to teach: and I draw on Mahatma Gandhi and my Catholic mission school in India in chapters 42 and 43 to show how my new country can learn from my old country.

The strengthening of the civil society through reasoned discourse as well is another, more familiar, side of this coin. So, when confronted by the hysteria over Japan's "insidious" infiltration of our society and our economy, I have reacted strongly, seeing the prejudice for what it is and as unworthy of us. While I have written on Japan a great deal, and I turn to it when I discuss trade policy in this volume in Part Five, I include my review (chapter 45) of Pat Choate's *Agents of Influence*, published by no less a publisher than Knopf, and my expression of unhappiness (chapter 46) with James Fallows's unduly generous review of it in the *New York Review of Books*, whose liberalism has not protected it from succumbing much too often to varying levels of Japan-baiting by its stable of writers, in Part Nine. I do so because both deal with the demonization of Japan and the fact that, by encouraging Americans to think that the Japanese are "buying out" our think tanks, our academics, our schools, our politicians, and our retired bureaucrats, writers such as Choate come close to substituting calumny for reasoned discourse, undermining our civil society and the quality of our democracy.

Part Nine also has a claim, for reasons I state below, on my little essay on the inappropriateness of the exclusionary rule (chapter 47), commitment to which is almost a litmus test for a liberal. In writing this piece, in a contrarian mood, I must confess that I felt that I was risking my reputation as an intellectual with socially liberal views. This venture into legal theory just happened, however, to receive approving nods from Professor Akheel Amar, the distinguished constitutional lawyer at Yale, and from Jeffrey Rosen, who edits legal affairs at the *New Republic*. Drawing on the theory of economic policy, I had argued why the the pursuit of two objectives—the punishment of the guilty and the discouragement of illegal search—could not be effectively undertaken by one policy instrument, namely the exclusionary rule that threw out illegally collected evidence. The elimination of that rule, so that evidence would be admitted, and the punishment of those who conducted the illegal search would instead constitute two policy instruments that would jointly achieve both objectives more effectively. Since the dismissal of charges in criminal prosecutions on "technicalities" has increasingly tended to bring law into contempt and hence undermine the respect for the rule of law that is a key ingredient of a well-functioning democracy, the elimination of the exclusionary rule and its replacement by a more appropriate two-headed policy clearly constitute a matter of some importance: hence my inclusion of that piece in the part of the volume on democracy.

Trade: Free and Multilateral

But while these intellectual writings reflect my views on the importance of a good society within which economic policy must be set, the definition of that efficient policy while wearing my hat as an economist has naturally been the central preoccupation of my writings. Within that broad agenda, the pursuit of freer, multilateral trade for the world economy, and for each nation within it, as the organizing principle of an efficient economy characterizes my writings.

That serious theorists of the gains from trade, over two centuries, have thought of possible theoretical exceptions to the case for free trade is not news to a sophisticated theorist of international trade. Indeed, the infant industry argument for protection goes back to John Stuart Mill; and equally the argument that a country that can influence its terms of trade can also profit from restricting its trade was the subject of Robert Torrens's writings and debated fiercely in the British Parliament in the late 1840s. In the early 1930s, Keynes broke away from the free trade ranks because he argued that the prevalence of massive unemployment—a huge market failure—justified doing so. Indeed, ever since Adam Smith discovered the virtues of free trade, economists have made their scientific reputation by inventing new market failures that are held to justify departing from free trade.

I learned all this when I studied under the great international economist, Harry Johnson, whose obituary portrait at the time of his early death (chapter 53) I have included here as it provides reflections on the sociology of knowledge and of public policy, on the influential Chicago School of economics, and on the remarkable group of economists who turned Cambridge economics during the postwar years through 1950s into a phenomenon that recalled what the unique constellation of Moore, Russell, and Wittgenstein in one place and one time had done for Cambridge philosophy.

But my main act of contrariness was to argue, in 1963, from India, to which I had returned two years earlier from Oxford, that if the market failures were in domestic markets, the "optimal," that is, the best, way to address them was through domestic policies, *while maintaining free trade*.[6] This immediately and substantially narrowed down the scope for protectionism in the policy arena. It was thus a blow for free trade: no longer could economists assert as they had done for nearly two centuries that, just because there was a market failure in the economy, we should indulge in protection.

Hence, my policy preference turned increasingly toward free trade as the central thrust of an efficient policy. This was only reinforced by living in India, which had turned to an autarkic, import-substituting policy that, I soon felt, was imposing huge costs on the economy: a judgment that would finally be accepted almost a quarter of a century later by the Indian government when it turned boldly to reform policy and to jumpstart a badly damaged economy. My early writings on India in the 1960s (for example, *India* and a 1966 report that I did on trade reform for the Indian government) and also on the costs of autarky (as in the Frank Graham Lecture I gave at Princeton in 1967) were thus characterized by a distinct view that protectionism was not merely bad but expensive.[7]

Thus, in both respects, when the air became thick in the United States in the 1980s with demands for protectionism of one variety or another as the crying need for the United States, I was mentally ready to fight the good fight again, this time for good policy, not in the developing countries, but in the world's most developed country!

The immediate context of the rise of protectionist sentiment was the new concern over oligopolistic competition among the big firms in the United States and their rivals in Japan, coupled with the scientific developments in the theory of international trade under such "imperfect competition" and its implied market failure. Now, as a scholar of international trade, I greatly admired (and believe that one day the Nobel Prize committee will share my admiration for) the scientific merit of the new advances in the theory of trade with imperfect competition and the way in which they illuminated the implications of oligopolistic markets so that we understood better exactly how market failure arose in such markets. I was certain, however, that none of this work had re-shaped *either* the central anti-free-trade insight of the two-century-old literature that market failures required one to reexamine the case for free trade *or* the key pro-free-trade insight of the postwar theory of commercial policy that free trade would cease to be the best policy only if the failure extended (beyond domestic) to external markets.

In fact, on the very subject matter of imperfect competition that these scientific advances of the 1980s focused, free trade had already been called into doubt after the first major advances in the theory of imperfect competition by Joan Robinson and Edward Chamberlin sixty years ago, as Nobel laureate John Hicks had noted years ago in a famous lecture to the Manchester Statistical Society on the successive crises faced by free traders.

One therefore only strengthened the protectionist hand by arguing altogether wrongly, as Paul Krugman did to my surprise in his popular writing on the subject and in quotations by the media, that until the imperfect-competition theory arrived on the scene there had been no "theoretical" argument for protection, that now finally there was, and that the case for free trade would from now on have to be argued on practical grounds. His words are best reproduced, from a widely read popular 1987 piece:[8]

[T]he case for free trade is currently more in doubt than at any time since the 1817 publication of Ricardo's *Principles of Political Economy*.... In the last ten years the traditional constant returns, perfect competition models of international trade have been supplemented and to some extent supplanted by a new breed of models that emphasizes increasing returns and imperfect competition. These new models ... open the possibility that government intervention in trade via import restrictions, export subsidies, and so on may under some circumstances be in the national interest after all ... free trade is not passé, but it is an idea that has irretrievably lost its innocence. Its status has shifted from optimum to reasonable rule of thumb. There is still a case for free trade as a good policy, and as a useful target in the world of politics, but it can never again be asserted as the policy that economic theory tells us is always right.

Krugman was a young star when he wrote these astonishing words, so he could not have been suffering from senility; and his good health precluded the affliction of amnesia. A possible explanation was that he had learned nothing about the theory of commercial policy and its evolution since he had been to the wrong school: but then I had to discard that explanation since he had learned it all in my own classroom! So the likely conclusion was that he had been carried away by enthusiasm and that the editors had been guilty of dereliction of duty. Or, he was simply perpetrating a hoax.

If so, he had plenty of victims, more enthusiastic than himself. A generation of journalists, among them Robert Kuttner and James Fallows, and economists, among them Lester Thurow, and think tankers, among them Laura Tyson and her band at the Berkeley Roundtable known as BRIE and Clyde Prestowitz at the newly founded Economic Strategy Institute, fell for the hoax. It is clear that none of them quite understood the nuances of the scientific work in question: indeed, having seen their references to the work, popularly known as "strategic trade theory," I can state categorically that Krugman was simply a wild flag they waved when they stormed the Bastille, seeking to destroy free trade and its guardians.

The media was naturally responsive. In my files I find a striking, but not atypical, example of this situation in a *Business Week* column by Karen Pennar, on February 27, 1989, proclaiming, "The Gospel of Free Trade Is Losing Apostles," with three economists displayed as in a Wanted List: a pensive me, a Krugman with an enigmatic hint of a Mona Lisa smile, and a nearly gleeful Tyson. The article is premised wholly on Krugman's discovery of "the imperfectly competitive world" and how "[a]mmunition for protectionism is coming from economists doing research in an area called strategic trade."

The quotations from Tyson in the story are interesting:

"We should be thinking about using trade policies to promote and protect industries and technologies that we believe to be important to our
well-being," says Laura D'Andrea Tyson, an economist at the University
of California at Berkeley.... She argues that the U.S. government could
have moved far more quickly to protect, and perhaps promote, the
semiconductor industry, for instance. Instead, the U.S. was "late and
reactive."

The column then states:

Lester Thurow, dean of the Sloan School of Management at the Massachusetts Institute of Technology, argues that the U.S. must follow some
form of "managed trade" as the Europeans do, trying to secure shares in
certain markets.

And, so the progeny of Krugman, and to be sure the wayward
ones whom one cannot blame the parents for, became the new
apostles of industrial policy, of managed trade, of aggressive actions against Japan in the interest of strategic trade gains. In turn,
they became Clintonites who would counsel the new administration and even get to lead it from inside down the path that
would devastate our trade policy. Later, when Krugman would
disown the bunch in *Foreign Affairs* in April 1994 in a provocative
attack on the administration's conceptual and policy errors, based
on a zero-sum rather than a mutual-gain approach to trade, their
response was swift and impassioned, though no match for Krugman's superior expertise: they were being mercilessly deflated
with brutal stabs by the very master who had ballooned them up
earlier.

But, those years, from late 1980s until the end of President
Clinton's first term, were witness to those follies, widely shared
and turned into a fog of mendacity that few could penetrate. Indeed, even many trade economists were bamboozled since few
knew the details of the policy changes that were happening and

many believed that they must be sensible because Clinton was a policy wonk and because the professional skeptics must surely be those who were "not with" the new Krugmanesque developments in trade theory, victims of the "conventional wisdom" that must now be abandoned.

So I took up the challenge. It was many-sided. I directly responded to Krugman's essay "Is Free Trade Passé?" by taking up the theme in my 1988 Bernhard Harms Prize speech, "Is Free Trade Passé after All?"—a piece read by economists, for whom it was intended.[9] For the general public, I treated the questions in my little 1988 book *Protectionism*, arguing the case against using strategic trade theory for making policy. But I also went directly to the magazines and the newspapers, as seen in this volume.

The "industrial policy" and "fair trade" notions to ensure level playing fields with Japan that Laura Tyson clearly favored became a focus of concern once she made it to the chairmanship of the Council of Economic Advisers. I therefore subjected her views, as expressed in her latest book, to a detailed critique in the *New Republic* (chapter 8). To spare Tyson and her BRIE colleagues— whose book on the subject I reviewed in the *Journal of Economic Literature* (chapter 7)—the full brunt of espousing industrial policy, I should add that many others have embraced such notions as that manufactures matter more than other activities or that semiconductor chips are better to make than potato chips, so we should want to use trade and other policies to influence market outcomes in those better directions. Thus, for instance, Eastman Kodak, a manufacturing firm, put out a pamphlet written by a team of well-known economists that endorsed the importance of manufacturing with many arguments that I must say were simply unpersuasive. My MIT teacher and colleague Robert Solow, with his customary wit, identifies well the problem with basing policy on the argument that some activities have greater social worth than others because of nice spillover effects: "I know for sure that some activities are better than others; unfortunately, I do not know which ones they are."

Since declinism, or the diminished giant syndrome as I have called it, was also driving U.S. trade policy in those unwise, "level-playing-fields," reciprocity-obsessed directions, I treated the theme in several pieces, many among them now collected in Part Three. Here, I noted also the historical parallel with the reaction of Britain to the rise of Germany and the United States at the end of the nineteenth century in a *New York Times* op-ed and drew specific implications for the direction in which it was driving U.S. trade policy in a fuller piece in *Foreign Affairs* (chapter 4).

The diminished giant syndrome, as in nineteenth-century Britain, led many to believe that it was our openness relative to our new rivals' protection that had led to our unfortunate relative decline. That view took hold especially in relation to Japan, whose lack of level playing fields became quickly a matter of faith and the main weapon of the Silicon Valley's lobbying efforts. It translated immediately into what I have called aggressive unilateralism, under which, using Section 301 legislation, we would threaten Japan with tariff retaliation if she did not agree to our demands.[10] And pretty soon, those demands took the shape, especially under the Clinton administration, of managed trade: Japan was asked increasingly to accept firm import targets or what I christened as VIEs (voluntary import expansions in symmetry with VERs, voluntary export restraints). Both the terms, *aggressive unilateralism* and *VIEs*, have now become part of the economist's linguistic repertoire; and both policies have now been discredited, thanks to the numerous critical commentaries addressed against them and Japan's rejection of our demands because of the arguments against them.

Part Four reprints three pieces on the use of aggressive unilateralism. Part Five addresses first the issue of Japanophobia,

Japan-baiting, and Japan-fixation on the U.S. scene. A *New York Times* op-ed on Pat Buchanan (chapter 12), which drew the Clintonites' wrath, notes how this hateful presidential candidate's precise trade prescriptions on Japan were taken literally from the writings of mainstream journalists such as James Fallows, who drew in turn from the intemperate Japan-baiting writings of well-known economists who were close to the Clinton administration. Indeed, by contrast, Buchanan's demands were moderate and his language less inflammatory.

The piece was bound to draw the loyal Clintonites' wrath. But I might add that a contributing factor to their rage was surely the headline chosen by the caption writers of the *Times*. It was inflammatory: "What Buchanan Owes Clinton." As anyone who has written for the media knows, we writers have no say in what headline will grace our essay: it is a hazard we must live with. But I did call up one of the editors and say that, if we had to zero in on the president, surely a better caption would have been: "Buchanan S. O. B. [Son of Bill]." Surprisingly, Michael Lind reacted in the *New Republic* to the op-ed with a hilarious charge of smear and libertarian conspiracy directed at me (as well as Charles Lane), to which I reacted in a letter to the editor, also reprinted here (chapter 13).

To be fair to James Fallows, one of our most gifted journalists and an astonishingly acute observer of United States, I also reproduce (chapter 14) a fawning review of his earlier book, *More Like Us*, written before he went to Japan and lost his cool, where he writes with eloquence that the way to compete with Japan is to exploit the United States' strength and cultural ways rather than to bash the Japanese or seek to transplant their ways (as many including Tyson and Thurow were recommending on the compelling principle of "monkey see, monkey do"). And I cap it off (chapter 17) with a letter to the *New Republic* on Thomas Friedman, the brilliant Pulitzer Prize–winning *New York Times* reporter who was stationed in Washington to learn about economics and trade before becoming an op-ed-page columnist on foreign affairs in the slot that Leslie Gelb of the Council of Foreign Affairs used to have. Untutored in economics, he took the Clintonites' propaganda against Japan's trade hook, line, and sinker, to a point where the resulting sentiment and invective against Japan would flood his influential column with such frequency that it became customary among many of us to call him the unofficial spokesman for Mickey Kantor and his PR machine. After my letter, Friedman has written several fascinating columns, but not one about Japan's trade. I would like to take credit for this, but I have no doubt that he realized all on his own that he had been had.

Part Five (chapters 15, 16, and 18) also draws together many pieces showing how grotesque is the characterization of Japan as culturally so different that Adam Smith did not apply, as a wicked trader that excluded imports and dumped exports, and as a formidable mix of Superman and the evil genius Lex Luthor.

Then Part Five concludes with a set of writings in which I argue how, in consequence of those mischaracterizations, we have gotten our trade policy toward Japan hopelessly wrong. On the economics of those policies, especially on the seeking of VIEs, I had written extensively for my peers but had also exposed in a letter to the *Financial Times* the errors in the arguments of Fred Bergsten, the director of the Institute of International Economics, who had hastily climbed on board with the Clinton administration on both aggressive unilateralism and VIEs.[11] The pieces reprinted here, on the other hand, are varying exhortations, with pertinent arguments, to the Japanese to say no to the U.S. demands for VIEs. Those exhortations started with a prominent op-ed in the *Financial Times* (chapter 19) just before the Miyazawa-Clinton summit that was dramatically but accurately entitled "Japan Must Now Say 'No'."

In the end, the Japanese did say no, breaking up the later Hosokawa-Clinton summit over the issue and prompting me to write the *Foreign Affairs* piece, "Samurais No More" (chapter 18), explaining why the summit failed, why that could have been anticipated, and how the habit of treating Japan as an "outlier" off the curve, and as an "out and out liar," must be abandoned in favor of a normalized trade relationship. Next, the Japanese turned us down summarily on the car dispute (chapters 20 and 21). Even the renewal of the semiconductor chips agreement with governmental specification or monitoring of numerical market shares was denied in the summer of 1996.

These policy postures are, of course, precisely what I had long advocated, not just in Japan's interest but more in that of the WTO-centered, rules-based world trading system, and they formed the subject matter also of a long interview that I had with Vice Minister Sakamoto of the Ministry of International Trade and Industry shortly after our debacle in Geneva in the car dispute.[12] I argued that Mr. Sakamoto should refuse to sign any more special trade agreements, should reject VIEs and numerical approaches of any kind whatsoever, and should insist firmly on normalizing the trade relationship between the two countries such that disputes with Japan in the future would be handled precisely the way those with the European Union are handled, for example. The merit of that script having been seen by the Japanese side, the Clinton administration's descent into managed trade, into aggressive unilateralism, and into repeated flirtation with Japan-baiting policies appears to have finally ended after repeated failure, just as I had anticipated and encouraged.

But the life of free traders will never be one of leisure since governments will keep them busy with new follies to fight. The ability of the Clinton administration to be innovative in this way has been truly impressive. Whereas the demands for "fair trade" among the developed, rich countries that are members of the

Organization for Economic Cooperation and Development—principally our complaint against Japan—have marred our trade policy, those demands are now beginning to be matched by the chorus of complaints against the developing, poor countries because of the "unfair" trade resulting from their lower environmental and labor standards.

Thus, while the Bush administration again had begun to weaken somewhat, the Republicans have subsequently resisted (though not necessarily for the nuanced arguments that I advance) such demands. But the Clintonites have succumbed to the union pressures to accept and advance as their international agenda the enactment of a social clause into the WTO whose main objective would be to turn the practice of the specified labor standards into preconditions for WTO-guaranteed access to the markets of other member countries. A similar flirtation with the notion that any difference in labor and environmental standards implies "social dumping" and "ecodumping," respectively, has repeatedly surfaced in the U.S. Congress, especially at the hands of Congressman Richard Gephardt, who has tried to enact legislation known now as the "blue" and "green" protectionist legislation.

The mistaken arguments underlying such demands, their potential to undermine free trade and to recreate a divide between the rich and the poor countries, and the need for alternative proactive policies in pursuit of a better world in regard to the environment and labor practices are the subject matter of many of the pieces in this volume. They form part of the subject matter of chapter 2; and they are the entire focus of Part Six. In particular, the *Scientific American* essay (chapter 22) lays out the correct way to understand the relationship between free trade and environmental protection and to pursue efficiently those two great agendas of our time. This is an essay whose principal objective was to build a bridge between two otherwise hostile groups and may well have made a small contribution to the greater mutual understanding, though not consensus, that has now broken out.

But that does not exhaust my trade battles on the policy front. In the teeth of a massive shift in the 1980s in favor of pursuing free trade areas, which are certainly not the same as free trade but are constantly presented as such by the media and by the politicians whether free traders or protectionists, I have felt constrained to draw the line and ask the difficult question, Is it wise to pursue the formation of more such FTAs, which are really preferential trade agreements (PTAs) because they offer free trade to members but inherently discriminate against nonmembers to whom they are therefore protectionist? Over a number of scholarly writings, culminating in a book released in Washington in 1996,[13] I have argued ceaselessly against this pro-PTA policy change, which is a retreat from the essential tenet of multilateralism in trade— the absence of discrimination—to which the United States was strongly wedded in the postwar period.

The writings collected in Part Seven are a fair sample of many of my popular writings, ranging from critical analysis (as in the *Foreign Policy* article, which is chapter 27) to ridicule of PTAs (as in the spoof, "The Watering of Trade," reprinted as chapter 29). The flip side of the pro-PTA shift has been the antimultilateralism, anti-GATT school of economists, led in the 1980s by the MIT economists Lester Thurow and Rudiger Dornbusch. So, in response to Thurow's cry that the "GATT is dead," and the prescription of others that the "GATT should be killed," I often wrote in defense of multilateralism, the Uruguay Round multilateral trade negotiations, and the GATT (as in the *Wall Street Journal* op-ed, chapter 25). I should say that, with the successful conclusion of the Uruguay Round, the upgrading of the GATT into the WTO, which is now clearly alive and alert, and the questions increasingly raised concerning the wisdom of PTAs now that the WTO exists, my writings, often dismissed in the 1980s by the anti-GATT school as the "mutterings of the multilateral mantra," do not look so bad.

Immigration

Of course, the most difficult policy act for a free trader is to be also a free immigrationist. There is usually, however, an affinity between the two views in the recesses of one's heart. It exists, to be sure, also in economics, which recognizes that both phenomena can (that is, if one does, the other will) put pressures on the wages of workers if the trade and immigration in question are with an economy such as Mexico's, which is abundantly populated by poor workers. Moreover, in the historic debate on the 1905 Immigration Act in the United Kingdom that introduced national quotas on immigration virtually for the first time anywhere, it is interesting to observe that the free traders were generally free immigrationists and the protectionists were for immigration restrictions.

The symmetry, of course, cannot be carried excessively far in practice because, while trade is usually judged in terms of a utilitarian logic that stresses economic gains, immigration is judged also by the added ethical yardstick of communitarianism. I must nonetheless confess that I have always taken the public stance that legislation must err on the side of a relaxed attitude toward immigrants, whether legal, illegal, or refugees—the three categories to which our various legislative efforts have been directed. This is at the heart of my review in the *New Republic* (chapter 32) of two major books on immigration: one by Julian Simon, whose main thrust I greatly liked for its generosity and empathy while disagreeing with some of its excessively optimistic judgments about the economic benefits from immigration, and the other by

George Borjas, whose focus was narrower and the economics tighter but whose views on illegal immigration, falsely based on his statistical findings, have helped give a mean edge to the issue of illegal immigration.

The view I have taken is that, in post-Renaissance, Western societies, it is (fortunately) not possible to enforce employer sanctions for hiring illegals or Draconian penalties against illegals themselves. Hiring illegals, provided you treat them decently instead of exploiting them, is simply not going to be regarded as heinous and warranting stiff punishment. So, adding more such measures will not deter the inflow of illegals in any significant manner while affecting their well-being at the workplace, intimidating many among them into exploitative conditions of work that Labor Secretary Robert Reich then expects Kathie Lee Gifford to stop through band-aid gestures. Besides, increased attempts at enforcement against illegals require civil-liberties-risking ID systems so that illegals can be effectively set apart from the natives and the legal immigrants. In turn, that can only promote discrimination against look-alike natives and legal immigrants in the Hispanic and other minority communities.

Instead, therefore, of trying to chase the illegals through ever more sanctions and enforcement, it is best to leave them alone through a freeze in enforcement, virtually looking the other way once they are in, and to concentrate on stopping them at the border. Such border enforcement will not be overly effective either; but clearly public policy requires that a substantial and plausible attempt be seen to be made if the government is to be considered credible. Control of the border is, after all, the flip side of the nation-state and of associated notions of sovereignty. Thus, my solution to the illegal immigration situation is to try to stop them at the border, but, once they are here, to treat them with the humanity that we, especially as a nation of immigrants, owe them (chapter 33). I thus wholly disagree with the recent advocacy by

Borjas and others of immigration policies that are hugely popular across both the Democratic and the Republican parties and look to greater domestic enforcement and increased attention to ways of identifying the illegals within our society (chapter 39).

Among the other themes in the part of the volume on immigration policy is the treatment of foreign students. Chapters 36 and 37 take a benign, welcoming attitude to them, debunking fashionable arguments that are current concerning their adverse impact on scientists' earnings and on the progress of blacks in advancing toward higher education.

Chapter 31, the lead piece in Part Eight, is an op-ed from the *Christian Science Monitor*, which advances an idea that I hold with great passion: that the world needs a World Migration Organization to complete the international superstructure of "governance." The organization could not tell nations what to do, since control of the border is regarded as an essential pat of a nation-state. But what I would like it to do is to review systematically and periodically, for each country, its policy in its entirety on legal and illegal migrant and refugee inflows. The WMO should ask and answer questions such as how migrants and refugees are admitted, treated, and expelled, what expenditures are undertaken to assist them, and what the country regards as their rights and obligations. Such a review would bring every country to accountability by exposure of its own practices and by comparison with the better practices of other nations, and one would hope the review would embarrass and shame countries into better behavior. At the moment, except for the United Nations High Commission for Refugees, which is doing a splendid job on refugees, we have literally no organization of the stature of WTO on trade or of the International Monetary Found on macroeconomic stability that addresses the immigration policies and performance of countries, so that each country is sovereign in those important matters that should not any longer be left beyond scrutiny, free from scorn and beyond chastisement when deserved.

While I have had some successes in the policy campaigns that I have sketched in this introduction, nothing would please me more than if this idea of a WMO took hold. As people walk, fly, and swim across borders, as migrants or refugees, fleeing or simply seeking a better life, and their numbers steadily rise, the time has come to address institutionally the ethics and economics of this flow of humanity instead of leaving it to the whims of individual nation-states. Anything less would be a shame.

Notes

This selection of essays, op-eds, reviews, and letters to the editor has been chosen from a much larger set. In the interest of maintaining the internal integrity and coherence of a larger argument, some overlap has been avoidable. Specifically, the analysis in chapter 24 overlaps with a fraction of the contents of chapters 1 and 2, as do very small segments of chapters 20 and 21, of chapters 31 and 34, and of chapters 36 and 37.

1. See, in particular, Irwin (1996). Bhagwati (1988) also discusses the British repeal of the Corn Laws that ushered in free trade, and the debates at the time, as well as extensive participation by the great economists of the day when the issue of British abandonment of unilateral free trade was debated at the end of the nineteenth century as that nation experienced its own "diminished giant syndrome" as we did in the 1980s in the United States: a parallel that was first noted by me in Bhagwati (1988).

2. Mill (1944, chap. 4) recalls that the "first writings of mine which got into print were two letters published towards the end of 1822, in *The Traveller* evening newspaper.... There was a reply by Torrens [the great economist and owner of the *Traveller*], to which I again rejoined" (61). He writes next of publishing three more letters soon after in the *Morning Chronicle* in January and February 1823, under the signature of Wickliffe.

3. Herzen (1982, 666).

4. In fact, the problem of poverty amelioration was at the heart of Indian planning, with accelerated growth being regarded not as an objective in itself but as a policy instrument to reduce poverty, unlike what some self-serving economists have asserted when turning belatedly to poverty issues decades later. Growth was regarded as a way of getting the underemployed poor into jobs that would

give them increased income on a sustained basis. I have therefore described this growth-oriented approach to removing poverty as an activist "pull-up" rather than a conservative "trickle-down" strategy in my writings. See, in particular, my 1987 Vikram Sarabhai Lecture, "Poverty and Public Policy," reprinted in Bhagwati (1991a, chap. 25).

5. See Weiner and Field (1975, chap. 3).

6. This paper was published in the celebrated Chicago journal, the *Journal of Political Economy*, and was coauthored with V. K. Ramaswami, who was then chief economic adviser in the Indian Ministry of Commerce and an economist of remarkable ability.

7. Unfortunately, here I part company again with Paul Krugman, who took the position in Krugman (1991) that the cost of protection is small, if not negligible. That book was commissioned by the *Washington Post* at the end of the 1980s, and it is revealing of the climate on Capitol Hill that this influential newspaper decided to excerpt precisely the "protection does not matter" section of Krugman's book as an op-ed! I believe that I am fair in saying that, in light of much recent work on the issue, most economists in the younger generation today have returned to my view that the cost of protection is significant: among them are some of today's brightest, young trade (for example, Robert Feenstra) and growth (for example, Paul Romer) economists, whether theorists or policy types.

8. Krugman (1987, 131–32).

9. It has been variously reprinted but is accessible in Bhagwati (1991a, chap. 1).

10. Bhagwati and Patrick (1991).

11. By now, there is a great deal of scholarly examination of the question. My own work in this area and other contributions have been beautifully reviewed and extended in a full-scale treatment of the subject by Irwin (1994), whereas my work on the subject by my and other students continues to appear in professional journals such as the *Journal of International Economics*.

12. The interview was the cover story in the 1996(1) issue of the *Journal of Japanese Trade and Industry*.

13. See Bhagwati and Panagariya (1996).

References

Bhagwati, Jagdish. 1988. *Protectionism*. Cambridge: MIT Press.

———. 1991a. *Political Economy and International Economics*, vol. 5. Edited by Douglas A. Irwin. Cambridge: MIT Press.

———. 1991b. *The World Trading System at Risk*. Princeton: Princeton University Press.

———. 1993. *India in Transition*. Oxford: Clarendon Press.

Bhagwati, Jagdish, and Padma Desai. 1970. *India*. Oxford: Oxford University Press.

Bhagwati, Jagdish, and Robert Hudec, ed. 1996. *Fair Trade and Harmonization: Prerequisites for Free Trade?* Cambridge: MIT Press.

Bhagwati, Jadgish, and Arvind Panagariya. 1996. *The Economics of Preferential Trade Agreements*. Washington, D.C.: AEI Press.

Bhagwati, Jagdish, and Hugh Patrick. 1991. *Aggressive Unilateralism*. Ann Arbor: University of Michigan Press.

Choate, Pat. 1990. *Agents of Influence: How Japan's Lobbyists in the United States Manipulate America's Political and Economic System*. New York: Knopf.

Herzen, Alexander. 1982. *My Past and Present Thoughts*. Berkeley: University of California Press.

Irwin, Douglas A. 1994. *Managed Trade*. Washington, D.C.: AEI Press.

Irwin, Douglas A. 1996. *Against the Tide*. Princeton: Princeton University Press.

Krugman, Paul. 1987. "Is Free Trade Passé?" *Journal of Economic Perspectives* 1 (2): 131–44.

———. 1991. *The Age of Diminished Expectations*. Cambridge: MIT Press.

———. 1996. *Pop Internationalism*. Cambridge: MIT Press.

Mill, John Stuart. 1944. *Autobiography*. New York: Columbia University Press.

Soros, George. 1987. *The Alchemy of Finance: Reading the Mind of the Market*. New York: Simon and Schuster.

Weiner, Myron, and John Field, eds. 1975. *Electoral Politics in the Indian States*. New Delhi: Manohar Book Service.

I

Trade in the Global Age

1   A New Epoch?

As this millennium ends, confusion reigns. Are we in the midst of a rather virulent form of mutant capitalism, prompted by the spread of markets and the arrival of the Global Age, that permanently imperils the earnings of the blue-collar workers, accentuates economic insecurity among white-collar workers, undermines our sense of personal identity and autonomy, endangers democracy, and is ushering in a New Epoch that requires us to rethink the economic and social institutions of an earlier era? Or are we witnessing transitory difficulty and distress, whose magnitude is hyped by the media, with the consequence that pessimistic perceptions so induced in the populace have overtaken the optimistic reality that promises that this too shall pass?

The tug of war between the two contrasting views is momentous in its consequences. If the dismal view is correct, and we stand aside as silent witnesses to an unfolding history that we complacently disregard or whose import we fail to grasp, then

---

Originally published, in slightly shorter form, in the *New Republic* (May 19, 1997): 36–41, under the title "Fear Not: Why the Global Economy Shouldn't Scare Americans." Reprinted with permission.

This chapter reviews Robert J. Samuelson's *The Good Life and Its Discontents: The American Dream in the Age of Enlightenment 1945–1995* (New York: Times Books, 1997), Jeffrey Madrick's *The End of Affluence: The Causes and Consequences of America's Economic Dilemma* (New York: Random House, 1997), and Sheldon Danziger and Peter Gottschalk's *America Unequal* (Cambridge: Harvard University Press, 1997).

we could unleash chaotic responses by the distressed who are denied the benefits of a significant and appropriate societal response. On the other hand, if we rush in to fix what ain't broke, and even wind up denying ourselves through unjustified interventions the undoubted economic benefits of markets and participation in the global economy, we would be shooting ourselves in the foot.

The incentives for intellectuals are stacked, of course, in favor of choosing the former option. The world is dominated by best-sellers, talk shows, and op-ed pages crowded with the images and words of the thinkers with celebrity status acquired for "bold" thinking that proclaims new ages and epochs. And, their status, once acquired, seems to be immune to the tests of time and refutation. Even when they are felled by body blows, delivered by careful critics and unfolding realities that contradict rather than corroborate, their celebrity survives in the media. The fifteen minutes of Andy Warhol are a lifetime in this game.

Thus, ask yourself, where *did* the Affluent Society go? An unsuspecting environmentalist may well be forgiven for thinking that John Kenneth Galbraith had written about the Effluent Society! Or, you may persist and ask whatever happened to the arrival of "technostructure" and the consequent new era of the long managerial view in corporate planning and of permanent jobs, announced again by Galbraith? Indeed, with many today lamenting the crippling dominance of shareholders bent on "short-termism" and many others blasting the downsizing phenomenon as the "low road" undermining permanent jobs, the big-think proponents of the epoch of technostructure and "managerial capitalism" have surely lost now to the serious scholars who scoffed at them then.

The success of the new entrants in this game has been often as shortlived. Thus, recall the declinism, or what I have called the "diminished giant syndrome," that swept through the United

States in the 1980s and contrast it with America's relative prosperity today as Japan, once feared as omnipotent and touted as a
role model to us by many, is now seen in its long-standing distress as having joined the human race after all. Again, as Europe,
with its low growth rates and high unemployment rates, has become in its entirety the "sick man of Europe," where must Lester
Thurow hide his confident prediction that, of the three economic
giants today, Europe would emerge the "winner"?[1] No lesser fate
has overtaken his famous declaration that the "GATT is dead," a
diagnosis that was wrong even when he made it in Davos at the
World Economic Forum: just as he spoke, the GATT was being
besieged by lobbyists wanting to include their causes on its
agenda while nonmember nations were queuing up to join, suggesting that necrophilia must have broken out if Thurow was
right! Yet, the public reputations of these savants are intact—their
new works and views treated with deference in the media.

The scholars and policy specialists, especially the economists
among them, who offer skepticism for the changing-epoch theory,
on the other hand, face a certain risk. They sound callous, at
worst, and silly, at best, if they question the strength or persistence of the economic phenomena that are so "obviously" the
defining and distressing characteristics of the new epoch. At the
same time, such skepticism must now face intellectual resistance
because, in fields as different as political theory, philosophy, international relations, and sociology, the assumption that we are
now at a critical epoch-changing moment of capitalism, defined
principally by the Global Age, has sprouted a veritable renais-
sance, and anything that produces skepticism on the critical economic foundations of these speculations is not good news. Indeed,
the lost sense of personal identity and the new anguish of diminished economic prospects, presumably induced by the Global
Age, underlie the growing fascination with varying forms of flirtation with communitarianism in political theory.

This is evident in the Harvard political theorist Michael Sandel's recent work,[2] advocating a return to a "republican community," typified by his remarkable suggestion, repeated approvingly by the Pulitzer Prize–winning columnist Thomas Friedman in the *New York Times*, that the answer to NAFTA is the PTA (American schools' parent teacher association): a prescription that is strange, not merely because it is hard to think of NAFTA as adding in any way to the fragmentation and isolation now endemic to American society—beautifully captured in Saul Bellow's novella *Seize the Day* and lamented in the insightful sociological writings of Robert Bellah—but also because the recommended response to it by joining the excruciatingly boring PTA activities rather than by listening to music or visiting with agreeable friends or working at the local soup kitchen or curling up on your sofa with an interesting book seems to me like a prescription for torture.

Equally, Oxford's political philosopher John Gray has argued for a new politics with a communitarian liberal perspective in Britain, citing the inherent contradiction of Thatcherism: that its economic policies created the initially supportive voters among the "aspiring working class" who profited from these policies but who now are the fearful skeptics that face "middle-class pauperdom" and want refuge in a policy framework that does not rely exclusively on markets and globalism. Besides, markets and globalism have eroded the capacity of the state to promote social solidarity by providing for common life and by catering to locally shared norms or "understandings" of fairness and justice that are tangential to what markets achieve. Gray has then argued that "[i]t may be that meeting the human need for enduring forms of common life will ultimately require the imposition of political limits on aspects of globalization, such as global free trade."[3]

Again, sociologist Richard Sennett, in his 1996 Darwin Lecture at Cambridge on "Disturbing Memories," has written of the alienation, the delinking of the worker from his "place," and the consequent loss of identity that globalism has presumably produced, even suggesting that the revival of religion in the United States may be seen as a response:

[M]ammoth government and corporate bureaucracies are becoming both more flexible and less secure institutions; they employ new technologies to connect globally whilst ridding themselves internally of layer upon layer of managers and skilled workers. The character of work has thereby shifted, away from fixed functions or clear career paths towards more limited or shifting tasks. Work is ceasing to provide the worker a stable identity.[4]

And, as if that were not enough, the Global Age is seen as a threat to democracy itself. Forces beyond democratic control within the nation-state are seen now as dominating one's economic life. Sharing this view, the American consumer activist and political gadfly Ralph Nader also sees international institutions as constraining and overturning the gains made on environmental and health issues through grass-roots democracy. Thus, in his view, the GATT (now transmuted into the more powerful World Trade Organization), a creature of multinationals that have been routed in hard-fought battles at the local level, devises agreements behind nongovernmental organization backs that win the war for these very corporations in an end run around democracy.

Indeed, a veritable flood of popular books is now on the market, chewing at these questions and painting on a wide canvas with varying success. The World Economic Forum—which meets annually for a week in Davos, where a few academics act as the court jesters to the political leaders of second-level countries who seek foreign investment by convincing the assembled hordes of mediocre businesses that "economic reforms" in the shape of integration into the world economy are firmly in place—has also adopted "globalization" as its buzzword: therefore, the vulgar are also caught up in the fever as much as the elite intellectuals. Indeed, the most popular cliché today, after the "end of the cold war," is globalization: everything must presumably change because of it!

So what is really going on? There are three questions that are begged by all this tumult. Is there increased distress? What is producing it? And what can we do about it?

Distress

The different elements of distress need to be unbundled. Two main phenomena are now seen widely to have afflicted the recent economic scene. On the one hand, the real wages of unskilled blue-collar labor appear to have declined in the United States through the 1980s and stagnated in the 1990s. On the other hand, the vulnerability of the educated white-collar workers there seems to have increased.

The evidence for both phenomena has been challenged, not by American conservatives and the *Wall Street Journal* editors alone, and has survived intact in its broad thrust. Thus, real wages have fallen, but not quite so much if adjustments are made for the recent revision in the consumer price index (which shows a lower inflation and hence a lower deflation of the observed nominal wage to the estimated real wage) and for fringe benefits: even further revisions recommended by the Boskin Commission on the inflation adjustment, a controversial business, would leave real wages looking better but not good. Again, whatever has caused American real wages to fall during the 1980s and virtually to stagnate in the 1990s to date, appears to have operated equally in Europe, causing higher levels of unemployment there since the European labor markets—especially in Germany and France—are generally more "inflexible" than America's. Indeed, the contrast has added fuel to the demands by efficiency-seeking reformers to free up the European producers from the welfare-state protections and benefits that have been built into their hiring-and-firing system even as the American trade unions, reduced to managing less than 12 percent of the labor force now, increasingly seek to go in the other direction and oppose what sociologists call the "commodification" of labor.

The decline in real wages in the United States has been set against the backdrop of a rise in income and wealth inequality, well documented by Edward Wolff of New York University and paralleled by studies for several other developed countries. This is not necessarily a socially explosive contrast, however, even though it may offend the egalitarian sensibilities of the analyst observer. For one thing, the economists' measures of inequality are abstract concepts with little meaning to nearly all of us. Besides, even easy-to-grasp news such as the large and increased share of income and wealth going to the top 5 percent of households has little power to offend in itself. Thus, whether U.S. Treasury Secretary Robert Rubin has wealth that I have seen estimated at a sizable $100 million, or if it increased far more dramatically than mine in the 1980s, and whether the entire tribe of stockbrokers is unconscionably affluent and besides has dramatically gained recently in income and wealth as a class, produces in me—as a citizen rather than as an economist—nothing more than a ripple of titillation. Nor is that news of interest to the populace at large and of any consequence to its economic anguish or political actions: the numbers are way out of our normal cognitive range.

What does matter, however, is the coexistence of fallen and stagnant real wages at the bottom and conspicuous consumption at the top, with substantial remuneration of management—especially a downsizing management—at the workplace itself and with a sense that mobility upwards into the more prosperous ranks above is diminished. On these dimensions, the facts do not look altogether good in the United States, where the debate on the consequences of globalization has been the most heated.

Thus, as Simon Schama has reminded us, the embarrassment of riches among the Dutch burghers provided capitalism with a human face: the burghers pursued wealth, creating prosperity, but the wealth was not spent on personal self-indulgence. What Calvinism and Puritanism produced in an earlier era, however, is hard to imagine as defining the lifestyles that we see in the Style sections of the American newspapers such as the *New York Times* and the *Washington Post*. I suspect that the new visual technologies, bringing the lavish consumption of the rich and the superrich into our bedrooms, do not simply satisfy vicariously the proletarian appetites for the feasts they see on others' tables but, given today's distress, feed frustration and resentment instead.

It is the sense that you cannot improve yourself so as to get at the higher income, consumption, and wealth that you see others enjoying that may be the ultimate problem: for that would undermine the unique basis of American capitalism. Capitalism survives best when, as in the Calvinist model, it encourages accumulation but requires from the successful a restraint in consumption and an abundance of altruism. Or it works when, despite unequal outcomes, it offers the social and economic mobility, the equality of opportunity, that is often called the American Dream. It would seem, however, that the perception has grown in recent years that one's probability of getting up to a higher rung of the income ladder has declined in the United States.

This perception is not entirely out of line when checked against the objective reality. As Peter Gottschalk of Boston University, who has written a careful scholarly analysis of poverty and inequality in the United States with Sheldon Dantziger,[5] has argued recently, there are now five studies of earnings and income mobility in the United States, using longitudinal data that trace incomes over time: while two suggest that the trend is down, three indicate that there is no trend. In none of the studies, how-

ever, is there any indication of improved upward mobility out of
one's income level that would soften the blow from stagnant
wages.

But the perception does seem to exaggerate the reality. Part of
the reason for this phenomenon, of course, is that such perceptions are often formed by the popular media that are handicapped
in two ways: bad news is good news and breaking news pays
more dividends that repeating it. The result has been to overplay
greatly the notions that good jobs are disappearing, that the new
service-sector jobs doom us to a destiny of hamburger flippers,
and that we are now the "overworked" Americans making two
ends meet by holding down three jobs. The President's Council of
Economic Advisers, in a brief but incisive study[6] that was held
back for some time as the administration's political advisers confronted the obvious difficulty in reconciling the strategy of shared
angst with the desire to claim that Clintonomics was producing
results, has in fact dealt a mortal blow to such ideas. In particular,
the council shows that the vast majority of net new jobs—jobs
produced minus those destroyed—created during the early 1990s
were full-time rather than part-time, that nearly two-thirds of
these during February 1994 through February 1996 were in sectors
and occupations that paid above-average wages, and that the
share of workers holding multiple jobs has remained approxi-
mately constant since the late 1980s.

Moreover, we know from the work of Henry Farber, a labor
economist at Princeton, that those who are permanently displaced, including the ones caught up in the downsizing at the big
firms that hit the headlines, have not faced a bleaker prospect of
finding a new job now than in the early 1980s: the dismal trend
has no basis. Then again, generalization from the sad stories of the
downsized managers who would up bagging groceries or delivering liquor to their neighbors, taking in earnings hugely down
from their former levels, while indulged even by the talented task

force of journalists who put together the blockbuster seven-part front-page series, "The Downsizing of America," in the *New York Times* in February 1996[7] has no counterpart in statistical reality: the average reduction in American wages earned from 1981 through 1993 by the displaced was a sad, but still not devastating, 14 percent.

And even the extent of downsizing is greatly overblown. Recent studies in both the United States and the United Kingdom show that the average "length of tenure," by which we mean the length over which a job is held, has not declined substantially and that the Global Age has not ended or devastated "jobs for life." Simon Burgess and Hedley Rees of Bristol have analyzed British data from 1975 through 1992 and shown that, while the length of time has declined, the reduction has been rather small. The average tenure for men remained around 10.5 years, reached 10.8 years in 1982, and then fell to about 9.4 years by 1991. And the picture does not change much if the data are broken down by age groups, although the slight decline is more apparent in the young and the old rather than among those aged thirty-one to forty-five. This is more or less the finding of economists for the United States as well in recent years: the length of time over which jobs have been held has not shown a precipitous decline in the past two decades.

To understand at a deeper level, however, why the public at large has nonetheless fallen prey to the grossly exaggerated complaints about the vanishing American Dream, we could do no better than read the brilliant and vastly optimistic book, *The Good Life and Its Discontents*,[8] by Robert Samuelson, the columnist for *Newsweek* and the *Washington Post*. He too destroys some common stereotypes: among the more melodramatic being that, as Juliet Schor of Harvard argued in a much-cited 1992 book,[9] the American worker today is "overworked" and presumably stressed. Samuelson (1995, 214) cites data from a later study that show that this conclusion was "simply wrong" because "[w]omen work more on jobs, but the increase is fully offset by doing less homework. Men's working hours have remained roughly stable."

But his main and original contribution is to advance the argument that despondent Americans have been the victims of what is best described, by borrowing from the literature on the developing countries in the 1950s, as the "revolution of rising expectations." The prosperity of the 1950s and 1960s, which is often called by economists the Golden Age, was set against the memory of the devastation the Great Depression, the austerity of the Second World War, and the fears of depression thereafter, and unleashed a sense of exaggerated optimism about both the future and the government's ability to keep us steady and rising upwards on the escalator with the aid of the newfangled Keynesian economics and the confident new tribe of economists. By contrast, the obvious limitations to the economists' ability as seen from their failure to fine-tune the economy and eliminate the scourge of recessions, the emerging tradeoff between inflation and employment that made the earlier goal of a low-unemployment economy yield to the notion of the higher "natural" rate of unemployment, and the slower growth of GNP since the 1970s in the post-OPEC era, contrasted with the immediate past of great optimism, producing the exaggerated pessimism that afflicts the populace today. Although we are doing better, we are not doing so well as we thought we would, and so there is immoderate despair where there should be moderate joy.

Samuelson assigns a small role in this complex and richly nuanced story also to the indirect effects of slow growth: less growth implies less revenue, and less revenue puts a damper on the growth of public spending on entitlement programs, even as the demands for such expenditures have increased sharply. But he certainly does not see in slow growth the root cause of all evil. By contrast, Jeffrey Madrick's thin and shallow book, *The End of*

Affluence,[10] despite the hype accorded to it in the *New York Review of Books* (which shares the editorial services of Jason Epstein with Random House), is crippled, not merely by a wholly implausible explanation of what had caused economic growth to be slow since the early 1970s, but also by a simplistic surrender to economic determinism. Madrick wants his readers to believe that, if only growth since the 1970s had been higher, all American problems would have disappeared. Consider this strange assertion:

Our health-care expenditures, our fastest-growing major expense, would have been more affordable if we had continued to grow at the historic [faster] rate. (P. 11)

This is good arithmetic but bad economics. Suppose that expensive new technology is invented to attack cardiovascular disease. GNP should grow with that invention because growth reflects "fundamentals" such as capital accumulation and technical change. But if the health care system is set up in a way such that most patients cannot be denied the benefits of the best technology, the increased medical expenditures can outstrip substantially the greater economic growth and revenues. Indeed, there is no dispute that this is partly what explains the recent explosion in medical expenditures. Or consider this outrageous claim:

Slow economic growth may increasingly set old pensioners against young workers, homeowners against renters, suburbs against cities, natives against immigrants, light-skinned Americans against dark-skinned ones, debtors against creditors, and those with power, by virtue of their own wealth or their paid representation in Washington, against those who have none. (P. 163)

Really! So "all bad things go together," a dangerous flip side of the conventional liberal fallacy that "all good things go together," and we are are in danger of civil war or civil wars.

Samuelson is thus illuminating about why Americans now exaggerate their sense of impotence at bettering themselves through good jobs and upward mobility, and the true realities are far more sanguine than these fears imply. But, as I have argued, the realities and the fevered perceptions are not totally at odds. Todd Idson of Columbia and his coauthor Robert Valletta, as also Farber, have shown that the overall probability of getting displaced, meaning permanently laid off, has certainly increased somewhat in the United States. This is specially true for the educated and older workers. Mind you, here we are talking of losing your shirt, not of going on to buy a new suit: at issue here is the downward mobility that the fear of involuntary job loss implies rather than the prospect of upward mobility. The focus of the displacements on the educated, older group explains, of course, the differential preferences between security and opportunity that seem to get reflected in some American polls. Thus, in a January 1996 *Washington Post* column James Glassman reported an August 1995 survey by Luntz Research that, when asked to choose between "the opportunity to succeed" and "security from falling," 88 percent of the Generation Xers (those born between 1965 and 1980) chose the former, a distinct difference from the older generation's less gung-ho response.

This is perhaps inevitable: where the young tend to see opportunity and seek variety and change, while dreading the prospect of being stuck in lifetime jobs, the older workers naturally see difficulty in finding new jobs and seek continuity of the job they have. But the latter group's preference may well have been accentuated as the displacement rates have increased for them and created a more acute sense of job insecurity. Indeed, as I argue presently, the job insecurity may be properly seen as having increased if people begin to feel, for objective reasons such as a familiarity with the presence of increased foreign competition, that the probability of their holding onto jobs has diminished even though few displacements have actually occurred.

The Explanation

So, something has indeed changed. Real wages of the unskilled have fallen: at minimum, they have failed to rise as they did before. Job insecurity of the skilled has risen. The conjunction of the two phenomena, however moderate, underlies the current reality, and the perception (even if disproportionate), of distress.

There are two schools of thought on why we ail thus: those who focus on domestic factors such as technological change and those who lay the blame on the Global Age. I believe that the real wage decline is to be explained as the product of unskilled-labor-saving technical progress within our own economies, and we are going down the wrong track if we take the route of worrying, as many do, about seeking external explanations, chiefly the opening of our trade and investments to the developing countries of the South. On the other hand, the question of job insecurity indeed has much to do with the Global Age. Let me explain.

Consider the decline in real wages of the unskilled. The evidence that globalism—in the form of trade with and investment in poor countries—is a significant cause of that decline is not compelling. Those who think otherwise do not come to grips with a central fact: if such trade is at the heart of the explanation, then the import prices of the labor-intensive goods should have fallen relative to those of other skilled-labor-intensive goods. For that is the mechanism by which, obviously, the pressure on real wages of labor would arise. But all serious researchers now agree that such was not the case in the 1980s, when the real wages of unskilled labor fell in the United States. In fact, if you look at the behavior of the prices of labor-intensive goods in the 1970s, when real wages kept rising, those prices actually fell. Thus, when prices of labor-intensive goods were falling (in the 1970s), real wages kept rising; and when those prices were rising, real wages fell.

That is not so surprising as one might think. After all, the intuition that falling prices of the goods that one produces will necessarily prevent one from sharing in the gains from trade sounds like common sense. But, as Wolfgang Stolper and Paul Samuelson showed half a century ago, it takes heroic assumptions to turn intuition into an ironclad law. Economic theorists typically gain recognition by proving a "possibility" theorem that overturns the notion that something is unprovable or by proving an "impossibility" theorem that overturns the view that something may be possible. The Stolper-Samuelson theorem, that the real wage of labor could be shown *necessarily* to fall when the price of labor-intensive goods fell, belonged to the former class; there were few economists for whom the notion was anything more than a theoretical curiosity.

One need not be an economist to grasp the argument that falling prices of labor-intensive goods can increase the real wage of labor. Consider that my wage at work falls because the shoes that I produce fall in price. But then I may also be spending a lot of my income to buy shoes and other labor-intensive goods that have become cheaper, so that my gains as a consumer outweigh my losses as a worker, leaving my "real" wage and my economic welfare higher. As it happens, working people do spend a much higher portion of their budget on such goods than, say, an average reader of the *New Republic*. Again, increased international competitive pressure could snap our industry into greater efficiency, as the Japanese did for Detroit: all productive factors then profit from that increased efficiency. Increased economies of scale in production as freer trade expands markets could also profit all factors. Indeed, modeling the effects of NAFTA in that fashion, economists Drusilla Brown, Alan Deardorff, and Robert Stern had calculated during the debate on NAFTA that its passage would improve, not worsen, our workers' real wages.

I should add that the popular nightmare that our unskilled workers are destined to be swamped by rapidly expanding supplies of labor-intensive products, made in "gigantic" countries such as China and India, ignores two elementary facts. China and India are large; but their economic size, which is the relevant statistic, is not so large. The United States, in some estimates of national income, is six times the size of India and three times the size of China. A "large" rate of growth of supply in the poor countries can be absorbed without difficulty by a "small" rate of growth of rich-country demand. Besides, the world is a continuum of exporters and importers of labor-intensive products, and countries move from one role to another as time passes and incomes change. Hence, we have no reason to think that the expansion of the Chinese and Indian supply of labor-intensive goods will necessarily take place in American markets—or for that matter in the traditionally rich OECD country markets—exclusively.

Indeed, as Australian economist Ross Garnaut has shown (see figure 1.1), the ratio of net exports to world imports of labor-intensive manufactures has indeed risen dramatically since 1980 (from negligible levels to roughly 14 percent) for China, but it has simultaneously and symmetrically fallen (from about 14 percent to virtually zero by 1994) in East Asia, so that the Chinese expansion of such manufactures has been absorbed during the 1980s mainly within the Asian region itself, thus avoiding substantial pressure on structural adjustment in the "old industrial countries." Aggregating those counties into a "South" or an "East" that will come at us like gangbusters is an ugly fallacy that ignores how countries progress up a ladder in comparative advantage.

Thus, the argument about trade with poor countries producing paupers in our midst is hard to sustain empirically. And so is the contention that investment is also such a source of the distress of our unskilled. During the 1980s, the United States received more

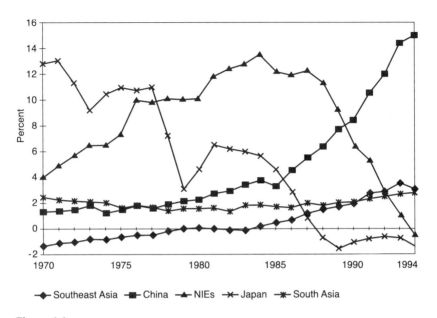

Figure 1.1
Ratio of net exports to world imports of labor-intensive manufactures, East and South Asia 1970–1994 (%).
Source: UN trade data, International Economic DataBank, Australian National University. Compiled by Ross Garnaut, ANU, Australia.
Note: Southeast Asia includes ASEAN (excluding Singapore) and Vietnam; NIEs include Taiwan, Hong Kong, Korea, and Singapore; and South Asia includes India, Pakistan, Bangladesh, and Sri Lanka.

direct foreign investment than it sent out. And if we look at all foreign investment as the flip side of our current account deficit, then we also received net investment. The conclusion is inescapable: economic integration with the South does not lie at the core of the difficulty facing our unskilled; and the obvious culprit then has to be unskilled-labor-saving technological change.

But isn't that technological change itself prompted by global competition? Some analysts, such as Ethan Kapstein, think so, but they are wrong. If global integration with the South is driving wages down, then the resulting technological change should be biased toward increasing the use of the cheaper labor. What we see is the opposite. The tendency of technological change is to diminish the reliance on cheaper labor.

But if I reject the view that globalization with the poor countries imperils our workers, I am not suggesting that the Global Age makes no difference in our economic life. Quite the contrary. The Global Age is increasingly, and in a systematic and systemic fashion, beginning to change the landscape in a way that contributes to job insecurity. We have to reckon with what is popularly described as increased foreign competition. More precisely, what we are facing now is a new and steadily encroaching economic universe in which the nature of comparative advantage is becoming thin, volatile, and kaleidoscopic and is creating vulnerabilities for industries, firms, and workers.

In world trade and world investment, there are now greater transactions and greater flows. Trade in goods and services has continued to grow faster relative to national incomes throughout the postwar period. More pertinently, the share of trade within the (hugely tradable) merchandise and primary goods sector has grown perceptibly, compared with the prewar and the immediate postwar levels. By the 1980s, as economic historian Douglas Irwin has noted, there was a vast increase in the exposure of tradable industries to international competition: a situation that was more true of primary industries in the prewar period but now characterizes most manufactures today. The substantial exposure to international competition, the fact the few industries today can pretend that they are immune from international competition: that reality is making itself more and more keenly felt.

The continuing integration of the world's financial markets, the increased transnationalization of production by multinationals, and the convergence in technological ability among the OECD countries have all combined to make competition among firms across nations fierce. Companies in different countries can avail themselves of similar technologies, borrow at similar interest rates, and produce where it pays a little more to do so, in a manner that was difficult only a decade ago. The margins of competitive advantage have, therefore, become thinner: a small shift in costs somewhere can now be deadly to your competitiveness. We used to call such industries "footloose"; the ability to hold onto them was fragile, as the "buffer" or margin of competitive advantage was not substantial. In the old days, few considered such industries to be the norm. Today, they are the norm.

There is no better proof of this sense of increased vulnerability in international competition—reflecting what I have called the "kaleidoscopic comparative advantage" of the Global Age—than the fact that firms (the managements and the workers) are increasingly tempted to look over their foreign rivals' shoulders to see whether differences in their domestic policies and their domestic institutions are giving them that extra edge in competition that then amounts to "unfair trade." That growing perception of the new volatility of economic advantage also animates all the "fair trade" demands to harmonize the institutions and the policies of other countries with the institutions and the policies of our own, so as to impose "equal burdens" and to "level the playing field." It fuels the lobbying to raise environmental and labor standards in developing countries, and exacerbates our continuing "system friction" with Japan.

The increased international competition, I suspect, also explains to a degree the tendency to displace the older, educated workers that Farber has documented and hence also the general rise in displacement rates from 1980 through 1993 that Idson and Valletta have documented. While the incentive to let those workers go, in favor of younger educated workers, follows from technical change to which the older education is not equally well suited, there is also an additional, subtle reason linked to the new competition as to why firms will let them go. That follows from the labor-market theory that explains why firms will often rationally prefer wage profiles for an employee such that wages are below productivity early in tenure and above productivity later in tenure. But then what prevents the firm from firing the senior workers, thus collecting what economists call in jargon "rent" and what is better described as a rip-off from those workers, is simply the "reputation costs" that would then stigmatize the firm as an unreliable employer that cheats you out of your greater-than-your-current-productivity wages in the later years. In short, the loss from reputation costs if the firm cheats is what prevents it from breaking that "implicit contract" between itself and its employees. But if a firm can say, "I would love to keep you, but international competition leaves me with no choice except to fire you," the firm can leave its reputation intact. Moreover, if the norm of downsizing as the way to survive spreads through the system, and "mean" is married to "lean," that makes the firm just like Joe Blow down the road: a survivor in the fierce Darwinian struggle in the Global Age. Perhaps that is the reason down-sizing seems to be almost uniquely rampant in big multinational corporations.

Thus, the Global Age explains the increased job insecurity in two interlinked ways. The changed external environment of a kaleidoscopic comparative advantage does it directly by increasing job displacements; it also does it indirectly by inducing a change in the behavior of the firms in the direction of firing workers to collect the rents without penalty. The former phenomenon is a definite and enduring change; the latter should prompt, over time, the replacement of breakable "implicit contracts" by explicit contracts that are enforceable and cannot be violated without penalty.

The Wrong Response: Isolationism and Intrusionism

The pressure on the wages at the bottom is then overwhelmingly due to domestic technical change; the job insecurity in the middle

and at the top is primarily due to the Global Age. For both phenomena, we need, however, a mature, far-seeing, unpanicked
intellectual and institutional response. Instead, we have the distractions and delusions of isolationism and intrusionism.

A typical *isolationist* response is that of Pat Buchanan, the Republican contender for the presidential nomination in the 1996
U.S. election. He favored withdrawing from the external threat,
hiding behind protection even if it meant loss of the gains from
trade. Fearing a typhoon, you get out of sunny Florida and withdraw to a safer, even if dreary, locale. The "moderate" protectionists would like to halt further freeing of trade with the poor
countries, as does the maverick millionaire and European parlia-
mentarian Sir James Goldsmith, who wants free trade only among
"like-wage" countries so as to protect the wages of our workers.
The "extreme" protectionists would like to unravel even the
existing trade treaties such as NAFTA. Either way, we close the
door to freer trade with the poor countries, denying them and
ourselves the certain benefits of a more open economy.

But, if you are a great power, you may be able to indulge an
intrusionist response that the Clintonites favor: you may be able to
moderate the typhoon itself. Thus, the United States has the option of cajoling, bamboozling, and punishing other nations into
adopting policies that limit the competition that the Global Age
offers. That may not work very well when the United States faces
off against other rich and powerful countries. Thus, the American
attempts to force Japan, for instance, into abandoning its institutional structures have generally met with failure except when
domestic forces within Japan already leaned in the direction desired by the United States.

But matters are better stacked in its favor, especially when the
United States faces the poor countries of the South, since it can
mobilize as its allies the other rich nations that share its concern
and objective: the rich together form a powerful group. That is

precisely how we must interpret the recent growth of "unfair trade" demands addressed to the poor nations and our attempts to raise their environmental and labor standards: that would presumably raise the production costs of rivals abroad in the South to levels that make their competition more tolerable.

Intrusionism, however, is no less of a chimera than isolationism. It seeks to restrain trade, but from the other end: it is tantamount to "export protectionism." The problem is that the foolishness of intrusionism is less transparent. That is partly so because those concerned with competitiveness are often allied with groups that seek to advance the legitimate, moral agendas that set us apart from many other nations. The latter groups perhaps act on John Stuart Mill's remark that no great cause was advanced without someone's special interest being mixed up in it. But they are wrong.

For, the anticompetition lobbies have weakened the moral agenda by selectively tilting it against the poor nations and shielding the rich nations, and by linking it closely to trade access instead of advancing it in other ways that are more effective. Thus, our demands for a social clause at the World Trade Organization, making conformity to it a precondition for market access, have been reduced to an emasculated "core." The right to unionize and to bargain collectively is included—but then why omit strictures on the restrictions on secondary boycotts and on the practice of hiring replacement workers, both of which can cripple the strikes of workers and have helped reduce American unions to a minuscule membership of the workforce? Again, there is nothing about the sweatshops that are rampant in our garment manufacture or about the rights of migrant workers, who are often subject to abject abuse here if investigative television reports are to be believed. The heavy hand of "export protectionism" is all too manifest in the United States, and it arouses strong objections from poor countries, which suspect that the Clinton administration is disguising American interests as American values.

Those values are better advanced instead by the political and financial support of the numerous and growing NGOs, both here and abroad, that work ceaselessly to nudge the world in the right direction. Appropriate international institutions such as the International Labor Organization on labor rights, and the United Nations Children's Fund on rights in the Convention of the Child, could be assigned to produce systematic and periodic reviews of member states' conformity to those conventions, just as the trade policy review mechanism does most usefully and effectively for trade policy now at the WTO. That, in turn, would enable governments to use public censure, and NGOs to use campaigns, labeling, and boycotts to shame and pressure firms and nations, both poor and rich symmetrically, to change their offending ways. Used in that way, today's "civil society" can be a very powerful instrument of change. But the Clinton administration, whose public silence over China's egregious violations of human rights is deplorable, has embraced intrusionism instead, in the shape of the social clause—a bone thrown to the unions in an abandonment of genuine commitment to the cause of human rights—and a surrender to export protectionism.

Trade is then not the cause of declining real wages; it likely improves them. The Luddite solution to the problems of the unskilled is similarly flawed. The solution to the economic problem that is distressing us has to lie, rather, in a domestic institutional response: in more and different governmental action and architecture, designed so that we can profit less painfully from the new age. Political scientist John Ruggie wrote in 1982 of what he called "embedded liberalism," arguing that the New Deal had embedded liberalism of the marketplace into the "social order," making it tolerable and survivable. The same argument, Ruggie suggested, could be extended to the integration of nations into the world economy.

The flux and adjustment costs seen to be imposed by forces beyond the nation-state create a particularly acute demand for state relief. The communitarian legitimacy of such relief is plain. Writing in *Protectionism*,[11] I had argued a decade ago for the creation of "institutional support mechanisms to ease the consequences of, and hence to facilitate, the decline and the exit of firms in the context of a vastly more integrated world economy"; the most compelling such institution would be the provision of adjustment assistance. Robert Reich, following in those footsteps, has insisted on workers' retraining and educational upgrading. In a time of accelerating technological advancement, enhancing the acquisition of skills through educational reforms, including vouchers, is the right kind of thinking.

Moreover, in a world where we now do not have, whether we want them or not, steadily increasing jobs with the conventional probability of long tenure, we need to break the historically derived tight links between employment and the benefits that provide basic needs: a problem that is acute in the United States because of its provision of health care that has been tied into employment by quirk of wartime. But as long-held jobs cease to expand robustly and will become scarcer, the young workers also need to become adept at the art of planning their financial future, because pensions and other benefits that traditionally developed as the package provided by one's long-term employers have also become increasingly scarce in tandem: you are now more likely to be planning your retirement on your own, and the sorry fate of the hapless widow who let her husband do "finances and taxes" while she minded the family awaits many in the new economy, adding greatly to their anxieties, if we sit back and do nothing to educate the young to manage their future.

Institutions often do evolve on their own in response to needs, of course. But will they necessarily evolve without the states steering in the necessary direction? And even then, will they evolve fast enough? Only a romantic belief in the virtue of laissez faire and a cynical disbelief in the possibility of useful state action can lead one to answer those questions in the affirmative.

Besides, a state that stands aside as society undergoes difficulties such as those that now afflict the economy will be seen as careless and even callous, lacking in the extended empathy that is surely at variance with the generous impulses that led to the welfare state. When President George Bush talked of a thousand points of light, urging that private philanthropy replace public spending, those appeared more like the fires in a burning republic while the president fiddled in Washington. Thus, we must remember what the market-only libertarians have forgotten: extending a hand, even if bearing few gifts, to the poor, rather than demonizing and dismissing them as "undeserving"—a phenomenon brilliantly described and decried by sociologist Herbert Gans[12]—and to the victims of economic and social dislocation not merely is good for the soul but also is good politics.

One thing can be said with confidence of the Global Age: it is no time for antigovernment politics in the world's rich democracies.

Notes

1. See Thurow (1992).

2. See Sandel (1996).

3. See Gray (1996, 33).

4. See Sennett (1996).

5. See Dantziger and Gottschalk (1996).

6. See Council of Economic Advisers (1996).

7. The series was subsequently published as *The Downsizing of America* (New York: Times Books, 1996).

8. Samuelson (1995).

9. See Schor (1992).

10. See Madrick (1995).

11. See Bhagwati (1988).

12. See Gans (1995).

References

Bhagwati, Jagdish. 1988. *Protectionism*. Cambridge: MIT Press.

Council of Economic Advisers. 1996. *Job Creation and Employment Opportunities: The United States Labor Market, 1993–96*. Washington, D.C.: Government Printing Office, April 23.

Dantziger, Sheldon, and Peter Gottschalk. 1996. *America Unequal*. Cambridge: Harvard University Press.

Gans, Herbert. 1995. *The War against the Poor*. New York: Basic Books.

Gray, John. 1996. *After Social Democracy: Politics, Capitalism and the Common Life*. London: Demos.

Madrick, Jeffrey. 1995. *The End of Affluence*. New York: Random House.

Samuelson, Robert. 1995. *The Good Life and Its Discontents*. New York: Times Books.

Sandel, Michael. 1996. *Democracy's Discontent: America in Search of a Public Philosophy*. Cambridge: Harvard University Press.

Schor, Juliet. 1992. *The Overworked American: The Unexpected Decline of Leisure*. New York: Basic.

Sennett, Richard. 1996. "Work, Place, Polity." New York University. Photocopy.

Thurow, Lester. 1992. *Head to Head*. New York: Warner Books.

2   The Global Age:
       From a Skeptical South
       to a Fearful North

Prebisch and UNCTAD

I am both honored and pleased by the invitation to give the Raul Prebisch Lecture.

The honor comes from recalling an exceptional man. Prebisch was an eminent scholar and a prominent actor on the policy stage, a preeminent figure who carried his great stature with charm, grace, and wit. The honor is the greater because of where I give the lecture. The emergence of the new South Africa under Prime Minister Mandela, wedded to the rule of law and a commitment to producing racial and ethnic harmony in a world pulling in more dissonant and destructive directions, has been a ray of hope for all of mankind.

But it is not geography alone that lends added honor to my lecture. History does as well. Put within the UNCTAD IX program, it inevitably recalls the glory of UNCTAD under the able leadership of Raul Prebisch at the creation. At the same time, UNCTAD IX is also of historic significance as this institution now confronts its destiny under the leadership of yet another major Latin American personality, Mr. Rubens Ricupero, underlining that continent's great gifts to the rest of us.

Originally presented as the Raul Prebisch Lecture at UNCTAD IX in Johannesburg, South Africa, on April 29, 1996.

But my honor goes also with pleasure. The pleasure is immediate and personal. For, as it happens, my very first policy experience on the international stage was at UNCTAD over three
decades ago, when Raul Prebisch was the first secretary general,
and I was invited, a young professor of international trade in
Delhi, at the tender age of twenty-nine to serve on an expert
group preparing a report on trade liberalization by and among
developing countries.

I recall this early event in my and in UNCTAD's life also
because it has many aspects that bear on Raul Prebisch and on
UNCTAD itself. The expert group—or what we would today call
an eminent persons' group in our age of vanity, if not silliness: I
remember being on an eminent persons' group at the UNIDO
several years ago when Gunnar Myrdal, a member, looked around
and said "I see no one eminent here!"—was chosen by UNCTAD,
not nominated by governments, so it had the independence to
chase ideas unconstrained by governmental directives. It also had
on it, not as subsidiary staff but as coequal members, established
scholars with real expertise in the subject, so that the problem
could be examined in depth and with a sense of vision that tran-
scends immediate political constraints: contrast this with the practice today when, much too often, we have expert groups and
commisssions whose members are almost exclusively politicians
out of office or bureaucrats in office and whose own undoubted
abilities go unaided by interaction with coequal members who
have the necessary knowledge based on reflection and scholarship. Also, the scholars were by no means concerted in their opinions: they represented diverse views. In short, Raul Prebisch, and
UNCTAD under him, were characterized by intellectual curiosity,
and by willingness to examine, cross-examine, and reject all and
even Prebisch's own views. The institution was ahead of the
curve: seizing leadership on issues and pronouncing on them
with the best intellectual resources then available.

In fact, let me recall that issues such as the international migration of skilled manpower and its economic implications for the rights and obligations of migrants and of the countries of origin and destination, the questions raised by intellectual property protection in a world with growing importance of technology, and trade issues such as tariff escalation and value-added protection (now known as effective protection) were first recognized and discussed within UNCTAD and became matters for further analytical contribution in the academe. A personal reminiscence again illustrates the point I am making: it concerns the fact that UNCTAD raised the question of services in world trade long before it got onto the GATT. When some years ago, I was invited to give the annual Geneva Lecture of the International Insurance Association, I chose the topic of the GATT and trade in services. Dr. Giarini, secretary of the association, told me later that when he had told the chairman of his council, a leader in Britain's insurance industry and member of the House of Lords about my subject, he had asked "Hmmm, GATT. What is it? Some kind of UNCTAD?"

This is hard to appreciate as the memory of this institution and of Prebisch has faded in the OECD countries, and it has become commonplace in some influential quarters to think of UNCTAD as if it was instead UNWASHED and UNKEMPT. The irony is that, just as this unfortunate view has gained ground, the academic evaluation of the role of more respected agencies such as the World Bank as the fountainhead of new ideas has become skeptical. Thus, a much-cited recent study, coauthored by macroeconomist Michael Gavin, now the principal economist with the Inter-American Development Bank, and one of today's most distinguished young developmental economists Dani Rodrik (who, I might add, started out his career at UNCTAD), has argued that the social rate of return in terms of innovative ideas on the

World Bank's massive expenditures to date on research has been negligible.[1]

Nonetheless, there is no smoke without fire. UNCTAD did indeed allow the early openness and stress on expertise to lapse progressively. It also increasingly made the mistake of assuming that intellectually weak argumentation by radical economists on the fringe, just because it was outside the mainstream, was therefore also the appropriate way to think about the developing countries: a non sequitur that would be fatal to its health. Instead, UNCTAD should have exploited the enormous diversity of views within the mainstream itself, drawing on a range of reputed economists as Prebisch did, to advance the intellectual debate in ways that could have complemented by counterpoint the orthodoxies prevailing in other agencies with agendas defined by their own composition and interests.

The era that lies ahead under Mr. Ricupero's leadership is poised now to return UNCTAD to that ambitious role, and the creative mode, that characterized the Prebisch era as many of us "friends of UNCTAD" fondly recall it. But the definition of that role cannot be that UNCTAD would reflect a particularistic and unique "developing country viewpoint" as often in the past. Paradoxically, that approach, if it ever made any sense earlier, certainly makes no sense today for two contrasting but complementary reasons.

The developing countries are now too *diverse* in their economic and political circumstance and context to make generally possible a unified viewpoint as "theirs" (that is, that of the "South"). This changed reality surely played a principal role in the rapid demise in the 1970s of the global negotiations that were predicated on the premise of North-South confrontation.[2]

At the same time, the earlier notion that the developing countries are divided from the developed countries (the "North") in

terms of their economics, justifying special and differential treatment at the GATT and elsewhere has yielded to the view that
economics is *universal* and that ideas and policies such as trade
protection, extensive regulation by a bureaucratized state, generic
restraints on inward foreign investment, and the stifling of markets
generally are bad for everyone, whether developing or developed.

In fact, the universalism extends to politics as well, and not
just to economics today. Thus, the notion that democracy is
fine for the developed countries but that development requires
authoritarian structures of governance is no longer considered
plausible.[3] Since we meet in south Africa, which is a meritorious
example of a functioning democracy today as India has been in
the postwar decades, let me dwell on this important issue a trifle
longer.

I suspect that the defunct claims in support of authoritarianism
for the developing countries were a result of the prevalent style of
economic thinking when the postwar period of planning began. It
was argued, following the influential model of the English economist Roy Harrod and the American economist Evsey Domar,
that the rate of growth depends on what you invest and what you
get out of it by way of increased income. It thus depends on the
savings (and investment) rate as also on the investment (that is,
"marginal capital") to output ratio. If one treated the marginal
capital–output ratio as more or less a technological parameter, as
the gifted development economists of the time such as Paul
Rosenstein-Rodan and Jan Tinbergen did, then all policy action
was concentrated on raising the average savings rate to increase
investment and hence the growth rate. Moreover, if public-sector
saving was considered to be the principal agent for raising the
savings ratio, as it was at the time, then it was evident that the
authoritarian states would be at an advantage over democracies:
the former could create the necessary surplus through heroic fiscal

efforts that the latter, dependent on popular support, could not. Interestingly, both the Marxist and the Harrod-Domar models produced the same presumption.

But, of course, the reality turned out to be otherwise. The variations in growth performance across countries have tended to reflect, not just differences in rates of investment, but also dramatic differences in the marginal capital–output ratio. The latter, in turn, reflects the policy framework and its effects on the efficient use of resources.[4] Again, I would argue that the policy framework relevant here includes incentives and democratic processes that both enable and motivate effective participation by the citizenry in the growing economy. And recent arguments further suggest that the combination of economic markets and political democracy is unbeatable as a prescription for sustained, long-run growth.

So, confronted by this new universalism, the intellectual niche that UNCTAD can occupy with success must be embedded within it, instead of being built on the exceptionalism of the developing countries. Within this broad universalism, UNCTAD can nonetheless advance perspectives, informed by scholarly research, that reflect better the *interests* of the developing countries (on questions and answers to common problems) that other institutions are unlikely to offer if past experience and present realities are a guide.[5]

Such a redefined role is necessary, and must be supported, because an overriding and central effect of the Global Age, has been that, alongside the huge opportunities for economic prosperity that it presents, it also creates fears. But, ironically, these fears of integration into the global economy that afflicted the developing countries in Prebisch's time, just as the developed countries busily were embracing globalism, have now in Ricupero's age been surmounted by the developing countries but have instead come to afflict the developed countries. These fears, and the often harmful demands they generate to amend the rules of world trade and investment, constitute a threat to the well-being of the developing countries just as they have embraced the Global Age.

UNCTAD can make its unique contribution to "trade and development," its original terms of reference and its rationale at the creation, in several ways such as the tasks that Mr. Ricupero has been outlining recently: for example, the provision of technical assistance in trade matters to developing countries that lack the capabilities to operate in the increasingly complex trading regime today.[6] But it can do so also by examining these fears of the developed countries, seeking to lay them to rest where they are exaggerated and unwarranted (as seems often to be the case), while also probing the rationale and the wisdom of the measures (such as the proposed social clause in the WTO) that these fears have prompted, exposing them to unbiased, scholarly and apolitical scrutiny.

UNCTAD's history and mission as an institution focused on the developing countries' problems should ensure that its perspectives will *complement* those of the OECD, whose history and mission focus its research and agenda so as to reflect more closely the political concerns and the economic interests of the developed countries that constitute its membership.[7] Both should serve to inform and assist in friendly cooperation the WTO as it prepares, under Mr. Ruggiero's leadership, to extend and strengthen the world trading regime to meet the challenges of the Global Age as we enter the twenty-first century.[8]

So, I turn to the theme of this lecture: the Global Age and its consequences. I shall begin with my central observation and the organizing principle of my analysis: the irony of the role reversal that has occurred between the developing and the developed economies on fears of integration into the global economy. I shall highlight the fact that these fears of the developed countries are heavily, and destructively, focused on integration with the developing countries, just as the fears of the developing countries in the postwar decades were focused symmetrically on the imagined dangers of integrating with the developed countries.

I shall then argue that these fears are, at best, exaggerated and, at worst, ill-informed. In addition, I shall suggest that the current, fear-fed demands in the major developed countries for changes in the rules and regimes that govern the world economy are much too often ill-designed. It is time for the leaders of the developed world to defuse these fears and, where the fears have some basis, to act less like politicians lazily compromising with lobbies to accept whatever demands they make and then forcing the international adoption of their proposed harmful changes in the world economy, and instead to act more like statesmen who recognize these pressures but deflect them into more creative proposals that strengthen, rather than weaken, the architecture of the world economic regime.

The Global Age: The Ironic Role Reversal

The dominant feature of the world economy is its increasing globalization and the growing fear of its consequences in the developed countries. The latter, a consequence of *actual* globalization or integration into the world economy on several dimension, is in sharp contrast to the warm embrace of the Global Age by the policymakers in a large number of the developing countries.

It also represents a marked reversal of attitudes in the two sets of countries from the time of Prebisch. At that time, in the early postwar decades, the developing countries were skeptical, even afraid, of *potential* globalization, shying away from such international integration, while the developed countries were into the Liberal International Economic Order, tearing down trade barriers in successive GATT rounds, liberalizing direct investment flows (despite the occasional protests such as that of Mr. Servan-

Schreiber of France on *The American Challenge*), and forging ahead on securing currency convertibility.

The developing countries' attitude of fear of global integration is best evoked by a celebrated Latin American formulation of the time: "integration into the world economy leads to disintegration of the national economy." In place of the agreeable conclusion of conventional economics that international trade, investment, etc. were mutual-gain, *benign-impact* phenomena, constituting an opportunity rather than a peril, the developing country intellectuals and policymakers, for the most part, subscribed to a zero-sum view of the integration process that involved what Prebisch called the center and the periphery in his early writings. Thus, they either had a *malign-impact* view of globalization: as in the influential *"dependencia"* thesis of Latin America's most renowned sociologist, President Cardoso of Brazil. Or they even believed in *malign-intent* paradigms where trade and aid were regarded, for instance, as instruments of neocolonialism that would continue colonial control in new ways.[9]

Today, those attitudes have yielded to the benign-impact views as developing countries, one after another, have changed economic-philosophical beliefs and their policies to seek fuller integration into the global economy. Three examples should suffice to illustrate. President Cardoso, the *dependencia* theorist of yesteryear, is today's mastermind of Brazil's economic reforms that take her ever more into the global economy. President Salinas led Mexico into NAFTA, turning on its head former President Porfirio Diaz's famous dictum: "Poor Mexico: how far from God and how near the United States!" Looking across the Rio Grande, Salinas saw a colossus that he viewed as Mexico's opportunity, not as a threat. Finally, even India, mired in inward-oriented policies for over a quarter century, has begun a deliberate and systemic change of gears to move its economy into the Global Age.[10]

But, as globalization has proceeded apace on virtually every dimension of international interaction, whether trade or direct investment or capital flows or migration, the developed countries have witnessed growing alarm from their citizens over its implications for a variety of issues, among them the real wages of workers, economic security, political autonomy and democracy, and the ability to maintain high labor standards. I shall elaborate.

That globalization has accelerated is hard to dispute. Thus, in both world trade and investment, there are greater transactions and flows, often even when adjusted for increased national incomes, suggesting that the economic activities of nations are increasingly in the global arena. But even this index misleads, at least for the implications of globalization of trade and investment: these averages tell you little about the "margin" and about what global competition offers in terms of both opportunity and about "vulnerability" to producers.

Let me begin by detailing the changing realities on *trade* flows, as some of the principal fears of the developed countries today, and their unfortunate demands, follow precisely from this phenomenon. Now, trade in both goods and services has continued to grow faster relative to national incomes throughout the postwar period, even despite the OPEC-induced macro crisis in the 1970s and the deflation during the early 1980s. The successive rounds of reciprocal tariff and nontariff-barier reductions under GATT auspices have been a major contributory factor that the Uruguay Round will strengthen as it brings freer markets to new sectors while opening the doors wider in the old sectors.

But more can be said. In some respects, as historians have noted, the rise in the share of trade to GNP has mostly restored the world trade to its prewar situation. Thus, for the United States, the share of merchandise trade in national income was 6.1 percent in 1913 and 7.0 percent in 1990: the difference is not compelling. But the shares were 3.6 percent in 1950 and 3.8

percent in 1960, so the perceptions today have been defined undoubtedly by the postwar rise, not by the fact that this rise is
more or less back to "normal" levels interrupted by the period
between the Great Depression and the end of the Second World
War.[11]

More pertinently, this share hides the important reality that the
share of trade within the (hugely tradable) merchandise and primary goods sectors has grown perceptibly, compared with both
the prewar and the immediate postwar levels. In fact, by the
1980s, there was a vast increase in the exposure of tradable
industries to international competition: a situation that was more
true of primary industries in the prewar period now characterizes
most manufactures today. It is not true that these shares continue
to increase explosively; in fact, the recent research of economists
Magnus Blomström and Robert Lipsey suggests that they may
have stabilized in the past decade. But the reality of substantial
exposure to international competition, the fact that few industries
today can pretend that they are proof from international competition, and the consciousness thereof in defining issues and demands
for governmental action are major factors that we ignore at our
peril.

Indeed, the increased integration of the world's financial markets, and the increased transnationalization of production by
multinationals, both phenomena of globalization that have run a
parallel as also a supportive course, have combined with the
convergence in technological ability and know-how among the
OECD countries, as documented by many economists such as
William Baumol, to make competition among firms across nations
fairly fierce. Firms in different countries can access similar technologies, borrow at similar interest rates, and produce where
it pays a little more to do so, in a manner that was still difficult
in the mid-1980s. The margins of competitive advantage have
therefore become thinner: a small shift in costs somewhere can

now be deadly to your competitiveness.[12] In the old days, we used to call such industries "footloose": the ability to hold on to them was fragile, as the "buffer" or margin of competitive advantage in them was not substantial. But few considered such industries to be the norm. Today, because of the factors I have mentioned, they are. I have called this the phenomenon of *kaleidoscopic comparative advantage*, a concept that gives meaning to the notion that globalization of the world economy has led to fierce competition: slight shifts in costs can now lead to shifting comparative advantage, which is therefore increasingly volatile.

This argument has the advantage of contributing to the explanation, in a unified way, of three important phenomena today that are in evidence as the source of the fears of the Global Age in the developed countries:

1. The vulnerability of one's competitiveness and viability in international competition that has so arisen, reflecting the newly volatile, kaleidoscopic comparative advantage in the Global Age, means that firms are increasingly tempted to look over their foreign rivals' shoulders to see whether differences in their domestic policies and their domestic institutions are giving them that fatal extra edge in competition which then amounts to *"unfair trade."* The proliferation of "fair trade" demands in the developed countries to harmonize domestic institutions and policies as prerequisites for free trade among trading nations reflects, among other lesser reasons, this growing perception of kaleidoscopic comparative advantage.[13]

2. The globalization-led kaleidoscopic comparative advantage also reinforces, albeit in a small way, the substantial sense of *economic insecurity* ensuing overwhlemingly from the rapid growth of information technology and now overtaking the citizens of the developed countries, for it must add to the labor turnover that makes for layoffs and, more important, to the increased rate of

permanent dismissals that now afflicts even the white-collar workers.[14]

3. In the same fashion, it likely contributes in some small way to the *decline in real wages* of the unskilled. For, increased labor turnover must mean that workers stay less on the average on a job, so that they acquire less on-the-job-training and employers also give them less of it as they expect the workers to move on, thus flattening their lifetime earnings curve: just as a rolling stone gathers no moss, a moving worker gains few skills and earns fewer increments in wages.[15]

Of course, this rise of fierce competition and the attendant sense of economic vulnerability relate to the *globalization* itself and are not focused on integration with the *developing countries* as the source of the difficulties in the developed countries. But this is not true if I were to complete the sketch of the developed countries' fears of the Global Age by noting that they have been accentuated by the fact that international capital and labor flows vis-à-vis the developing countries in particular are also seen as increasingly compounding the problems posed by the expanded trade shares. Let me just sketch the principal themes.

Direct foreign investment (DFI) has expanded greatly, with North-North DFI becoming during the 1980s as important as North-South DFI, a phenomenon noticeable in the case of Japan especially as her DFI partially replaced her exports to the European Union and to the United States, initially in response to protectionist threats in specific sectors such as automobiles and then later in response to the rising yen. While the Servan Schreiber variety of anguish at DFI inflows did surface in the United States when Japanese investments began to rise in the late 1980s, the main agitation has arisen from the labor unions that have always seen the developing countries as their principal foes in the game of economic competition. Long opposed to "losing jobs" to the developing countries because multinationals move production abroad, unions in the United States have focused their attacks increasingly on the DFI going from the North to the South as a major problem posed by the Global Age.

A matching fear for jobs and wages has arisen from the increased flows of refugees and illegal immigrants from the developing to the developed countries. In a world increasingly of "borders beyond control,"[16] if I might exaggerate for effect, most developed countries are now unable to fully regulate their immigration inflows: illegal immigration (heavily biased in composition toward the unskilled and hence the more resented for its feared economic impact on the real wages of the natives) has been for some time an issue in the United States and other countries.[17] The liberal traditions of the developed countries, where basic humanity prompts citizens to shield and judges to exonerate those who violate the immigration laws (including prohibitions on employing illegal aliens) and where government cannot (rightly) bring themselves to shoot at people crossing the border illegally by land, by sea, by air, increasingly confront the agitations of those who fear the economic consequences of such an influx.

What is remarkable about these fears of the developed countries is that they mirror so well the fears of the developing countries almost a half century ago. At that time, recall that the countries on the periphery feared the center. Global integration with countries with unequal power, in that instance the developed countries of *greater* strength, would lead to predation rather than to mutual gain: skilled nationals would leave; multinationals would earn more than they would contribute; free trade would bring about the perpetuation of backwardness and destroy nascent industrialization; income distribution would grow worse; and loss of autonomy and a situation of *dependencia* would follow. Today, the critics of the Global Age equally maintain that continued integration with countries of unequal power, in this instance the developing countries of *lesser* strength, would cause predation: unskilled migrants would arrive; mutlinationals would leave to create jobs elsewhere; free trade with countries with lower labor and environmental standards would lead to deindustrialization and loss of one's own standards; income distribution would worsen; and loss of autonomy to external forces beyond one's control and to institutions such as the WTO where the Third World has an equal vote, God forbid, would threaten one's sovereignty. Indeed, the world has come full circle!

Phantoms More than Reality: Real Wages and Jobs

But just as the developing countries have surmounted their fears and learned that the global integration with the developed countries promises more than it threatens, the developed countries need to do the same today in regard to their own global integration with the developing countries. In fact, let me remind you that I plan to argue that these fears are not merely exaggerated but also do not justify some of the proposed measures to deal with them at the international level. Since time is the scarcest resource today, let me argue this by concentrating on the single but large question of fallen wages and risen unemployment.[18]

The Facts

Consider, for instance, the argument that the decline in the real wages of the unskilled in the United States and the rise alternatively in their unemployment in Europe in the 1970s and 1980s, continuing into the 1990s, is a consequence of trading with the South with its abundance of unskilled labor. By enhancing the possibility of such trade through trade liberalization, the contention goes, the North has put its own unskilled at risk. The demand for protection that follows is then not the old and defunct "pauper-labor" argument which asserted falsely that trade between the South and the North could not be beneficial. Rather, it is the theoretically more defensible, income-distributional argument that trade with countries with paupers will produce paupers in one's midst, that trade with the poor countries will produce more poor at home.

Now, it is indeed true that the real wages of the unskilled have fallen significantly in the United States during the previous two decades. In 1973 the "real hourly earnings of non-supervisory workers measured in 1982 dollars ... were $8.55. By 1992 they had actually *declined* to $7.43—a level that had been achieved in the late 1960s. Had earnings increased at their earlier pace, they would have risen by 40 percent to over $12."[19] The experience in Europe has generally been similar in spirit, with the more "inflexible" labor markets implying that the adverse impact has been on jobs rather than on real wages.

But the key question is whether the cause of this phenomenon is trade with the South, as unions and many politicians feel, or rapid modern information-based technical change that is increasingly substituting unskilled labor with computers that need skilled rather than unskilled labor. As always, there is debate among economists about the evidence; but the consensus today among the trade experts is that the evidence for linking trade with the South to the observed distress among the unskilled to date is hard to find. In fact, if real wages were to fall for unskilled labor owing to trade with the South, a necessary condition is that the goods prices of the unskilled-labor-intensive goods would have to have fallen; and subsequent examination of the U.S. (and recently of German and Japanese) data on prices of goods shows that the opposite happened to be true in the critical period of the 1980s.[20]

While, therefore, the consensus currently is that technical change, not trade with the South, has immiserized the Northern proletariat, the fear still persists that such trade is a threat to the unskilled. In Europe, there has thus been talk of the difficulty of competing with "Asiatic ants."

Alongside that is the fear that multinationals will move out to take advantage of the cheaper labor in the poor countries, as trade becomes freer, thus adding to the pressure that trade alone, with each nation's capital at home, brings on the real wages of the unskilled. Of course, that too is an unsubstantiated fear: but it has even greater political salience since the loss of jobs to trade is less easily focused on specific competing countries and their characteristics than when a factory shuts down and opens in a foreign country instead. As it happens, I suspect that, at least in the United States, the flow of capital also is in the wrong direction from the viewpoint of those who are gripped by such fear. For, during the 1980s, the United States received more direct foreign investment than it sent out elsewhere, both absolutely and relative to the 1950s and 1960s. Besides, if foreign savings are considered instead, the 1980s saw an influx, corresponding to the current account deficit that has bedevilled U.S.-Japan trade relations for sure.

But, regardless of the true realities that make it difficult to assign a significant, if indeed any, role in the present predicament of the Northern unskilled workers to trade and investment in this Global Age with the developing countries, the general feeling persists in many influential quarters that trade with the developing countries is a problem and the resulting demands on policy change have more political salience than one would care to have and would be foolish to ignore.

The Demands: Isolationism and Intrusionism

These demands take two contrasting forms. First, there is the traditional protectionist response. Here, there are those who would raise trade barriers against the developing countries: a battle cry of the erstwhile presidential candidate Pat Buchanan in the United States, who wanted an across-the-board 20 percent tariff on imports from China and an unravelling of NAFTA. Then, there are the "moderates," who would only stop liberalizing trade further with the developing countries: here, we must count (Sir James Goldsmith among them, I believe) the proponents in the North of free trade areas among "like-wage" countries as against free trade generally as the latter would include lower-wage countries.

These protectionist pressures are not so hard for the leaders of the developed countries to resist: the advantages offered by free trade, and the ideological triumph (at least for now) of the open-markets alchemy for efficiency and growth in a highly competitive world economy, make it virtually impossible for responsible leadership to embrace such *isolationist* ideas and attendant protectionist pseudosolutions. But, unfortunately, that is not true of the alternative response, no less desirable, that we observe on the part of some of the leading governments in the North.

This second alternative is best understood by an analogy. Faced by the prospect of typhoon, you may move out of its range, shifting from sunny but typhoon-prone Florida to dreary but safe locales: this is the isolationist, withdrawing, protectionist response to the fears (in the developed countries) of the developing countries in the Global Age. But, if you have read your Malinowski or Radcliffe Brown, you may also pray to the weather gods and get the typhoons to go elsewhere. This interventionist or *intrusionist* option is one that can be contemplated, as a response to the threats imagined from elsewhere, only by the economically and politically powerful countries: they can aspire to force the developing countries, by using a variety of punishments and inducements, to adopt domestic institutional and policy changes so that the competitive threat is moderated.

This is how we must interpret the chorus of demands that have spread in the United States and in Europe for inclusion of environmental and labor standards in the WTO, requiring that either they be moved up in the developing countries or else the developed countries be allowed to countervail the "implied subsidy" represented by these lower standards. Proposals for such legislation have already been introduced from time to time in the U.S. Congress, as in Congressman Gephardt's "blue" and "green" bill, which would have authorized the U.S. administration to impose "ecodumping" duties against lower environmental (that is, *green*) standards abroad and "social dumping" duties against lower labor (that is, *blue*-collar workers') standards abroad.

Several factors, including moral ones, undoubtedly contribute to the emergence of one or more of these "fair trade" demands. But a principal one among them surely is the desire to raise, in one way or another, the costs of production of your rivals abroad: and what is more easy to do than to say that they are deriving advantage by having lower environmental and labor standards and therefore free trade with them amounts to "unfair trade"? This complaint, and attendant agitation for penalizing those foreign firms with import taxes if their countries do not raise their standards toward one's own, then have the advantage that *either* you will be able to get your rivals' costs up and reduce the pressure of their competition by forcing them to raise their environmental and labor standards *or*, if they do not do so, you will get protection against them as trade barriers are raised against the continuing unfairness of competition. This agitation therefore offers a foolproof method of meeting your foreign rivals' competition: it therefore accounts also for its popularity.

But let me argue in plain language that these demands, prompted in large part (but by no means exclusively) by the fact of international competition and reflecting the view that lack of identical standards amounts to "unfair trade," are properly being resisted by the developing countries and are inappropriately being accommodated by some of the governments in the developed countries, as in the recent pressures emanating from the United States and France, in particular in favor of a social clause at the WTO.

Intrusionism: Environmental and Labor Standards

These demands are unwisely recreating the North-South divide which we had put behind under what I described earlier as the universal recognition of economic markets and democratic politics, and of the mutual advantage from integration into the world economy, as the principles on which to found a sound economy and a good society. To understand the folly of these developed countries, and the dangers they pose to the developing countries and to the world trading regime, let me now address in succession the parallel but still contrasting issues of ecodumping and of the social clause at the WTO.

The Legitimacy of Diversity and the Folly of Ecodumping Demands

If we are dealing with "global" environmental problems, when there are transborder externalities, as with the global warming and ozone-layer problems, it is now recognized that we need global solutions that avoid free-rider problems and punishments for defection. The disagreements among countries that universally accept the need for such solutions arise only from differences in their views of what is a "fair" allocation of the burden of pollution avoidance, especially as there is an understandable tendency on the part of the worst offenders, some of the developed countries, to shift the burden of adjustment disproportionately to the developing countries.[21]

The ecodumping allegation, on the other hand, extends plainly to what economists call "domestic" environmental problems: as when effluents are discharged in a lake or a river that is entirely within a nation's own borders, and there are no transborder spillovers into other jurisdictions.

Now, in this latter set of domestic pollution cases, economists would generally expect to find diversity rather than uniformity of environmental standards in the same industry in different countries—that is, in what I shall call cross-country intraindustry (CCII) differences in standards, typically in the shape of pollution tax rates. This diversity of CCII standards will follow from differences in tradeoffs between aggregate pollution and income at different levels of income, as when richer Americans prefer to save dolphins from purse-seine nets whereas poorer Mexicans prefer to put people first and want to raise the productivity of fishing and hence accelerate the amelioration of Mexican poverty by using such nets. Again, countries will have natural differences in the priorities attached to which kind of pollution to attack, arising from differences of historical and other circumstances: Mexicans will want to worry more about clean water, as dysentery is a greater problem, than Americans, who will want to attach greater priority to spending pollution dollars on clean air. Differences in technological know-how and in endowments can also lead to CCII diversity in pollution tax rates.

The notion, therefore, that the diversity of CCII pollution standards and taxes is illegitimate and constitutes "unfair trade" or "unfair competition," to be eliminated or countervailed by eco-dumping duties, is itself illegitimate. It is incorrect, indeed illogical, to assert that competing with foreign firms that do not bear equal pollution tax burdens is unfair. I would add three more observations.

First, we should recognize that if we lose competitive advantage because we put a larger negative value on a certain kind of pollution whereas others do not, that is simply the flip side of the differential valuations. To object to that implication of the differential valuation is to object to the differential valuation itself, and hence to our own larger negative valuation. To see this clearly, think only of a closed economy without trade. If we were to tax pollution by an industry in such an economy, its implication would be precisely that this industry would shrink: it would lose competitive advantage vis-à-vis other industries in our own country. To object to that shrinking is to object to the negative valuation being put on the pollution. There is therefore nothing "unfair" from this perspective, if our industry shrinks because we impose higher standards (higher pollution taxes) on our industry while others, who value that pollution less, choose lower standards (lower pollution taxes).

Second, it is worth noting that the attribution of competitive disadvantage to differential pollution tax burdens in the fashion of CCII comparisons for individual industries confuses absolute with comparative advantage. Thus, for instance, in a two-industry world, if both industries abroad have lower pollution tax rates than at home, both will not contract at home. Rather, the industry with the *comparatively* higher tax rate will. The noise that each industry makes on basis of CCII comparisons, aggregated to total noise by all industries, is then likely to exaggerate seriously the effect of different environmental valuations and CCII differences on the competitiveness of industries in higher-standards nations.

Third, the legitimacy of the diversity may be suspect if the governments that are making the decisions on pollution tax rates are unrepresentative. Clearly, one cannot attribute such legitimacy to the Soviet-bloc governments, which, in fact, polluted wantonly and whose citizens had no voice. But fortunately, democracy has broken out almost everywhere: just a few countries, either the stragglers from the communist era (China, North Korea, and Cuba) or the nonideological one-leader or one-party states (Iraq and Syria), now lie wholly outside the democractic pale.

Besides, between nongovernmental organizations and television, the ability to be summarily indifferent to voices that articulate ecological concerns has fallen drastically. Albeit, democracies differ in their structures and their quality; but there is no reason to think that the developed countries uniformly have advantage over the developing countries in this regard.

An Unjustified Fear of the "Race to the Bottom"

But one more worry needs to be laid to rest if the demands for upward harmonization of standards or ecodumping duties in lieu thereof are to be effectively dismissed. This is the worry that free trade with countries with lower standards will force down one's higher standards. The most potent of these worries arises from the fear that "capital and jobs" will move to countries with lower standards, triggering a "race to the bottom" (or more accurately a race toward the bottom), where countries lower their standards in an interjurisdictional contest, below what some or all would like, to attract capital and jobs. So, the solution would lie then in co-ordinating the standards-setting among the nations engaged in freer trade and investment. In turn, this *may* (but is most unlikely to) require harmonization among countries to the higher standards (though, even then, not necessarily at the levels already in place), or perhaps there might be improvement in welfare from simply setting minimum floors to the standards.

Unlike the just-rejected argument that dismisses diversity of standards as illegitimate and therefore unfair per se, this is undoubtedly a theoretically valid argument. The key question for policy, however, is whether the empirical evidence shows, as required by the argument, that: (1) capital is in fact responsive to the differences in environmental standards and (2) different countries or jurisdictions actually play the game then of competitive lowering of standards to attract capital. Without both these phenomena holding in a significant fashion in reality, the "race to the bottom" would be a theoretical curiosity.

As it happens, systematic evidence is available for the former proposition alone, but the finding is that the proposition is not supported by the studies to date: there is very weak evidence, at best, in favor of interjurisdictional mobility in response to CCII differences in environmental standards. There are in fact many ways to explain this lack of responsiveness: (1) the differences in standards may not be significant and are outweighed by other factors that affect locational decisions; (2) exploiting differences in standards may not be a good strategy relative to not exploiting them; and (3) lower standards may paradoxically even repel rather than attract direct foreign investment.[22]

While we do not have similar evidence on the latter proposition, it is hardly likely that, as a systematic tendency, countries would be actually lowering environmental standards to attract capital. As it happens, countries, and even state governments in federal countries (for example, President Bill Clinton, when governor of Arkansas), typically play the game of attracting capital to their jurisdictions: but this game is almost universally played, not by inviting firms to pollute freely but instead through tax breaks, holidays, and land grants at throwaway prices that result most likely in a "race to the bottom" on business tax rates, which wind up below their optimal levels! It is therefore not surprising that there is little systematic evidence of governments' lowering environmental standards to attract scarce capital. Contrary to the fears of the environmental groups, the race to the bottom on environmental standards therefore seems to be an unlikely phenomenon in the real world.

I would therefore conclude that both the "unfair trade" and the "race to the bottom" arguments for harmonizing CCII standards or else legalizing ecodumping duties at the WTO are lacking in rationale: the former is theoretically illogical, and the latter is empirically unsupported. In addition, such WTO legalization of ecodumping will facilitate protectionism without doubt. Anti-dumping processes have become the favored tool of protectionists today. Is there any doubt that their extension to ecodumping (and equally to social dumping), where the "implied subsidy" through lower standards must be inevitably "constructed" by national agencies such as the Environmental Protection Agency in the same jurisdiction as the complainant industry, will even more surely lead to the same results?

The "fixing" of the WTO for environmental issues therefore should not proceed along the lines of legitimating ecodumping. The political salience of such demands remains a major problem, however. One may well then ask, Are there any "second-best" approaches, short of the ecodumping and CCII harmonization proposals, that may address some of the political concerns at least economic cost?

A Proposal to Extend Domestic Standards in High Standards Countries to Their Firms in Low Standards Countries, Unilaterally or Preferably through an OECD Code

The political salience of the harmful demands for ecodumping duties and CCII harmonization is greatest when *plants are closed* by one's own multinationals and shifted to other countries. The actual shifting of location and the associated loss of jobs in that plant magnify greatly the fear of the "race to the bottom" and of the "impossibility" of competing against low standards countries. Similarly, when investment by one's own firms is seen to go to specific countries that happen to have lower standards, the resentment gets to be focused readily against those countries and their standards. When jobs are lost simply because of *trade* competition, however, it is much harder to locate one's resentment and fear on one specific foreign country and its policies as a source unfair competition. Hence, a second-best proposal could well be to address this particular fear, however unfounded and often illogical, of outmigration of plants and investment by one's firms abroad to low standards countries.

The proposal that I would like to make, most appropriately in Johannesburg, is to adapt the so-called Sullivan principles approach to the problem at hand. Under Sullivan, U.S. firms in South Africa were urged to adopt U.S. practices, not the South African apartheid ways, in their operations. If this principle that the U.S. firms in Mexico be subject to U.S. environmental policies (choosing the desired ones from the many that obtain across different states in that federal country) were adopted by U.S. legislation, that would automatically remove whatever incentive there was to move because of environmental burden differences.

This proposal that one's firms abroad behave as if they were at home—do in Rome as you do in New York, not as the Romans do—can be either legislated unilaterally by any high standards country or by a multilateral binding treaty among different high standards countries. Again, it may be reduced to an exhortation, just as the Sullivan principles were, by single countries in isolation or by several as through a nonbinding but ethos-defining and policy-encouraging OECD code.

The disadvantage of this proposal, of course, is that it does violate the diversity-is-legitimate rule (whose desirability I argued). Investment flows, like investment of one's own funds and production and trade therefrom, should reflect that diversity. The proposal therefore reduces the efficiency gains from a freer flow of cross-country investments today. But if environmental tax burden differences are not so different, or do not figure prominently in firms' locational decisions, as the empirical literature that I cited seems to stress, the efficiency costs of this proposal could also be minimal while the gains in allaying fears and therefore moderating the demand for bad proposals could be very large indeed.

Yet another objection may focus on intra-OECD differences in high standards. Since there are differences among the OECD countries in CCII environmental tax burdens in specific industries for specific pollution, this proposal would lead to "horizontal inequity" among the OECD firms in third countries. If the British burden is higher than the French, British firms would face a bigger burden in Mexico than the French firms. But then such differences already exist among individuals and firms abroad since tax practices among the OECD countries on taxation of individuals and firms abroad are not harmonized in many respects.

Other problems may arise. Monitoring of one's firms in a foreign country may be difficult; and the countries with lower standards may object on grounds of "national sovereignty." Neither problem seems compelling. It is unlikely that a developing country would object to foreign firms' doing better by its citizens in regard to environmental standards (that it itself cannot afford to impose, given its own priorities, on its own firms). Equally, it would then assist in monitoring the foreign firms.

If I may be cynical, this eminently reasonable proposal, which I made at the time of NAFTA in an article in the *New York Times*, was not received with enthusiasm by the corporate sector, and hence by either the U.S. administration or Congress, because the well-guarded little secret of the multinationals is that their demands on their governments and hence on what they want included in the WTO, as with trade-related investment measures and now the more ambitious Multilateral Agreement on Investment, concern the removal of impediments to their expansion, not the imposition of restrictions on their freedom to maneuver.

The Question of Labor Standards and the Social Clause

The question of labor standards, and making them into pre-requisites for market access by introducing a social clause in the WTO, has both parallels and contrasts to the environmental questions that I just discussed.

The contrast is that labor standards have nothing equivalent to *transborder* environmental externalities. One's labor standards are purely *domestic* in scope. In that regard, the demands for "social dumping" for lower labor standards that parallel the demands for ecodumping have the same rationale and hence must be rejected for the same reasons.

But a different aspect to the whole question results from the fact that labor standards, unlike most environmental standards, are seen in moral terms.[23] Thus, for example, central to much thinking today on the question of the social clause is the notion that competitive advantage can sometimes be morally "illegitimate." In particular, it is argued that if labor standards elsewhere are different and unacceptable morally, then the resulting competition is morally illegitimate and "unfair."

Now, when this argument is made about a practice such as slavery (defined strictly as the practice of owning and transacting in human beings, as for centuries before the Abolitionists triumphed) and its other forms, such as bonded labor, including the abhorrent practices of mortgaging one's children to de facto servitude to employers and of abusively exploiting prisoners in the labor camps in the gulag, there will be nearly universal agreement that if such slavery produces competitive advantage, that advantage is illegitimate and ought to be rejected as posing unfair competition to one's workers in competing industries.

The moral argument may, however, be not merely to consider such slavery-based competition as unfair to our industries and workers. It may also be that we as a nation do not wish to profit from such trade: we will not sup with the devil, even though we miss a free meal. Or it may be a consequentialist moral argument that we wish to punish *others* who permit such slavery and, by denying them trade in such slavery-produced goods, we seek to induce them to change such slavery.[24]

The insertion of a social clause for labor standards into the WTO can then be seen as a way of legitimating a compelling and universally accepted moral exception to the otherwise sensible GATT rule that prohibits the suspension of a contracting party's trading rights concerning a product simply on the ground that another contracting party objects to the process by which that product is produced.

The real problem with the argument, however, is that universally condemned practices such as slavery are rare indeed. True, the ILO has many conventions that many (but far from all) nations have signed. But many have signed simply because in effect those conventions are not binding. Equally, and for the opposite reason that (since it is a nation that takes its international obligations seriously) the signing of the conventions may produce conflicts with its own legislations, the United States has signed no more than a tiny fraction of those conventions.

The reality is that diversity of labor practices and standards is widespread in practice and for the most part reflects, not necessarily venality and wickedness, but rather diversity of cultural values, economic conditions, and analytical beliefs and theories concerning the economic (and therefore moral) consequences of specific labor standards. The notion that labor standards can be universalized, like human rights such as liberty and habeas corpus, simply by calling them "labor rights," ignores the fact that this easy equation between culture-specific labor standards and universal human rights will have a difficult time surviving deeper scrutiny.

I might illustrate the fundamental difficulties we face by taking the United States (since it is a principal proponent of the social clause) and demonstrating immediately that the U.S. logic on the question can lead to a legitimate demand for a widespread and sustained suspension of its own trading rights if a social clause reflecting labor standards in a comprehensive way were established.

Thus, for instance, worker participation in decisionmaking on the plant, a measure of true economic democracy for both unionized and nonunionized labor that is surely *more* pertinent than the mere unionization of labor, is far more widespread in Europe than in North America. Would we then condemn North America to denial of trading rights by the Europeans? Migrant labor is again ill-treated to the level of brutality and slavery in U.S. agriculture owing to grossly inadequate and corrupt enforcement, if investigative shows on U.S. television are a guide. Does this mean that other nations should prohibit the import of U.S. agricultural products? Sweatshops exploiting female immigrants with long hours and below-minimum wages are endemic in the textile industry, as documented amply by several civil-liberties groups and now appreciated widely because of the discovery of an establishment in California that employed virtual slaves and the subsequent admission by Labor Secretary Reich that monitoring and enforcement were appallingly weak and would remain so because of lack of funds. Should the right of the United States to export textiles then be suspended by other countries as much as the United States seeks a social clause to suspend the imports of textiles made by child labor?

Even the right to organize trade unions may be considered to be inadequate in the United States if we go by "results," as the United States favors in judging Japan: only about 12 percent of the U.S. labor force in the private sector today is unionized. Indeed, it is not secret, except to those who prefer to think that labor standards are inadequate only in developing countries, that unions are actively discouraged in several ways in the United States. Thus, it does not require deep knowledge to see that the restraints in place on secondary boycotts and the freedom to have replacement workers can cripple a union's ability to strike, rendering the union impotent and making its existence a formality rather than a matter of real substance. Indeed, in essential industries, even strikes are restricted. Moreover, the definition of such industries also reflects economic structure and political realities, making each country's definition only culture-specific and hence open to objection by other. Should other countries have then suspended U.S. flights because President Reagan had broken the air traffic controllers' strike?

Lest you think that the question of child labor is an easy one, let me remind you that even this raises complex questions. The use of child labor, as such, is surely not the issue. Few children grow up even in the United States without working as babysitters or delivering newspapers; many are even paid by parents for housework in the home. The pertinent social question, familiar to anyone with even a nodding acquaintance with Chadwick, Engels, and Dickens and the appalling conditions afflicting children at work in England's factories in the early Industrial Revolution, is rather whether children at work are protected from hazardous and oppressive working conditions.

Whether child labor should be altogether prohibited in a poor country is a matter on which views legitimately differ. Many feel that children's work is unavoidable in the face of poverty and that the alternative to it is starvation, which is a greater calamity, and that eliminating child labor would then be like voting to eliminate abortion without worrying about the needs of the children that are then born.

Then again, insisting on the "positive-rights"-related right to unionize to demand higher wages, for instance, as against the "negative-rights"-related right of freedom to associate for political activity, for example, may also be morally obtuse. In practice, such a right could imply higher wages for the "insiders" who have jobs, at the expense of the unemployed "outsiders." Besides, the unions in developing countries with large populations and much poverty are likely to be in the urban-industrial activities, with the industrial proletariat among the better-off sections of the population, whereas the real poverty is among the nonunionized landless labor. Raising the wages of the former will generally hurt, in the opinion of many developing-country economists, the prospects of rapid accumulation and growth, which alone can pull more of the landless labor eventually into gainful employment. If so, the imposition of the culture-specific developed-country-union views on poor countries about the rights of unions to push for higher wages will resolve current-equity and intergenerational-equity problems in ways that are then *morally* unacceptable to those countries. Indeed, in such cases, such an imposition may itself be legitimately regarded with indignation as morally obtuse, if not wicked.

The Social Clause: A Bad Idea

One is then led to conclude that the idea of the social clause in the WTO is rooted generally in an ill-considered rejection of the general legitimacy of diversity of labor standards and practices across countries. The alleged claim for the universality of labor standards is (except for a rare few cases such as slavery and its close variants such as labor in bondage and in the gulag) generally unpersuasive.

The developing countries cannot then be blamed for worrying that the recent escalation of support for such a clause in the WTO in United States and France, among the leading OECD countries, derives instead from the desire of labor unions to protect their jobs by protecting the industries that face competition from the poor countries. They fear that moral arguments are produced to justify restrictions on such trade since they are so effective in the public domain. In short, "blue protectionism" is breaking out, masking behind a moral face.

Indeed, this conclusion is reinforced by the fact that none of the major OECD countries pushing for such a social clause expect to be the defendants, instead of the plaintiffs, in social clause–generated trade-access cases. On the one hand, the standards to be included in the social clause to date are invariably presented as those that the developing countries are guilty of violating, even when some transgressions thereof are to be found in the developed countries themselves. Thus, according to a report in the *Financial Times*, a standard example used by the labor movement to garner support for better safety standards is a disastrous fire in a toy factory in Thailand, where many died tragically because exits were shut and unusable. Yet, when I read this report, I recalled an example just like this (but far more disconcerting when you noted that the fatalities occurred in the richest country in the world) about a chicken plant in North Carolina where also the exits were closed for the same reason. Yet, the focus of the international agitation has been on the poor, not the rich, country.

At the same time, I must say that the argument that the social clause should contain "core" standards sounds fine until you realize that this is also tantamount to a choice of standards for attention and sanctions at the WTO that is also clearly biased against the poor countries in the sense that none of the problems where many of the developed countries themselves would be more likely to be found in significant violation—such as worker participation in management, union rights, and rights of migrants and immigrants—are meant to be included in the social clause. Symmetry of obligations simply does not exist in the social clause, as contemplated currently, in terms of the coverage of the standards.

This theme may be pursued further. The choice of the WTO as the repository of a social clause, stacked against the developing countries, is also a way of additionally proofing oneself against the possibility of being a defendant. This is so because the standing to bring cases at the WTO lies with the member governments, not with NGOs as in the public interest litigation such as in India or in the case of human rights if a nation has signed (as the United States has not done) the Optional Protocol on the International Covenant of Civil and Political Rights (the basic international compact on human rights). India and Egypt, for instance, may be expected to be bamboozled by threats and inducements, political and economic, by major powers into not pursuing social clause–led cases against them; but the NGOs would not so easily back away from such a scrap. If, indeed, the demands are being truly inspired by a moral viewpoint that genuinely seeks symmetric, universal rights and their enforcement, the selection of the WTO as the institution of choice for sanctions is hardly credible.

Indeed, both the choice of standards to be included in the social clause and the choice of the institution where the social clause will be situated cannot but leave serious analysts in the developing countries convinced that the movement is a prime example of what I called intrusionism, inspired by the desire to moderate competition from the developing countries by raising their costs of production. This view is further reinforced when the unions allied to these demands are often seen to be those in industries directly threatened by such competition, or when the morality underlying the demands for a social clause is couched in terms of a universalist language that asserts transborder moral concerns by groups that equally support immigration controls that deny the universalism they assert.[25]

If Not a Social Clause, What Else?

If this analysis is correct, then the idea of a social clause in the WTO is not appealing; and the developing countries' opposition to its enactment is totally reasonable. We would not be justified then in condemning their objections and unwillingness to go along with such demands as depravity and "rejectionism."

But if a social clause does not make good sense, is everything lost for those in both developed and developing countries who genuinely wish to advance their views of what are "good" labor standards in a decent society? Evidently not.

It is surely open to them to use other instrumentalities such as NGO-led educational activities to secure a consensus in favor of their positions. In fact, if your ideas are good, they should spread without coercion. The Spanish Inquisition should not be necessary to spread Christianity; indeed, the pope has no troops. Mahatma Gandhi's splendid idea of nonviolent agitation spread, and was picked up by Martin Luther King, and finds strong resonance in the practice and precepts of President Mandela, not because Gandhi worked on the Indian government to threaten retribution against others otherwise; it happened to be just morally compelling.

I would add that one also has the possibility of recourse to private boycotts, available under national and international law; they are an occasionally effective instrument.[26] They constitute a well-recognized method of protest and consensus creation in favor of one's moral positions. Indeed, given both the rise of CNN and the explosion of NGOs, the ability to mobilize public opinion in support of morally inspired positions truly supportive of human rights with a deep universalist appeal through exposure, persuasion, and private boycotts has increased enormously. There is also a growing consensus on the use of labeling to provide consumers with the information that enables them to discriminate more effectively against products using processes they disapprove of.[27]

Where, however, a nation has unmarketable culture-specific moral views[28] on the production and import of certain products and is under domestic political pressure to go alone with official suspension of such imports, it is worth stressing that there is nothing in the current international regime to prevent it from doing so. It can simply suspend the trade of another country and "pay" for it by making trade concessions, or it can put up with matching retaliation by the other country in the form of its own withdrawal of market access to the punishing country. The latter is, in effect, what the European Union did over its politically necessary suspension of hormone-fed beef trade and the subsequent retaliation by Ambassador Carla Hills of the United States.

The Global Age: Transcending Fears to Construct a New Architecture

The new international architecture that we must build to secure the gains from the Global Age must then not be founded on faulty foundations inspired by exaggerated fears. It must also not be one that begins by creating a North-South divide when we have just managed to put such dissensions behind us in a common vision reflecting the universalism of both economics and politics that I drew your attention to. What vision, then, should we embrace? Or perhaps, if I may recall Raul Prebisch at the end as I did at the beginning, where would he, simultanoeusly a visionary and a builder, have led us at this historic juncture?

Evidently, we need to reject the folly of including a social clause and ecodumping varieties of trade and environmental agendas into the world trading regime: the WTO would surely be handicapped, and the developing countries harmed, by such measures.

Instead, recognition of the important role of NGOs as agents that can use suasion effectively, a careful and fairminded design of labeling approaches that are applied symmetrically to both developing and developed countries (so that Rugmark is matched by extension of effective labeling to harmful products that developed countries ban in their own markets but allow their multinationals to export to the developing countries),[29] and a shift of international analysis and encouragement of improved environmental and labor practices in all countries to appropriate institutions such as the United Nations Environmental Program and the International Labor Organization, are among the proper ways to bring these great tasks to attention and fruition today.

Moreover, instead of moving the world into a foolish strait-jacket of "deep integeration"—a shallow concept when it comes to the social clause and environmental tax burden harmonization —and forcing it on the WTO and the developing countries, to whose disadvantage it must work, it is better to finish the task of creating a world of free trade, an essential component of the Global Age that still remains a job undone.

This task is all the more important as the trading system has now been afflicted by a huge and increasing proliferation of free trade areas, which are better called by their true name: prefer-ential trading arrangements (PTAs). These PTAs now crisscross the world economy, creating a "spaghetti bowl" phenomenon of trade tariffs and nontarift barriers that depend on where products come from: numerous rates apply in the European Union and United States alone, depending on source, with "rules of origin": producing a maze messing up the international division of labor in the Global Age.

These PTAs are politically driven: no politician is happy unless he has put his signature on at least one of them. It gives them a place in the sun and, while going preferential, you can still pre-tend that you are for free trade since no one in the media under-stands the distinction. We economists now have a CNN theory of regionalism or PTAs: you can get onto world television through an APEC or a Mercosur summit, which you cannot do at Geneva at the WTO!

So, the only way to kill this growing maze of preferences is, not through ingenious changes in Article 24 at the GATT/WTO, which sanctions PTAs, since it is doubtful that they will be paid much attention to in practice when virtually everyone is in the game, or by prohibiting PTAs, which simply cannot be suppressed when the political demand for them is so overwhleming, but through going to worldwide free trade (which effectively kills the preferences since a preference relative to zero is zero).

So, the nations of the world must unite behind such a vision and such a target: worldwide free trade by, say, 2010. Mr. Renato Ruggiero and Mr. Rubens Ricupero can be natural allies in propagating such a target, for it would galvanize both the WTO and UNCTAD—both at a critical defining moment in their history, the WTO beginning to create it and UNCTAD struggling to survive it.

Mr. Ruggiero's task will be to bring the reluctant United States on board: cajoling it away from its current folly of embracing the social clause and rejecting an activist further-freeing-of-trade role for the WTO in the matter of setting its new agenda.[30] On the other hand, remembering that the era of exceptionalism is over, Mr. Ricupero must unhesitatingly bring the developing countries on board behind such a target.

I am afraid that, ironically, Mr. Ruggiero's task is likely to be the more difficult since the United States, and indeed France, are in the throes of Intrusionism inspired by the phantom fears of the Global Age. By contrast, Mr. Ricupero should find his task much easier as the developing countries now find in the Global Age the virtues that they could not see in the earlier years. But, it is my fond hope that the two will be able to lead, hand in hand, in shared partnership, the nations of the world into a truly Global Age with worldwide free trade. Indeed, one could not hope to find better leadership than what they offer. After all, by a remarkable coincidence, the names of both these men can be initialized to

R.R.: a symbol of exceptional quality to us in the former colonies of Great Britain, where R.R. stood, of course, for Rolls Royce!

Notes

1. See Gavin and Rodrik (1995). These authors do say, however, that the World Bank has done a good job of disseminating (as against creating) good ideas, an area where UNCTAD took the back seat over time. In accounting for the latter, the willingness of the World Bank to draw on mainstream economists and their increasing neglect over the years by UNCTAD must be considered the chief culprit. Of course, I am describing only the central thrust of each institution's merits and demerits in regard to using and disseminating good ideas. There are important exceptions, especially in regard to UNCTAD's recent work, particularly on the so-called "trade and" issues, such as the interface of trade and the environment.

2. So did the recognition that "commodity power," based on an extension of OPEC's success to several other commodities, was an illusion even though it had been embraced as a new phenomenon redefining the relationship between developing and developed countries by shrewd politicians such as Henry Kissinger and by policy wonks such as Fred Bergsten before the Nairobi UNCTAD. For a fuller analysis, see Bhagwati and Ruggie (1984, chap. 2).

3. I have considered this question in depth in my 1994 Rajiv Gandhi Memorial Lecture (Bhagwati 1995).

4. We should not forget that the policy framework affects the rate of investment as well. In fact, this played a central role in my view in accounting for East Asia's phenomenal growth in the postwar period, as argued in my keynote speech to a Cornell University conference on East Asia (Bhagwati 1996).

5. One example might illustrate, lest you might think that I am putting up a straw man. When the question of intellectual property protection (IPP) was being extensively debated at the GATT, the overwhelming view in the scholarly community was that the IPP being demanded in Geneva was being pushed by lobbies in the developed countries to the point where it was far too high. But, to my knowledge, this predominant scholarly view was not forcefully adopted and disseminated by the leading international agencies, whether the OECD or the World Bank. It is doubtful that Prebisch's UNCTAD would have remained so indifferent, abandoning both good economics and the interests of the developing countries, if it had been confronting the IPP question instead. Indeed, the GATT must be complimented for having permitted its staff to pursue precisely the skeptical research, even if in a very small way, that others were unable or unwilling to provide.

6. The requirements here are enormous, especially as legal fine print has invaded everything concerning trade to a degree where even large and highly skilled

developing countries such as India are handicapped by their lack of trade-law expertise in looking out for their interests.

7. This view contrasts, I suspect, with that of some OECD governments, chiefly the United States, which would rather emasculate the research capabilities of UNCTAD (and, for that matter, of the WTO) and concentrate them exclusively in the two Bretton Woods institutions, the IMF and the World Bank. The research leadership of these two institutions, one might observe without caricature, has been jealously guarded by the leading developed countries.

8. Indeed, the redefinition of the UNCTAD role also implies a close working relationship between it and the WTO, putting behind the two institutions the indifference, even hostility at times, that marred their relationship in the early days when the GATT was considered to be the playground of the wealthier nations and UNCTAD the champion of the poorer ones. (The witticism went that the UNCTAD Secretariat was deliberately sited so as to obscure the GATT's view of the lake from its earlier location, in an ultimate act of defiance!)

As the WTO, with the developing countries active players within its own new universalism, now seeks to enlarge its minuscule institutional research capability to support its creative efforts on behalf of the multilateral trading system (in which efforts we can only support it), it can also reach out for research cooperation with agencies such as UNCTAD on issues of common concern. Again, under the leadership of Mr. Ricupeo and Mr. Ruggiero, signs of such cooperation can already be found.

9. The analytical categories, benign-impact, benign-intent, malign-impact, and malign-intent, as ways of categorizing the different schools of thought on the effects of integrating into the global system were developed by me in my introductory essay in Bhagwati (1977).

10. The reasons why the developing countries have moved to reforms are the subject of extensive analysis by economists today. Among these reasons, the value of example in the form of success (of other nations following different policies) and of failure (of one's own policies) is certainly an important factor. In addition, we must reckon with the effect of proreform aid conditionality, although the impact of one's policy failures will play a role in turn, since such failures are what drive countries into the Bretton Woods institutions that enforce such conditionality.

11. See Irwin (1996).

12. Economists call this a "knife edge" phenomenon, as in the case of Ricardian comparative advantage, where a small shift in comparative advantage can lead to substantial shift in production.

13. These other reasons include moral ones, as represented by human rights NGOs, which seek to stamp out domestic differences in conformity to universal human rights notions. I have discussed the different philosophical, economic,

structural, and political factors underlying variously the many demands for harmonization that are breaking out today in Bhagwati and Hudec (1996, chap. 1).

14. This phenomenon of increase in the rate of permanent dismissals has now been demonstrated in the U.S. context to be afflicting more the older and educated workers. See Farber (1996) and Valletta (1996, esp. fig. 1).

15. I have developed this theory in several recent articles, including in Bhagwati and Dehejia (1994). Note that this theory relates to globalization, not to the allegedly deleterious effect of trade with poor countries which is the conventional factor price equalization argument.

16. This is the title of my forthcoming book, with the subtitle, *Immigration: Economics, Ethics, and Politics of Immigration*.

17. So has the explosion of refugees, some of them leading in turn to an overload on asylum claims in the developed countries even as the fear has arisen that illegal immigration seeks to misuse the asylum route to immigration. The refugee crisis today, as it must be called for it is no less, has been splendidly handled by Madame Ogata as the UNHCR chief, an appointment for which Japan can properly take credit.

Indeed, in view of the economic, ethical, and political implications of the expanding legal, illegal, and refugee flows that have now emerged on the world scene, and the absence of any international institution that oversees the entire phenomenon in totality the way the Bretton Woods and related institutions look after aid (IBRD), liquidity (IMF), and trade (WTO and UNCTAD), I have proposed for some time now the establishment of a World Migration Organization (WMO), whose function would be to provide such assessments of different countries' total policies on immigration and nudge them, through analysis and exposure, in the direction of evolving a consensus son some basic views of the rights and obligations, both economic and political, of countries and migrants. See, in particular, Bhagwati (1992). The caption of that article read, "A World Migration Organization could influence current negative developments, which are largely ad hoc and reflect diverse national responses to emerging immigration crises."

18. Unfortunately, I do not have the space here to analyze other claims such as the loss of autonomy, the growing sense of alienation, etc., which are also on the Northern scene and which I equally regard as largely exaggerated and fearful.

19. See the many empirical writings of Robert Lawrence on the subject.

20. This has been widely conceded now by those who were skeptical, including Ed Leamer of UCLA. The only dissident is Jeffrey Sachs, whose claim to have overturned this finding is based on dubious procedures, which, even then, produce results that, while cited by the unsuspecting media, are statistically worthless. For an evaluation of this question, see my "Trade and Wages: A Malign Relationship?," 1995, Columbia University mimeo, contributed to a forthcoming

volume, edited by Susan Collins, for the Brookings Institution, a think tank in Washington, D.C.

21. I should add that there is by now a clear recognition of this problem by all countries and a willingness by the developed countries to design burden distribution in a more just fashion.

22. The evidence and the basic explanations are advanced illuminatingly by Arik Levinson in Bhagwati and Hudec (1996, chap. 11) and summarized and systematized by Bhagwati and Srinivasan in Bhagwati and Hudec (1996, chap. 4).

23. Some environmentalists do think, however, in moral or at least philosophical terms and see nature as having its own autonomy and not being exploitable in the service of man. This viewpoint means, of course, that cost-benefit analysis and the concept of tradeoffs are both ruled out; and, in economic jargon, the valuation put on environmental objectives becomes infinite.

24. I have considered the alternative moral arguments in Bhagwati and Hudec (1996, chap. 1).

25. Recently, a senior economist with the U.S. Department of Labor has argued that polls show that moral concern over child labor cuts across states, whether affected by competition or not, and therefore protectionist intention cannot be inferred. This is, of course, a naive argument. Are these opinions independent of protectionist encouragement of such sentiments, based on crude propaganda that equates bonded child labor, for example, with child labor per se, among other distortions? If the dog is barking, you still must ask, What or who causes him to bark?

26. Though, here also, I must add that many NGOs and citizens in the developing countries are rightly concerned by the asymmetric power that can be exerted by private boycotts in countries that are economically more substantial and politically more powerful, thus lending greater weight to the moral concerns of the citizens of the strong as against those of the weak nations. So the time may well have come to examine whether organized private boycotts should be permitted without restraint when exerted against weaker, foreign nations rather than against their own governments.

27. The issue of labeling is not so easy as it seems. Who decides on the label? What language should be used? Would you use a label, POISON, or the present anemic one about the surgeon general's warning, in selling cigarettes? Would you simply use the label "Made with Child Labor," which necessarily evokes the image of child exploitation, or would you use a different description that is more differentiated and discriminating? Here, the recent research by the UNCTAD secretariat has been almost alone among the developmental international agencies in exploring systematically, with the aid of excellent experts, the deeper questions raised by ecolabeling and other forms of labeling, underlining the point I was making about the unique role that UNCTAD alone can play in examining issues with developing country interests in plain view.

28. Are the American love for dolphins, the Indian respect for cows, the English affection for dogs universalizable by moral suasion? They are rarely grounded in basic beliefs in animal rights but seem to reflect notions such as "cuteness" (dolphins look so human, look at their pretty snouts) or "loyalty" (a dog is man's best friend), which are surely culture-specific.

29. The word *effective* is important. Thus, where the population is largely illiterate, effective labeling is impossible and must be replaced by bans at source by the developed countries.

30. Indeed, at the QUAD trade talks in Kobe, the United States managed to bamboozle Canada and Japan into acquiescence on going to the December 1996 ministerial of the WTO with the demand that the social clause be included on that agenda. When a great power is set on a task, no matter how harmful, it is hard to offer continued resistance. I would predict, however, that this unhappy persistence by the United States will produce a major confrontation in Singapore.

References

Bhagwati, Jagdish. 1992. "A Champion for Migrating Peoples." *Christian Science Monitor*, February 28.

———. 1995. "Democracy and Development: New Thinking on an Old Question" (1994 Rajiv Gandhi Memorial Lecture). *Indian Economic Review* 30 (1): 1–15.

———. 1996. "The Miracle That Did Happen: East Asian Growth in Comparative Perspective." Department of Economics, Columbia University. Photocopy, May 2.

———. ed. 1977. *The New International Economic Order*. Cambridge: MIT Press.

Bhagwati, Jagdish, and Vivek Dehejia. 1994. "Freer Trade and Wages of the Unskilled—Is Marx Striking Again?" In *Trade and Wages: Leveling Wages Down?*, edited by Jagdish Bhagwati and Marvin H. Kosters. Washington, D.C.: AEI Press.

Bhagwati, Jagdish, and Robert Hudec, eds. 1996. *Fair Trade and Harmonization: Prerequisites for Free Trade?*, vol. 1. Cambridge: MIT Press.

Bhagwati, Jagdish, and John Ruggie, eds. 1984. *Power, Passions and Purpose: Prospects for North-South Negotiations*. Cambridge: MIT Press.

Farber, Henry. 1996. "The Changing Face of Job Loss in the United States, 1981–1993." Princeton University. Photocopy, March 21.

Gavin, Michael, and Dani Rodrik. 1995. "The World Bank in Historical Perspective." *American Economic Review Papers and Proceedings* 85 (May): 329–34.

Irwin, Douglas, 1996. "The United States in a Global Economy? A Century's Perspective." *American Economic Review Papers and Proceedings* 86 (May): 41–46.

Valletta, Robert G. 1996. "Has Job Security in the U.S. Declined?" *Federal Reserve Bank of San Francisco Newsletter*, no. 96–07, February 16.

II

On the Mat: The Poverty of Protectionism

3   The Poverty of Protectionism

Jagdish Bhagwati may be the world's most militant defender of free trade. Certainly the Columbia University economist is a highly conspicuous and effective polemicist against its many new adversaries. If you turn on a news program or look at an op-ed page when the General Agreement on Tariffs and Trade (GATT), the North American Free Trade Agreement (NAFTA), or an alleged new threat from Japanese "predatory trade" is on the national agenda, the odds are that you will see or read Jagdish Bhagwati.

The doctrine of free trade has long had a bad press with theorists of "underdevelopment." and Third World states were urged to shun it. Economists raised in poor countries or educated in waning ones were prominent in the ranks of the skeptics. So anyone seeking a champion of free trade would seem foolish to start by looking for a man born in India in 1934 and trained at Cambridge University in the 1960s, but those are indeed the intellectual origins of Jagdish Bhagwati, which helps make him so striking a figure. On the basis of hard experiences, he is convinced that free trade is a poor economy's only hope and a stagnant one's only chance. At a time when the self-inflicted wounds of Pacific Rim protectionism are becoming visible just as European and

---

Originally published as an interview by Frederic Smoler in *Audacity* 3 (Winter 1995): 16–26. Reprinted with permission.

American protectionism is gaining new intellectual respectability, I discussed these paradoxes with Professor Bhagwati in his office at Columbia.

Many people seem to think that both NAFTA and GATT are triumphs for free trade, while you have argued that NAFTA is much less of a good thing. What's the distinction?

I see NAFTA as an achievement because President Clinton fought for it despite all his initial hesitations, demonstrating that he had surmounted his fears—both political and ideological. That was a touchstone: He'd been sitting on the fence for so long that most of us thought rigor mortis had set in. Finally he found a voice and some conviction. But while the president understood NAFTA as free trade, NAFTA is in fact a free-trade *area*, which is not the same thing as worldwide free trade. Because the President saw NAFTA as a free-trade move, most economists were delighted that it passed, although the continuing and widespread fear that trading with poor countries hurts us is not very cheering. I hope the success of NAFTA will be seen as an affirmation that trade between rich and poor countries is by and large beneficial to the rich countries, and that is why rich countries do it.

What are the disadvantages of free-trade areas?

I remain uneasy about what FTAs mean for the United States as the major player in the world trading system. Since World War II we've articulated the goals for the world trading system and have held that FTAs, which are a club to which other people are not admitted, are a bad idea except when there are overpowering political needs for them. Our FTA with Israel, for example, was more a political affirmation than a policy shift. After 1982 we abandoned our great commitment to multilateralism by moving into regionalism, but you can't be enthusiastic about arrangements that discriminate against outsiders. During the NAFTA debate it was very hard to convey any of this without appearing to be against free trade, especially after Ross Perot got into the anti-NAFTA act. Large numbers of economists simply shut up because they didn't want to give aid and comfort to the protectionists.

You're also a heretic about GATT, the worldwide free-trade agreement. While most critics argue that far too many concessions were made by the United States, you believe that too many concessions were made to the United States.

My remark was a response to Congress's feeling that somehow we made too many concessions. Obviously, we've given up very real things to the developing countries—a chunk of our textile industry, for example—and a lot of them will benefit from the trade expansion that will follow agriculture's coming under greater market discipline. In the main, though, I believe that the GATT has been a win-win situation for the United States because we set the agenda when we pushed for the Uruguay Round to be launched in 1982. We didn't succeed until 1986, but the side that sets the agenda has the advantage. Also, I believe as an economist that you gain as much from your own import liberalization as from somebody else's. Unilateral reductions of your own tariff barriers let you exploit the gains from free trade more effectively.

People assume that if you make an import concession, the other party wins, and therefore you have to balance off the concessions. I think we went too far demanding certain concessions.

What does "too far" mean?

Our role is uniquely complicated: As the architect of free trade, we have to distinguish among internal domestic lobbying, the national interest, and the international interest. But it's only the last that an architect designing a world trading system should keep in mind: What will lead to maximum gains for all?

Now sometimes the architect may be able to rig the trading system. The United States normally wouldn't do that, but Nazi Germany or the old Soviet Union had no qualms about setting unfair rules for their spheres of influence, and had they designed a world trading system, it would have been the same thing on a grander scale. The United States isn't in that game, but as a result of lobbying pressures, some of the things that went into the new GATT are not mutual-gain propositions but simply ways of getting better returns for us.

Can you give an example?

Of course. Demanding extensive intellectual-property protection in fields we dominate as powerfully as we do: software and pharmaceuticals. We wanted this protection in the GATT so that we could use trade sanctions to benefit our own industry, and economists think a lot of this is protection in the bad sense of the word.

Your have to remember exactly what Congress means to do when it protects intellectual property. If knowledge came like manna from heaven, then its rapid diffusion would produce the greatest good for everybody. If vaccines were free, without payment to the people who invented them, then more children would benefit immediately. But knowledge doesn't fall like manna from heaven. People invest in creating knowledge, and if knowledge were constantly diffusing without paying those who created it, in the long run everybody would be worse off. It's a classic trade-off problem: The higher the returns to people who create new knowledge, the less the vast majority benefits right now.

There's obviously some optimum level of protection for achieving the best mix of creation and diffusion of knowledge. As it happens, economists looking into this have found very little damage from less protection. The creation-inhibiting supply-side effect is unimportant.

Why is that?

The reason is mainly competition. If Ciba and Pfizer, two gigantic firms, are in competition with each other, the fact that you and

I might be imitating their work in the garage doesn't seem too important. Even if we're a bit bigger, it'll take a little time for us to reverse engineer the stuff they invented, so there's a natural period over which Ciba and Pfizer will be able to get a good return. In any case neither can afford to sit back and say, "I'm going to stop plowing back profits into R&D because I'm worried about the fact that people are going to copy this without my getting any royalties from it." If Ciba sits back, Pfizer's going to go ahead and clean Ciba out, and vice versa.

So the supply-side argument essentially collapses.

Well, supply-side economics ultimately collapsed because the supplyside people thought that when taxes were cut there would be so much output expansion—despite lower tax rates—that there would be revenues coming out of the secretary of the Treasury's ears. And that didn't happen. There was some evidence of a supply-side effect, but it was rather small, and that misjudgment produced an enormous deficit. Similarly, I've seen no research suggesting that the supply-side effect on intellectual-property protection is worth a hill of beans. That is the view generally held by people who work in this area.

There are a lot of new theoretical arguments against this kind of intellectual-property protection. What are the practical downsides?

We are now using the GATT for the collection of royalty payments, which is not a mutual-gain transaction. In so doing, we have abandoned or diluted a very attractive philosophical basis for organizing the GATT—the idea that trade is mutually beneficial to all contracting parties and that therefore all parities should liberalize. Now we're saying that the GATT is in business to secure an unrequited transfer from the poor countries to the rich ones.

We have shifted from utilitarian logic to a rights-based argument: We invented the stuff, so it's ours, and anybody who doesn't agree to our terms and conditions for using it is engaging in piracy and theft. Once you use words like *piracy* and *theft*, you've effectively made your opposition very defensive. But we don't really seem to believe our own argument. If we did, we'd demand permanent patent protection rather than worry about raising it to twenty years, which is the formula we imposed.

What's the advantage of a utilitarian argument?

Economics is based on the utility principle. It attempts to secure the best life for everybody, and the pursuit of mutual gain is a better basis for reaching authentic agreements with strangers than a self-interested rights-based argument. But most people find it very uncomfortable even to mention the topic because rights have become so much a part of the Washington rhetoric that you immediately lose all credibility if you say, "I'm not for intellectual-property protection."

There are two arguments that might be made for the American positions on intellectual property. The first is that they embody a conception of fair play that seems obvious to most Americans. The second is that the United States' competitive advantage lies in the production of intellectual property. We're abandoning our greatest asset if we let it be freely appropriated by all comers. How would you reply to those arguments?

They're fair comments, and that is why our negotiators' demands were largely met. All I'm saying is that the level at which our demands were pitched was beyond what could be justified. We should have been able to say, "Look, what about twenty years? Let's discuss whether that makes sense for different industries," and so on. By putting it in such stark terms—*piracy*—we managed to drown out the really relevant question.

If protecting intellectual property has no important incentive effects, why did it become such a prominent feature of the American trade debate?

Well, we do invent know-how, and if we can collect a higher return on it, we add to the national welfare—but at the expense of the developing world. If protection did provide an incentive to innovation, then protecting American intellectual property would be to the advantage of a country like Taiwan because the more new knowledge comes out, the more Taiwan benefits. But everyone seems to agree that it's really a redistributive mechanism.

The money at stake is scarcely trivial, though. One hears eight-figure estimates of the value of pirated American software, pharmaceuticals, music, and video. Do you have any sense of the real numbers at issue?

If they were that big, then the transfer from the poor to the rich countries would be so dramatic that it would lead to evasion in the end! I believe the numbers are much smaller. Besides, there are *some* gains for poor countries. I come from India, and I played a role in getting the Indians to agree to intellectual-property protection on the ground that India, being a middle power that increasingly produces software and movies, is potentially a major exporter. Indian films are very popular in the Middle East, but they're pirated there as much as our American movies are in India. India is a major exporter of software because Indian mathematicians are very cheap. Given all that, I said, "Look, forget about the principles. India is right in the middle; we're not Zaire or Gabon. Yes, India will have to pay more for pharmaceuticals, but it's going to gain a great deal in other areas." Some countries were finally convinced that they had a much bigger stake here than they'd first thought. But usually in these talks, when another country proposes something, it's assumed that it's going to harm yours.

And you question this assumption?

It's simply wrong. The Europeans were against including the service sector in international trade negotiations simply because

American Express pushed for it so hard in 1982. If we wanted it so much, they reasoned, it had to be bad for them. But when they finally examined the question, they realized that they had a whole lot of terribly good banks, they had Lloyd's and other splendid insurance companies, and London's financial sector is nothing to sneeze at. So the Europeans changed their tune altogether and teamed up with us. So did many developing countries. A lot of them realized that their proposed trade liberalization in agriculture and textiles would be more effective if they could use advanced banking services, which their own banks could not provide, having been hamstrung by long-standing protection. So service liberalization was the best way to boost their own exports.

Can the French learn this lesson? They seem the most recalcitrant about giving up protection.

The French are not as into competition and free trade as we are, so they learn more slowly from the success that other countries, particularly America, have had with these policies. But there's no question that the value of our telecommunications example has been dramatic. Nobody asked us to break up AT&T, freeing up the American market in telecommunications, but we've gained enormously as a result. Others may take five years or ten years to follow our example, but they will.

Example works effectively today through globalization: World markets are very open, and the experience of competition in third markets can be a strong incentive for liberalization. You can't protect your own market if you want to play a global role. The developing countries' telecommunications markets are worth billions of dollars. If you're as inefficient because of excessive protection as the Japanese and the French are, it's going to hurt you there. We're seeing it happen.

So American deregulators are going to turn out to be the real heroes of the eighties?

We've really done dramatically well because of deregulation. The 1994 McKinsey study on recent American productivity growth may be slightly exaggerated, but it still underlines the point that deregulation makes our industries leaner and meaner than those of our regulated foreign rivals.

Protectionists claim that it's crazy for an open economy to try to compete with a protected one. Not so. I've been insisting to my friends in the service sector and telecommunications that this emphasis on reciprocity and refusal to open markets just because others have closed theirs is misguided. Example and competition will bring the rest of the world on board, or they'll be wiped out.

What about Motorola and its battle with the Japanese? The Japanese reaped the benefits of competition in third markets while retaining the benefits of protection at home. They partitioned their domestic market so that within six or seven years they had produced an exportable cellular product.

Because economics is about prevailing tendencies, you can always produce counterexamples. I had a teacher at Cambridge, Joan Robinson, who said that in economics virtually everything is true: You can find examples of both what you want to be true and its opposite. What you have to ascertain is the stronger tendency in a system.

Japan is one of the rare cases where protection has worked at all, and it worked largely because the Japanese have always set their minds on international markets and had complementary policies like investment in R&D and a very high rate of literacy, which made the theoretical possibility of learning under protection a reality. So it's a dangerous example. Nine-tenths of the world does not have those complementary policies, for political and other reasons, so that you get goofing-off effects rather than learning effects, and people just hide behind trade barriers, jack up prices, and stagnate in the sheltered domestic market.

If I build a model where I assume learning will happen, then of course I'll conclude that protection is efficient and protection can work. But typical world experience shows that only competition produces learning, and protection works very badly. Moreover, in the case of Motorola and Japan, yes, that was an industry where protection enabled specific Japanese firms to grow. But in electronics, as in other industries, there has also been a whole lot of intervention that hasn't worked out. The Japanese lost very badly with digital versus analog. In the car industry they tried to stop specific firms from expanding, and that didn't work out. There are lots of examples from across their economy.

Can we conclude from this that industrial policy does not work?

It's not that industrial policy doesn't ever work. After all, even private enterprise doesn't work perfectly and painlessly; it works by wiping out the failures. No method can give you 100 percent results. I believe in the value of intervention in many cases. We tend to judge public policy by an impossible test: It's supposed to work every time. I think we should allow for a failure rate at least similar to that of the private sector, which means maybe 30 percent.

My objection to industrial policy—an objection that I believe many economists are beginning to share—is that it is very, very difficult to decide which industries to support, and there's no reason to assume you'll break the 30 percent barrier. True, in the postwar years Japan grew rapidly by making relatively good choices. But the government didn't make those choices; Mitsubishi and Mitsui did. The private sector coopted the government into support of its vision, not the other way around.

You have more experience with industrial-policy bureaucrats than do many of their American admirers. What does it teach you?

My view, highly colored not only by the American example but particularly by India and the many developing countries I studied in my youth, is that bureaucrats are probably the people least likely to make wise choices. Their money is not at stake. They're able to use public financing to write off their mistakes whenever they're directly involved, and they typically don't have any micro-knowledge at all.

I am very skeptical of these people's abilities, not because of my early education as an economist, which was in fact left-wing and interventionist, but because I've observed them at work. Indeed, if Japanese bureaucrats produced the Japanese miracle, that's a miracle in itself. The entrepreneurs, the people of Japan, and the other folks who shaped modern Japanese institutions—many of them Americans—deserve the credit for having made wise choices.

And yet the Japanese government is consistently pointed to as a model of successful intervention.

A lot of Japanese government intervention fixes market failures that are peculiarly Japanese to begin with. For example, with Japan's permanent employment system it's very difficult to pool information because people don't move from industry to industry; they're stuck in one for a lifetime. In that situation you may need the government to induce a flow of information that is normal in the American labor market.

Again, as I said earlier, the successful part of the Japanese system may paradoxically have been to insulate the dynamic private sector from harmful interventions. They manage to get the government to say, "Look, we'll cordon off that area and not bother you." Governments do hundreds of things, because what do you get elected for except to meddle, right? A lot of government-corporate interaction in Japan is a mechanism for making sure the government doesn't energetically mess things up. There are channels for the private sector to tell the state, "If you screw around with something, make sure you leave out our sector. This is where Japan's future lies."

You've been skeptical that there was any such thing as an economically relevant cultural mix peculiar to Japan. You always put cultural *in quotation marks.*

I don't think I've ever denied the value of culture. I say, for example, that economics teaches us that people respond to prices. What culture does is determine the price at which you respond. So it's not *whether* you respond to economic conditions; it's *how* you respond to them.

Take India, and compare two areas: East Pakistan, which became Bangladesh, and West Pakistan. They were carved out of Bengal and Punjab respectively, with massive dislocation after the massacres that followed the partition. In Bengal it took forever and ever to put people back on their feet, and there are still refugees from that time. The Punjabis, on the other hand, never looked back. Now why was that? Well, I could say that the Bengalis were part of a feudal society where people were not used to seeking out economic opportunities. That doesn't mean that they lack economic motivation—they have plenty of it—but their cultural conditioning didn't make them run around and create opportunities. It made them look to the state, whereas the Punjabis weren't waiting for government to design anything.

So how do I explain that difference? Well, I can go back to what happened to Punjab under the British Empire. The British started irrigation works, recruited the Punjabis into the army to fight the Afghan wars, and then settled them at a very young age on the irrigated lands. So the Punjabis went through army discipline and became very successful farmers and a potential entrepreneurial class. Now that's a kind of quasi-cultural explanation.

But if you ask, "Why did these guys get coopted into the British Army when the Bengalis didn't?" I'll say, "Well, because they were martial, the British must have seen something. If you go back to Alexander's invasion, he got a pretty good fight in the Punjab and turned back. Maybe, as the contemporary accounts suggest, Punjabis have been very martial for two and a half thousand years; some cultures can be pretty durable. Maybe Alexander figured India was full of these guys and it wasn't worth going on. If he had, however, he would have conquered the country in a couple of weeks. Most of us have never been martial." Score one for a cultural explanation, but it's a question of how you use the cultural arguments. If you use them to say, "Economics doesn't matter," you probably don't understand the culture you're talking about. Cultures shape specific responses, but Punjabis and Bengalis both respond to markets.

Isn't it odd that a great enthusiasm for a Japanese model should arise in America just as it's fading in Japan, where its defects become painfully clear?

Yes. During the 1980s we Americans began thinking of the Japanese as either Supermen or Lex Luthors, or both—omnipotent or very wicked, or both. The omnipotence argument has been punctured, and now we've got to tone down the notion that they're so different from us. Once you understand their different circumstances, a lot of their practices can be explained in economics terms. The Japanese economy is far less culturally determined than we seem to believe, and the most important cultural factor is reactive nationalism—the desire to outdo foreigners—which is both diminishing and not uniquely Japanese.

American–Japanese trade negotiations seem to generate strong American nationalistic sentiment. What is your sense of the negotiations that are going on now?

I think that the Clinton administration believes that the Japanese market is used as a sanctuary. It thinks the Japanese exploit their internal market, grow strong there, then go out and take over the world. If you believe that, then you have to try to break into their market. The Japanese did to some extent use their home market that way to take over the D-RAM market in the 1980s. But we must remember that we've come back in a big way with higher value-added chips, underlining the fact that the sanctuary concern is exaggerated and even hysterical.

At the same time, there's no smoke without fire, and a lot of people have had unpleasant experiences trying to enter Japanese markets. Unfortunately, however, I think the president is completely conditioned by the experience of his economic advisers. If I'd spent all my time for the better part of a decade listening to Mr. Scully or the Motorola people, I wouldn't find out whether Japanese unfairness actually mattered very much. If you don't do some independent tests, you're just recording these stories from the point of view of industry.

Has that view had too much influence on the Clinton administration?

Well, there is little doubt that the president chose advisers who bought into this extreme view. As a result, our policy shifted rather dramatically, and we insisted that the Japanese government somehow deliver "results." Essentially, the president's men were saying to the Japanese, "Look, we think that you are excluding our imports in all kinds of unfair and inscrutable ways. We don't know exactly how you do it. But we know that you are doing it. So we are going to put your feet to the fire and ask you to deliver results in the form of more imports. It is up to you to decide how to do it."

One time I called up an eminent newspaperman who had bought into this line so much that he was known as the administration's unofficial spokesman. In response to my protests, he replied: "When it came to dealing with Middle East terrorist attacks on us, the smartest thing for us to do was to go to Syria, which was really behind it all, and say, 'We don't know how it's going on, but you have influence and you are encouraging it or doing nothing to stop it, so you work it out any way you can, or we'll bomb the hell out of you.'"

To him, dealing with Japan on trade was analogous to dealing with Syria on terrorism! If you buy such a diagnosis, the rest follows, but I don't buy that diagnosis, nor do a lot of other economists. We'd like to see Japanese deregulation; we'd like to see a stronger Fair Trade Commission; we'd like to be able to take the Japanese to GATT, so that the process would be symmetrical. If we take the Japanese to court, then the Japanese, on certain other things, should be able to take us to court.

Now, it would be nice if we could just tell the Japanese, as judge, complainant, and jury, "You're being unfair. Stop." That was possible when they were weak, and it may have been justifiable when their markets were closed, and it wasn't even a terrible idea when we were looking at specific and identifiable practices.

But when the Japanese are strong and they're becoming more open and they're ready to use impartial and symmetrical dispute settlement procedures, this is a very bad way to do business. Trying to get the Japanese to regulate their economy more (to fulfill import targets) when views in Japan have changed in favor of deregulation is perverse. My opinion is that the problem is exaggerated anyway, but even if it is not, our methods are not the right ones.

I think that President Clinton has really gotten off on the wrong foot. The Japanese system is changing culturally and economically, and we ought to be encouraging that change. We have extensive experience with deregulation, and we should be providing Japan with that expertise, which it can use.

Turning to the Uruguay Round of GATT, some Republicans now seem to be hesitant about it.

Yes, the first important one to break ranks was Newt Gingrich, who started talking last spring about how the Uruguay Round means that we will lose sovereignty. That is short-sighted.

The postwar movement of Republicans away from protectionist philosophies and of Democrats toward them was a historic switch in American politics. Do you think that they are beginning to flip again, with the crude nationalism of Pat Buchanan and now Newt Gingrich?

I don't know where that's coming from. I thought it was confined to a fringe, but Newt Gingrich is, after all, a historian, a well-read guy. He really bothered me because the Republicans on the whole played a very good role in NAFTA, and for them now to appear to be sabotaging the GATT is very worrying. It's hard for me to see what game Gingrich is playing.

Well, clearly Buchanan made an intelligent bet, if not yet a winning one: that isolationist, xenophobic politics have a future with the American people.

I think his fundamental notion is that the Third World consists of a lot of tinhorn dictatorships. This image is increasingly at variance with reality but, though outdated, it still plays very well. That is one of the legacies of the NAFTA debate. Mexico was also accused of sending hordes of paupers our way and stealing all the jobs, so free trade with Mexico was regarded as a suicide pact.

NAFTA created a mindset whose residue we still have to live with. The debate left a widespread conviction that our wages are going to be depressed by trading with poor countries, that they are going to diminish our sovereignty, and that they are not really legitimate governments.

You have argued that the fear of Third World competition driving American wages down and unemployment up is poorly supported by available data.

Yes, this is so. Nearly all research shows that these dynamics are powered not by trade with poor countries, but by technical change. The real pressure on wages is coming from massive technological change, which takes incomes away from the unskilled and redistributes them up the skill ladder. Unemployment and low wages are not inflicted on the North by the South; they are produced by the North's technical progress, which will create problems for the poor countries too. The new technology is so productive that it can create unemployment for unskilled people around the globe.

Is there a near- or middle-term solution to the unemployment wrought by this technical revolution?

Not really. Labor Secretary Robert Reich is grasping at the only idea anyone has, which is to make people better educated, but that's more easily said than done. Improving education is not a straightforward thing like building factories abroad to lower labor costs. It's more like population control. There is no easy solution.

Ultimately that is the threat to freer trade: When you can't do anything meaningful to help people, they'll grasp at straws. Even if competition with the South is only 10 percent of the problem, knocking off that 10 percent is politically appealing, especially if nobody has a clue about what to do about the other 90 percent.

III

The Diminished
Giant Syndrome:
The Obsessive Search
for "Fair Trade" and
Reciprocity

4   The Diminished Giant Syndrome: How Declinism Drives Trade Policy

The perception, far exceeding the reality, of American decline is having subtly harmful consequences for U.S. international economic policy. The curse of declinism, manifest from the mid-1980s but contained by the Bush administration, was indulged to excess by Bill Clinton's campaign. Its political success in ending Republican presidential reign adds a lethal edge to the prospect that U.S. leadership will be sacrificed to the myopic and self-indulgent pursuit of "what's in it for us" economic policies in the world arena.

The American mood parallels Great Britain's at the end of the nineteenth century. Germany and the United States had emerged on the world economic scene as major players, threatening the end of the British century. Today it is Japan that has emerged, threatening to open a Pacific century. As was Great Britain at that time, America has been struck by a "diminished giant syndrome"—reinforced by the slippage in the growth of its living standards in the 1980s. This affliction has caused a loss of confidence in America's inherited postwar trade policies.

When the syndrome hit Great Britain, unilateral free trade had been received doctrine, with Germany and the United States seen, correctly, as embracing tariffs to protect nascent industries.

Originally published in *Foreign Affairs* 72 (Spring 1993): 22–26. Copyright 1993 by the Council on Foreign Relations, Inc. Reprinted with permission.

Figure 4.1
The "diminished giant syndrome" afflicted the United States, as a result of
Japan's phenomenal rise, in the 1980s. It was manifest also in Great Britain at the
end of the nineteenth century, as the United States and Germany grew in the
world economy. Sir Howard Vincent, Member, entered the British Parliament,
Evelyn Waugh style, festooned with mops, pails, and brushes marked "made in
Germany," to alert his fellow Members to the German threat. Illustration by the
Punch cartoonist E. T. Reed.

The ensuing debate was about renouncing British unilateralism, which had been practiced with a passion for nearly half a century. In the United States a parallel view has grown—with presumably immense influence in the Clinton administration—that America too has disarmed itself unilaterally in trade while others compete "unfairly" and that the time has come to shift from being patsies who turn the other cheek to becoming aggressive traders.

The British reality of asymmetrical trade barriers, which survived that nineteenth-century debate, is matched today only by America's perception of the same. This perception is grossly disproportionate to the reality, but it is driving Washington toward trade policies that could well endanger the postwar trading system that it has so assiduously nurtured for more than forty years. It rests on a measure of self-serving exaggeration and distortion of facts, all a result of the panic and petulance that attend the diminished giant syndrome. Two examples should illustrate.

First, the belief is strong on Capitol Hill that, in the postwar period of nearly half a century, America gave away trade concessions and collected few in return. This was true in a few cases, as with developing countries and Europe right after World War II. But after the earliest rounds of multilateral negotiations, in every successive round America has sought and gained balanced concessions. Indeed, by most judgments the proposed "Dunkel draft" agreement for the Uruguay Round of the General Agreement on Tariffs and Trade (GATT) is heavily unbalanced in America's favor. Reciprocity, not unilateralism, has been America's motto in trade through nearly all its history. The contrary notion rests on a myth. But, held with conviction, it fuels the sense that America needs to switch from a multilateral exchange of concessions to unilateral demands for unrequited concessions by others. The earlier bargains were "unfair." Thus the new order should redress the imbalance that America's altruism spawned and which the aggrieved power can now ill afford.

Figure 4.2
Members of Congress gather on Capitol Hill on July 1, 1987, to smash a Toshiba radio cassette recorder to protest Japan's Toshiba Corp. sale of technology to the Soviet Union. They include Rep. Don Ritter, R-Pa., Rep. Helen Bentley, R-Md., and Rep. Elton Gallegly, R-Calif.

Second, the notion that Japan is "closed" is by now accepted among many as an article of faith. It continually leads to demands for managed trade in the shape of commitments by Tokyo for quantitative import targets and export concessions by Japanese industries. But these demands do not distinguish between "openness" and "penetrability." The Japanese market is open to manufactured imports, largely as a result of the trade liberalizations of the early 1980s. The U.S. market, on the other hand, is dominated by voluntary export restraints (on automobiles, among other items) and antidumping actions, from which Japan has abstained. But there remain many complaints of the difficulty of penetration resulting from Japanese institutions and practices that create witting and unwitting roadblocks to market access.

These cascading complaints are often a reflection of the fact that the Japanese economy has different institutional features that are a consequence of its history. Japan's success in escaping colonization and its policy of selectively importing foreign technology and ideas—and even of keeping foreigners at a distance within Japan —have prevented the extensive acculturation that other countries such as China and India went through over a century ago. Japan has been exposed to this process only since its postwar occupation. By now, however, the nation is changing rapidly. The new pace of acculturation is reflected in the prominent Japanese novelist Junichiro Tanizaki's poignant essay, "In Praise of Shadows," which laments the passing of the old Japan. But acculturation works not merely through the conventional diffusion of American culture. It also operates through the extensive presence abroad of Japanese multinationals, and hence Japanese executives and their families.

The perception that the Japanese market is open and substantial has finally led to an increased willingness to undertake the added fixed costs necessary to enter it. The complaints about Japan's impenetrability are a clear sign that Japan is, in fact, being penetrated effectively. The unfamiliarity of the terrain is generating unreasonable demands that the Japanese landscape be remade in America's own image. The results of this penetration are reflected in the unprecedented rise in the late 1980s in the ratio of manufactured imports to GNP and as a share of total imports. Demands for widespread changes in Japanese institutions and for managed trade, quite aside from their potential for damage to a rulesbased world trading regime, thus reflect a panic that is not justified by the unfolding situation.

Japan's chronic payments surplus is not a sign of its "closed" market or of predation by Japanese exporters in America's "open" market. Balance of payments surpluses and deficits reflect macroeconomic factors, not trade barriers. Occasionally, concerned congressional representatives will bow to this economic logic. More often, however, they revert to what they think is surely "obvious." Thus, many in Congress now seek to renew the Super 301 provision of the 1988 Omnibus Trade and Competitiveness Act, which would enable the Clinton administration to tag countries such as Japan as unfair traders—the criterion being that the competing nation accounts for more than 15 percent of the U.S. trade deficit. In her confirming testimony, even the president's chief economist, Laura D'Andrea Tyson, appeared to give a nod to this notion of a trade-barrier-caused payments deficit.

Of course, the Japanese trade surplus has grown even as its trade barriers have come down. Nor should one forget that, for a longer period than the "chronic" Japanese surplus, there existed the dreaded "dollar shortage" after World War II—and America would hardly accuse itself of being a closed or closing economy during those years of extensive trade liberalization. Nonetheless the Japanese surplus creates an inexorable sense that this "proves" that Japan is "closed" and, in turn, it drives demands for foolish changes in U.S. trade policy. The corrosive influence of these sentiments and misunderstandings is manifest in policy shifts that are already diluting the U.S. commitment to multilateralism, even as the president offers occasional support for the Uruguay Round.

Unilateralism Hurts GATT

Support for aggressive unilateralism has grown. Threats of protectionist retaliation when others fail to meet either multilateral or bilateral treaty obligations is not the issue. It is only an issue when Washington uses its economic power to attempt to secure new concessions or changes in established trade practices that it unilaterally declares unfair or unacceptable. Such trade threats create the impression, now worldwide, that America believes in the law of the jungle rather than the rule of law—especially when these trade retaliations themselves are illegal under the GATT.

The Clinton campaign unfortunately committed itself to reviving the lapsed Super 301 legislation in its manifesto, "Putting People First." This proposed legislation, alongside the attachment to the use of unilateralism, has added yet another objection to U.S. acceptance of the Dunkel draft to settle the Uruguay Round: Washington now seeks to make the use of 301-type trade retaliation legal under the GATT. This demand is most unlikely to be met since, as GATT chief Arthur Dunkel is supposed to have remarked, the best thing that the United States did for the GATT was to start down the 301 and Super 301 road, thus unifying an outraged and alarmed world behind the trading regime.

The problem with the embrace of aggressive unilateralism is that, in the end, other countries will not suffer it gladly. The use of Super 301 in 1989 did not work against India and Brazil, which both refused to bow to U.S. demands. Japan responded tangentially and eventually settled with few concessions. Taiwan and South Korea made small concessions to avoid being named. The European Community (EC) was left unmolested, having made amply clear its intention not to be browbeaten.

The reaction in Japan to the prospect of reviving Super 301 is likely to be more spirited this time. The Matsushita Committee report and business groups have argued for Japan to arm itself with Super 301 legislation of its own; there has been similar talk in Europe. Undoubtedly some countries would take the United States to the GATT dispute settlement process if it became clear that, unlike the Bush administration, which tended to moderate the use of such actions, the Clinton administration was enthusiastic for them.

Widespread use of Super 301–style tools would create an environment in which countries, even if not engaged in trade wars, would be charging each other unilaterally, with unfair trade practices, psyching each other out with tough talk and threatened action. The atmospherics would become conducive to a breakdown of the trust and confidence necessary to maintaining an orderly, predictable trading system—precisely the climate in which protectionism may flourish. An excellent illustration is provided by the threatened use of the antidumping clause by Detroit's Big Three automakers. Once they thought that the Clinton administration favored aggressive action against foreign competition, they resorted to the "unfair trade" mechanism to secure their ends, as would be expected. But once foreign firms are unilaterally characterized as predatory or as being unfairly assisted by their own governments, or once foreign governments are accused of protecting their home turf—as indeed the Clinton people are given to doing—the outbreak of real trade wars looms that much larger.

Danger of Trade Blocs

Declinist sentiments may push the United States dangerously close to regionalism. Again there is an interesting parallel with Britian. In nineteenth-century Britain those who wanted to resort to (reciprocal) protection often also favored imperial preference, which would reserve British colonies for British goods, against Germany and America.

Today the enthusiasm for regional free trade areas is dressed up as a great free trade move. But it is evident that the main motivation is protectionist: Mexico becomes America's preferential market, with Japan and the EC at a disadvantage. Surely the relatively lukewarm enthusiasm among most American business groups for the Uruguay Round—as compared with passionate support for the North American Free Trade Agreement—can be attributed in large part to the fact that any advantages America gains under the GATT are equally doled out to rivals in the EC and Japan, while under NAFTA they flow asymmetrically to the United States.

As long as the talk of "head to head" confrontation with the EC and Japan drives U.S. policy—with its zero-sum implication that their success means America's failure—Washington will move toward preferential trading arrangements. As it pushes yet further into South America, Washington will certainly provoke an Asian trading bloc. Unless the United States stops NAFTA at Mexico and turns firmly toward GATT-based multilateralism, a likely consequence of its obsession with decline will be a fragmented world of four blocs: an augmented EC; NAFTA extending into the Americas; a Japan-centered Asian bloc; and a fourth "bloc" of marginalized nations such as those of South Asia and Africa whose recent shift toward outward trade will be frustrated by preferential trade arrangements. That would be a tragedy.

Pessimism about America's ability to lead in the teeth of its diffidence and declinism is only accentuated when one focuses on the prospects it faces in trade policy. Economists, whose science is soft rather than hard, are inordinately pleased when their predictions come true. Nonetheless, in the present instance my failure would please me all the more.

5   Hormones and Trade Wars

Hormones can be dangerous. Imprudently used, they could ruin our lives and infest the Olympics. But—would you believe—they can even start trade wars. When the European Community's ban on hormone-fed beef went into effect on January 1, 1989, we imposed retaliatory tariffs, thus firing the opening shots of what may turn into a battle, perhaps a war, before the dust settles.

This round of punch, counterpunch is only the latest consequence of the ugly mood that has afflicted our trade policymakers recently and is reflected in full measure in the trade legislation enacted last summer. The potential for more mischief, for multiple births of trade conflicts following in the footsteps of the flap over hormones, is real.

The Bush administration will have to hang tough. It will have to face down lobbies armed with the new trade law or the United States will be increasingly engaged in the heavy-handed pursuit of narrow trade interests.

Both the year-old dispute over hormones and the 1988 legislation reflect an illogical conviction that our trade problems are a response to unfair practices of our trading rivals, rather than to our own macroeconomic folly and the inevitable rise of new nations to shared prominence in world trade.

Originally published in the *New York Times* (January 9, 1989). Copyright © 1989 by The New York Times Co. Reprinted by permission.

The refrain on Capitol Hill may well be a variation on Macbeth's witches: Your fair is foul and our foul is fair. The suspicion of our rivals' perfidy, of their insidious closing of their markets while exploiting ours, is unshakable.

The dispute over beef illustrates this only too well. The Europeans are fully within their rights, under the General Agreement on Tariffs and Trade, in defining their social policy to ban consumption of hormone-fed beef. What they cannot do is to ban such imports while allowing domestic production.

Other nations such as Australia and Argentina, which are far more dependent on agriculture than the United States, have accepted this. Indeed, these nations and Europe accept our own social-policy-based restrictions such as the ban on nonpasteurized cheese. The Europeans even delayed the imposition of the ban by a year and made an exception for imports of the banned beef for consumption by pets, thus easing adjustment problems for exporters. Why the fuss then?

Essentially, our complaint is that there is no scientific evidence to justify the ban. There is the suspicion, therefore, that the Europeans are really out to restrict our exports. But none of this is sensible; it reflects petulance and paranoia.

Social policy does not always reflect compelling scientific evidence. Often, in fact, confirming evidence trails the concern. Evidence which triggers action varies across countries; indeed, we ban drugs that others don't for evidence they find insufficient. It is ludicrous therefore to make war over the issue of scientific evidence. The Europeans have imposed the ban in response to internal social demands from health groups, not from any desire to protect domestic producers.

The 1988 Omnibus Trade and Competitiveness Act, better rechristened the Ominous Trade Act, only makes matters worse. Section 301 (under which the beef dispute was pressed) has been firmed up. Popularly known as Super 301, invoking the image of Superman taking on the evil genius Lex Luthor, it has been greatly expanded and forged into a lethal instrument of harassment of our trading rivals.

As amended, it urges the President to respond to any foreign policy or practice that is "unreasonable," regardless of contractual rights and treaty obligations. The long illustrative list of "unfair and inequitable" practices, decided upon unilaterally by ourselves, includes the mere "toleration" by foreign governments of "systematic anticompetitive practices," phrasing that should make legal practice in Washington particularly lucrative.

The Bush administration can certainly expect a busy season. It will have to resist the veritable flood of demands for willful and aggressive actions against foreign industries and governments that the new trade law will generate. It will have to fight the misguided attitude that the fault lies with our trading partners rather than with ourselves and a changed international scene.

.

6 The Dangers of Selective Safeguards

The trading nations are engaged, in the Uruguay Round, in the Herculean task of rebuilding the General Agreement on Tariffs and Trade (GATT). New sectors (for example, services) are to be included; new disciplines (for example, intellectual property) established; old failures (for example, textiles) corrected.

Compromises will be inevitable. But they should come through failures of accomplishments, not by surrender to those who seek to legitimate, rather than outlaw, the trading practices that flout the very principles whose embodiment makes the GATT worth fighting for. And yet, on the critical question of rewriting the traditional "safeguard" provisions in the GATT, the negotiations seem poised to do precisely that.

Currently, GATT Article 19 permits member states to increase protection temporarily for a domestic industry seriously injured by unforeseen import increases. The protection must not discriminate among different suppliers, however. But, with the support of the European Community and the United Sates, the chairman of the safeguards negotiating group has now tabled a draft agreement which—while giving general endorsement to nondiscriminatory application—states that the group should consider

Originally published in the *Financial Times* (January 10, 1990), with Robert Baldwin.

permitting country-selective restrictions in certain situations. This invitation should be rejected.

Nondiscrimination is economically sound. If imports must be restricted, it is efficient to restrict them from the inefficient sources. Tariffs that apply equally to all will ensure this result. Selective quotas will not. Selective restrictions are politically targeted at countries that are vulnerable because they are weak. Political clout, not economic efficiency, becomes the key to gaining access to international markets.

Selective restrictions encourage more protectionism. If politically weaker exporters can be selectively hit, restrictions will cause less international fallout for governments than if all exporters, strong and weak, must be hit. The cost of indulging protectionism thus falls, and the incidence of protection correspondingly rises, with selectivity.

Selective quotas are also unfair to those in injured industries the protection is aimed at helping. Producers in uncontrolled countries expand their export to take up much of the slack in supplies from the targeted countries. Even these latter countries upgrade the quality of their products so the value of their exports falls less than the quantity. As experience demonstrates, the result is that output and employment in the injured domestic industry rise less than expected. This sets off new political pressure for extending import restrictions to additional foreign suppliers. Ironically, this process can continue until all potential suppliers are covered—a result that nondiscriminatory protection gives immediately and more efficiently.

The folly of selectivity is further manifest now that the world economy is increasingly globalised. The "spider's web" of crisscrossing investments makes it ever more difficult to target imports from specific sources. Are imports from Japanese companies producing, with or without local partners, in the United States also to be targeted by the Community when it targets their exports from Japan? This question has indeed arisen and threatens a pro-liferation of trade conflicts and of solutions with new and in-herently arbitrary bureaucratic rules about "rules of origin" and "local content." Thus, does selectivity add more to the Kafkaesque maze that threatens to overwhelm the trading nations, illustrating anew the wisdom of GATT's architects in choosing nonselectivity.

Why then are the United States and the European Community calling for an examination of the circumstances under which selective safeguards might be applied? For answers, consider the following.

It is easier to secure legitimacy by changing the law rather than the errant behaviour. Evidently, existing GATT-illegal, selective export restraint arrangements in such sectors as steel, semicon-ductors, automobiles, videotape recorders, and machine tools are difficult to discard. Permitting selectivity would confer legitimacy on these protective measures, even though this is hardly what was meant by the Ministerial Resolution launching the Uruguay Round, when it was agreed that they would be brought into con-formity with GATT rules.

An explanation for the weakened commitment to nonselectivity by the United States can also be found in the recent growth of pressures for "managed trade." Exploiting the continuing trade deficit, powerful business and labour lobbies have chiselled away at traditional commitments to GATT principles, encourag-ing import protectionism, unilateralism, regionalism, and man-aged trade. The fear of the Far East has also prompted members of Congress to seek an aggressive trade policy with special U.S. privileges as America's only salvation. Selectivity in restricting imports, the oldest form of managed trade, poses no problem in this climate. It becomes an added tool for isolating the "unfairly" successful exporters, while sparing those one seeks to favour.

But the cost of legalising selectivity would be exceptionally high. Its inadequacies are evident. But selectivity is also correctly viewed as a particular threat to the developing nations: they are weak and vulnerable. At a time when new disciplines are to be imposed on them in services and elsewhere, it would be mockery indeed to remove from them the legal protection of nondiscrimination in the use of safeguards.

Above all, the fact is that managed trade is the antithesis of GATT principles. "Saving GATT" by sacrificing its tenets would be a triumph of form over substance.

7　　　　　　　　　　　Brie for Breakfast

Messrs. Cohen and Zysman are political scientists. They are the resident gurus at BRIE (Berkeley Roundtable on International Economy). While they doubtless enjoy imported French cheese, especially with the Zinfandel from the local vineyards, they get the goose pimples watching movies on their Japanese VCRs. They are worried sick by America's alleged deindustrialization. This book is their effort to say why and to startle a complacement nation into an active policy to defend its industries.

Economists will want to look at the book since it has become the bible of the manufacturing lobby and is also a favorite of the Congressmen who gave us the retrograde U.S. Trade Bill of 1988. But I should warn them that they will find the book exceptionally irritating. The reason is that the authors display throughout an unmitigated scorn for, and an ignorance of, what economists and their craft have to say about the matter at hand. It has been aptly said that familiarity breeds contempt but contempt does not breed familiarity. The unfortunate result is that the authors occasionally engage in unjustified critiques that detract from their case and will distract the reader.

Originally published in the *Journal of Economic Literature* 27 (March 1989): 121–23. Reprinted with permission.

This chapter reviews Stephen S. Cohen and John Zysman's *Manufacturing Matters: The Myth of the Post-Industrial Economy* (New York: Basic Books, 1987).

In particular, trade theorists, whose works are not cited but who are nonetheless systematically berated, will not be amused to find their writings and views misstated. For example, the authors argue that "[t]he Heckscher-Ohlin theory assumes . . . given factor endowments in each country" (p. 276), when every graduate student has read Findlay's classic (1970 *Journal of Political Economy*) article on endogenizing the growth of capital and successful extension of the theory to the long run. On the normative side, the authors evidently have not read the work of Samuelson, Smith, Srinivasan, Dixit, and others on the gains from trade in an intertemporal setting, and continue to argue as if the theory of commercial policy is wholly static and inappropriate.

These lapses do not help. But the reader should be patient, for Cohen and Zysman have a thesis that is serious. Essentially, they contend that (1) America's manufactures are in jeopardy; (2) manufactures matter for prosperity; and, therefore, (3) active governmental intervention, including "strategic" trade policy, is necessary. I am afraid, however, that I am not persuaded by their arguments.

Thus, faced by Robert Lawrence's compelling contention that the share of manufactures in U.S. value-added has remained steady in recent decades, the authors pour scorn on him and proceed to look for other evidence that would justify their fears. Thus, for instance, they ask the reader to eye-scan charts such as the one (figure 5.3) on real wages in manufacturing, which shows a post-OPEC halt, possibly even a decline—we are unable to determine which since the authors do not use statistical tests—and to accept assertions (again without statistical documentation and analysis) that "the price elasticity of imports has increased" (p. 67), suggesting increased competition. The latter argument will please offended economists as they proceed to read that "this shift in elasticity helps account for the failure of the dropping dollar to bring American trade back towards balance" (p. 68)!

Manufacturing may indeed be in trouble in the United States, but the authors do not provide a plausible analysis as to how and why.

As for manufactures mattering, the Cohen-Zysman arguments are not more persuasive. The authors seem to believe in key sectors, recall historical episodes of growth around industries such as autos, produce French intellectuals in support of the view that we are now at such a juncture where semiconductors and high-tech must be produced at home to retain economic prosperity, and cite Japan as an example of a state that has accepted such beliefs, acted on them, and prospered. Economists will recognize this argument as implicitly one of externalities attached to manufactures (though the authors, like virtually every noneconomist, seem wrongly to consider linkages as necessarily implying externalities); they will also recognize that this is one of the hardest arguments to make empirically convincing.

In fact, the difficulties that Cohen and Zysman face here are familiar to economists since the deindustrialization thesis is by no means a novelty to them. Long before the local version offered by Cohen and Zysman, a British deindustrialization school had made waves. Led by Nicholas Kaldor, the great Cambridge economist, that school emerged in the same psychological climate as the one that has prevailed in the United States of the 1980s: one of a sense of diminishing greatness as an economic power. The British school assumed, citing the "Verdoorn Law," that manufactures were more progressive than services. Their prescriptions led in turn to Britain's adopting for a time the Selective Employment Tax, differentially taxing employment in the service sector to propel people into the manufacturing sector. The case for "reindustrialization" by protection or promotion that was proposed in Britain was never convincing to most, though it should be emphasized that economists bravely tried with patience, a priori logic, and econometrics to test its underlying premises. I am persuaded that, even if Cohen and Zysman had tried to emulate these economists, they would have failed equally: the issues are unusually intractable, and hypotheses and convictions in this gray area tend to remain just that.

As for policy intervention, I am glad to note that the authors are smart in rejecting trade protection to encourage "reindustrialization": Robert Reich has preceded them in this move to a sensible renunciation of protectionism. But they endorse "strategic" trade policy: a phrase that is now loosely used by many, experts and laymen alike, since it sounds like being clever or pursuing optimality and hence a policy that surely the "best and the brightest" can only embrace. As it happens, Cohen and Zysman mean by it simply monitoring and removing foreign interventions, trade or domestic, that give our rivals an artificial advantage in manufacturing production. As with classical infant-industry protection, especially in its Kemp-Bardhan version where technical change costlessly accrues from learning by doing, these interventions may give permanent advantage, ceteris paribus, even though the interventions themselves are transitory, and thereby reduce our level of invaluable manufacturing production. The main problem with this prescription, as embodied in the 1988 Trade Act, is that the United States would have itself decide whether foreign rivals enjoy such artificial advantages. Given the present "diminished giant" syndrome in the United States, the tendency to see such "unfair" practices by our economically successful rivals is inevitable; and given our strength, our capacity to confront our politically weaker rivals with corresponding harassments and to coerce them into trade-distorting measures such as "voluntary import expansions" (VIEs), where they divert trade from others to the United States, is considerable. But there is no comprehension of this and related threats to the postwar international trading regime to be found in the circles that feed on a steady diet of prescriptions for a "tough," a "strategic," trade policy. I have dealt with these issues at length in the 1987 Ohlin Lectures (Bhagwati 1988), while exploring further recent developments in the theory of commercial policy, and their bearing on the question of free trade, in the Harms Prize Lecture (Bhagwati 1989).

Warts and all, however, this book has the considerable merit of being relevant, possessing a clear thesis and an engaging style that the practitioners of our dismal science can no longer command and have almost forgotten to value. It is certainly worth your time, if not your money.

References

Bhagwati, Jagdish. 1988. *Protectionism.* 1987 Ohlin Lectures, Cambridge: M.I.T. Press.

———. 1989. "Is Free Trade Passé after All?" Bernhard Harms Prize Speech, *Weltwirtschaftliches Archiv* 125 (1): 17–44.

8   Rough Trade

Laura Tyson, the chief of President Clinton's Council of Economic Advisers, is anything but uncontroversial. She is also immensely smart. Her economist critics err when they cite her lack of academic distinction relative to their own as evidence of folly in the president's choice.

And yet good policy judgment comes in two varieties. You recognize it in others when they reach conclusions identical to your own, or when they persuade you to change yours. It is not a quality that many economists have, but it is desirable, certainly, in the president's chief economist. Unfortunately, if Laura Tyson's new book on trade policy is any guide, there is cause for concern.

The book displays a certain political skill. Tyson hedges by describing herself as a "cautious activist," and by making accommodating noises to keep critics at bay. Still, for all her disarming and disclaiming, her economic views emerge all too clearly. Tyson would overturn the basic premises of our postwar trading policies. And her arguments fail to persuade.

Concentrating on "high-tech" industries, Tyson declares herself in favor of three kinds of government action to help these

Originally published in the *New Republic* (May 31, 1993): 35–40. Reprinted with permission.

This chapter reviews Laura D'Andrea Tyson's *Who's Bashing Whom?: Trade Conflict in High-Technology Industries* (Washington, D.C.: Institute for International Economics, 1993).

industries: first, selective subsidies; second, the use of "aggressive unilateralism" in the form of threats to close our markets and to pry open foreign markets that we unilaterally judge to be closed to us unfairly; and third, a resort to "managed trade," which economists define as the setting of restrictive quotas on imports and targets to expand exports, Tyson choosing the latter.

All of this she urges with "caution," and under "appropriate" conditions. But these policies would undermine, for a sizable and growing segment of world trade, the current international trading system. Under that system, the use of subsidies has been increasingly constrained. New trade obligations have been established through reciprocal concessions rather than through using intimidation to extract one-way concessions; and the trend is toward settling trade disputes in impartial multilateral tribunals. Moreover, managed or "results-oriented" trade, where bureaucrats fix quantities to be traded, has increasingly given way to "rules-based" trade, where the quantities traded reflect competition, just as in a game it is the rules that are fixed and not the final score.

Fearing Tyson's beliefs, which they have gleaned mostly from her reputation for being "against free trade" rather than from a close reading of her work, economists have reacted in two defensive ways. Herbert Stein, a former chairman of the Council of Economic Advisers, let his hopes triumph over his expectations, and in the *Wall Street Journal* he predicted that Tyson would return to the fold. Robert Barro of Harvard University, in the same newspaper, took an outlandish line: it did not matter who ran the Council of Economic Advisers, since it influenced nothing.

But such reassurances will not suffice. Tyson is a powerful figure now, and as her book makes clear, she has an agenda. Indeed, the most likely explanation for Tyson's appointment is the most obvious one: the president finds that her views broadly coincide with his own. (The president's unrehearsed statements on trade policy at his first press conference only confirmed this impression.) The importance of high-tech industries and the need to promote them in all necessary ways: these appear to be home truths that only impractical "theorists," who are out of touch with "reality," ignore. Few politicians remember, of course, that common sense is precisely the quality that makes people assert that the earth is flat, since that is how it appears to the naked eye.

The president can also be expected to be responsive to the high-tech executives who flocked around him during the campaign. And a president who won the campaign preaching an exaggerated message of economic decline will be vulnerable to economists who can equate high-tech special pleading with socially desirable policy. Tyson certainly plays that tune. The policy program of her book rests on the following logic. High-tech industries are more important than others; international trade and competition in them are skewed, because our trading rivals intervene more heavily than we do; when others intervene to help their high-tech industries, we must intervene, too; and the appropriate policies include subsidies, trade retaliation, and managed trade.

Each of these assertions is unconvincing at best, flawed at worst. Consider, first, her infatuation with high-technology industry. Being high-tech is popularly thought to be synonymous with occupying the high ground; making semiconductor chips is better than making potato chips, as Clyde Prestowitz put it. Ross Perot loved Prestowitz's motto so much that he used it in the presidential debate. And Bill Clinton found Prestowitz's support so important that he cited it in the final debate as proof of his own Silicon Valley virtue. And yet, for all these endorsements, and Tyson's, the argument is shallow.

The definition of high-tech industry, for a start, is much too nebulous for purposes of policy. One favored criterion is above-average spending on research and development; but there are different ways of defining averages, and the period over which you calculate the average will yield different groups of high-tech industries. Also, if you think high-tech means using advanced technological know-how and highly skilled labor, then you may be in for some surprises. Michael Schrage has written in the *Los Angeles Times* about how potato chips are actually made by PepsiCo.'s Frito-Lay subsidiary. It turns out that those guys are not slouches chewing tobacco on an assembly line that has seen no changes since Chaplin's days. Potato chips are made by pretty sophisticated technology these days.

Prestowitz has clearly bitten off more than he can munch; and so has Tyson. It is also not enough to say, as Tyson does, that R&D has beneficial spillovers for society at large, and that economists agree that those spillovers are often uncompensated. At best, that argues only for a general, rather than industry-specific, subsidy for research and development. Tyson is also guilty of concentrating only on R&D in manufactures as a source of uncompensated spillover effects. But don't doctors earn less than the happiness they provide simply by being accessible when you fall sick? Banks provide valuable infrastructure: Is this reflected in their profits? Are teachers' salaries a measure of their true worth? If I had to hazard an informed guess, I would say that services are at least as prone on the average as manufactures to yield uncompensated spillover effects, maybe more.

But Tyson wants to make a very specific case for singling out particular industries for support. She argues that certain high-tech industries have greater cachet in creating uncompensated externalities than do industries not on her list, and are therefore deserving of governmental support. But she does not bother to look at the evidence, sparse as it is, on where the uncompensated externalities are, and whether they correspond to her pecking order of favored industries. Economist Edwin Mansfield did careful work on the returns from seventeen industrial innovations, and he found that the highest discrepancy between social and private returns from innovation was in "thread innovation" and then in "stain removers," neither of which would rank high on a high-tech list, or even appear on such a list at all. Besides, these discrepancies are so different across industries, and so difficult to predict, that selecting any one industry, or any one bunch of industries, for prior support is nothing more than an act of faith. The empirical basis for such a selection is shaky indeed.

Unless Tyson has a crystal ball and can plausibly foresee, which she cannot, which industries are most deserving of a subsidy, we must stick to tax breaks for all R&D. It is a policy about which we may agree, since all we can tell for sure is that R&D in general turns out to have a social rate of return that vastly exceeds its private rate of return. This may favor the "high-tech" industries on Tyson's list. But it may not, since "over the last decade, the ten ... industries classified as high-technology industries by the U.S. Department of Commerce funded nearly 60 percent of private industrial R&D in the United States." That more than 40 percent of American R&D is funded by non-high-tech industries suggests that the net effect of a general R&D subsidy may well be to pull resources to these industries rather than to Tyson's preferred ones. And this would likely be the better outcome.

Moreover, recent research by economists David Dollar and Edward Wolff has shown that Japan's particular industries, including high-tech industries, "emphatically" contribute nothing to explaining why Japan's aggregate productivity has been catching up with ours. Although "much of the American obsession with Japan arises from that country's success in some highly visible [mostly high-tech] lines: automobiles, television, VCRs and computers," they conclude that "Japan caught up with the United States because its relative productivity increased in every industry." The same basic result holds for other OECD countries, and therefore "there is not some key industry or product line that has to be captured as the means to economic success."

I suspect that the preference for computer chips over potato chips is, in the end, also a form of quasi-Marxist technological determinism. Surely it is not what you produce that determines what you are; it is what you do with yourself. You could be producing semiconductor chips, fitting boards mindlessly, exporting them in order to import potato chips, eating them as you watch television, and turning into a society of morons. Alternatively, you could be producing potato chips with advanced technology, exporting them to import semiconductor chips embedded in PCs that you use imaginatively to improve yourself, turning into a society of creative citizens. It is the "fundamentals," your education and your aspiration, that finally matter, not your work station and your industry.

Proceeding from the unproved premise that the high-tech industries must be preferred, Tyson argues that we are sitting by idly while others intervene sensibly to seduce high-tech to their shores. Why do we tie our hands while others fight? Partly because we refuse to admit that others do fight; and partly because we subscribe to the defunct doctrine of free trade, turning the other cheek.

Tyson's contention that others fight and we don't rests on case studies that are selective; they do not reflect an unbiased sample. Sure enough, Motorola pagers had a difficult time breaking into Japan, and the European airbus was subsidized with dogged determination. But you would not know from Tyson that the Japanese government's subsidies for private sector R&D, for example, are no more than $1 billion annually, running at about 3 percent of the $30 billion in R&D subsidies dispensed to private companies by our government. Indeed, as Gary Saxonhouse has noted, our government spends far more, in absolute and proportional terms, than Japan's on civilian R&D even when our defense-related expenditures are ignored.

The selectivity of Tyson's empirical research is also evident in her discussion of the complex issue of Japan's "closed" markets. Tyson cites only those who favor her own position, ignoring the work of Saxonhouse and Robert Stern, who have shown that Japan's average tariffs and nontariff barriers have fallen to negligible levels, perhaps even to levels lower than ours. Indeed, in manufactures, our extensive use of voluntary export restraints (for example, on Japanese autos) and our resort to antidumping actions, given Japan's virtual self-denial of these protectionist devices, put our manufacturing protection well ahead of theirs.

The debate has shifted, therefore, to "structural" barriers in Japan's market. To understand this issue, recall the Tarzan movies of your childhood. The jungle may be closed to you because the natives, led by the chief, are shooting poisoned arrows at you. But if they are not, and the jungle is open (and inviting because of the gold that it promises), the progress of the safari through the jungle is constrained by the tall grass and the thick vegetation. Then again, the path through the jungle is hazardous because of the dangers posed by traps, laid by natives to hunt animals but inadvertently dangerous to the safari as well. In short, openness and penetrability are different things.

The focus of the debate about Japan has now shifted from openness to penetrability, even though politicians and sloppy economists continue to talk of Japan's "closed" market. Is the penetrability of the Japanese market for manufactures unusually low? Attempts at proving that Japan is impenetrable are a growth industry in the high-tech economics sector, but it is the rare study that is not in dispute. The most cogent analyses have been directed at showing how Japan's *keiretsus* (or close-knit business groups) reduce imports from abroad by buying preferentially from their own domestic suppliers. But even these studies run into serious conceptual problems. *Keiretsus* are informal groupings, and hence hard to work into statistical analysis. They come in many different varieties. Moreover, vertical *keiretsus* (closely linked suppliers and users) are only an informal counterpart of vertically integrated companies, far more common here. Do we complain about IBM making its own semiconductor chips (and hence preventing Hitachi from selling them to IBM by "denying access"), or about General Motors, which produces more than 75 percent of its parts itself (while the share of the average in-house production of parts in Japanese auto plants is closer to 25 percent)? Indeed, some of the same factors that encourage close supplier relationships among firms there stimulate vertical integration here. Can the same thing be bad in Japan and good in America?

To be sure, those who find others to be competing unfairly rarely examine their own backward. It is not just that similar roadblocks can obtain at both ends. Rather, what we consider to be perfectly reasonable, given our culture and our history, will often present obstacles to others who evolved differently. If the safari finds the jungle difficult to penetrate, the debut of the Earl of Greystoke in London and the entry of Crocodile Dundee into New York were no walkover, either. Think of how the older-generation Japanese must have struggled to get a toehold in our markets, which presented both perils and opportunities: the English language was an imposing barrier to entry, and residues of racism were widespread.

Tyson ignores all such complications of perspective, advocating that the United States respond head-to-head, matching each ploy with a ploy of our own. As the Clinton campaign promised in *Putting People First*, if they do not play by our rules, we will play by theirs. Tyson suggests that this "eye for an eye" response has been inhibited in the United States by the doctrine of unilateral free trade, now defunct because of a "new" theory of trade. She errs. We have never been unilateral free traders. The "old" theory of trade allows amply for shared embrace of free trade. The

GATT, designed and supported by the most distinguished free traders of the postwar generation of international economists, is premised on the mutuality of trade obligations and concessions. The reasons for not going along with Tyson's prescriptions are far more complex and nuanced than mere reflexive commitment to unilateral free trade.

The lament that our markets are open when others are closed has its flip side in the current self-indulgent view that we have been altruists in our trade policy, giving concessions that are not matched by those we receive. This belief does not sit well with the facts. Unlike nineteenth-century Britain, with its passionate commitment to unilateral free trade, we have generally insisted on reciprocity of concessions. Even the Trade Act of 1934, which began trade liberalization after the disastrous Smoot-Hawley Tariff of 1930, has the word "reciprocal" in its title. What we did in the postwar period was to provide leadership in creating and sustaining a GATT-based multilateral trading system, geared to opening markets through successive rounds of negotiations. But you can lead without being altruistic. In virtually all rounds (except the very earliest, when the others were prostrate after the war), we collected as much as we gave.

It is also incorrect to assert that free traders have generally been unilateralists because that is what the "old" trade theory of Adam Smith taught them. Yes, we do teach our students that if others harm themselves and us through trade barriers, that is not reason to compound the damage by erecting our own. As Joan Robinson used to say, if others throw rocks into their harbor, why throw rocks into your own? But then we also know that Adam Smith had clearly advanced the argument that there are times when we may usefully threaten to impose tariffs to get others to remove theirs. You may be able to throw rocks at others and thereby to force them to dredge up the ones they have thrown into their own harbor.

Cosmopolitan free traders also have argued for symmetry of free trade obligations. I might gain if you subsidize and cheapen the goods that I import; but your subsidy distorts the incentives shaping the allocation of activity among different nations. Cosmopolitan free traders prefer free trade for all to unilateral free trade by oneself, just as one may gain by receiving stolen property but object to doing so because of the effect that would have on the system at large. In fact, the GATT, overseeing world trade since 1947 and now 108 nations strong, embodies precisely these "systemic" views of free trade. In both trade obligations and concessions, the institution seeks symmetry and reciprocity.

Tyson, then, need not fear free traders. Few free traders are for unilateral disarmament. But they need fear her. For she goes well beyond the suspension of belief in unilateral free trade to embrace aggressive unilateralism against our rivals. She endorses our use of (even GATT-illegal) tariffs against countries whom we have unilaterally decided are "unfairly" competing with us; she wants to enforce corrective measures, including a commitment from them to import targeted quantities of specific items such as semiconductor chips. Thus, she challenges (and, as the president's chief economist, endangers) multilateralism as the process for establishing and enforcing trade discipline. She is an enemy of rules-based trade.

The heavy hand of American industries is evident in Tyson's thinking, not least in her failure to consider that the interventions of foreign governments may have been foolish and our failure to match them may have been wise. The Concorde, a commercial disaster, gets only one mention in her book. She fails to probe thoroughly the story of high-definition television, told by Cynthia Beltz, in which the Japanese government was "proactive" but backed the wrong (analog) horse, while we were passive and won by betting on the (digital) winner. Clearly, this is the highest profile test case for those in favor of selective industrial policy. Its proponents clamored for intervention: influential business, labor, and congressional leaders sent an open letter to President Bush and Congress, urging that the government support this crucial technology, warning that our trading rivals were already investing hundreds of millions of dollars in it.

On the European airbus and on Japanese semiconductors, there are many studies now suggesting that governmental support produced disadvantageous results. But Tyson either ignores them or dismisses them summarily with agile footnotes. The grounds on which she rejects the well-known study by Richard Baldwin and Paul Krugman, which concluded that the Japanese policy on semiconductors had harmed the Japanese economy, are telling. Tyson argues that the Japanese government's first priority was to support and attract the semiconductor industry, rather than to worry about the costs to consumer welfare, and that in any case, thanks to the spillover effects from producing one's own chips, the disadvantages of intervention were exaggerated.

But this will not do. Surely Tyson would not want to evaluate industrial policy in terms of industry-defined or government-defined objectives such as protecting production, rewarding friends, and satisfying lobbies, without asking whether the policy was socially desirable or undesirable. And the broad appeal to spillovers, without any attempt at calculating whether they are large enough to offset Baldwin and Krugman's findings, is a trifle disappointing in a work that advocates a shift in our policies on the basis of economic analysis. Tyson's attitude plays into the hands of those who facetiously argue that spillovers and externalities are the last refuge of the scoundrel, and of others, more cynical, who maintain that they are the first.

But if Tyson, along with American industries, exaggerates the need to match what others do by mistaking their occasional folly for beneficial intervention, she is also overzealous in emphasizing the importance of taking the lead. In analyzing oligopolistic industries in which a few players compete, economists often analyze "first-mover" advantages and the ability to make it difficult for latecomers to enter the market. Tyson fears, for the most part, that foreign actions (for example, subsidies) and inactions (for example, failure to break up *keiretsus*) will create irreversible first-mover advantages for foreign high-tech firms at the expense of American firms. If we wait to negotiate agreed rules, as at the GATT, on matters where we have concluded that others already may be seizing the opportunity to gain ground, then Tyson concludes all will be lost. Therefore, we must act unilaterally and immediately.

Tyson panics too much. Has she not heard of the "latecomer's advantage"? Developing countries in the postwar period grew at unprecedented speed because they increased their investment rate, but also because they could profit by taking vast technological know-how off the shelf. Many firms leapfrog ahead of the first-movers. Recent theoretical work demonstrates the possible wisdom of "better late than early." Many real-world stories, carefully recorded by economist F. Michael Scherer, also document how U.S. firms have successfully fought back when others have moved ahead.

Tyson's policy prescriptions are nonetheless in tune with the petulance that attends the "diminished giant syndrome" as we face the competition from the Pacific: the suspicion that they are gaining thanks to unfair trade practices is hard to dispel, even to moderate. Her positions also dovetail nicely with the inclination to interventionism that attends declinism. The great economic historian Alexander Gerschenkron once observed that state interventionism increases the more you are behind. Declinism fits the pattern: the fear of falling behind strengthens the visible hand as much as the reality of being behind.

In a declinist ethos, moreover, corporate interests become important bedfellows of the proponents of the general interest.

Though John Kenneth Galbraith exaggerated in saying that what was good for General Motors was (necessarily) bad for the United States, it is no exaggeration to note that much of the country is now in a mood to assert the opposite, that what is good for General Motors is (necessarily) good for the United States. Thus have panic and petulance, ideology and interests combined to make Tyson the woman for this season. A long, northern winter is on its way.

9   An Unhealthy Obsession with Reciprocity

In 1846, Prime Minister Robert Peel, speaking in the Parliament for a British policy of unilateral free trade, argued eloquently: "I trust the Government ... will not resume that policy which they and we have found most inconvenient, namely, the haggling with foreign countries about reciprocal concessions, instead of taking that independent course which we believe to be conducive to our own interests. Let us trust to the influence of public opinion in other countries—let us trust that our example, with the proof of practical benefits we derive from it, will at no remote period insure the adoption of the principles on which we have acted."

As U.S. trade policy founders on the shoals of reciprocity, crippling the postwar leadership of that great nation on the world trading system, the "proof of practical benefits" from her "first-mover's advantage" in unilateral deregulation and openness in modern sectors such as finance and telecommunications is indeed beginning to move other nations to follow the U.S. course. President Clinton needs to ponder Prime Minister Peel's words, abandon the counsel of his current advisers, and change course.

Indeed, except when it aggressively seeks unrequited trade concessions from others under threat of sanctions, U.S. trade

---

Originally published, in slightly shorter form, in the *Financial Times* (August 24, 1995), under the title "President Clinton versus Prime Minister Peel: The Obsession with Reciprocity."

policy has become a prisoner of the doctrine of reciprocity, where no trade concession is made unless matched by the other nation's and access to one's market must be equal to that offered by others.

This was manifest in the withdrawal of the United States from the WTO pact on banking and financial services in 1995 because there were "insufficient" reciprocal concessions by other countries and it wished to discriminate against these nations. Remarkably, leadership on the issue was seized by Sir Leon Brittan and the European Union; their efforts rescued the pact until 1997 with its nondiscriminatory MFN feature intact.

The same exaggerated concern with reciprocity, reflecting the assertion that the Japanese markets are closed whereas the U.S. markets are open, has prompted the Japan-baiting Section 301 tactics, with demands for instant gratification in the form of managed-trade targets as on purchases of car parts. It led to the thinly disguised debacle at Geneva in the U.S.-Japan car dispute. By threatening Japan with punitive tariffs which were bound and whose imposition would thus be manifestly WTO-illegal, and by demanding that Japanese firms in the United States buy more U.S.-made parts when in fact the TRIM agreement at the WTO forbids such domestic-content pressures, the United States wound up with the predictable outcome where the Japanese government faced down these tactics and demands almost contemptuously. The United States not merely lost face; it also lost the respect of the world community as a trade leader, mindful of rules and respectful of multilateralism.

But even as this obsession of the Clinton administration with reciprocity is carried well beyond that required by the political necessity which dictates that *some* element of reciprocity is inevitable when governments work on the twin assumptions that trade is good but imports are bad, economists have come to recognize that Peel's assertion of the virtues of unilateralism is coming into its own.

Thus, for some years now, many inward-looking developing countries, having learned from the example of the success of the outward-oriented economies of the Far East, have been opting for "autonomous" trade liberalizations outside the reciprocity framework of the GATT negotiations.

Then, again, cross-country studies of manufacturing firms by McKinsey & Company's Global Institute (1993), as recently reported by economists Martin Neil Baily and Hans Gersbach (1995), have confirmed the obvious: that vigorous competition in open markets is a sure-fire recipe for the adoption of best-practice production methods that make firms truly competitive.

In the financial sector as well, the openness and flexibility of London and New York, maintained regardless of reciprocity to date, have clearly enabled them to attain and retain status as world-class financial centers. By contrast, the excessive and counterproductive regulations of Tokyo have now created the serious prospect of Tokyo's loss of business to the more deregulated Singapore.

For these reasons, and not because of 301 pressures, one now detects considerable nervousness and desire for deregulation and freeing of protected markets in Japan and, for that matter, in Europe and elsewhere. One may be able to protect one's own markets, developing what the Europeans call "national champions." But these champions will have puny muscles; they will not be able to compete against the lean and mean firms of the United States, which is ahead of the curve in openness and deregulation. This recognition is now manifest in Japan's famed MITI, where visitors, including myself, have observed that old-style concerns with industrial policy have now been replaced with concerns to ensure industry's foreign competitiveness by deregulation that would match that of the United States. While *gaiatsu* (foreign pressure) exerted through 301 tactics has failed miserably in recent years, evidently the *gaiatsu* of external example is beginning to work well instead!

Unfortunately, the infatuation with reciprocity that grew to gargantuan size on the U.S. scene in the late 1980s will not disappear easily. Declinism, the "diminished giant syndrome" as I called it then, had partly prompted it, just as it had when many similarly urged reciprocity on unilateralist Britain at the end of the nineteenth century when Germany and the United States emerged as rivals. Fortunately, declinism has disappeared with America's economic turnaround and Japan's economic difficulties.

But there is also the insidious legacy of both amateur and professional economic theorizing of the time. The amateur theorizing concerns the repeated claims that Japan's "sanctuary" markets unfairly threaten U.S. firms. Behind their barriers, the Japanese firms are assumed to earn sizable monopoly profits, which then are used to compete their rivals into bankruptcy, thus lending force to our demands for reciprocal access. The problem with this contention is simply that it has no factual basis. Serious analysts agree that most of the Japanese industries are fiercely competitive; besides, their rates of return are generally low and below ours.

But the professional theorizing in favor of reciprocal access is more serious. It comes from my brilliant MIT student, Paul Krugman, who formalized the Silicon Valley entrepreneurs' reciprocitarian complaints. In essence, they argued that, with their own markets closed while the U.S. markets were open, the Japanese firms had two markets (and hence larger production) while the U.S. firms had one. So Japanese firms would have lower costs, reflecting the higher production levels because of learning by "doing."

Whatever the model's merits at the time, it can be seen now to be as ludicrous as its assumptions. Learning depends critically on the environment. A policy of openness and deregulation, especially in modern industries such as present-day finance and tele-communications, leads to the learning and efficiency that build competitiveness. The model, and the unfortunate support it provided for hypersensitivity to reciprocity, only serve to remind us of the witticism that illogic alone can protect the economist from the unfortunate consequences of making wrong assumptions.

References

Baily, Martin Neil, and Hans Gersbach. 1995. "Efficiency in Manufacturing and the Need for Global Competition." *Brookings Papers on Economic Activity: Microeconomics*: 307–47.

McKinsey Global Institute. 1993. *Manufacturing Productivity*. Washington, D.C.: McKinsey & Company, Inc.

IV

Aggressive Unilateralism: Playing at High Noon

10   Super 301's Big Bite Flouts the Rules

In her confirmation hearings, Carla A. Hills, the United States trade representative, used the imagery of a crowbar to underline her intention to pry open foreign markets. After her testimony, capital insiders rushed to reassure the world that Ms. Hills needed to talk rough on Capitol Hill but that she will hang tough against Section 301 of the 1988 Omnibus Trade and Competitiveness Act, which is known as Super 301.

Super 301 is a section of the law that enables the trade representative to single out a country as an unfair trader, begin trade negotiations with that country and, if the negotiations do not conclude to America's satisfaction, impose sanctions. Super 301 builds on Section 301 of the earlier Trade Act of 1974. On May 25, under Super 301, Ms. Hills listed Japan, India, and Brazil as unfair traders.

When the 1988 Trade Act was debated, the tired opposition to Super 301 was finally muted by giving the president the ultimate discretion in the enforcement of this section of the law. The president would stop the folly of Super 301 in its tracks, some critics of the legislation hoped. But that incorrectly assumed that the president would be able to resist pressure from the public, the influential American manufacturing and export lobbies, and Congress.

Figure 10.1
America's policy of "aggressive unilateralism" is illustrated by David and Fred
Zinn, inspired by both Lewis Carroll's *Through the Looking Glass* and Lord
Randolph Churchill's remark in the late nineteenth century that foreign markets,
like oysters, need to be opened with a "strong clasp knife, instead of being
tickled with a feather."

The task now before those of us who believe in a free trading
system is not merely to fight the use of Super 301, but to contain
the damage that has already resulted from its use.

Why is it wrong to use the crowbar of Super 301 to open
foreign markets?

The essential problem is that Section 301 of the 1974 law and
Super 301 command the executive branch to open foreign markets
through the use of unilateral retaliation. But under the rules of the
General Agreement on Tariffs and Trade—which is built on the
principles of symmetrical obligations and rights between countries—claimed violations of trade must be judged by a multi-

lateral dispute resolution panel, whose authority the complaining government must accept. Objectionable trade practices not covered by the GATT's rules must be dealt with by negotiating what are called new "disciplines," where acceptance of a new obligation by one country must be paid for by an equal concession from the other. As Section 301 of the 1974 act and Super 301 are being applied, the United States is rejecting these basic tenets of the GATT and claiming a unilateral right to judge others and to impose new disciplines on them without offering any concessions of its own in fair exchange.

It is necessary, therefore, to defeat the effects of this dangerous law. But how? Evidently, presidential leadership offers no escape. And the Trade Act is unlikely to be erased—Congress is the problem, not the solution.

The answer to changing this law has to be in the collective mustering of opposition to the use of Super 301 by the trading nations of the world. The Japanese have, for the moment, declared that they will not negotiate under the Super 301 threat of retaliation. Their best bet, given their muscle, is to make this stick by offering to continue negotiations at the Uruguay Round of the GATT in all trade areas other than those under which they were cited on May 25, 1995—supercomputers, commercial satellites, and forest products.

At the GATT council meeting in January 1995, fifty-one nations condemned the United States for violating the GATT's rules—which is also a violation of one of America's treaty obligations—in using Section 301- and Super 301-induced tariff retaliation. Japan must now throw its considerable weight behind the many nations that seek to declare Super 301 retaliations illegal in the context of the GATT.

There is little doubt that such retaliations are indeed illegal under the GATT. But a formal determination to that effect would surely stop Super 301 in its tracks unless President Bush is prepared to sustain a domestic law that violates America's international commitments. It has been rightly said that Americans are at their best when they feel strong, at their worst when they feel weak; the Japanese vice versa. In the past decade there has been a strange conjunction of an American sense of decline, and the continuing, though declining, notion of economic insignificance in Japan. Both perceptions encourage an aggressive highhandedness by the United States in trade polity and low-key compliance by the Japanese. Hitting Japan with Super 301 and branding it as an unfair trader may have unforeseen consequences when the Japanese wake up to their true economic strength—as they seem to be beginning to do—smarting under the insult.

The friends of an open trading system believe in rules that apply to all. They can only hope that fear of retribution from the United States will not prevent the world from the only course of action that can rescue it from the consequences of Super 301's folly.

11　　It's The Process, Stupid!

Aggressive unilateralism is returning to centre stage in American trade policy. In particular, Super 301 is about to strike again. Unveiled in the 1988 Omnibus Trade and Competitiveness Act, this broadened version of the earlier Section 301 legislation allows America, in effect, to designate specific countries as unfair traders and to threaten them with higher tariffs unless they change their trading practices. Super 301 sounded splendid: the name evoked Superman, taking on Lex Luthor, as the virtuous United States battled unfair traders abroad.

Super 301, approved by the Bush administration, expired in 1990. The Clinton administration, it appears, wants to bring it back to life. Certainly, the statements Bill Clinton's team has made so far on trade are consistent with its underlying philosophy. Mr. Clinton backed the idea during his campaign, and the congressmen with the most influence on trade policy are for it: two proposals to revive Super 301 are already before Congress. Laura Tyson, the president's chief economist, endorsed the ideas in a recent book. The Institute of International Economics and its chief, Fred Bergsten, are regarded on Capitol Hill as lobbyists for free trade: they also have thrown in the towel and embraced the policy.

Originally published in the *Economist* (March 27, 1993): 69. © 1993 The Economist Newspaper Group, Inc. Reprinted with permission. Further reproduction prohibited.

America pointed its Super 301 weapon in May 1989 at Japan, Brazil, and India. Japan was the main target: many in Congress had pressed for the legislation with Japan explicitly in mind. Japan was the classic "unfair trader": a predatory exporter and an exclusionary importer. All "normal" efforts to persuade it to change had failed. India and Brazil were thrown in, mainly because they had irked America's trade negotiators at the Uruguay Round by objecting strenuously to American positions on services and intellectual property.

The results have been hailed as a great success. In reality, India and Brazil refused to negotiate under duress over practices that were fully compatible with their treaty obligations under the GATT. Brazil, after a change of government, changed many of its policies anyway. India was named again under Super 301 in 1990. But America did not retaliate—perhaps because India would surely have taken the case to the GATT, which in all likelihood would have ruled America's action illegal. Japan, which manages its political and economic relationship with America with understandable care, nonetheless refused to bargain with Super 301 pointing in its face. In another forum it offered minor concessions, mainly on supercomputers and satellites: this enabled the Bush administration to fight off renewed action against Japan in 1990.

The administration backed away from confronting the EC—the Community made it clear it would be no pushover. America's only success came with South Korea and Taiwan: both made concessions specifically to avoid Super 301 action. Both are heavily dependent on America for their security. Neither at the time was a proper democracy, and so did not need to worry about popular resentment at giving in to American bullying.

Despite all that, Super 301 is regarded by many Americans as a success. According to this delusion, it would have been an even bigger one if the timidity of the Bush administration had not undermined it. The new administration, many hope, will be bolder. As America's trade representative, Mickey Kantor, put it: the Clinton people are interested in results.

Fair enough: but in that case other countries will be interested in results too. The Clinton administration's gung-ho talk makes an angry response from the rest of the world much more likely. There are already signs that this time Japan will be less accommodating.

Are countries right to resent America's threatened recourse to Super 301? It is necessary to distinguish between two sorts of trade measures. First, actions that are taken to enforce the trading rights that the United States has acquired under trade treaties (such as the GATT) but which impartial adjudicators have found to be "nullified and impaired" by a foreign nation. Second, actions that are taken to win entirely new trading rights, based on a unilateral finding of unfair practices, and under threat of retaliation which is often GATT-illegal in design (as when America threatens to raise tariffs which are bound under the GATT).

The first category raises no hackles. Recall the recent oilseeds dispute. America convinced two impartial GATT panels that the EC had nullified earlier trade commitments. Next, the EC blocked the adoption of those findings by the GATT council—which, incidentally, would be impossible under the rules proposed in the Dunkel draft of the Uruguay-Round agreement. When Carla Hills announced retaliation against the EC, she was widely supported by many GATT members—the EC was successfully backed into a corner. If that action had been taken after a unilateral finding that the EC had behaved improperly, you can be sure that many other countries would have disapproved—and that the EC would have fought back.

So the case against the second sort of action can be aptly put in campaign Clintonese: It's the process, Stupid. When America decides unilaterally that a foreign trading practice is unacceptable, and threatens to close its markets—disregarding its own

GATT commitments—the rule of law has been replaced by the law of the jungle. What could be more unfair? The weak cannot use Super 301 the way Washington can; and when the strong use economic power in that way, politics rather than markets governs trade.

Some argue quaintly that America will use its power prudently to reform the trading system for the benefit of all. Perhaps that was the aim of the "reluctant" Bush-Hills era. In fact, the power tends to be seized—as it was in those earlier years—by domestic lobbies, which then use it to run American policy for their own advantage. With producer interests triumphant in Washington, as they now are, the ides of the benign dictator acting for the common good looks silly.

What should the rest of the world do? The only effective answer to Super 301 is a firm and total refusal to negotiate under its threat. Only a united response by everybody engaged in world trade will cut this cancer out of the system.

V

Japan on One's Mind:
The Clintonites down the
Precipice

The Obsession

12   What Buchanan Owes Clinton

Patrick J. Buchanan's stump speeches calling for trade protectionism have taken on a life of their own even though they have been denounced by most mainstream policy wonks and politicians. He has used the issue to win the New Hampshire primary and has found that even Senator Bob Dole has borrowed part of his platform.

Yet Mr. Buchanan's specific prescriptions owe much to those very wonks and politicians—many in the Clinton administration—who find his agenda appalling. He found the ammunition for his campaign without difficulty in his opponents' backyards.

Mr. Buchanan thinks that Japan is an unfair trader. His prescription: Bash it with 10 percent tariffs on every Japanese import.

I have a sense not of outrage but of déjà vu. James Fallows once wrote a pair of influential articles in the *Atlantic Monthly* urging the "containment" of Japan. Among his remedies: precisely the retaliatory tariff that Mr. Buchanan espouses!

And Mr. Fallows's idea was not new. It had been suggested by Rudiger Dornbusch, a Massachusetts Institute of Technology economist.

Their conviction that Japan was an exclusionary importer and a predatory exporter has since been shared by other left-of-center

Originally published in the *New York Times* (February 22, 1996). Copyright © 1996 by The New York Times Co. Reprinted by permission.

journalists, including Robert Kuttner of the *American Prospect* and Michael Lind and John Judis of the *New Republic*.

As a presidential candidate, Bill Clinton sought votes by catering to this prejudice. His platform, *Putting People First*, promised legislation that would permit us to name Japan an "unfair trader" and to unleash retaliatory tariffs against it.

As president-elect, he appointed economists such as Laura Tyson, head of the National Economic Council, who shared these views. Unsurprisingly, Washington's think tanks suddenly had surprising converts to the cause of punitive tariffs against Japan.

But the get-tough policy with Japan failed miserably. The February 1994 summit meeting between Prime Minister Morihiro Hosokawa and President Clinton in Washington collapsed over our demands that Japan meet numerical import targets in specific sectors.

So did the May 1995 automobile trade talks. President Clinton threatened punitive tariffs on thirteen models of Japanese luxury cars. In the end, he capitulated, with only a few paltry face-saving "concessions" from the Japanese.

Thanks to a passive press, somehow these failures turned into public relations successes. And the politics seemed to work to President Clinton's advantage. The thought that Japan-bashing pays politically could not have escaped Mr. Buchanan. He simply is much more forthright about it.

Such bashing is not the only element of his protectionism that derives from mainstream ideas. He also opposes the General Agreement on Tariffs and Trade and the World Trade Organization, multilateral trade agreements first opposed by environmental and labor groups.

These groups first vilified the GATT as Gatt-zilla. They may shudder at Mr. Buchanan's prominence now, but he has taken their issues and turned them into a presidential campaign.

13   Trade Wars

Michael Lind (1996) displays a thin skin while turning to innuendo to justify a silly charge of "smear tactics" against me for my *New York Times* op-ed and against Charles Lane.

Lind should know that you cannot have it both ways: take a striking position on an issue and have it taken seriously by only those you admire and not by those you despise. Indeed, one's fate is often to have one's ideas vulgarized and misused by those one despises and ignored by those one admires.

That Pat Buchanan's specific trade policy ideas on Japan were not merely the results of such misuse but came directly from the mainstream policy wonks, many walking the corridors of the Clinton administration, is both undeniable and is what I argued. Did Buchanan invent for himself the notion that Japan is a "threat," that its trade policies are "unfair," that Japan ought to be "contained," that (in view of all this) we ought to levy an across-the-board tariff on Japan of 10 percent? No, Mr. Lind: go and read James Fallows in the *Atlantic Monthly,* and you will find that he discusses with warmth a Bush *shokku* that would enact a 20 to 25 percent, not just Buchanan's modest 10 percent, across-the-board tariff on Japan, citing sources such as Rudiger Dornbusch, a well-known advocate of the use of such weaponry. Buchanan clearly has read these gentlemen. If Buchanan is a mad bomber,

Originally published as a letter to the editor in the *New Republic* (May 27, 1996): 6. Reprinted with permission.

he certainly found his bombs, not just their components, on our front porches, not even our backyards.

And it would be a heroic folly to assume that the administration's vote-seeking, flamboyant, and assiduous adoption of a confrontational if ineffective policy on trade with Japan, and the influential writings in the media of the Japan-worriers such as Lind, did not serve to water the fields which Buchanan ploughs.

Instead of growing up and accepting this reality, Lind whines. He sees me as part of a "libertarian" attempt to "associate liberals with a particularly noxious far-right extremist." This will appear as hilarious to my friends as to my foes.

I must confess to being a registered Democrat, a social liberal, and even a happy member of the MIT diaspora who was also for twelve years on the MIT faculty. I used the description (he puts it in quotes) of Dornbusch as an MIT economist because he is not a celebrity and needs identification, not because I wished to imply, as Lind clearly thinks, that he was a "liberal."

Lind charges me with creating an "enemies list." But academics call the "naming of names" the citing of sources. Lind's ignorance of this culture is equally manifest when he wrongly cites my affiliation, to reinforce his libertarian conspiracy thesis, as the American Enterprise Institute. Of course, I am at Columbia University. Like many academics, I have found it useful to work briefly with or at several reputed institutions, including both Brookings and the AEI (with whom I terminated my periodic visits last year). But Lind would not understand that, would he?

Reference

Lind, Michael, 1996. "Smear Tactics." *New Republic*, April 29, p. 421.

14   Facing the Japanese Challenge

James Fallows has long been my favorite American journalist. He observes what many miss, often shaping a mosaic of luminous and compelling design. He can cut through complexity, yielding fresh insights where none seemed possible. Even when he fails to persuade, he succeeds in changing our perceptions of problems and phenomena we thought we had understood. This splendid volume confirms me in my Fallowsphilia.

More Like Us starts with the celebrated cliché of the decade: The Far East threatens our premier status in the world economy. But it ends with an original response.

Some want to take a leaf from the exotic Pacific book. The new Democrats urge us to adopt the industrial policy that Japan presumably practices and we do not. Others would rather burn the book. Congress has just pressured President Bush into becoming a latter-day Commodore Perry, threatening Japan with retaliation under the 1988 Omnibus Trade and Competitiveness Act if it does not change to suit our interests.

Fallows, who spent a year in Japan recently for the *Atlantic Monthly*, urges us instead to look closer at ourselves, to renew

Originally published in the *New Leader* (May 15–29, 1989): 17–18. © American Labor Conference on International Affairs, Inc. Reprinted with permission.

This chapter reviews James Fallows's *More Like Us: Making America Great Again* (Boston: Houghton Mifflin, 1989).

our economic strength by recognizing our "abnormality"—our uncommon virtues, or "culture"—and fashioning solutions that build directly on it. "A society that is true to its own culture will usually have a healthy economy," he points out. "It will have found the right way to elicit people's best efforts. The economic progress it makes will, in turn, allow many people to have more satisfying lives."

America's uniqueness lies in the pervasiveness of "possibility," the principle of social mobility that has led to continuous seeking of new chances in a tradition where constraints inspire challenge and not accommodation—a virtual celebration of disorder. "Japan gets the most out of ordinary people by *organizing* them to adapt and succeed. America, by getting out of their way so that they can adjust individually, *allows* them to succeed."

Fallows paints telling portraits of migrants who sought the second chance this country offers, reinventing their lives as only America enables them to do. He describes his own family's move when he was five from the East Coast to the small town of Redlands, California. This is the California that was devastated by Joan Didion in the *Saturday Evening Post* as a wasteland "where it is easy to Dial-a-Devotion, but hard to buy a book ... the last stop for all those ... who drifted away from the cold and the past and the old ways." Fallows celebrates the flip side—the seizure of new opportunities, the remaking of one's destiny—with greater insight. He adds three sketches of people who turned themselves around by "not knowing their place": Buddy and Judy Ginn, who moved from the Midwest to oilrich Alvin, Texas; the Nguyens, who fled from Vietnam to Los Angeles; and Wyman Westbury, who fought at great odds against the establishment in a company town in St. Mary's, Florida.

America has been weakened, Fallows argues, whenever it has denied the concept of possibility—and the attendant notion that anyone can succeed, therefore no one is inherently better or entitled to deference. When social mobility gave way to class in enabling the educated to avoid the Vietnam draft, the consequence was the prolonged continuation of a serious and debilitating war. More important, racial discrimination has deprived blacks of access to the American dream, leaving the nation with an intolerable social stain and economic burden. And discrimination against women has had much the same effect.

Fallows further warns against recent trends that restrict various groups in our society. He alerts us to the increasing educational prerequisites demanded by the professions on entry, although in fact there is little evidence that this education correlates with performance; to the IQ tyranny which, unscientifically but forcefully, reduces large numbers to a falsely "objective" inferiority that limits their sense of the possible; and to the myriad ways, such as yuppie life-styles, Americans today tend to define themselves as different from their fellow countrymen.

What we have to do, says Fallows, is "reopen America"—revive the optimism that Americans are capable of to stimulate personal gain and benefit the public good. He urges a shift in government spending from entitlements to insurance, because a safety net is needed, not sinecures. The poor deserve workfare, not welfare, and public school reform to improve their prospects. Substantial deregulation of the professions is necessary so that competence, not formal educational background, becomes the relevant entry factor. We must also continue the inflow of immigration that so much of our unique principle of possibility derives from.

These sweeping conclusions invite little disagreement, for they are essentially marked by good sense and that peculiarly un-American quality associated with older civilizations, wisdom. Indeed, it is easy to miss the freshness of Fallows's prescriptions precisely because they appear so reasonable. Congressmen, who look after the larger American interests and accept honoraria from the narrower ones, should instead be paid by Common Cause to read this book. They and we would both be better for it.

The Democrats would profit from the author's insistence on flexibility of response to pressing domestic problems, reinforced by suitable social policies. Their flirtation with protectionism and the itch to pursue a course of "managed trade" that would confuse what is good for Motorola with what is good for the country and the world trading system, runs wholly against the thrust of Fallows thesis.

The Republicans would profit equally. Flexibility implies that opening world markets is not enough. This must be accompanied by adjustment assistance to displaced workers, giving them training and funds to grasp the second chance. Civil rights enforcement and affirmative action, which provide the entree and the role models that help extend the principle of possibility to blacks and women, acquire credibility from *More Like Us*.

If Fallows is to be faulted, it is for excessive concessions he makes concerning the primacy of culture and its stranglehold on economic behavior. Certainly the Japanese are different from us. One only has to read Junichiro Tanizaki's beautiful book, *In Praise of Shadows*, to see how different they truly are. But it is wrong to infer that they do not belong to the human race whose economic behavior Adam Smith fashioned into the principles of political economy. It is precisely this non sequitur that Fallows's fascination with cultural difference is likely to encourage. The result will be a regrettable strengthening of the nonsensical claim that the "containment of Japan" requires unconventional restraints.

Clyde Prestowitz, an indefatigable proponent of "managed trade," has asserted that Japan, by virtue of cultural factors, is impenetrable, and consequently there will always be a tendency toward a Japanese surplus in the balance of trade. If that is true, it is astonishing that it took nearly a century after Commodore Perry opened up Japan for this inevitable surplus to develop! The reality is that the Japanese trade surplus has come at the end of a period when Japan has been integrating more closely into Western culture.

The widely held belief that Japan's trade barriers—some overt, many inscrutable and covert—account for our trade deficit is not validated by any economic theory. Nor can this view survive the fact that Japan's trade barriers did not increase, but actually diminished, during the period that our deficit emerged.

The Japanese trade surplus reflects the excess of high personal savings over domestic investment that began to occur in the late 1970s, thanks to a reduced investment rate in the wake of the economic upheavals caused by OPEC. The American trade deficit reflects, by contrast, President Reagan's budgetary profligacy. Japan's culture and Japan's trade barriers are not the problem, and bashing Japan is not the solution to our troubles.

Fallows is fundamentally correct in asking us to look within ourselves for our strength. But the challenge from the Far East for the next century cannot be met entirely by enhancing the principle of possibility. We need to do much more, to complement individual striving with social action in many other ways. Our savings and investment rates have collapsed to levels less than half those in Japan. The pace at which we implement technical change has slowed. Our children are lapsing increasingly into illiteracy. If we do not address these underlying sources of our long-term economic malaise, we shall without question lose the race with the Pacific nations.

Getting Japan Wrong

15   The Japanese—Not So Inscrutable to Adam Smith

Under the terms of the Super 301 provision of the 1988 Trade Act, President Bush must decide which countries to target as unfair traders. A word of advice: Lay off Japan. The charges about Japan's supposedly unfair trading practices are an unfair condemnation of a friendly ally.

The Japan-bashers' arguments against Japan's supposed trade perfidy have undergone a series of self-interested metamorphoses. The original complaint was that Japan's visible trade barriers were much higher than ours. When it became apparent that this was not so, the criticism shifted to the charge that the Ministry of International Trade and Industry somehow was managing to prevent the lower trade barriers from increasing imports. Empirical scrutiny failed to sustain this charge too.

Now the argument has shifted again. The current charge is that the problem is not the efficacy of MITI's visible (import-restraining) hand but the inefficacy of Adam Smith's invisible (import-enhancing) hand. In short, Japan is too bizarre and exotic, in its culture and in its economic organization, for markets (and therefore GATT-style market access) to work as they do in the West.

Originally published in the *Wall Street Journal* (April 26, 1990).

The culturalists have had a field day with this view. But their assertions of Japan's cultural uniqueness and how normal "rules-based" trade with Japan is impossible, don't hold up under economic scrutiny. As is often the case, economics can explain differences glibly attributed to culture. A few examples should suffice:

Take the popular view that Japan's familial culture leads to the "permanent-employment" system. Few know that this system came to Japan only after the Second World War. Indeed, as argued recently by Columbia Professor Jacob Mincer, the labor turnover rates in Japanese manufacturing before the war and in American manufacturing since the war are broadly similar. It wasn't until after the war that the decline in employee turnover in Japan occurred. The explanation seems to be that the rapid economic growth in postwar Japan was based on rapid technical change that called for intensive formation of human capital specific to an enterprise. This encouraged lower turnover.

Or take the frequent complaint that the Japanese are wedded to their own for supplies of intermediates. Evidence? In the United States, Japanese companies' ratio of imported intermediates to value added is twice as high as that of other foreign investors. But think again. If protection, or the threat of it, induces foreign firms to enter a market, they will typically import as many components as they can from their home base, where production is cheaper. Who can deny that our actual and threatened trade restraints against Japan have been substantially greater than those against other nations? The astonishing thing may well be that Japanese investors have not wound up showing a yet higher ratio of imports to value added.

James Fallows of the *Atlantic Monthly* writes about Japan's inability to play by "rules," and its preference for "quantities." These cultural abnormalities make it impossible for Japan to have rules-based, GATT-type trade and makes "managed trade" (with specified quantities traded) the best solution. Japanese trade negotiators presumably ask the United States: How much do you want us to import? Mr. Fallows attributes this query to "Japanese discomfort with the very prospect of abiding by abstract principles." This is nonsense. Is it not more likely that, faced with Americans' repeated complaints, the Japanese ask: "How much do you want us to import," wisely muting the rest of the sentence: "to get you off our backs?" Since the 1930s, the United States has imposed quantitative limits on Japan's successful exports, starting with "voluntary" export restraints on electric lamps and textiles. Could not the Japanese have learned, thanks to us, the wisdom of asking about quantities?

Clyde Prestowitz, former U.S. trade negotiator and an ally of Mr. Fallows in the angst over Japan, is doubly wrong when he asserts that Japan "plays a different game" and that therefore the United States cannot have beneficial trade with it under a rules-based multilateral trading regime. For one thing, the sports analogy is inappropriate: In games, one party loses and the other wins; in trade, both often win. His second error, shared by other culturalists, is to exaggerate the exotic nature of the Japanese game. In his incomprehension, he's like the Indian maharajah who, taken to a polo match, turned to his English host in puzzled consternation to say: " It is so sad to see them fighting over that ball. Why don't you give each their own?"

What then about the view, often ascribed to Chalmers Johnson, professor at the University of California at San Diego, that Japanese companies believe in "predatory" competition?

The notion that American companies, by contrast, compete in a benign fashion is faintly romantic and fully foolish. What the Cambridge economist Joan Robinson used to call the "animal spirits" of capitalist entrepreneurs surely are manifest in both countries. The successful always appear more predatory. This was exactly the stereotype of British entrepreneurs during the nineteenth century and of the "ugly" American in the 1950s and 1960s. With success, one gets one's share of envy and resentment.

The hawks in Congress would like to hit Japan again this year with Super 301, seeing Japan's latest concessions at the Structural Impediments Initiative talks as a defendant's admission of guilt. But these concessions are nothing of the kind. Most, such as the promise of more infrastructure spending, have little relationship to trade: none can be a substitute for our own actions in improving our trade deficit.

Rather, the concessions are designed to cap the increasingly strident Japan-bashing from getting altogether out of hand. They give the administration a sporting chance to face down a bellicose Congress by citing Japan's agreeable accommodation of our needs. The president should seize that chance.

16

The Fraudulent Case against Japan

The inclusion of the feisty Lee Iacocca in the president's entourage on his Asian travels reminded me of Mr. Iacocca's television ads last year, asserting that his cars were now as good as Japan's.

Mr. Iacocca managed only to make a new car salesman look like a used car salesman. The ad also reflected what is wrong with his, and unfortunately many others', approach to competing with the Japanese: The consumer's vote in the marketplace does not count. The producer knows he is making a quality product. If, despite that, the Japanese outsell him, they have to be "unfair" traders.

The perception of the Japanese as unfair traders is more than half a century old. The rising tide of Japanese exports of textiles, electric lamps, safety matches and pencils in the 1930s led even then to charges of unfair trade. "Voluntary export restraints" were imposed on Japan by Australia, Britain, the United States, and others, even when Japan ran bilateral trade deficits with them.

Fear of Japan

After World War II, the fear of Japan remained so strong that U.S. efforts at getting Japan admitted to the General Agreenent on

Originally published in the *Wall Street Journal* (January 6, 1992).

Tariffs and Trade succeeded only in September 1955, eight years after the agreement was signed. Even then, fourteen counries, 40 percent of GATT's then-membership, invoked Article 35 under which they need not extend GATT-defined rights (such as market access) to a new member. For years thereafter, Japan would be negotiating for its full GATT rights with these countries, many of them European.

America's freedom from fear of Japan at the time reflected no doubt its emergence as a dominant power, while war-devastated Europe lived up to the Russian proverb: Fear has big eyes. Now, however, the U.S. economic situation has changed. The "diminished giant" syndrome that spawned in late nineteenth-century Britain demands for fair trade against newly emerged Germany is now manifest in the United States.

The panic has produced petulance. A small but influential school of "revisionists" endlessly repeats fallacies about America's trade with Japan. Two are particularly pernicious.

"The Japanese will make semiconductor chips while we make potato chips." This metaphor of former U.S. trade official Clyde Prestowitz electrifies his audiences. The metaphor does not merely exaggerate grossly U.S. deindustrialization (which is still negligible in real terms) or its loss of modern high-tech industries. It also is a form of vulgar, Marxist technological determinism.

Where you work is surely not decisive in determining how productive you will be and how satisfying your society will be. You can be fitting semiconductor boards mindlessly like Chaplin in *Modern Times*, exchanging them in trade for potato chips that you munch watching television in a witless stupor. Or you could be running a superautomated potato chip factory, exchanging your chips in trade for personal computers that you use to become a more productive and intellectually innovative member of your society.

- "[W]hen foreign competitors ask Japan to embrace the principles of free trade, they run up against ... a broader Japanese discomfort with the very prospect of abiding by abstract principles," revisionist James Fallows observed in the *Atlantic* in 1989. Therefore, instead of futilely pressing Japan to conform to the rules of free trade, the United States should demand that Japan accept targeted quantities of U.S. goods.

But a simpler and wholly plausible explanation of the Japanese behavior in trade negotiations seems to be that, since the 1930s, they have not been allowed to trade by rules. Their export successes have always been met by demands for quantitative restraints. Other countries' political preferences, not the cultural afflictions of the Japanese, seem to have molded their attachment to quantities.

If Japan is widely regarded as an unfair trader, it may be because the successful often appear to be predatory. A recent *World Economic Forum* survey of 2,000 CEOs around the world asked: Who is the unfairest of them all? Predictably, the Japanese topped the list, followed by South Korea. The third place of honor went to the United States, still a major exporter, and successful beyond its fears.

Perhaps those who are bamboozled by the allegations against Japan would be surprised to learn that Japan's nontariff barriers do not look so bad compared with those of the United States. The United States does badly on autos, iron and steel, and textiles; Japan is significantly worse on agriculture and on footwear. It is fair to say that while Japan is more protectionist in agriculture than the United States, it is less protectionist in manufacturing. And while the United States, Australia, Canada and the European Community use antidumping actions liberally (between 1980 and 1985, the four sponsored 280, 393, 219, and 254 actions respectively), Japan has almost totally abstained from these measures.

Many who are convinced that Japan does not offer market access have therefore moved from the clearly false position that Japan has high trade barriers to the complex contention that Japanese institutions are so "different" that they effectively impede imports. This view is psychologically most comforting to fairminded Japan-bashers: "I don't think that Japan is deliberately unfair; it is just playing a different game from mine and so, when we play at free trade, this unwittingly helps it and hurts me. I must therefore give up free trade and impose managed trade on Japan."

But there are serious problems with this view. Simply looking at Japan's low ratio of manufactured imports to gross national product, as is often done, is naive. Sophisticated economists would want to estimate, according to their theories, what Japan "should" be importing. As it happens, there are at least three good reasons for Japan to have an unusually low ratio of manufactured imports to GNP:

1. It relies more than most countries on imports of raw materials, which it pays for with manufactured exports.

2. It has a skewed demand pattern for its own goods. This comes from having had over a century of "controlled openness" to foreign influences.

3. Since over long periods exports will broadly pay for imports, the low import ratio implies a low export ratio; and the latter may, in turn, reflect protection against Japan.

Regardless, the substantial econometric studies of cross-country import ratios that are now available fail to support unequivocally the contention that Japan's imports are below what can be expected along conventional lines. Indeed, the econometric studies of Ed Leamer of UCLA and Gary Saxonhouse of the University of Michigan support Japan's "normality."

The alternative approach of examining directly Japan's institutions, such as its *keiretsu* (groups of "associated" companies) and its retail distribution system to see whether they hamper market access is marked by serious conceptual and inference problems. A recent study by Robert Lawrence of the Brookings Institution used a classification that grouped Japan's major companies into seventeen keiretsu in 1986 but, only three years later that same classification scheme found forty-seven.

President Bush is ill-advised in choosing the rhetoric of unfair trade as he arrives in Tokyo. Even if the president believes that Japan's market is a difficult one because of institutional differences from the United States, difference cannot be automatically condemned as "unfair."

Besides, the Japanese scene is changing rapidly and the "problem" of market access is already beginning to loss its cogency. As Japan liberalized its economy through the 1970s, there were three reasons why the import response would be sluggish: the high cost of entering the Japanese market; the lack of assurance (given Japan's reputation as an unfair trader) that successful entry would not somehow be reversed; and the sense that the market was not large enough.

All these reasons have virtually vanished, and the results are starting to come through. Japan's ratio of manufactured to total imports has practically doubled in the 1980s. Patience to let the process take hold, vigilance to ensure that the Japanese do not lapse into protectionism as imports surge, and the macro policies of yen revaluation and U.S. budget deficit reduction to reinforce the working of the international adjustment mechanism are the policies that the president should opt for.

To countervail the populists and the protectionists who want controls on Japan's exports and guaranteed shares of Japan's markets, the president also needs substantial trade successes. The Uruguay GATT Round is just what the president needs, even in a recession.

U.S. Exports Gain

U.S. exports gain from Uruguay's deals on services, on intellectual property and within agriculture. The United States "loses" only on textiles, but there the U.S. commitment is stretched out over ten years and most of the pain comes only at the end.

The president can also seize the opportunity in Tokyo to break out of America's "piecemeal regionalism" that looks only south of Rio Grande, and to move instead to "programmatic regionalism" that would boldly aim at bringing the Pacific region rapidly into a U.S.-sponsored Free Trade Area, en route to multilateral free trade with all at GATT. If Mexico's President Salinas has the courage to embrace America, President Bush should have the courage to embrace Japan. As for Mr. Iacocca, don't worry: He will get his golden parachute, count on it.

17 On Boiling Frogs

While your occasional debunking of celebrities in the scatological fashion of Lytton Strachey fails to enthuse me, I must admit that the piece by Nader Mousavizadeh (1995) on Thomas Friedman's foreign policy writings made me understand why this distinguished *Times* columnist has often left me flabbergasted even when he writes, as he does frequently, on international economic questions.

The moral insensitivity that is charged to Friedman, and is illustrated with his remarkable commentary on Bosnia and the Kurds, can be seen as scarring Friedman's views on trade policy as well. He has taken uncritically to the confrontational "geo-economics" that provides a thin veneer of pseudo-Hobbesian intellectualism to Washington's current preoccupations driven by petty politics and puerile economics. It is particularly evident in the unceasing fulminations against Japan that explode like a burst of gunfire in his columns.

Japan, in these columns, becomes a gigantic conspiracy practicing predatory exports and exclusionary imports: there is no nuance, no regard for the complexity of the question at hand, no doubt. Friedman's Japan is an ahistorical, unscholarly abstraction that must be confronted and its evil trade empire destroyed. One

Originally published as a letter to the editor in the *New Republic* (August 14, 1995): 4–5. Reprinted with permission.

fails to see here a judicious, probing, thoughtful, liberal temperament, mindful of crossing the line into, and fueling, morally indefensible paranoia and prejudice; the affinity with Pat Buchanan
is much too plain.

Indeed, the story that he started a column with once, to rejoice
how Japan, faced with a continually rising yen, has been coping
with the heat without opening its "closed" markets but will finally
have no option except to do so, reveals more than he intends. He
recalls an experiment in his school where a frog is being boiled
alive. The heat rises; the frog jumps but not enough to escape the
confining glass; things get hotter, the frog leaps and leaps, lin-
gering in the glass until the boiling water makes him finally jump
to safety.

As I read this column, my thoughts turned, not to Japan or its
trade, but to Friedman himself. What kind of school did this kid
go to where they boiled frogs?

Reference

Mousavizadeh, Nader. 1995. "Not Two Cents." *New Republic*, July 10, pp. 12–13.

18   Samurais No More

The failure of the February 11, 1994, Hosokawa-Clinton summit in Washington to produce a trade agreement on U.S. terms was marked by theatrics on the American side. Deputy Treasury Secretary Roger Altman's banter was typical. He declared, with the bluntness that Wall Street breeds, that the United States would wait "until hell freezes over" for the Japanese to accept U.S. demands. When Prime Minister Hosokawa finally said no to them, the American anger was palpable.

U.S. Trade Representative Mickey Kantor brought to center stage the Motorola cellular phones dispute, which the administration had readied to coincide with the summit by speeding up ongoing negotiations. Amenable to manipulation as "proof" of Japan's perfidy, the dispute was also the one most likely to be settled at a low cost, financial and political, by the Hosokawa government to save U.S. face: a crumb thrown to the United States, it could be called a cake.

Indeed, Japan ended the dispute by bribing Motorola with investment outlays while affirming the dispute's uniqueness and reiterating the policy of saying no. The Clinton administration, predictably, performed a war dance, celebrating a victory in a skirmish as if it had won the war, attributing the Motorola

Originally published in *Foreign Affairs* 73 (May/June 1994): 7–12. Copyright 1994 by the Council on Foreign Relations, Inc. Reprinted with permission.

settlement to American resolve and threats, particularly to the president's revival in March 1994 of the "Super 301" weapon, which authorizes the administration to highlight countries it determines are trading unfairly and, if it chooses, to impose trade sanctions in retaliation.

Breaking Its Own Rules

The Clinton administration, however, cannot conceal the reality that its policy is fatally flawed. The policy makes demands that are inconsistent with the very principles on which the United States has itself provided leadership in shaping the world trading system over half a century. As important, the policy fails to grasp the significant changes that make both the style and the substance of these demands unacceptable to the new Japan. American policy is thus both unworthy and unworkable.

The problems with that policy concern "quantities" and "process." The United States wants managed trade: specifically, it wants the Japanese government to accept numerical benchmarks and targets for increased imports in specific sectors. It is also pressing for one-way concessions from Japan in areas where the United States has judged Japan to be either closed to imports or in violation of treaty obligations, acting unilaterally instead of using impartial procedures to which Japan would also have recourse. In both respects, the United States has the double disadvantage of having been roundly condemned by other nations and of having not the remotest chance of acceptance by Japan.

Benchmarks are only a weasel word for targets (that is, quotas), and these import targets quickly turn into export protectionism: they work to guarantee for American firms a share of the foreign market just as conventional import protectionism gives firms a guaranteed share of the domestic market.

These targets will multiply because they are open to manipulation by domestic firms that seek assured export markets. When Japan unwisely accepted the Reagan administration's demand for a numerical benchmark (for the first time in U.S.-Japan trade negotiations), economists had forecast that other firms and industries would soon jump on the bandwagon. It was too rewarding a precedent not to exploit, and indeed that is exactly what has happened. Now a complaisant administration has become the agent for the lobbyists of industries such as autos, auto parts, and medical equipment, seeking to impose many more such agreements on Japan.

The proliferation of such import targets to several sectors would also bring other countries onto the scene demanding their own guaranteed share of the Japanese market. The reason is plain enough: Japan must be fully aware that if it opens up to imports but those imports do not come from the United States, the pressure from Washington will continue. So Japan will have a powerful incentive to divert its imports from other nations to the United States, even if the United States pretends that its objective is to open the Japanese economy, not throw contracts the way of American firms. Hence, properly fearing trade diversion, the European Union has always said that if Japan concedes import targets to the United States, the EU will be right behind.

If numbers rather than rules are accepted as the way to conduct trade, the prospect is then certain that Japanese industry would soon be subject to heavy regulation and compelled to produce the politically agreed market shares. This would be bad enough for Japan. But it would also be a low blow to the rules-based world trading system that the United States has professed to uphold at the General Agreement on Tariffs and Trade.

In consequence, the United States, traditionally the leader on trade issues to the applause of economists, has found itself opposed by economists, whether Democrats or Republicans.

There is also little support for America's Super 301–aided unilateralism. Washington is isolated when it wants to take the law
in its own hands, especially now that the Uruguay Round has
produced a binding settlement procedure. Even if Japan were
guilty as charged, it is unacceptable that the United States should
become complainant, judge, and jury.

The New Japan

Japan's resistance to U.S. demands was urged worldwide—from
Europe in particular—undoubtedly strengthening Hosokawa's
resolve to say no. But that resolve comes from within Japan itself,
reflecting the nuanced yet remarkable changes that Japan is
undergoing. The Clinton administration simply does not get it:
the new Japan is trying to be like the old United States just as
the new United States, with its flirtation with industrial policy,
embrace of demands for managed trade, and (as in the president's
announcement of the Saudi purchase of U.S. aircraft) unabashed
use of political muscle rather than economic competitiveness to
succeed in world markets, is trying to be like the old Japan.

Hosokawa, and the large numbers of reform-minded Japanese
who voted the Liberal Democratic Party out of power, wish an
end to old-fashioned regulation. Managed trade would turn the
clock back when they want to push it forward. The reformers also
believe in reciprocal rights and obligations; they reject unilateralism and want multilateralism; they want due process, not the
peremptory judgments of the United States (which reflect the self-
serving finger-pointing of individual U.S. companies).

Ironically, but predictably, these are American ideas. They have
spread rapidly to Japan because, among other reasons, Japan has
large numbers of its young citizens abroad. Over 40,000 Japanese
students are in the United States today, learning to put their feet
on the table in the classroom instead of meekly bowing to the

sensei (the venerable teacher). With the dramatic shift in the 1980s in the share of Japanese direct foreign investment away from the poor countries to the rich, prompted in part by the outbreak of protectionism in the EU and in the United States that restricted export access to these markets, great numbers of Japanese women and children also live in the West. They are a subversive, modernizing force. Increased numbers of Japanese academics can now be found on U.S. campuses, speaking English fluently and working with Americans at the frontiers of science when only a decade ago there were practically none.

The Japan that was so set on what the historian Henry Smith has aptly called "controlled openness"—drawing carefully on what it liked in other cultures rather than abandoning itself, like the United States, to free cultural influx and experimentation— is now beyond such control. The globalization of the Japanese economy and modern communications imposes its own logic on the nation. But the Clinton aides in charge of Japan policy, mainly Wall Street luminaries and high-profile lawyer-lobbyists with lifestyles that leave little room for reflection and put a premium on going for the jugular, appear to be ignorant of this historic transformation. These Clinton warriors think they are fighting the samurai when they are facing GIs.

Indeed, these aides manifested their lack of comprehension of the new Japan with tactical errors in negotiations leading up to the summit. The bureaucrats in Japan were assumed to be the problem. The new politicians, keen on reform, were assumed to be U.S. allies in seeing the manifest virtue of demands for managed trade to "open Japan." But the new politicians were the ones who had principled objections to managed trade and also to U.S. unilateralism.

While the United States was pretending that benchmarks were different from targets, Kantor did not even bother to dissimulate when, in the semiconductor agreement, the U.S. market share fell

Figure 18.1
View of Yokohama, ca. 1860, ink and color on paper, dramatically shows Japan's policy of what the historian Henry Smith has called "controlled openness." The five "black ships" in the harbor are for each of the five nations, the original G-5 as it were, which had forced Japan into trade treaties. Yokohama, to which the foreigners were restricted, is shown as connected to the mainland by a single bridge on the upper right side: a thin and controlled link to the guarded mainland. Today, however, Japan's openness has vastly increased: they are "samurais no more."

recently below the 20 percent benchmark; instead he came out swinging with both hands, complaining about the shortfall as if the benchmark were a target and demanding corrective action. Moreover, the president, indulging in Japan-bashing to promote the North American Free Trade Agreement, had already promised revival of Super 301, taking the incentive away from the Japanese to settle on U.S. terms in order to avoid the provision's reenactment. The Clinton aides failed to understand that their twin assumptions about Japan—that nothing but bluster can succeed and that bluster cannot fail—were no longer valid.

In the end, the flaw in U.S. policy derives from the exaggeration of Japan's differences of yesterday as much as from an ignorance of its rapid convergence to the United States today. Washington is obsessed with the view that Japan is different and special, a predatory exporter and an exclusionary importer that must be dealt with as an outlaw, what Jonathan Rauch has called an "outnation," with tough external *gaiatsu* (foreign pressure) and targets to restrain exports and expand imports.

Economic analysis hardly supports such stereotypes. The simpleminded assertion coming from the Clinton administration that, because Japan's share of manufactured imports in GNP is below the average of the Group of Seven industrialized nations, Japan "underimports" and has a closed market requiring special measures is nonsense. By that token, since Canada's share is substantially higher than the United States', the United States should be judged closed relative to Canada. Sophisticated econometric studies of the question are badly divided; the better-crafted of these certainly do not support the thesis that Japan imports too little, nor do they indicate a special and extraordinary effect of informal trade barriers that make Japan a fit case for unusual treatment in the world trading system.

Even the imports by Japan of manufactured goods, a persistent source of complaint, have grown in the past decade to over half of its imports. Moreover, the foreign share in many of Japan's high-tech markets, so dear to Clintonites, is by no means static or small. Figure 18.2, based on recently released data from the National Science Foundation, shows that in seven important high-tech markets, the U.S. and Japanese import shares look pretty similar, so much so that if the industries and the countries were blacked out, one could well mistake the U.S. chart for Japan's.

The notion of Japan's overwhelming difference nonetheless persists because it is reinforced by the egregious fallacy, often repeated by the president and his aides in public, that Japan's huge bilateral surplus with the United States is surefire proof that Japan's markets are closed, requiring a concentration of one's

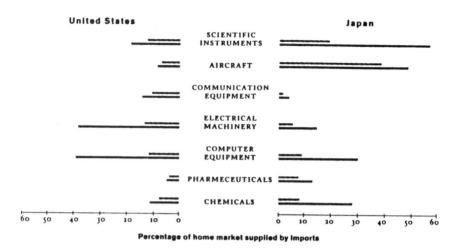

Figure 18.2
Import penetration of seven high-tech markets: 1981 and 1992.

wrath and energy on Japan. Occasionally, counterintuitive economic sense will prevail for a moment, but then fallacy, so
compelling to the untrained mind, resurfaces. Convincing Washington that bilateral surpluses are no index of the openness of
markets is as difficult as convincing a peasant that the earth is
round when it appears flat to his naked eye.

Nor does Japan's multilateral surplus set it apart as wicked and
bizarre. Its persistence is shorter-lived than America's own surplus
in the two decades after the Second World War. Japan's surplus
reflects its excess of domestic savings over investment and is
generally to be applauded as a contribution to world net savings
at a time of huge demand for investable funds in the developing
and the former socialist countries. In the immediate short run,
Japan can certainly contribute to its own recovery and indirectly
help the United States by undertaking the significant fiscal stim-
ulus that Hosokawa had worked to get. But all macroeconomists
agree that the spillover or "locomotive" effect of Japanese stim-
ulus on U.S. prosperity will be small, making even this obsession

of the Clinton administration seem strange. In short, nothing here requires that the United States think that Japan is "off the curve" in responsible macroeconomic management: its mistakes are no more gargantuan than those of the United States, for example, during the decade of fiscal irresponsibility from which it has just emerged.

Cooperation, Not Confrontation

The cancer at the core of U.S. policy then is the view that the United States needs a differential treatment of Japan and a special framework agreement. The justifications for that premise, never strong, are particularly implausible today. They must finally be abandoned.

There is nothing extraordinary even about the specific trade disputes with Japan. Similar complaints can be made with regard to other nations. The accounts of the delays experienced by Motorola in getting its cellular phone system adopted in the Tokyo-Nagoya corridor (one of two in Japan), for example, must be set against the facts that Motorola was not allowed to set up its own system at all in France and Germany and had to adapt to a different system there, and that entry into the U.S. market itself had been impeded by antidumping harassment. Such examples can be readily multiplied.

The time has come to admit that Japan must be allowed to trade by rules rather than quantities, and that the rules must include the adjudication of disputes by impartial procedures available to both parties. The notion that U.S.-Japan trade issues are so special that they must be dealt with bilaterally in a framework that permits the United States to impose one-way demands on Japan and to pronounce unilaterally its own verdicts that Japan has "failed to live up to its agreements" must finally be laid to rest.

Will the president, no stranger to principled and bold changes of course, rise to the occasion? It will not be easy: the failed trade policy toward Japan is most likely his own. After all, the North America Free Trade Agreement and the Uruguay Round were Republican initiatives; he needed one of his own. The Silicon Valley entrepreneurs were the first to swing to him during the campaign; he bought their view of Japan. He chose advisers that shared these jaundiced views. He chose a U.S. trade representative and a commerce secretary who proudly say that they disdain economic "theology" and want results; so they reflect interests, not principles, as they confront Japan.

The president may have fancied that he would have the glory of "opening Japan," as a sort of modern-day Commodore Perry. That historical parallel will not work. The tragedy is that, by persisting in the current policy, he may put two great nations on a course that may repeat history in less agreeable ways.

*Getting Trade Policy
toward Japan Wrong*

19   Japan Must Now Say No

When Shintaro Ishihara, the maverick Japanese politician and noted literary figure, wrote in anguish an essay asking the Japanese to learn to say no to America's unceasing trade demands, it touched off a storm in the United States.

Many in the United States display symptoms of a "diminished giant" syndrome in the face of Japan's rise as an economic superpower, just as the British did when Germany and the United Stated emerged as rivals at the end of the nineteenth century. These symptoms are so severe that rational discourse about Japan has become nearly impossible.

The time has come for Japan to draw its line in the sand in response to the Clinton administration's plans to muscle its way to a new, tough-minded trade policy on Japan. This would set quantitative import shares (similar to those for semiconductors) as targets for Japanese industries and so seek "results" in place of rules.

Japan needs to say no to such demands, which rest on fallacious economics and are destructive of the rules-based world trading system that America's presidents have nurtured since the Second World War. But this negative response needs to be combined with positive actions to establish Japanese leadership of the multilateral trading system.

Originally published in the *Financial Times* (April 16, 1993).

The present U.S. drive to expand "managed" or "results-oriented" trade with Japan, by setting quantitative import targets, derives from the conjunction of a false premise with an unpleasant fact.

The false premise is that Japan's persistent trade surplus is proof that its markets are closed: if manufactured goods could be sold to Japan, it is argued, the surplus would not exist.

The unpleasant fact is that the Japanese market for manufactured goods is open. It is even more open than those of the United States and the European Community, both of which have made copious use of voluntary export restrictions (VERs) and anti-dumping and countervailing duties, the favoured instruments of protectionists today. Japan has largely abstained from using such measures.

This combination of the false premise with the unpleasant fact implies that Japan's imports must be expanded "somehow." The Bush administration, in principle sensible in trade matters, decided that the problem lay in Japan's unique cultural and institutional characteristics. The Clinton administration, generally intemperate about trade questions, has decided that Japan is incorrigible. Its preferred solution is to impose import targets.

Yet the underlying premise is wrong. It is wrong even though President Bill Clinton embraced it in his untutored remarks about Japan at his first press conference.

Students of economics should hardly need reminding that trade barriers, as distinct from macroeconomic policies, do not determine trade balances. But this is not an argument that can be easily sold to politicians. Where abstract arguments fail, examples might work instead. A graph of Japanese trade deficits and surpluses since the Second World War would show an oscillation, as is true of most countries, even though its trade policies have become steadily more liberal. Americans should also recall that the United States itself ran a trade surplus for many years after the Second

World War, even though the United States was not particularly protectionist at the time.

Japan is being unjustifiably blamed. But its acceptance of import targets in response to a charge that is flawed in conception would be a still greater folly. As the semiconductor case has shown, such targets would be inherently arbitrary. There would also be no effective way for Japan to ensure that its private industries would fulfill them. The targets would also be seen as "export protectionism," allowing any industry with political clout to secure guaranteed shares of foreign markets.

If the United States were to obtain Japanese agreement to such targets, the EC would not be far behind. Soon, Japan's trade would be governed by politics, not by competition and rules. Success with an economically powerful country such as Japan would whet the appetite for use of the same policy vis-à-vis other, less powerful countries. The practice would spread as businesses, seeking guaranteed market shares abroad, pressured a complacent administration toward ever more managed trade.

Japan needs to be firmly "rejectionist" when the Clinton administration makes a push for managed trade. It should learn from its semiconductor experience and heed the adage that if one gives way once, one will be asked to yield again. But Japan should also be positive. It should propose an international process to assess complaints of "nullification and impairment" of trade obligations. Such a procedure should serve as a substitute for the establishment of import targets in industries where the US possesses only prima facie complaints, which it too readily treats as final proof.

The suggested process could be bilateral, as in the U.S.-Canada Free Trader Agreement, or, better still, multilateral, as in the General Agreement on Tariffs and Trade. The process would, in turn, be available symmetrically to Japan as a complainant, a feature that is absent from the U.S. Congress's favourite weapon: the 301 and Super 301 legislation of the Omnibus Trade and

Competitiveness Act of 1988. The chance of such a role reversal would itself moderate the Clinton administration's enthusiasm for what would otherwise be one-way demands on Japan.

The GATT is the right institution because it is based on symmetrical rights and obligations among its contracting parties. The GATT has to be Japan's, and indeed the world's, ultimate defence against managed trade imposed by—and for the interests of—strong nations.

Japan's prime minister, Kiichi Miyazawa, has not, contrary to some assertions, held up the conclusion of the Uruguay Round. It was the EC's unwillingness to make agricultural concessions acceptable to the Cairns Group of agricultural exporting countries that was the main early stumbling block. At the same time, Japan has not given an energetic push toward concluding the round either. Mr. Miyazawa should use today's summit to proclaim that he is willing to compromise on opening rice markets.

Mr. Miyazawa should also announce that his strategy would be to close the round within the year and immediately have a new round to pursue unfinished business, such as the interaction between liberal trade and environmental protection. On this issue Japan is already at the centre of the stage with its success at the Rio Earth summit.

Japan should say no to unreasonable and unwise demands for manage trade. But it needs also to say "full speed ahead" to finishing the round, to starting a new one, and to strengthening the multilateral trading system, now in severe jeopardy.

20   Is This Showdown Necessary?

Here we go again! Just when the Clinton administration's trade policy with Japan had settled into a saner mode and we'd abandoned the "aggressive unilateralism" of threatening to impose tariffs to secure Japan's acceptance of our demands, U.S. Trade Representative Mickey Kantor is back on the war path, belting out the same old battle cries.

Punitive tariffs of 100 percent on thirteen models of Japanese luxury cars will be imposed by June 28 1996, if Japanese firms do not capitulate to our demands, including a guarantee that they buy a set amount of American auto parts. This policy has no more chance of success now than it did in 1994 when, at the summit meeting that February beween Clinton and Japan's then–prime minister, Morihiro Hosokawa, Japan flatly refused to accept numerical import targets.

If the Clinton folks go through with them, these tariffs will put us on the wrong side of international law, since they violate World Trade Organization rules to which we have agreed. We cannot unilaterally raise tariffs that have been fixed by negotiation at the WTO at levels of 2.5 to 25 percent.

Ironically, this is happening even before the ink dries on the Uruguay Round of multilateral trade negotiations that established the WTO, and whose success President Clinton proudly trumpeted

Originally published in *Newsday* (June 11, 1995). Reprinted with permission.

Figure 20.1
Source: *Newsday* (June 11, 1995).

a few months ago as his administration's triumph. Such a colossal blunder could not have been committed except under a unique conjunction of factors, each pulling policymakers in the same misbegotten direction.

The politics is manifest. Representatives Richard Gephardt (D-Missouri) and David Bonior (K-Michigan), powerful foes of free trade who passionately opposed NAFTA and almost cost the president its passage in Congress, represent constituencies where the car industry is important. Trade unions, though now representing under 12 percent of the private labor force, are still an important constituency for Democrats, and the United Auto Workers a major player.

The Mexican bailout has also put Clinton on the defensive. Ross Perot and opponents of NAFTA in the Democratic Party are busy saying, with little logic but a great deal of populist plausibility:

We told you so. The best defense is a good offense. By diverting his critics' attention to exports and Japan, the president is seeking to turn his foes on trade into friends hunting a common quarry.

Japan-baiting, crude or sophisticated, has always been fair game in U.S. politics. The ceaseless repetition by the administration and some influential columnists that Japan's markets are "closed" continues to poison the domestic atmosphere and skew public opinion in favor of industry lobbyists' outrageous demands. But many scholars, including Gary Saxonhouse of the University of Michigan and David Weinstein of Harvard, have reminded us that Japan's tariffs and import restrictions have been lower than ours since the mid-1980s. We have slapped restraints on Japan's U.S. exports since May 1981, while Japan has never imposed such limits on our cars.

True, Japan's unique culture of "controlled openness" drives our businessmen up a wall. It is said, aptly, that you can buy from Japan in English, but you must sell there in Japanese. It is hard for us to settle in for the long haul and concentrate on cultivating customers rather than on making instant sales.

But other nations have, and our own smart industries have as well. The results are obvious: Kantor, who keeps citing import shares as proof of Japan's impenetrability, neglects to mention that manufactured goods now represent well over half of Japan's imports. In seven high-tech markets, such as electrical machinery, scientific instruments, and pharmaceuticals, the percentage of the home market supplied by imports is very much like ours. But Kantor panders uncritically to domestic lobbies that want a free lunch on the political gravy train.

Bureaucratic factors also play a role here. Embattled Commerce Secretary Ron Brown is worried about Republican threats to close down his shop. The best thing going for him politically is to land American CEOs contracts in foreign markets. Piggybacking on Kantor's assault on Japanese markets is a wonderful opportunity.

The failure of the Hosokawa-Clinton summit in 1994 was a black mark against proponents of the hard line against Japan. Then, these trade hawks in the U.S. trade representative's office and the Commerce Department unsuccessfully pressured the Japanese government to accept our demands; now they're attempting to pressure the Japanese car firms directly. They are demanding that the automobile industry agree to numerical targets for purchasing both new and used American car parts, and that it open its showrooms and car dealerships to Detroit's models.

The high yen has already made a shift to more imported components profitable for Japanese firms. For them to accept a formal, numerical obligation is deemed an inexpensive proposition by our hawks. Moreover, the high yen is hurting their sales overseas. The Clinton strategists figure that financial difficulties, coupled with punitive U.S. tariffs, ought to be sufficient to make the Japanese capitulate. The bird, wounded badly, will fall into our lap.

Indeed, if the Japanese car industry caves in quickly, it will not matter that our threatened tariffs are illegal under WTO rules, and that the Japanese government has promised to take us to court there. Having procured from the Japanese car firms what we want, we could simply sheathe the sword without bloodletting— by not imposing the tariffs. The Japanese case against us at the WTO would become moot.

Unfortunately, our policy mavens seem to have miscalculated. For even if the car firms themselves have an economic incentive to yield to our blitzkrieg, no one should expect the Japanese government to remain passive. If blackmail against its car industry were allowed to prevail, there is every prospect that other extortionists would emerge from the woodwork. The Japanese government has merely to scan the long laundry list of complaints against Japan's "unfair trade practices," lodged by lobbyists queued up outside Kantor's office, to fear the worst. So it is not surprising that Ryutaro Hashimoto, Japan's minister for international trade and industry, has stood fast; nor that his ministry (MITI) is reportedly about to announce subsidies to the Japanese car firms, to tide them over their financial difficulties.

Our strategists have also forgotten that the chairman of Toyota is also the president of Keidanren, the Japanese Chamber of Commerce, this year. He has reportedly assured his business colleagues that the car industry will not fold, opening the door to offensives against other sectors of the economy. In this official capacity, he will take the heat in the public interest.

In short, the Clinton administration's best and brightest have landed themselves in a terrible mess. With neither the car firms nor the Japanese government blinking, we are left with two options: reversing policy and suspending the proposed tariffs, or imposing them and inviting Japan's inevitably successful appeal to the WTO. Neither is a pleasant prospect. Clinton's trade warriors are clearly worried about a policy failure that could make the Hosokawa-Clinton summit breakdown look like a minor blip.

Indeed, otherwise hawkish Republicans such as Newt Gingrich and Phil Gramm have already begun to distance themselves from the administration's hard line, claiming they would have taken Japan on differently. When we finally stumble, they are likely to demand, not that the United States get out of the WTO, but that an incompetent president get out of the White House.

The administration needs face-saving exit. Fortunately, one already exists, because Japan, wisely considering the importance of its bilateral relationship with us, has already agreed to assist our penetration of its automobile market. MITI, for example, has offered low-interest loans to our car firms to develop smaller models appropriate to the Japanese market. Just this past week, the European Union and Japan reached a substantial agreement, easing several market-entry problems posed by safety inspection requirements. These could apply to us, too. It should be noted that several European car manufacturers, such as BMW, have penetrated the Japanese market successfully and have built their own dealership networks there. We could do the same.

The Clinton administration could announce such developments as trade goodies its bluster has won, while taking the more intractable issues to the WTO for arbitration. The Japanese government would certainly play along. Its leaders know that saving face is as important in the Occident as in the Orient.

When the dust has settled on this latest skirmish, we should draw back and ask: Does it make sense to conduct trade diplomacy with Japan in such *High Noon* fashion? Surely it is time to normalize our dealings with Japan: seeking bilateral resolution of our (and their) complaints, and turning to the WTO for rulings when we cannot agree among ourselves.

Japan has changed irrevocably. The new generation, many of its members trained in our universities and as independent-minded as we are, will no longer accept our highhanded ways and one-sided demands. The Clinton warriors are discovering, painfully, that they are not fighting samurai anymore, but other GIs.

21   The U.S.-Japan Car Dispute: A Monumental Mistake

In Washington, U.S. trade policy is often asserted by official spokesmen, and accepted widely by the media and (I am sorry to say) by several economists who are unfamiliar with the issues and are bamboozled by the rhetoric, as one of President Clinton's success stories. In reality, when one probes deeper and looks for necessary nuances, it is almost a disaster area.

The popular approbation derives, of course, from the fact that President Clinton saw the Uruguay Round and NAFTA through a divided Congress and opposition within his own party. This was a welcome development for many supporters of free trade who had been deeply concerned by the president's initial ambivalence on the matter, whether due to lack of conviction or divisions among his political advisers. In fact, I was sufficiently distressed by the initial presidential fence-sitting on trade to remark in an afterdinner speech that, while the problem with President Bush had been that one could not read his lips, the problem with President Clinton was deeper: one did not know whether to read his lower lip or his upper lip.

But if President Clinton deserves applause for finding his convictions on freer trade over the Uruguay Round and over NAFTA, the same cannot be said of his administration's actions in regard

---

This article first appeared in *International Affairs* (London) 72, 2 (1996): 261–79, and is reproduced with permission.

to the principles of multilateralism. In particular, the administration's record can be faulted on (1) the use of aggressive unilateralism, in the form of unilateral threats of tariff retaliation illegal under the GATT; (2) its willingness to demand "managed trade" in the shape of import targets or what I called, and now others also call, VIEs (voluntary import expansions) from Japan; and (3) its obsession with the extension of preferential trade arrangements (PTAs) under GATT Article twenty-four, even when the GATT has been jump-started and its successor, the WTO, is in forward gear.

I have dealt extensively with the last issue in several recent writings; and many economists have now come to raise objections to the Clinton administration's desire to "walk on both legs" and to suggest that we may instead wind up "walking on all fours" if we enter into both MTN (multilateral trade negotiations) and PTAs instead of reverting to exclusive reliance on MTN under WTO auspices.[1] In this article, however, I plan to examine the U.S.-Japan car dispute as a prime example of what has been wrong with U.S. policy in relation to the two issues mentioned above: aggressive unilateralism, and demands for managed trade in the form of VIEs and their virtual equivalents.

The General Background

The Clinton administration took office on the basis of a campaign among the elements of which were an obsession with Japan's trade surplus and its trade practices and a declaration of intent to revive the lapsed Super 301 provision of the 1988 Omnibus Trade and Competitiveness Act so as to bring Japan to book for its wittingly wayward presence in the world economy. The major figures on whom the administration relied in its early days for advice in these matters were the well-known former bureaucrat Clyde Prestowitz, scarred by battles with the Japanese over years of trade negotiations and a Republican who threw his support behind Clinton as presidential candidate on these issues, to the latter's great delight and gratitude; the noted journalist James Fallows, whose splendid early judgment that the best U.S. response to the rise of Japan and the Far East was to be "more like us" (that is, to accentuate reliance on what was best in the U.S. system rather than to imitate the alleged Japanese virtues) had yielded to frantic demands to "contain Japan" after he had spent a year there (whereas familiarity is said to breed contempt, in the case of Japan it often seems to breed panic); and the articulate and influential columnist Robert Kuttner, a new Suslov in the Democratic Party and founding editor of the *American Prospect*, about whom a Washington wit had remarked that "Kuttner had not yet met a tariff that he did not like."

The main economists chosen by the Clinton administration were also known to be sympathetic to these views: the current deputy secretary of the Treasury, Lawrence Summers, an economist of great ability, had expressed hawkish views on Japan's trade policy and alarmist views on the consequences of Japan's trade surplus; and the choice of Laura Tyson as the chairwoman of the Council of Economic Advisers, to the chagrin of others who aspired to the job, was evidently inspired by her sympathetic views on industrial policy and the Super 301 provisions, and by her clear declaration of support for an aggressive policy toward Japan on high-tech industries in her 1992 book *Who's Bashing Whom? Trade Conflict in High-Technology Industries,* published with superb timing and with dividends for the author.[2]

Mickey Kantor's appointment as the U.S. trade representative (USTR), succeeding Carla Hills, also turned out to be a major shot across the bows in the new era of confrontation with Japan and aggressive pursuit of U.S. trade demands. In a characteristic statement, he announced early on that he had no time for "theology" and that he would instead go for "results": in short, he was a litigator out to win a case, with no interest in jurisprudence. Free trade and multilateralism were not the issue; the goal was to advance U.S. trade interests. He proudly claimed that he talked to Prestowitz on Japan; no reputable scholars on international trade generally or on Japan's trade in particular appear to have had the benefit of sharing their views with Mr. Kantor.

If there was any prospect of dissent, it yielded to the fierce loyalty that the new trade policy toward Japan seems to have required within the administration. High officials who had been moderate and "cosmopolitan" on Japan opted for silence and prudently gave ground. The effect of the aggressive tactics on the influential outside critics too, may have been chilling. Fred Bergsten, head of the Institute for International Economics in Washington, long unfairly attacked by James Fallows and Pat Choate (the author of the anti-Japan screed, *Agents of Influence*) as being soft on Japan because of Japanese financial support for his institute, now found Super 301 revival a good idea and also changed his mind in the administration's direction on how closed Japan's markets were: changes that were presumably prompted by more reflection but were certainly welcome to the new administration.

The new, tough policy on Japan was not entirely new, of course, since elements of it can be found in the Bush administration as well. But the Bush administration had been opposed to the tough versions of the 301 provisions in the 1988 Trade Act. The use of Super 301 against Japan represented a surrender to strong congressional pressures, given the fact that the 1988 act had landed the Bush administration with a very difficult situation vis-à-vis Congress; but it was effectively undercut in several ways by the USTR. Similarly, the Bush administration's use of import targets was minimal: the numbers cited in the Tokyo communiqué on the purchase of U.S. parts by Japan's automakers, for example, were clearly not meant to be firm targets.

The Clinton administration, by contrast, wanted to revive the lapsed Super 301, wished to elevate indicative numbers in some cases to a firm principle of managed trade with Japan more broadly, and saw the confrontation with Japan as a necessary shift of gear in trading with that country. It was ideologically dressed in the garb of what has been called *realekonomic*, a concept propagated by those such as Ed Luttwak who contend that economic rivalry is important "now that the cold war has ended" (a school of lazy minds that mechanically asserts that everything must change because the cold war has ended) and by others who argue that trade is a zero-sum game (a notion that the economist Paul Krugman now derides but himself encouraged in the 1980s by a careless translation of the principles of trade policy under imperfect competition into public discourse).[3]

The shift in policy toward Japan that the Clinton administration wished to execute was based on the following premises:

1. Japan was unfairly closed while the United States was open, giving Japan's firms considerable competitive advantage vis-à-vis U.S. firms.

2. This assessment could be made unilaterally by the United States and did not have to be validated by impartial procedures.

3. The closure of the Japanese markets was "informal" and hence the remedy for it was to ask Japan to accept a "results-oriented" VIE or "managed trade" approach to its imports.

4. The way to get Japan to accept such an approach was to use 301-sanctioned tariff-retaliatory threats against Japan, even if these were illegal under the terms of the GATT.

These premises, however, were either based on faulty economic analysis or politically unrealistic. With regard to the first premise, the view that Japan is so asymmetrically closed that it is an outlier, wildly off the curve, in its exclusionary import policies or situation, is far from generally agreed among economists. The Clinton administration's simplistic reliance on indicators such as Japan's lower share of imports in GNP vis-à-vis the OECD average, a bad habit they picked up from a fortunately minuscule but much-cited group of Japan-obsessed economists such as Rudiger Dornbusch (MIT) who rely wholly on such sloppy arguments, can be easily countered by noting that the fact that Canada has a vastly greater share of imports in GNP than the United States does not make Canada a vastly more open economy! As it happens, over a dozen econometric studies by different economists, put together by the Japan scholar Gary Saxonhouse at Michigan, have examined the question much more subtly and concluded that it is hard to characterize Japan's import share as "too low."

The second premise is neither good for the world trading system nor politically sensible. It is bad for the trading system because every such complaint should be assessed by impartial authorities rather than by the country making the complaint: the alternative to such a rule of law is subservience to the law of the jungle. Indeed, the office of the USTR is so captive to lobbying interests, as against the general interest, and its famous annual report on unfair trading practices abroad is so much a farrago of uncensored, unexamined industry complaints and assertions, that it is hard to credit the U.S. methods with any degree of legitimacy or credibility. Such unilateralism has been received by the world community with as much approbation as vigilantes, who seek to take the law into their own hands, receive from thoughtful citizens.

As for the third premise, the notion that a unilateral determination of Japanese "informal barriers," regarded as revealed in "too low" imports, should be fixed by setting VIE targets, flies in the face of the fact that only markets can determine what appropriate market shares and imports will be. No bureaucrat or economist can determine what the market will or will not do; in fact, arrogance in assuming that one could was the source of the massive inefficiencies that characterized planned economies such as India and the Soviet Union. The only valid procedure is to identify the alleged barriers and then to address them directly. It is also the case that, given this inherent impossibility of bureaucratically predetermining market shares, VIEs will turn into "export protectionism": export lobbies will use VIEs to carve out guaranteed shares in export markets in just the way that VERs and import quotas, constituting "import protectionism," seek to carve out guaranteed shares in the domestic markets.[4]

The fourth and final premise that Japan will succumb to unilateral threats is politically unrealistic. As I argued in an article entitled "Samurais No More" in the May–June 1994 issue of *Foreign Affairs* right after the failure of the Hosokawa-Clinton summit in Washington in February 1994 when Prime Minister Hosokawa refused to accept VIEs despite the threat of retaliatory retribution (much as Prime Minister Miyazawa had indicated in an earlier, friendlier summit), the Clinton warriors thought they were fighting the samurai when in fact they were fighting GIs. The Japanese have been changing rapidly: their students, now in the United States in vastly increased numbers, no longer bow before the revered *sensei* but put their feet on the table like the American students; and the women and children living abroad with the executives who populate the increased numbers of Japanese multinationals in the EU and the United States are agents of quick and powerful change. Once paralysed at the red and amber traffic lights by their traditional discipline, the Japanese can now be seen crossing against the light. These are no longer patsies who can be pushed around with trade demands justified by unilateral, lobby-led accusations. Yes, they will make even difficult trade concessions within reciprocal frameworks such as MTN at Geneva; but the notion that the Japanese can continue to be intimidated into making one-way trade concessions when the standard game is for such concessions to be made with some reciprocity—I give you some and you give me some—is to ignore the compelling reality that those days are past.

What is astonishing is that the Clinton administration, which had been badly chastened by the stubborn refusal of the Japanese government to cave in to the demands for managed trade and the attendant failure of the Hosokawa-Clinton summit, and whose policy toward Japan had become better informed and more mindful of the damage inflicted on the United States by earlier demands for managed trade, suddenly gave way in the dramatic dispute over cars. The reappearance at centre stage of a policy that had been discredited and discarded must be explained; and its consequences for the multilateral world trading system must be examined. As I argue below, the revival failed miserably, as was to be expected; but there is no assurance that the Clinton administration will not try again; indeed, the rhetoric of success in the car talks is so assiduously spread by the administration, and believed by so many, that it may well work itself into a mis-perception of a true victory rather than an ignominious defeat for which the true supporters of the multilateral trading system can only be thankful to the successful Japanese negotiators.

Explaining the U.S. Action

The central fact was that the United States explosively elevated its car dispute with Japan to centre stage with the unilateral declaration of 100 percent punitive tariffs on thirteen models of Japanese luxury cars if the Japanese negotiators did not capitulate on demands for "voluntary" import expansion (VIE) targets. In-terestingly, while the rest of the world (especially the EU spokes-men such as Sir Leon Brittan) predictably voiced their outrage and their criticisms of this move, Mr. Kantor, with characteristic delicacy of language, proclaimed that his critics could "scream, like pigs stuck on a gate" for all he cared. The crude analogy was more apt than he thought: pork was indeed a prime mover behind the action that he announced, flanked by the commerce secretary (Ron Brown) and the National Economic Council chairwoman (Laura Tyson).

An action that predictably destroyed the credibility of the administration's respect for the rule of law and its commitment to multilateralism, and brought the United States into disrepute and disgrace,[5] could only have been taken under a unique conjunction of several factors, all pulling in the same direction and all leading the United States down the low road. These factors were both political and bureaucratic; and they were translated into action because the economics of the car industry, both in Japan and in Detroit, combined with the rise of the yen to make the "managed trade" demands for VIEs (and other numerical targets such as those on dealerships), backed by aggressive unilateralism in the shape of punitive tariffs on Japan's car manufacturers, an irresistible proposition to the administration's strategists. Let me explain.

The Political Factors

The political aspect of the revived policy is manifest. President Clinton's political advisers saw great advantage in targeting the Japanese car industry. Representatives Gephardt (D-Missouri) and Bonior (D-Detroit), powerful foes of the administration over NAFTA, represent constituencies where the car industry is important. At the same time, the trade unions, while now representing under 12 percent of the private labour force, are nonetheless an important Democratic constituency, with the UAW an important player. Furthermore, with Mexico's bailout having revived the politics of NAFTA, and the illogical but influential "I-told-you-so" charges leveled by Ross Perot and the unions, the administration clearly hoped to deflect the antitrade sentiment to the perennial

Japan-baiting arena. Indeed, the president unabashedly used anti-Japanese sentiment to sell NAFTA: the United States would have privileged access to Mexico's market, whereas Japan would not.

The ceaseless repetition by the administration—and by some influential columnists who have become de facto unofficial spokesmen for the USTR—of the assertion that Japan is "closed," in blatant disregard of the widely shared huge scepticism in respect of this claim among major Japan scholars in the United States,[6] had continued to poison the domestic atmosphere in favour of ceaseless one-way demands on the Japanese, as in the car negotiations. Ironically, the United States has protected its own cars, having imposed voluntary export restraints (VERs), now virtually outlawed by the WTO, on Japanese exports in May 1981 and continued them de facto until recently. Of course, you never hear about them when Mr. Kantor takes to the hustings.

The result is that it is impossible for elected U.S. politicians to attack the administration's demands on Japan without appearing to be condoning Japan's "closed markets," as was evident in the nearly unanimous nonbinding resolution that was passed quickly in the Senate in support of the administration's policy.

The Bureaucratic Factors

The politics of pork was not the sole driving force behind the Clinton administration's action. Bureaucratic interests were equally important. Commerce Secretary Brown's enthusiastic and visible support for the action is to be explained in part by his and his department's predicament: he was under a cloud and his department was threatened with extinction by the Republican Congress. Manifestly, "opening markets" is a slogan and a goal whose appeal no politician could discount in a town where there are two overriding principles of trade policy: imports are bad; and exports are good. Piggybacking Mr. Kantor on the anti-Japan offensive gave him cachet and his department the rationale for survival; and it correspondingly gave the anti-Japan policy extra clout and support.

In addition, the question of petty bureaucratic pride must not be forgotten. When the Hosokawa-Clinton summit collapsed, as some of us had predicted it would, so did the reputation of the proponents of the new hard line toward Japan, premised on the fallacy that aggressive unilateralism and demands for VIEs are desirable policy instruments. Evidently, these proponents had taken the president down the wrong path. It was not great for them, no matter what excuses they offered up, to have such a failure on their record! There is little doubt that they were sulking, waiting, looking for an opportunity to outwit and waylay Japan so that the principle of VIEs would be conceded, and that too in the context of the use of the Section 301 variety of aggressive unilateralism. Roger Altman (the former deputy secretary of the Treasury) had threatened that he would wait "until hell freezes over" for Japan to yield to U.S. demands—unfortunately, he himself could not as the U.S. Congress had different plans for him[7]—and this was certainly the sentiment and aspiration of all bureaucrats of his ilk: one day, some time, some way, we would "get them."

Opportunity finally presented itself in the case of the car industry, offering these discredited bureaucrats a chance to push again for the failed policy, de facto abandoned in 1994 and 1995 and, in fact, certified to be so by Thomas Friedman of the *New York Times*, a vigorous critic of Japan.[8] Vindication was finally at hand.

The Irresistible Opportunity

It is easy to think that the car industry was the natural choice for the recent U.S. action. After all, it was the last of the sectors under the Framework Agreement. Perhaps the office of the USTR and its allies thought that the Japanese government might accede to demands for VIEs, under 301 tariff threats, as a way of getting the last remaining dispute out of the way and then settling down to a normalized trade relationship. If so, they did not, of course, understand that there was little reason for the Japanese government to expect that this would indeed be the "end game." Just look at the USTR's annual report on the unfair trade practices of others and the litany of complaints against Japan by several industries: would it really be reasonable for the Japanese trade ministry, MITI, to think that demands for VIEs, under threat of 301 tariffs, would disappear, instead of spreading to these numerous other industries, especially after the car industry's success? In fact, if MITI had any doubts, they should have been squashed by CEO George Fisher's firing of his own Eastman Kodak salvo against the Japanese soon after Kantor's action for the car industry.

The more reasonable assumption has to be that Kantor's clear expectation was that the car negotiation would end with Japanese acceptance of VIEs (and other demands), and that he expected this to be beneficial, not just for the political and bureaucratic reasons noted above, but also because it would establish the precedent with Japan that VIEs were the way to gain access to the Japanese market for several more industries.

The question to be answered, then, is, Why was the car industry chosen for Kantor's blitzkrieg? That negotiations were already under way in the car industry is hardly a sufficient reason. The answer has to be that the car industry offered the best prospect of winning the war that Kantor would declare. And, on reflection, it is obvious that the car industry offered him the best prospect for success, especially as, learning from the failure of the Hosokawa-Clinton summit, he had brilliantly shifted from seeking the VIEs from a Japanese ministry and *government* that had learnt to say no (to VIEs) to forcing the Japanese car *firms* instead to capitulate to these demands, while MITI minister Hashimoto would be left on the sidelines, wringing his hands.

The high yen had already increased the incentive for Japan to shift to imports of more components for new cars and of "aftermarket" replacement parts, quite regardless of any VIE commitments; under these circumstances, the U.S. demand that the Japanese car firms accept VIEs for increased imports of components was not exactly the imposition that it would otherwise have been (although, of course, the firms were also being asked to accept other loss-causing obligations, such as letting their Detroit competitors have numerically guaranteed access to their own single-agency dealers in which they had invested over the years). However, while the cost of *compliance* with the USTR demands was not particularly exorbitant, thanks to the high yen, the USTR strategy was to make the cost of *noncompliance* with the demands extremely high, thus making the prospect of capitulation by the Japanese car firms appear inevitable. The high yen had already put the Japanese car firms under serious strain. Why not impose huge financial penalties on them for noncompliance? The obvious way to do this was to levy punitive tariffs on their successful exports: in essence, hit them hard so that they hurt bad. Hence, the tariff retaliation was aimed at the car industry itself, violating the GATT injunction not to raise the bound tariffs and therefore making the action manifestly illegal under the GATT (if and when the tariffs were actually levied).[9]

Clearly, the strategy was to intimidate the Japanese car firms into capitulation as quickly as possible under threat of financial sanctions. This also explains the decision to make the tariffs retroactively effective almost immediately after the announcement of the intention to levy them, even though they would be imposed

only in late June (if at all): this was calculated to increase the
pressure on the firms to settle forthwith. The refusal to let the fast-
track procedure operate on Japan's suit against the 301 action at
the WTO was also similarly motivated and violated the spirit of
the Uruguay Round accord since the fast-track procedure was
taken from the earlier GATT practice on perishable agricultural
products where delay would be costly and unjust to the targeted
nations: the same principle clearly should have applied in this
case, for the Japanese car firms that were targeted would suffer
market disruption because of the backdating of the potential levy
of the illegal retaliatory car tariffs.[10]

The tactical shift to making the car firms, rather than the
Japanese government, the target of the punitive tariffs was a brilliant move in the sense that the evil genius Lex Luthor's moves
are brilliant in the *Superman* movies. It pitted the full power of a
sovereign government, and a superpower to boot, against private
foreign firms operating under strict hard budget constraints.
It was an inherently unequal contest. But, as I argue more fully
below, this was not a move that could escape the attention of the
government of Japan whose private firms were thus being intimidated and whose general trading interests would be directly
jeopardized if this outrageous action were allowed to succeed and
to set a precedent. Nor could economists who are interested in the
design of an appropriate world trading system, as distinct from
the successful pursuit of narrow and self-serving interests by
myopic bureaucrats and politicians, be indifferent to what the
USTR and the Clinton administration had done.

The Role of Detroit

I must also explain why the Detroit car firms lobbied for this set
of demands and actions, instead of getting into the open Japanese

car market as the European car firms have done, successfully and without using any such tactics. For, even though it has become customary in the United States to dismiss Japan's repeated claims that its car market is open, the fact remains that it is. Indeed, the executives of several European car firms have frankly said so, and many economists who have looked at the subject agree.

While I detail below the reasons why the Detroit car lobby's demands, taken over uncritically by the USTR,[11] were based predominantly on unsupportable complaints about the Japanese car market, let me state immediately that these demands made ample economic sense from Detroit's viewpoint, lending therefore further salience to a policy that reflected the compelling political and bureaucratic factors detailed above. The facts are that Japan's car market is expensive to enter and the sales prospects are unexciting, thus making it a considerably less attractive market to put one's marketing and other resources into than those of developing countries such as China, India, Indonesia, etc. (which the erstwhile under secretary for commerce, Jeffrey Garten, called the "emerging markets" around the world). If you sell cars in Japan, you *are* free to open up your own distribution system, advertise, cajole, and seduce your customers. But, in an advanced country, the costs of setting up such a distribution system of your own dealers are going to be hugely higher than in India and China, for instance. Of course, if you can use politics to piggyback on someone else's distribution system, you can cut down that cost of entry substantially. Hence the demands for such a "multiple-agency" system to be forced, with targets, upon Japan's car manufacturers: a demand that these firms have generally resisted much as the Detroit transplants in the European Union have strongly resisted such demands there. Then again, the market-determined sales-growth curve in Japan cannot be expected to be even fractionally as promising, whether for finished cars or for components, as virtually anywhere else. After all, you would be competing with the world's most formidable car manufacturers on their home ground. Hence, it would be a great help if the USTR could guarantee robustly growing sales through VIEs and such numerical targets.

These economic fundamentals, then, immediately defined the economic underpinnings of Detroit's demands, while the bureaucratic and political factors defined the reasons why these demands came to be embodied in the current policy.

The U.S. Demands: Ill-Conceived Stipulations Based on Dubious Complaints

It is not surprising, therefore, that nearly all of the Clinton administration's complaints were dubious at best; its demands, whether on the after-sales parts market or the sales of new cars or the purchase of components and parts for car manufacture, were therefore ill-conceived and inconsistent with the spirit of the WTO. Let me indicate why.

"Aftermarket" Replacement Parts

The United States complained that Japan required excessive car inspections, every two years, going well beyond what is necessary for safety in the U.S. judgement, and also that Japanese car manufacturers had captured the inspection stations which then did not carry U.S.-made spare parts. The U.S. objection to the inspection system is about as sensible as Japan telling the United States that American torts liability rules impose excessive burdens, including some on Japanese businesses in the United States, and therefore ought to be changed. The American public properly expects Congress, not MITI or Mitsubishi, to be concerned with that agenda.

The United States also wanted the garages to carry U.S.-made parts, though it is hard to see how the inventory policy of private businesses can be effectively prescribed by any government. The obvious and efficient solution is rather to set up U.S.-owned garages, carrying U.S.-made parts, and to ensure that these garages are readily certified for inspection (which, if denied, would be quickly adjudged to be an effective barrier to U.S. entry and therefore an excellent case to win before the WTO). But that would mean making the investment necessary to capture this market, which is where the real difficulty lay.

Access to Dealerships

The administration insisted that the Japanese car dealers, affiliated to specific Japanese firms, carry U.S. cars as well. Nothing prevents the U.S. firms from setting up their own single-agency distribution systems, as they used to, and as the Europeans continue to do (having only just renewed the exemption from the European directive on competition policy for the car industry, with American transplant car firms in Europe in tune with that decision, of course). Admittedly, if Nissan and Toyota were to hire someone to break the legs of those who work for U.S. dealerships, that would be a legitimate reason to allege barrier to American entry. But they do not. And other entrants, such as BMW, have indeed made the investments necessary to set up their own dealers.[12]

Chrysler spokesmen's familiar complaint that they would have to buy land at exorbitant prices while the Japanese firms bought their land at low prices makes as much sense as Governor Clinton's telling Mayor Koch that free trade between Little Rock and New York is unfairly stacked against the former because rents are exorbitantly higher in New York. Besides, an accountant would lose her licence if she allowed Japanese firms to continue costing their land at historic, rather than market, prices. Shall we hear next that, because Toyota, for the same reason, manages to produce more cheaply in Japan than U.S. firms entering the market could today, its production facilities in Toyota City should be opened up to produce U.S. cars?

Parts in New Cars

The administration also demanded that the Japanese car manufacturers set up "voluntary purchase plans" for expanded purchases of U.S.-made components. The United States has already coerced the Japanese transplants in the United States into buying more U.S.-made components, while inconsistently lecturing other countries for doing the same more formally and also building into the WTO prohibitions against "local content" requirements. Now, the United States was saying: if you can buy U.S.-made parts for your cars in the United States, why not for cars made in Japan? In short, the United States used one forced enhancement of sales of U.S.-made parts to justify another!

Never did the United States confront the critical issue, namely: if *keiretsu* are barriers to entry, what do we do about vertical integration which we have conventionally preferred? In fact, it is easier to maintain that the *keiretsu* by relying usually on multiple and changing suppliers, are easier for outsiders to crack than vertically integrated firms (such as IBM making and "buying" its own chips and General Motors buying nearly 75 percent of its parts from within).[13] Again, if markets are contestable, as they certainly are in the outside world—and, in my view, within Japan too; but this is not essential to my argument in an industry where markets are global—no Japanese firm can afford to buy from its favoured Japanese suppliers to the exclusion of more efficient foreign suppliers without being mown down in a tough, competitive environment.[14]

Publicizing the Case: The Los Angeles Lawyer Syndrome

Needless to say, the American public did not hear the truth of these matters. Instead, it got a barrage of half-truths and obfuscations, delivered with a calculated and cynical flourish to the media to gain propaganda advantage and to mislead the country into support of a disgraceful policy.

Since Mr. Kantor was the flamboyant star of this show, it is helpful to recall that he is not merely an American lawyer; he is also a Los Angeles lawyer. For those who watched the O. J. Simpson trial, Mr. Kantor seems far less of an original than he appears to the untutored eye.

Aside from his continual banter, he threw in the occasional red herring. To justify his actions, he argued also that history owed Detroit an apology and Japanese acceptance of the U.S. demands. This "down payment" was necessary because "through high tariffs, allocations of capital, and a range of other measures, the government of Japan in essence kicked foreign producers out of the market."[15] Quite aside from the inaccuracy of this claim, surely Kantor did not plan to make history a handmaiden for his claims on other nations. If so, the United States owes Britain a hefty down payment since the United Kingdom was a unilateral free trader through the decades in the latter half of the nineteenth century when the United States was protectionist. Indeed, consider that, having not afforded intellectual property protection to others when it was behind on innovation during its early history, the United States is happy to accuse others, now that it is among the innovators, of theft and piracy. Should it not instead, according to the new Kantor doctrine of contrition for one's past, offer "down payment" to the world for its earlier bad behaviour?

Mr. Kantor's lawyerly expertise was best seen, however, not in the specious arguments which he concocted with the utmost apparent sincerity, but rather in the suit that he declared he was

bringing against Japan at the WTO for nullification and impairment of its trade concessions and of America's corresponding
rights in the car industry. In fact, such a suit, under Article
23(I)(b) or perhaps 23(I)(c), targeted at narrowly and carefully
specified Japanese practices that were considered to be pertinent,
had been proposed as the correct course of action by many for
some time. The long-standing decision not to mount such a suit
had been a result of objections from two sources: first, from those
who thought the United States would lose (and so, presumably it
would be better to browbeat the Japanese into submission
through aggressive unilateralism instead; after all, the United
States "knew" they were guilty of nullification and impairment,
even though it could not prove it at the WTO); and second, those
who thought the United States would win (in which case the law
so made could come back to haunt the United States as well).

The change of mind about an Article 23 suit certainly had
nothing to do with a change of mind on the matter at issue.
Rather, the suit had every mark of being what American lawyers
call a "countersuit." If I take you to court on something wicked
that you have done to me, your lawyer will usually advise you to
start a suit against me, for bargaining purposes. Kantor's proposed suit against Japan was clearly such a countersuit. It had the
advantage of tying up the Japanese in a defensive mode just as
they were preparing themselves for their own, far more compelling, suit against the proposed U.S. punitive tariffs, illegal under
the WTO. But that is not all. It also could be expected to blunt, in
the uninformed public eye, the criticism that the punitive actions
against Japan were unilateral and illegal under the WTO by suggesting that the United States was going to the WTO and seeking
multilateral remedies for its complaints. In short, it was an effective diversionary tactic: in fact, if the United States did mean to
take the multilateral route to getting its complaint adjudicated, it
would have had no reason to press ahead with the illegal and

aggressive unilateralism. Indeed, since the game plan was to get the Japanese car firms to capitulate quickly, so that the Japanese suit and the U.S. countersuit would become moot, the U.S. strategists had clearly gambled that they would not have to face the consequences of actually confronting Japan in litigation at the WTO. These consequences were not pleasant to contemplate; hence, the bluster got louder as the deadline for the threatened imposition of punitive tariffs came closer, just as it did during the Hosokawa-Clinton summit.

In the end, the U.S. strategy failed: the Japanese, as should have been expected by informed analysts, yielded nothing of consequence, explicitly rejecting (for the first time) VIEs in any form. The U.S. threat to use punitive tariffs illegal under the WTO had simply not been credible: the WTO would have found against the United States some time during the election year, badly exposing President Clinton to the charge, not that he was wrong to stand up against Japan (that is politically a nonstarter), but that his chosen method of doing so had been incompetent and had hurt the United States instead.

In particular, the notion that the car firms in Japan would capitulate under financial pressure, forcing capitulation in turn by MITI, turned out to be wrong. MITI could surely not be expected to stand by while the car firms caved in: the consequences for Japan's trade would be too dramatic, reaching well beyond the car industry itself, for MITI to stand idly by. An obvious answer therefore, which I sketched in an op-ed piece in May 1995 in the *Journal of Commerce*, was for MITI to provide financial subsidy to the car firms to offset the punitive tariffs. There is evidence that this was actually done, using the R&D subsidy provisions of the Uruguay Round Subsidies Code to make the support compatible with WTO rules. Moreover, the U.S. strategists did not allow for the fact that Mr. Toyoda, chairman of Toyota, was also the president of Keidanren that year and was reported to feel that, while his car firm would find it easier to capitulate than to fight, he owed it to Japanese industry in general, in his presidential capacity, to fight instead. Suffice it to say that the U.S. strategists were oblivious to these complexities, were ignoring the lessons of the failed Hosokawa-Clinton summit, and continued to be generally unmindful of the new Japan with which they were dealing. Their failure came as no surprise to me. Nor did the fact that Mr. Kantor, true to form, declared victory and Mr. Hashimoto's political stock rose in Japan, where propaganda had not obscured the true facts of the car accord reached in Geneva.

The Consequences of the U.S. Action

The consequences of the U.S. action in the car dispute are certain to be contrary to the benign ones clearly assumed, and even asserted, despite the failure of the U.S. strategists.

Damage to the World Trading System

(1) The 301 action (even though the threat of punitive tariffs was withdrawn on June 28, 1996) has already damaged the cause of multilateralism. The general assumption at the end of the Uruguay Round was that the United States had renounced unilateralism and would abide by the rule of law at the WTO. This assumption was laid waste by Mr. Kantor, creating bitterness in Geneva and cynicism among members of the WTO.

The assertion that no action illegal under the WTO actually took place, because the threat of punitive tariffs was not actually translated into their imposition on June 28, is strictly correct. But this is a technicality; and the assertion that the United States would in fact go ahead and undertake such illegal action unless its demands were met is certainly an indication of the U.S. willingness to flout WTO rules to its advantage.

In fact, given the U.S. willingness to use unilateral threats against WTO members under the technical protection that only actual violations of the WTO are illegal, it is time to consider whether this distinction should not itself be outlawed. In international relations, the presence of a sufficiently credible threat is itself treated as justification for preemptive response. It should be treated thus in the 301 type of threats: perhaps a WTO dispute settlement panel will in future make such a finding at a suitable opportunity, putting the U.S. practice of making such a self-serving distinction out of bounds.

(2) Damage to the WTO also derives from the fact that the U.S. action put the credibility of the new institution in jeopardy. The new director general, Mr. Renato Ruggiero, who must be congratulated for having made the right move earlier in rejecting the call for a TAFTA (Transatlantic Free Trade Area) in favour of concentrating on multilateralism at the WTO, cannot but have noticed, though he refrained from saying so, that the U.S. handling of the car dispute with the instrumentality of aggressive unilateralism was incompatible with the spirit, if not the letter, of multilateralism. For his part, Sir Leon Brittan did unhesitatingly voice his own and the EU's forthright and unambiguous condemnation of the U.S. action.

(3) The U.S. action also damaged the world trading system by using the threat of punitive tariffs against Japanese car firms in the attempt to get them to capitulate to its demands. As I observed above, this pitted a government with huge political and economic resources against foreign companies subject to stringent budget constraints. This introduces an extraordinary new source of instability and unpredictability into world trade: when multinationals are present in many countries under the conditions of increased globalization of investment and production, the use of such intimidation exposes all to potential threats of disrupted markets and "takings" by blackmail.[16]

(4) It is worth recalling also that a policy of demanding VIEs, no matter what euphemisms are used, is also damaging to the world trading system since it is a sure-fire way of creating trade diversion: Japanese firms forced by the United States to accept VIEs could be counted upon to satisfy them by diverting market-determined orders away from others to U.S. exporters.[17] This is precisely why the Europeans were up in arms against any deal along these lines between Japan and the United States. It is also the reason why Australia (one of whose components firms had just lost its traditional sales to a Japanese car manufacturer who said that he had no choice but to shift to an inferior U.S. supplier because of the political pressure) wanted to join the EU in sitting at the table if there were going to be new talks between the United States and Japan on the car dispute.[18]

(5) Of course, VIEs are no less than "managed trade," despite the administration's expressions of outrage when this is stated. By now, the downside of such import targets is well understood by economists. I would reiterate in particular that these targets amount to "export protectionism": conventional import protectionism assures your firms a guaranteed increase in the domestic market, whereas VIEs assure such an increase in the export market.

Damage to the Clinton Administration

(6) It is clear enough that this action by the USTR has done serious international damage to the reputation of the Clinton administration in relation to the credibility of its commitment to multilateralism, given the demonstration of its continued attachment to a policy of aggressive unilateralism. This is fine when the United States is exercising moral leadership on an issue and is widely perceived to be doing so. It is not fine when the United States is seen universally as failing in probity and good sense simply in pursuit of short-run advantage for itself.

(7) That the administration allowed itself to be so badly out-witted by Japan in the dispute also bears witness to the inaptitude of the Clinton advisers.

The Future of U.S.-Japan Trade Relations

Even as this episode has closed, the Clinton administration must confront the question, What profit does the United States derive by conducting its trade relations with Japan in this way? These bilateral negotiations tied down to a one-way stream of demands, in which the United States casts itself simultaneously as com-plainant, jury, and judge, constantly yelling at the Japanese, seek-ing concessions, and offering none, contain absolutely no element of the reciprocity and symmetry that define virtually all other suc-cessful negotiations among trading nations. It is an approach whose days are numbered. Indeed MITI's forceful rejection of the proposed illegal actions and of unreasonable, one-way demands on its car firms, and its clear message to the United States that "we will see you in court," is exactly what the U.S. response would be if another nation were to attempt to push it around. Just imagine what would happen if the French government were to zero in and blackmail IBM or Xerox the way Mr. Kantor went after the Japanese car firms: Congressmen would be calling for French blood.

As soon as the present dust has settled, the Japanese can be expected to tear up the 1993 Framework Agreement between the two countries. If either nation has specific complaints, and indeed Japan has problems with the United States too (see the Matsushita Report on others' unfair trade practices), resolution must be sought bilaterally. If this does not work, recourse to the WTO for impartial resolution of the conflict must be made.

Proceeding with Japan as if it were an outlier and an outlaw is not merely unjustified by the facts; it is also a politically futile policy, doomed (thank heavens) to failure. In short, the chief lesson of the car dispute and its resolution for U.S. trade policy toward Japan is that trade relations with Japan need to be normalized.

Notes

1. See, in particular, the two essays in Bhagwati and Krueger (1995). See also Bhagwati and Panagariya (1996, esp. chap. 1), which effectively challenges the popular notion that PTAs among countries with high initial volumes of trade or which are geographically proximate are somehow "natural" and most unlikely to cause harm despite their being preferential. These contributions make a strong case that the Clinton administration's continuing embrace of PTAs is a folly.

2. The book, while successful in political circles, where it played to popular prejudice, and in the electronics industry where it served their lobbying interests, received more critical notice in the professional journals. I also reviewed it in Bhagwati (1993).

3. It is often argued that the "new" trade theory, based on imperfect competition in product markets, hurt free trade policy by strengthening the case for protection. There is some evidence that it may have, especially in the way Krugman et al. were cited by Kuttner et al. in support of their demands for protection. However, this was true only of economic illiterates who were unaware that the case for free trade depends on market prices reflecting social costs and that market failures can compromise that case (though, as I and others noted in the postwar contributions to the theory of commercial policy, trade interventions are not always the first-best way to fix these market failures): see, in particular, the historical analysis in my 1993 Harry Johnson Lecture to the Royal Economic Society: Bhagwati (1994a).

The real damage that Krugman et al. did to the trading system in the 1980s was rather by reviving the old argument that import protection could lead to export promotion, so that if my market was open and yours was not, then I could get hurt and you could benefit: precisely the zero-sum proposition that many chief executives in international industries and the Japan-baiters latched on to! This argument led to the excessive preoccupation with reciprocity and the insistence on the folly of MFN, which the United States currently exhibits just when unilateral opening of markets and deregulation are beginning to be seen as great engines for competitiveness and the insistence on reciprocity of openness makes little sense! On this issue, see Bhagwati (1995a).

4. These and other problems with VIEs I have noted in several writings. The best single current source, however, is Irwin (1994).

5. It can fairly be said that the editorial comments in important newspapers and magazines, such as the *Financial Times*, the *Wall Street Journal*, the *Economist*, the *New Republic*, among numerous others, were unusually scathing, and that the action taken was sufficiently momentous in its import for the world trading system to make many economists wonder whether this was not an occasion when the leading economists in this administration should have resigned in protest. A letter to the president, asking him to withdraw the tariff threat and to use the WTO dispute settlement process instead, was also signed by nearly 100 prominent U.S. economists.

6. See, in this context, my critical review of Laura Tyson's book, *Who's Bashing Whom? Trade Conflict in High-Technology Industries* Bhagwati (1993), (Washington, D.C.: Institute for International Economics, 1992), and Bhagwati (1994b).

7. He fell victim to the Whitewater investigation, having come uncomfortably close to perjury in his testimony before Congress and lost his viability in the administration in consequence. His piece in *Foreign Affairs* (Altman 1994), paired with mine (Bhagwati 1994b), is a defence of the Clinton administration's Japan policy that I can safely leave the reader to assess without assistance and confidently expect her to dismiss without reservation.

8. Interestingly, the Japan-baiters and Japan-worriers of yesteryear were the so-called revisionists: Chalmers Johnson (a scholar), Clyde Prestowitz, James Fallows, and Pat Choate (subsequently Ross Perot's in-house economist). They seem to have been replaced in prominence by John Judis (*New Republic*), Michael Lind (a journalist), Thomas Friedman, and Pat Buchanan.

9. It is noteworthy that tariff retaliations prompted by Section 301 have previously always been designed so as to make them legal under the GATT. This time, the USTR deliberately chose clearly GATT-illegal retaliation, not because it enjoys violating the rule of law (though it is disturbing that most trade economists and lawyers are convinced that Mr. Kantor has no respect for the rule of law, having frequently asserted that all that he cares about are "results," and having now demonstrated clearly that he means what he says), but because the strategy of getting the Japanese car firms to capitulate meant that the bound tariffs on their exports had to be raised illegally, as I explain in the text.

10. This is but one of the several aspects of the USTR's defiance of the spirit, even at times the letter, of the rules agreed to at the Uruguay Round that made the U.S. policy in the car dispute a cause of distress among those who are wedded to multilateralism and the rule of law.

11. In this context, it is interesting to contrast the USTR's annual report on unfair trade practices with that issued by MITI. The former, as I remarked earlier in the text, is a list of self-serving complaints by lobbies. The latter, by contrast, is written by a team led by Professor Matsushita, Japan's leading expert on GATT law and an internationally respected scholar now on the Appellate Board at

the WTO, who focuses on unfair trade as defined by a strict criterion—the WTO-inconsistency of other nations' trade policies. Besides, the MITI report includes at the end the EU and the USTR reports on Japan's unfair trade policies! You would think that the United States, a transparent and fair-minded nation, would be publishing a MITI-type report whereas Japan, which is nontransparent and unfair according to the ceaseless U.S. complaints, would be issuing the USTR type of report!

12. Since several European car manufacturers have already made the necessary investment in their own dealerships, this also added to the EU objections (discussed below) to the U.S. demands. In particular, they regarded it as unacceptable that the Detroit car manufacturers be given less expensive entry into Japan by forcing the Japanese car firms to open their own distribution networks to the U.S. firms. That would mean that the EU firms would have been treated disadvantageously vis-à-vis their U.S. rivals.

13. The work of economist Robert Lawrence, which suggests that Japanese vertical *keiretsu* are exclusionary, has been questioned by Gary Saxonhouse; besides, it does not compare the effects of U.S. vertical integration with those of a *keiretsu* structure.

14. This is the effective answer to the much-cited remark by a Toyota-U.S. spokesman that the Toyota transplants would like to buy more parts made in the United States but were buying them from Japanese suppliers to maintain employment in Japan. That may well be true now; but if so, this would cut into Toyota's profits quickly by hitting the firm's costs in a highly competitive and contestable global industry and in that case Toyota would soon abandon such an altruistic policy. The reality, as distinct from the spokesman's concern for his compatriots' employment, may well be that Toyota may be expecting the high yen to fall soon, which would explain the desire not to disrupt existing and efficient supply relationships for short-run advantage.

15. Quoted by Latham (1995), who offers a strong critique of this claim, arguing its essential historical inaccuracy. Even if one does not accept Latham's critique fully, it persuades one that, at minimum, the claim is misleadingly simplistic.

16. See the critique of the U.S. action by Douglas Irwin, the noted analyst and critic of VIEs, in Irwin (1995) and my earlier op-ed on the same point in the *Journal of Commerce*.

17. I had noted this problem in Bhagwati (1990).

18. Despite the public relations rhetoric that the United States wants imports into Japan to go up regardless of whose exports increase, there is no doubt whatsoever that the USTR wants its own lobbies to benefit from the highhanded 301 tactics and that the Japanese understand this.

References

Altman, Roger, C. 1994. "Why Pressure Tokyo?" *Foreign Affairs* 73 (May/June): 2–6.

Bhagwati, Jagdish. 1990. *The World Trading System at Risk*. Princeton: Princeton University Press.

———. 1993. "Rough Trade." *New Republic*, May 31: 35–40; chapter 8.

———. 1994a. "Free Trade: Old and New Challenges." *Economic Journal* 104 (March): 231–46.

———. 1994b. "Samurais No More." *Foreign Affairs* 73 (May/June): 7–12; chapter 18.

———. 1995a. "An Unhealthy Obsession with Reciprocity." *Financial Times*, August 24; chapter 9.

———. 1995b. "Japan, Again." *Journal of Commerce*, May 16.

Bhagwati, Jagdish, and Anne O. Krueger. 1995. *The Dangerous Drift to Preferential Trade Agreements*. Washington, D.C.: AEI Press.

Bhagwati, Jagdish, and Arvind Panagariya, eds. 1996. *The Economics of Preferential Trade Agreements*. Washington, D.C.: AEI Press.

Irwin, Douglas A. 1994. *Managed Trade: The Case against Import Targets*. Washington, D.C.: AEI Press.

———. 1995. Letter to the Editor. *Financial Times*, May 26.

Latham, Scott. 1995. "Animal Farm 1995." Photocopy, May 25.

VI

The Folly of "Fair Trade before Free Trade": Environment and Labor Standards

22   The Case for Free Trade

Economists are reconciled to the conflict of absolutes: that is why they invented the concept of tradeoffs. It should not surprise them, therefore, that the objective of environmental protection should at times run afoul of the goal of seeking maximum gains from trade. In fact, economists would be suspicious of any claims, such as those made by soothsaying politicians, that both causes would be only mutually beneficial. They are rightly disconcerted, however, by the passion and the ferocity, and hence often the lack of logic or facts, with which environmental groups have recently assailed both free trade and the General Agreement on Tariffs and Trade (GATT), the institution that oversees the world trading system.

The environmentalists' antipathy to trade is perhaps inevitable. Trade has been central to economic thinking since Adam Smith discovered the virtues of specialization and of the markets that naturally sustain it. Because markets do not normally exist for the pursuit of environmental protection, they must be specially created. Trade therefore suggests abstention from governmental intervention, whereas environmentalism suggests its necessity. Then again, trade is exploited and its virtues extolled by corporate and multinational interests, whereas environmental objectives

Originally published in *Scientific American* 269 (November 1993): 18–23. Copyright © 1993 by Scientific American, Inc. All rights reserved. Reprinted with permission.

are embraced typically by nonprofit organizations, which are generally wary of these interests. Trade is an ancient occupation, and its nurture is the objective of institutions crafted over many years of experience and reflection. Protection of the environment, on the other hand, is a recent preoccupation of national and international institutions that are nascent and still evolving.

Last year the environmentalists' hostility to trade exploded in outrage when an impartial GATT Dispute Settlement Panel ruled in favor of Mexico and free trade and against the United States and the welfare of the dolphin. The United States had placed an embargo on the import of Mexican tuna on the grounds that the fish had been caught in purse-seine nets, which kill dolphins cruelly and in greater numbers than U.S. law permits. The GATT panel ruled, in effect, that the United States could not suspend Mexico's trading rights by proscribing unilaterally the methods by which that country harvested tuna.

This decision spurred the conservationists' subsequent campaigns against free trade and the GATT. The GATT has no shortage of detractors, of course. In fact, some of its recent critics have feared its impotence and declared it "dead," referring to it as the General Agreement to Talk and Talk. But the environmentalist attacks, which presume instead GATT's omnipotence, are something else again.

An advertisement by a coalition of environmental groups in the *New York Times* on April 20, 1992, set a new standard for alarmist, even scurrilous, writing, calculated to appeal to one's instincts rather than one's intellect. It talks of "faceless GATT bureaucrats" mounting a "sneak attack on democracy." This veiled reference to Pearl Harbor provides an example of a common tactic in trade controversy: Japan-bashing. The innuendos have continued unabated and are manifest in the endless battles in Congress over the supplemental environmental accords for the North American Free Trade Agreement (NAFTA). The hostility is also intruding on the conclusion of the Uruguay Round of GATT talks, now in their seventh year, with the environmentalists opposing the establishment of the new Multilateral Trade Organization, which is meant to provide effective discipline and a necessary institutional structure for the GATT.

It is surely tragic that the proponents of two of the great causes of the 1990s, trade and the environment, should be locked in combat. The conflict is largely gratuitous. There are at times philosophical differences between the two that cannot be reconciled, as when some environmentalists assert nature's autonomy, whereas most economists see nature as a handmaiden to humankind. For the most part, however, the differences derive from misconceptions. It is necessary to dissect and dismiss the more egregious of these fallacies before addressing the genuine problems.

The fear is widespread among environmentalists that free trade increases economic growth and that growth harms the environment. That fear is misplaced. Growth enables governments to tax and to raise resources for a variety of objectives, including the abatement of pollution and the general protection of the environment. Without such revenues, little can be achieved, no matter how pure one's motives may be.

How do societies actually spend these additional revenues? It depends on how getting rich affects the desire for a better environment. Rich countries today have more groups worrying about environmental causes than do poor countries. Efficient policies, such as freer trade, should generally help environmentalism, not harm it.

If one wants to predict what growth will do to the environment, however, one must also consider how it will affect the production of pollution. Growth affects not only the demand for a good environment but also the supply of pollution associated with growth. The net effect on the environment will therefore depend on the kind of economic growth. Gene M. Grossman and Alan Krueger of Princeton University found that in cities around the world sulfur dioxide pollution fell as per capita income rose. The only exception was in countries whose per capita incomes fell below $5,000. In short, environmentalists are in error when they fear that trade, through growth, will necessarily increase pollution.

Economic effects besides those attributable to rising incomes also help to protect the environment. For example, freer trade enables pollution-fighting technologies available elsewhere to be imported. Thus, trade in low-sulfur-content coal will enable the users of less high-sulfur-content coal to shift from the latter to the former.

Free trade can also lead to better environmental outcomes from a shift in the composition of production. An excellent example is provided by Robert C. Feenstra of the University of California at Davis. He has shown how the imposition of restraints on Japanese automobile exports to the United States during the 1980s shifted the composition of those exports from small to large cars, as the Japanese attempted to increase their revenues without decreasing the number of units they sold. Yet the large cars were fuel inefficient. Thus, protective efforts by the United States effectively increased the average amount of pollution produced by imported cars, making it more likely that pollution from cars would increase rather than diminish in the United States.

Although these erroneous objections to free trade are readily dismissed (but not so easily eliminated from public discourse), there are genuine conflicts between trade and the environment. To understand and solve them, economists draw a distinction between two kinds of environmental problems: those that are intrinsically domestic and those that are intrinsically transnational.

Should Brazil pollute a lake lying wholly within its borders, the problem would be intrinsically domestic. Should it pollute a river that flows into Argentina, the matter would take on an intrinsically transnational character. Perhaps the most important examples of transnational pollution are acid rain, created when sulfur dioxide emissions in one country precipitate into rain in another, and greenhouse gases, such as carbon dioxide, which contribute to global warming wherever they are emitted.

Why do intrinsically domestic environmental questions create international concern? The main reason is the belief that diversity in environmental standards many affect competitiveness. Businesses and labor unions worry that their rivals in other countries may gain an edge if their governments impose lower standards of environmental protection. They decry such differences as unfair. To level the playing field, these lobbies insist that foreign countries raise their standards up to domestic ones. In turn, environmental groups worry that if such "harmonization up" is not undertaken before freeing trade, pressures from uncompetitive businesses at home will force down domestic standards, reversing their hard-won victories. Finally, there is the fear, dramatized by H. Ross Perot in his criticisms of NAFTA, that factories will relocate to the countries whose environmental standards are lowest.

But if the competitiveness issue makes the environmentalists, the businesses, and the unions into allies, the environmentalists are on their own in other ways. Two problem areas can be distinguished. First, some environmentalists are keen to impose their own ethical preferences on others, using trade sanctions to induce or coerce acceptance of such preference. For instance, tuna fishing with purse-seine nets that kill dolphins is opposed by U.S. environmental groups, which consequently favor restraints on the importation of such tuna from Mexico and elsewhere. Second, other environmentalists fear that the rules of free trade, as embodied in the GATT and strengthened in the Uruguay Round,

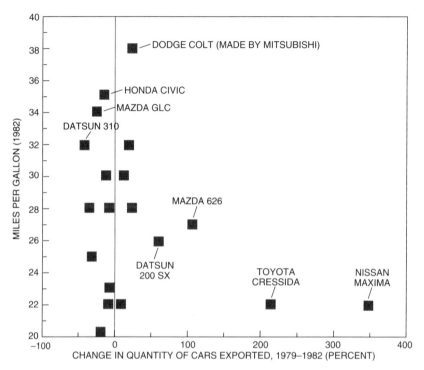

Figure 22.1
Perverse consequences for the environment may result from trade restrictions. This graph shows Japanese car exports to the United States before and after Japan's acquiescence in voluntary export restraints. Sales of small, fuel-efficient models declined, whereas those of the larger "gas guzzlers" soared.
Source: Robert C. Feenstra, University of California, Davis.

will constrain their freedom to pursue even purely domestic environmental objectives, with GATT tribunals outlawing disputed regulation.

Environmentalists have cause for concern. Not all concerns are legitimate, however, and not all the solutions to legitimate concerns are sensible. Worry over competitiveness has thus led to the illegitimate demand that environmental standards abroad be treated as "social dumping." Offending countries are regarded as unfairly subsidizing their exporters through lax environmental requirements. Such implicit subsidies, the reasoning continues, ought to be offset by import duties.

Yet international differences in environmental standards are perfectly natural. Even if two countries share the same environmental objectives, the *specific* pollutions they would attack, and hence the industries they would hinder, will generally not be identical. Mexico has a greater social incentive than does the United States to spend an extra dollar preventing dysentery rather than reducing lead in gasoline.

Equally, a certain environmental good might be valued more highly by a poor country than by a rich one. Contrast, for instance, the value assigned to a lake with the cost of cleaning up effluents discharged into it by a pharmaceutical company. In India such a lake's water might be drunk by a malnourished population whose mortality would increase sharply with the rise in pollution. In the United States the water might be consumed by few people, all of whom have the means to protect themselves with privately purchased water filters. In this example, India would be the more likely to prefer clean water to the pharmaceutical company's profits.

The consequences of differing standards are clear: each country will have less of the industry whose pollution it fears relatively more than other countries do. Indeed, even if there were no international trade, we would be shrinking industries whose pollution we deter. This result follows from the policy of forcing polluters of all stripes to pay for the harm they cause. To object, then, to the effects our negative valuation of pollution have on a given industry is to be in contradiction: we would be refusing to face the consequences of our environmental preferences.

Nevertheless, there is sentiment for enacting legislation against social dumping. Senator David L. Boren of Oklahoma, the proponent of the International Pollution Deterrence Act of 1991,

demanded import duties on the grounds that "some U.S. manufacturers, such as the U.S. carbon and steel alloy industry, spend
as much as 250 percent more on environmental controls as a percentage of gross domestic product than do other countries.... I
see the unfair advantage enjoyed by other nations exploiting the
environment and public health for economic gain when I look at
many industries important to my own state." Similarly, Vice
President Al Gore wrote in *Earth in the Balance: Ecology and the
Human Spirit* that "just as government subsidies of a particular
industry are sometimes considered unfair under the trade laws,
weak and ineffectual enforcement of pollution control measures should also be included in the definition of unfair trading
practices."

These demands betray lack of economic logic, and they ignore
political reality as well. Remember that the so-called subsidy to
foreign producers through lower standards is not given but only
implied. According to Senator Boren, the subsidy would be calculated as "the cost that would have to be incurred by the manufacturer or producer of the foreign articles of merchandise to
comply with environmental standards imposed on U.S. producers
of the same class of merchandise." Anyone familiar with the way
dumping calculations are made knows that the Environmental
Protection Agency could come up with virtually any estimates it
cared to produce. Cynical politics would inevitably dictate the
calculations.

Still, there may be political good sense in assuaging environmentalists' concerns about the relocation of factories to countries
with lower standards. The governments of higher-standards
countries could do so without encumbering free trade by insisting
that their businesses accede to the higher standards when they
go abroad. Such a policy lies entirely within the jurisdictional
powers of a higher-standards country. Moreover, the govern-

ments of lower-standards countries would be most unlikely to object to such an act of good citizenship by the foreign investors.

Environmentalists oppose free trade for yet another reason: they wish to use trade policy to impose their values on other communities and countries. Many environmentalists want to suspend the trading rights of countries that sanction the use of purse-seine nets in tuna fishing and of leg-hold traps in trapping. Such punishments seem an inappropriate use of state power, however. The values in question are not widely accepted, such as human rights, but idiosyncratic. One wonders when the opponents of purse-seine nets put the interests of the dolphin ahead of those of Mexico's people, who could prosper through more productive fishing. To borrow the campaign manifesto of President Bill Clinton: Should we not put people first?

Moreover, once such values intrude on free trade, the way is opened for an endless succession of demands. Environmentalists favor dolphins; Indians have their sacred cows. Animal-rights activists, who do not prefer one species over another, will object to our slaughterhouses.

The moral militancy of environmentalists in the industrialized world has begun to disillusion their closest counterparts in the undeveloped countries. These local environmentalists accuse the rich countries of "eco-imperialism," and they deny that the Western nations have a monopoly on virtue. The most radical of today's proenvironment magazines in India, *Down to Earth*, editorialized recently:

In the current world reality trade is used as an instrument entirely by Northern countries to discipline environmentally errant nations. Surely, if India or Kenya were to threaten to stop trade with the U.S., it would hardly affect the latter. But the fact of the matter is that it is the Northern countries that have the greatest [adverse] impact on the world's environment.

If many countries were to play this game, then repeated sus-
pensions of trading rights would begin to undermine the openness of the trading system and the predictability and stability of
international markets. Some environmentalists assert that each
country should be free to insist on the production methods of its
trading partners. Yet these environmentalists ignore the certain
consequence of their policy: a Pandora's box of protectionism
would open up. Rarely are production methods in an industry
identical in different countries.

There are certainly better ways to indulge the environmentalists' propensity to export their ethical preferences. The U.S.
environmental organizations can lobby in Mexico to persuade its
government to adopt their views. Private boycotts can also be
undertaken. In fact, boycotts can carry much clout in rich countries with big markets, on which the targeted poor countries often
depend. The frequent and enormously expensive advertisements
by environmental groups against the GATT show also that their
resources far exceed those of the cash-strapped countries whose
policies they oppose.

Cost-benefit analysis leads one to conclude that unilateral
governmental suspension of other's trading rights is not an
appropriate way to promote one's lesser ethical preferences.
Such sanctions can, on the other hand, appropriately be invoked
multilaterally to defend universal moral values. In such cases—as
in the censure of apartheid, as practiced until recently in South
Africa—it is possible to secure widespread agreement for sanctions. With a large majority converted to the cause, GATT's
waiver procedure can be used to suspend the offending country's
trading rights.

Environmentalists are also worried about the obstacles that
the current and prospective GATT rules pose for environmental
regulations aimed entirely at domestic production and consumption. In principle, the GATT lets a country enforce any regulation

that does not discriminate against or among foreign suppliers. One can, for example, require airbags in cars, provided that the rule applies to all automobile makers. The GATT even permits rules that discriminate against trade for the purpose of safety and health.

The GATT, however, recognizes three ways in which regulations may be set in gratuitous restraint of trade; in following procedures aimed at avoiding such outcomes, the GATT upsets the environmentalists. First, the true intention—and effect—of a regulation may be to protect not the environment but local business. Second, a country may impose more restrictions than necessary to achieve its stated environmental objective. Third, it may set standards that have no scientific basis.

The issue of intentions is illustrated by the recently settled "beer war" between Ontario and the United States. In 1988 the Canadian province imposed a 10-cents-a-can tax on beer, ostensibly to discourage littering. The United States argued that the law in fact intended to discriminate against its beer suppliers who used aluminum cans, whereas local beer companies used bottles. Ontario had neglected to tax the use of cans for juices and soups, a step that would have affected Ontario producers.

The second problem is generally tougher because it is impossible to find alternative restrictions that accomplish exactly the same environmental results as the original policy at lower cost. An adjudicating panel is then forced to evaluate, implicitly or explicitly, the tradeoffs between the cost in trade disruption and the cost in lesser fulfillment of the environmental objective. It is therefore likely that environmentalists and trade experts will differ on which weights the panel should assign to these divergent interests.

Environmentalists tend to be fearful about the use of scientific tests to determine whether trade in a product can be proscribed. The need to prove one's case is always an unwelcome burden to

those who have the political power to take unilateral action. Yet
the trade experts have the better of the argument. Imagine that
U.S. growers sprayed apples with the pesticide Alar, whereas
European growers did not, and that European consumers began
to agitate against Alar as harmful. Should the European Community be allowed to end the importation of the U.S. apples without
meeting *some* scientific test of its health concerns? Admittedly,
even hard science is often not hard enough—different studies
may reach different conclusions. But without the restraining hand
of science, the itch to indulge one's fears—and to play on the fears
of others—would be irresistible.

In all cases, the moderate environmentalists would like to see
the GATT adopt more transparent procedures for adjudicating
disputes. They also desire greater legal standing to file briefs
when environmental regulations are at issue. These goals seem
both reasonable and feasible.

Not all environmental problems are local; some are truly global,
such as the greenhouse effect and the depletion of stratospheric
ozone. They raise more issues that require cooperative, multilateral solutions. Such solutions must be both efficient and equitable. Still, it is easy to see that rich countries might use their
economic power to reach protocols that maximize efficiency at the
expense of poorer countries.

For instance, imagine that the drafters of a protocol were to ask
Brazil to refrain from cutting down its rain forests while allowing
industrialized countries to continue emitting carbon dioxide.
They might justify this request on the grounds that it costs Brazil
less to keep a tree alive, absorbing a unit of carbon dioxide every
year, than it would cost the United States or Germany to save
a unit by burning less oil. Such a tradeoff would indeed be economically efficient. Yet if Brazil, a poorer country, were then left
with the bill, the solution would assuredly be inequitable.

Before any group of countries imposes trade sanctions on a country that has not joined a multilateral protocol, it would be important to judge whether the protocol is indeed fair. Nonmembers targeted for trade sanctions should have the right to get an impartial hearing of their objection, requiring the strong defend their actions even when they appear to be entirely virtuous.

The simultaneous pursuit of the causes of free trade and a protected environment often raises problems to be sure. But none of these conflicts is beyond resolution with goodwill and by imaginative institutional innovation. The aversion to free trade and the GATT that many environmentalists display is unfounded, and it is time for them to shed it. Their admirable moral passion and certain intellectual vigor are better devoted to building bridges between the causes of trade and the environment.

23 American Rules, Mexican Jobs

Supplemental agreements are being negotiated with Mexico to raise and enforce environmental and labor standards as conditions for congressional approval of the North American Free Trade Agreement. But the proposals are, at best, debatable. Better suggestions can be made.

Because these proposals are largely driven by fear that we will lose jobs to the cheap Mexican labor, they seek to impose excessive environmental standards and have effectively become instruments for indirectly raising Mexican costs. The demands for tougher Mexican standards could be legitimately read as a ploy to undermine Mexico's ability to join the trade agreement and thus to kill the accord itself.

Demands that commit Mexico's scarce resources to improve environmental and labor standards are, however, not the end of the matter. Many congressmen and lobbies would go further. They would have Mexico also make similar commitments by each industry, matching them up to levels of regulation in corresponding industries in the United States. This would presumably yield level playing fields for our industries in the trade agreement; otherwise, it is reasoned, Mexico would reap unfair advantage in free trade with us.

But surely the manner in which Mexico divides its overall effort to meet environmental objectives among different industries and regions must reflect its own priorities just as ours reflect our own interests. Demands on Mexico to do exactly what we do are therefore not sensible. Since we would properly not submit to them if made by others, they are also unreasonable.

But we can address the chief concern of U.S. labor unions that our investments will flow to Mexico in industries where standards are lower than our own. For U.S. companies in Mexico, whether fully owned subsidiaries or joint ventures, we can legislate, not just exhort, that they act entirely up to our standards. Since our standards are often not uniform across different states, perhaps we might even overlegislate and make the toughest standards mandatory on our companies in Mexico. A rationale for this Draconian policy would be that industries in the states with the toughest measures are most likely to be influenced into moving to Mexico.

Such a policy, reminiscent of the Sullivan principles urging U.S. companies in South Africa to comply with American laws against racial discrimination, would respond to the fears of the unions about the loss of jobs to Mexico. It would thus strengthen the ability of the Clinton administration to reject the outlandish demands that Mexico, despite its poverty, do much more for the environment and labor than it can currently afford and that it replicate our regulations and standards on each industry.

This policy is in our jurisdictional powers. Our industries should be subject to our legislation, especially as no conflict with Mexican laws is at stake.

Proponents of tough environmental and labor standards, who desire them as good values that should apply to Mexican citizens, should also realize that the presence in Mexico of our companies adhering to the higher standards would encourage Mexican non-governmental organizations to agitate for an extension of such standards to all Mexican companies eventually.

24

Trade Liberalisation and "Fair Trade" Demands: Addressing the Environmental and Labour Standards Issues

I have long enjoyed an intellectual affinity with Sir Leon Brittan. He is the rare politician who reads what academic economists write—I have had the pleasure of many friends telling me about occasions when he quoted approvingly from my own writings—has a commitment to freer trade and is astute enough to translate that commitment into concrete action.

In what I say below, therefore, I find myself in the unusual situation of disagreeing with what I see as the main policy thrust of his remarks though of course Professor André Sapir will welcome the fact that the debate is joined explicitly and forcefully in the opening session itself.

In the following I propose to argue why many of the demands, emanating principally from the rich countries, for imposing "higher" environmental and labour standards on the poor countries as preconditions for trade liberalisation, ought to be rejected. Since practical policymaking cannot ignore political realities while statesmanship simultaneously requires that these realities must be confronted creatively and in a principled way, I suggest alternative ways in which these demands, which are politically salient as Sir Leon Brittan correctly observes, can be channeled

Originally published in the *World Economy* 18 (November 1995): 745–59. Reprinted with permission.

into policy proposals that are better crafted and more consonant with the principles of free trade.

Why Have Demands for Fair Trade Arisen?

The demands for imposing environmental and labour standards on the poor countries reflect several factors. Let me mention just a few of the more compelling ones that bear on the environmental and labour standards questions,[1] while addressing their merits later.

First, the fierce competition as the world economy gets increasingly globalised has led to increased sensitivity to any domestic policy or institution abroad that seems to give one's foreign rivals an extra edge. If then a country's producers have lower environmental and labour regulatory burdens, that is objected to as "unfair."

Second, protectionists see great value in invoking "unfairness" of trade as an argument for getting protection: it is likely to be more successful than simply claiming that you cannot hack it and therefore need protection. This has made the diversity of burdens for an industry among different countries appear illegitimate, making demands to reduce it look like a reasonable alternative to overt protectionism.

Third, some in the environmental and labour movements worry about the effect that competition with lower standards countries will have on their own standards. If trade shifts activity to where the costs are lower because of lower standards, and if additionally capital and jobs move away to exploit lower standards abroad, then the countries with higher standards may be forced to lower their own.

Fourth, aside from these "economic" and political concerns focused on their own society, the environmental and, especially, labour lobbies have moral concerns. They feel a sense of transborder moral obligation to human beings abroad: they would like child labour to cease abroad because they worry about children abroad; they do not want Mexicans to suffer from lower environmental standards; and so on.

These arguments cover a broad spectrum and are typically jumbled together in the popular and in political discourse. But they must be kept sharply distinct in our reflections and analysis if we are to arrive at proper policy judgments, as I hope to do now. Let me begin with environmental questions and then turn to labour issues, keeping in mind the proposals that are currently in the political arena.

The Question of Environmental Standards

Let me first distinguish between "domestic" environmental problems, as when a country pollutes a lake which is entirely within its own frontiers, and "global" environmental problems, when there are transborder externalities, as with the acid rain, global warming, and ozone-layer problems.

I shall consider the domestic problems initially, observing at the outset that normally an economist would not expect to object to different environmental standards in the same industry in different countries (that is, to what I shall call crosscountry intra-industry, CCII, differences in standards, typically in the shape of pollution tax rates).

Indefensible Demands for Ecodumping

The diversity of CCII standards will follow from differences in tradeoffs between aggregate pollution and income at different levels of income, as when richer Americans prefer to save dolphins from purse-seine nets whereas poorer Mexicans prefer to put people first and want to raise the productivity of fishing and hence accelerate the amelioration of Mexican poverty by using such nets. Again, countries will have natural differences in the priorities attached to which kind of pollution to attack, arising from differences of historical and other circumstance: Mexicans will want to worry more about clean water, as dysentery is a greater problem, than Americans who will want to attach greater priority to spending pollution dollars on clean air. Differences in technological know-how and in endowments can also lead to CCII diversity in pollution tax rates.

The notion therefore that the diversity of CCII pollution standards/taxes is illegitimate and constitutes "unfair trade" or "unfair competition," to be eliminated or countervailed by eco-dumping duties, is itself illegitimate. It is incorrect, indeed illogical, to assert that competing with foreign firms that do not bear equal pollution-tax burdens is unfair.[2] I would add two more observations.

First, we should recognise that if we lose competitive advantage because we put a larger negative value on a certain kind of pollution whereas others do not is simply the flip side of the differential valuations. To object to that implication of the differential valuation is to object to the differential valuation itself, and hence to our own larger negative valuation. To see this clearly, think of a closed economy without trade. If we were to tax pollution by an industry in such an economy, its implication would be precisely that this industry would shrink: it would lose competitive advantage vis-à-vis other industries in our own country. To object to that shrinking is to object to the negative valuation being put on the pollution. There is therefore nothing "unfair" from this perspective, if our industry shrinks because we impose higher standards (that is, pollution taxes) on our industry while others, who value that pollution less, choose lower standards (that is, pollution taxes).

Second, it is worth nothing that the attribution of competitive disadvantage to differential pollution tax burdens in the fashion of CCII comparisons for individual industries confuses absolute with comparative advantage. Thus, for instance, in a two-industry world, if both industries abroad have lower pollution tax rates than at home, both will not contract at home. Rather, the industry with the *comparatively* higher tax rate will. The noise that each industry makes on basis of CCII comparisons, aggregated to total noise by all industries, is then likely to exaggerate seriously the effect of different environmental valuations and CCII differences on the competitiveness of industries in nations with higher standards.

But one more worry needs to be laid at rest if the demands for upward harmonisation of standards or ecodumping duties in lieu thereof are to be effectively dismissed. This is the worry that I noted at the outset: that free trade with countries with lower standards will force down one's higher standards. The most potent of these worries arises from the fear that "capital and jobs" will move to countries with lower standards, triggering a *race to the bottom* (or more accurately a race towards the bottom), where countries lower their standards in an interjurisdictional contest, below what some or all would like, to attract capital and jobs.[3] So, the solution would lie then in coordinating the standards-setting among the nations engaged in freer trade and investment. In turn, this *may* (but is most unlikely to) require harmonisation among countries to the higher standards (though, even then, not necessarily at those in place) or perhaps there might be improvement in welfare from simply setting minimum floors to the standards.

This is undoubtedly a theoretically valid argument. The key question for policy, however, is whether the empirical evidence shows, as required by the argument, that: (1) capital is in fact responsive to the differences in environmental standards and (2) different countries/jurisdictions actually play the game then of competitively lowering standards to attract capital. Without both these phenomena holding in a significant fashion in reality, the "race to the bottom" would be a theoretical curiosity.

As it happens, systematic evidence is available for the former proposition alone, but the finding is that the proposition is not supported by the studies to date: there is very weak evidence, at best, in favour of interjurisdictional mobility in response to CCII differences in environmental standards.[4] There are in fact many ways to explain this lack of responsiveness: (1) the differences in standards may not be significant and are outweighed by other factors that affect locational decisions; (2) exploiting differences in standards may not be a good strategy relative to not exploiting them; and (3) lower standards may paradoxically even repel, instead of attracting, direct foreign investment.[5]

While we do not have similar evidence on the latter proposition, it is hardly likely that, as a systematic tendency, countries would be actually lowering environmental standards to attract capital. As it happens, countries, and even state governments in federal countries (for example, President Bill Clinton, when governor of Arkansas), typically play the game of attracting capital to their jurisdictions: but this game is almost universally played, not by inviting firms to pollute freely but instead through tax breaks and holidays, land grants at throwaway prices, and so forth, resulting most likely in a "race to the bottom" on business tax rates which wind up below their optimal levels! It is therefore not surprising that there is little systematic evidence of governments' lowering environmental standards to attract scarce capital. Contrary to the fears of the environmental groups, the race to the bottom on environmental standards therefore seems to be an unlikely phenomenon in the real world.

I would conclude that both the "unfair trade" and the "race to the bottom" arguments for harmonising CCII standards or else legalising ecodumping duties at the WTO are therefore lacking in rationale: the former is theoretically illogical, and the latter is empirically unsupported. In addition, such WTO-legalisation of ecodumping will facilitate protectionism without doubt. Anti-dumping processes have become the favoured tool of protectionists today. Is there any doubt that their extension to ecodumping (and equally to socialdumping), where the "implied subsidy" through lower standards must be inevitably "constructed" by national agencies such as the Environmental Protection Agency in the same jurisdiction as the complainant industry, will lead to the same results, even more surely?

The "fixing" of the WTO for environmental issues therefore should not proceed along the lines of legitimating ecodumping.[6] The political salience of such demands remains a major problem, however. One may well then ask, Are there any "second-best" approaches, short of the ecodumping and CCII harmonisation proposals, that may address some of the political concerns at least economic cost?

A Proposal to Extend Domestic Standards in High Standards Countries to Their Firms in Low Standards Countries Unilaterally or Preferably through an OECD Code

The political salience of the harmful demands for ecodumping duties and CCII harmonisation is greatest when plants are closed by one's own multinationals and shifted to other countries. The actual shifting of location, and the associated loss of jobs in that plant, magnify greatly the fear of the "race to the bottom" and of the "impossibility" of competing against low standards countries. Similarly, when investment by one's own firms is seen to go to specific countries which happen to have lower standards, the resentment gets to be focused readily against those countries and their standards. When jobs are lost simply because of *trade* competition, however, it is much harder to locate one's resentment and fear on one specific foreign country and its policies as a source of unfair competition.[7] Hence, a second-best proposal could well be to address this particular fear, however unfounded and often illogical, of outmigration of plants and investment by one's firms abroad to low standards countries.

The proposal is to adapt the so-called Sullivan principles approach to the problem at hand. Under Sullivan, U.S. firms in South Africa were urged to adopt U.S. practices, not the South African apartheid ways, in their operations. If this principle that the U.S. firms in Mexico be subject to U.S. environmental policies (choosing the desired ones from the many that obtain across different states in this federal country) were adopted by U.S. legislation, that would automatically remove whatever incentive there was to move because of environmental burden differences.[8]

This proposal that one's firms abroad behave as if they were at home—do in Rome as you do in New York, not as the Romans do—can be either legislated unilaterally by any high standards country or by a multilateral binding treaty among different high standards countries. Again, it may be reduced to an exhortation, just as Sullivan principles were, by single countries in isolation or by several as through a nonbinding but ethos-defining and policy-encouraging OECD code.

The disadvantage of this proposal, of course, is that it does violate the diversity-is-legitimate rule (whose desirability was discussed by me). Investment flows, like investment of one's own funds and production and trade therefrom, should reflect this diversity. It reduces, therefore, the efficiency of gains from a freer flow of cross-country investments today. But if environmental tax burden differences are not all so different, or do not figure prominently in firms' locational decisions, as the empirical literature (just cited) seems to stress, the efficiency costs of this proposal could also be minimal while gains in allaying fears and therefore moderating the demand for bad proposals could be very large indeed.

Yet another objection may focus on intra-OECD differences in high standards. Since there are differences among the OECD countries in CCII environmental tax burdens in specific industries for specific pollution, this proposal would lead to "horizontal inequity" among the OECD firms in third countries. If the British burden is higher than the French, British firms would face a bigger burden in Mexico than French firms. But such differences already exist among firms abroad, since tax practices among the OECD countries on taxation of firms abroad are not harmonised in many respects. Interestingly, the problem of horizontal equity has come up in relation to the demands of the poor countries (that often find it difficult to enforce import restrictions effectively) that the domestic restrictions on hazardous products be automatically extended to exports by every country. That would put firms in the countries with greater restrictions at an economic disadvantage. But agreement has now been reached to disregard the problem.

Other problems may arise: (i) monitoring of one's firms in a foreign country may be difficult; and (ii) the countries with lower standards may object on grounds of "national sovereignty." Neither argument seems compelling. It is unlikely that a developing country would object to foreign firms' doing better by its citizens in regard to environmental standards (that it itself cannot afford to impose, given its own priorities, on its own firms). Equally, it would then assist in monitoring the foreign firms.

Transborder Externalities: Global Pollution and WTO

The preceding analysis considered the trade issues which arise between countries even when the environmental problems are purely domestic in their scope. They can arise, of course, even

when these problems involve transborder spillovers or externalities. The latter, however, are generally more complex. Let me
consider only the problems that arise when the problem is not
just *bilateral* (as with, say acid rain, where the United States and
Canada were involved) or regional, but truly *global*.

The chief policy questions concerning trade policy when global
pollution problems are involved instead, as with ozone layer
depletion and global warming, relate to the cooperation-solution–
oriented multilateral treaties that are sought to address them.
They are essentially tied into noncompliance ("defection") by
members and "free riding" by nonmembers. Because any action
by a member of a treaty relates to targeted actions (such as
reducing CFCs or CO_2 emissions) that are a public good (in particular, that the benefits are nonexcludable, so that if I incur the
cost and do something, I cannot exclude you from benefiting from
it), the use of trade sanctions to secure and enforce compliance
automatically turns up on the agenda.

At the same time, the problem is compounded because the
agreement itself has to be *legitimate* in the eyes of those accused of
free riding. Before those pejorative epithets are applied and punishment prescribed in the form of trade sanctions legitimated at
the WTO, these nations have to be satisfied that the agreement
being pressed on them is efficient and, especially, that it is equitable in burden-sharing. Otherwise, nothing prevents the politically powerful (that is, the rich nations) from devising a treaty
that puts an inequitable burden on the politically weak (that is,
the poor nations) and then using the cloak of a "multilateral"
agreement and a new WTO-legitimacy to impose that burden
with the aid of trade sanctions with a clear conscience.

This is the reason the policy demand, often made, to alter the
WTO to legitimate trade sanctions on members who remain outside a treaty, whenever a plurilateral treaty on global environmental problem dictates it, is unlikely to be accepted by the poor

nations without safeguards to prevent unjust impositions. The spokesmen of the poor countries have been more or less explicit on this issue, with justification. These concerns have been recognised by the rich nations.

Thus, at the Rio Conference in 1992, the *Framework Convention on Climate Change* set explicit goals under which several rich nations agreed to emission-level-reduction targets (returning, more or less, to 1990 levels), whereas the commitments of the poor countries were contingent on the rich nations' footing the bill.

Ultimately, burden sharing by different formulas related to past emissions, current income, and current population are inherently arbitrary; they also distribute burdens without regard to efficiency. Economists will argue for burden sharing dictated by cost-minimisation across countries, for the earth as a whole: if Brazilian rain forests must be saved to minimise the cost of a targeted reduction in CO_2 emissions in the world, while the United States keeps guzzling gas because it is too expensive to cut that down, then so be it. But then this efficient "cooperative" solution must not leave Brazil footing the bill. Efficient solutions, with compensation and equitable distribution of the gains from the efficient solution, make economic sense.

A step toward them is the idea of having a market in permits at the world level: no country may emit CO_2 without having bought the necessary permit from a worldwide quota. That would ensure efficiency,[9] whereas the distribution of the proceeds from the sold permits would require a decision reflecting some multilaterally agreed ethical or equity criteria (for example, the proceeds may be used for refugee resettlement, UN peacekeeping operations, aid dispensed to poor nations by UNDP, or the WHO fight against AIDS). This type of agreement would have the legitimacy that could then provide the legitimacy in turn for a WTO rule that permits the use of trade sanctions against free riders.

The Question of Labour Standards and the Social Clause

The question of labour standards, and making them into pre-requisites for market access by introducing a social clause in the WTO, has parallels and contrasts to the environmental questions which I have just discussed.

The contrast is that labour standards have nothing equivalent to *transborder* environmental externalities. One's labour standards are purely *domestic* in scope: in that regard, the demands for "social dumping" for lower labour standards that parallel the demands for ecodumping have the same rationale and hence must be rejected for the same reasons.

But a different aspect to the whole question results from the fact that labour standards, unlike most environmental standards, are seen in moral terms. Thus, for example, central to American thinking on the question of the social clause is the notion that competitive advantage can sometimes be morally "illegitimate." In particular, it is argued that if labour standards elsewhere are different and unacceptable morally, then the resulting competition is morally illegitimate and "unfair."

Now, when this argument is made about a practice such as slavery (defined strictly as the practice of owning and transacting in human beings, as for centuries before the Abolitionists triumphed), there will be nearly universal agreement that if slavery produces competitive advantage, that advantage is illegitimate and ought to be rejected.

Thus, we have here a "values"-related argument for suspending another country's trading rights or access to our markets, in a sense similar to (but far more compelling than) the case when the United States sought to suspend Mexico's tuna-trading rights because of its use of purse-seine nets.[10] The insertion of a social clause for labour standards into the WTO can then be seen as a way of legitimating an exception to the wholly sensible GATT rule that prohibits the suspension of a contracting party's trading rights concerning a product simply on the ground that, for reasons of morality asserted by another contracting party, the process by which that product is produced is considered immoral and therefore illegitimate.

The real problem with the argument, however, is that universally condemned practices such as slavery are rare indeed. True, the ILO has many conventions that many nations have signed. But many have been signed simply because in effect they are not binding. Equally, the United States itself has signed no more than a tiny fraction of these conventions in any case. The question whether a substantive consensus on anything except well-meaning and broad principles without consequences for trade access in case of noncompliance can be obtained is therefore highly dubious.

Indeed, the reality is that diversity of labour practice and standards is widespread in practice and reflects, not necessarily venality and wickedness, but rather diversity of cultural values, economic conditions, and analytical beliefs and theories concerning the economic (and therefore moral) consequences of specific labour standards. The notion that labour standards can be universalised, like human rights such as liberty and habeas corpus, simply by calling them "labour rights" ignores the fact that this easy equation between culture-specific labour standards and universal human rights will have a difficult time surviving deeper scrutiny.

Take the United States itself (since it is a principal proponent of the social clause) and one sees that the proposition that its labour standards are "advanced" and that it is only providing "moral leadership" vis-à-vis developing countries, is hard to sustain. Indeed, the U.S. logic on the question can lead the United States itself into a widespread and sustained suspension of its own trading rights if there was an impartial tribunal and legal standing to file complaints was given to concerned citizens and NGOs rather than to governments that would be intimidated by the power of the United States from taking it to court.

Thus, for instance, worker participation in decision making on the plant, a measure of true economic democracy much more pertinent than the unionisation of labour, is far more widespread in Europe than in North America: would we then condemn North America to denial of trading rights by the Europeans? Migrant labour is ill-treated to the level of brutality and slavery in U.S. agriculture owing to grossly inadequate and corrupt enforcement, if investigative shows on U.S. television are a guide: does this mean that other nations should prohibit the import of U.S. agricultural products? Sweatshops exploiting female immigrants in textiles with long hours and below-minimum wages are endemic in the textile industry, as documented amply by several civil liberties groups: should the right of the United States to export textiles then be suspended by other countries as much as the United States seeks to suspend the imports of textiles made by exploited child labour?

Even the right to organise trade unions may be considered to be inadequate in the United States if we go by "results," as the United States favours in judging Japan: only about 12 percent of the U.S. labour force in the private sector is unionised. Indeed, it is no secret, except to those who prefer to think that labour standards are inadequate only in developing countries, that unions are actively discouraged in several ways in the United States. Strikes are also circumscribed. Indeed, in essential industries they are restricted: but the definition of such industries also reflects economic structure and political realities, making each country's definition only culture-specific and hence open to objection by others. Should other countries have then suspended U.S. flights because President Reagan had broken the air traffic controllers' strike?

Lest you think that the question of child labour is an easy one, let me remind you that even this raises complex questions as indeed recognised by the ILO, though not in many of the arguments heard in the United States today. The use of child labour, as such, is surely not the issue. Few children grow up even in the United States without working as babysitters or delivering newspaper; many are even paid by parents for housework in the home. The pertinent social question, familiar to anyone with even a nodding acquaintance with Chadwick, Engels, and Dickens and the appalling conditions afflicting children at work in England's factories in the early Industrial Revolution, is rather whether children at work are protected from hazardous and oppressive working conditions.

Whether child labour should be altogether prohibited in a poor country is a matter on which views legitimately differ. Many feel that children's work is unavoidable in the face of poverty and that the alternative to it is starvation, which is a greater calamity, and that eliminating child labour would then be like voting to eliminate abortion without worrying about the needs of the children that are then born.

Then again, insisting on the "positive rights"–related right to unionise to demand higher wages, for instance, as against the "negative rights"–related right of freedom to associate for political activity, for example, can also be morally obtuse. In practice, such a right could imply higher wages for the "insiders" who have jobs, at the expense of the unemployed "outsiders." Besides, the unions in developing countries with large populations and much poverty are likely to be in the urban-industrial activities, with the industrial proletariat among the better-off sections of the population, whereas the real poverty is among the nonunionised landless labour. Raising the wages of the former will generally hurt, in the opinion of many developing-country economists, the prospects of rapid accumulation and growth which alone can pull more of the landless labour eventually into gainful employment. If so, the imposition of the culture-specific developed-country-union views on poor countries about the rights of unions to push for higher wages will resolve current equity and intergenerational equity problems in ways that are normally unacceptable to these countries, and correctly so.

The Social Clause: A Bad Idea

One is then led to conclude that the idea of the social clause in the WTO is rooted generally in an ill-considered rejection of the general legitimacy of diversity of labour standards and practices across countries. The alleged claim for the universality of labour standards is (except for a rare few cases such as slavery) generally unpersuasive.

The developing countries cannot then be blamed for worrying that the recent escalation of support for such a clause in the WTO in major OECD countries derives instead from the desire of labour unions to protect their jobs by protecting the industries that face competition from the poor countries. They fear that moral arguments are produced to justify restrictions on such trade since they are so effective in the public domain. In short, the "white man's burden" is being exploited to secure the "white man's gain." Or, to use another metaphor, "blue protectionism" is breaking out, masking behind a moral face.

Indeed, this fearful conclusion is reinforced by the fact that none of the major OECD countries pushing for such a social clause expects to be the defendant, instead of the plaintiff, in social-clause-generated trade-access cases. On the one hand, the standards (such as prohibition of child labour) to be included in the social clause to date are invariably presented as those that the developing countries are guilty of violating, even when some transgressions thereof are to be found in the developed countries themselves. Thus, according to a report in the *Financial Times*, a standard example used by the labour movement to garner support for better safety standards is a disastrous fire in a toy factory in Thailand, where many died because exits were shut and unuseable. Yet, when I read this report, I recalled an example just like this (but far more disconcerting when you noted that the fatalities occurred in the richest country in the world) about a chicken plant in North Carolina where also the exits were closed for the same reason. Yet, the focus was on the poor, not the rich, country.

At the same time, the choice of standards chosen for attention and sanctions at the WTO is also clearly biased against the poor countries in the sense that none of the problems where many of the developed countries would be found in significant violation— such as worker participation in management, union rights, rights of migrants and immigrants—are meant to be included in the social clause. Symmetry of obligations simply does not exist in the social clause, as contemplated currently, in terms of the coverage of the standards.

The stones are thus to be thrown at the poor countries' glass houses by rich countries that build fortresses around their own. In fact, the salience which the social clause crusade has acquired in the United States and Europe, and its specific contents, owe much to the widespread fear, evident during the NAFTA debate in the United States, that trade with the poor countries (with abundant unskilled labour) will produce unemployment and reductions in the real wages of the unskilled in the rich countries. The social clause is, in this perspective, a way in which the fearful unions seek to raise the costs of production in the poor countries as free trade with them is seen to threaten their jobs and wages.

If Not Social Clause, What Else?

If this analysis is correct, then the idea of a social clause in the WTO is not appealing; and the developing countries' opposition to its enactment is justified. We would not be justified then in condemning their objections and unwillingness to go along with our demands as depravity and "rejectionism."

But if a social clause does not make good sense, is everything lost for those in both developed and developing countries who genuinely wish to advance their own views of what are "good" labour standards? Evidently not.

It is surely open to them to use other instrumentalities such as nongovernmental organisation (NGO)-led educational activities to secure a consensus in favour of their positions. In fact, if your ideas are good, they should spread without coercion. The Spanish Inquisition should not be necessary to spread Christianity; indeed, the pope has no troops. Mahatma Gandhi's splendid idea of non-violent agitation spread and was picked up by Martin Luther King, not because he worked on the Indian government to threaten retribution against others otherwise; it happened to be just morally compelling.

I would add that one also has the possibility of recourse to private boycotts, available under national and international law; they are an occasionally effective instrument. They constitute a well-recognised method of protest and consensus-creation in favour of one's moral positions.

With the assistance of such methods of suasion, a multilateral consensus must be achieved on the moral and economic legiti-macy of a carefully defined labour standard (and formally agreed to at the ILO today in light of modern thinking in economics and of the accumulated experience of developmental and labour issues date, and with the clear understanding that we are not just passing resolutions but that serious consequences may follow for follow-through by the signatory nations). The ILO is clearly the institution that is best equipped to create such a consensus, not the GATT/WTO, just as multilateral trade negotiations are conducted at the GATT, not at the ILO.

In turn, the annual ILO monitoring of compliance with ILO conventions is an impartial and multilateral process, undertaken with aid of eminent jurists across the world. Such a process, with changes for standing and for transparency, should be the appropriate forum for the annual review of compliance by nation states of such newly clarified and multilaterally agreed standards. Such monitoring, the opprobrium of public exposure, and the effective strengthening therewith of NGOs in the offending countries (many of which are now democratic and permissive of NGO activity) will often be large enough forces to prod these countries into corrective action.

In extraordinary cases where the violations are such that the moral sense of the world community is outraged, the existing international processes are available to undertake even coercive, corrective multilateral sanctions against specific countries to suspend their entire trading rights.

Thus, for instance, under UN embargo procedures, which take precedence over GATT and other treaties, South Africa's GATT membership proved no barrier to the embargo against it precisely because the world was virtually united in its opposition to *apartheid*. Even outside the UN, the GATT waiver procedure has permitted two-thirds of contracting parties to suspend any GATT member's trading rights, altogether or for specific goods (and now, services).

I must add one final thought to assure those who feel their own moral view must be respected at any cost, even if others cannot be persuaded to see things that way. Even they need not worry under current international procedures. Thus, suppose that (say) American or French public opinion on an issue (as in the tuna-dolphin case for the former and the beef-hormone case for the latter) forces the government to undertake a unilateral suspension of another GATT member's trading rights. There is nothing in the GATT nor will there be anything in the WTO, which will then compel the overturning of such unilateral action. The offending contracting party—the one undertaking the unilateral action—can persist in a violation while making a compensatory offer of an alternative trade concession, or the offended party can retaliate by withdrawing an equivalent trade concession. Thus, unless one resents having to pay for one's virtue (since the claim is that "our labour standard is morally superior"), this is a perfectly sensible solution even to politically unavoidable unilateralism: do not import glass bangles made with child labour in Pakistan or India, but make some other compensatory trade concession. And re-member that the grant of an alternative trade concession (or tariff retaliation) makes some activity other than the offending one more attractive, thus helping one to shrink the offending activity: that surely should be a matter for approbation rather than knee-jerk dismissal.

Notes

1. I have dealt with these factors systematically in my extended analysis in Bhagwati and Hudec (1996, chap. 1).

2. This conclusion is derived and extensively defended in Bhagwati and Srinivasan (1996).

3. Wilson (1996) demonstrates that there can be a "race to the top." This possibility is disregarded in the analysis above, as in the public discourse.

4. The evidence has been systematically reviewed and assessed recently by Levinson (1996).

5. These factors are analysed in Bhagwati and Srinivasan (1996).

6. There are other issues. One main class relates to the current GATT restrictions, as reflected in recent GATT Panel findings as in the two dolphin-tuna cases involving the United States, on "values"-inspired restrictions on imports of products using processes that are unacceptable, which will have to be clarified and will be the subject of new negotiations. My own views on the best solution to this class of problems, as also to the other main class of problems raised by environmentalists who fear that it is too easy for countries to challenge the higher standards which they have enacted in their own countries (an issue that was at the heart of the latest GATT panel finding, mostly in U.S. favour, in the EU-U.S.

case on differentially punitive U.S. taxes and standards on higher-gasoline-useage cars) are developed at length in Bhagwati and Srinivasan (1996); unfortunately, I have no space to address them here.

7. This of course, does not apply equally to trade in highly differentiated products like autos where one can get fixated on specific countries, for example, Japan.

8. See Bhagwati (1993).

9. This efficiency is only in the sense of cost minimisation. The number of permits may, however, be too small or too large, and getting it right by letting nonusers also bid (and then destroy permits) is bedeviled by free-rider problems.

10. I talk of the United States' suspending Mexico's trade rights since the GATT panel in the dolphin-tuna case upheld these rights for Mexico. If it had not, I should be talking simply of the United States' denying market access of Mexico.

References

Bhagwati, J. 1993. "American Rules, Mexican Jobs." *New York Times* (March 24); chapter 23.

Bhagwati, J., and R. Hudec, eds. 1996. *Fair Trade and Harmonization: Prerequisites for Free Trade?* 2 vols. Cambridge: MIT Press.

Bhagwati, J., and T. N. Srinivasan. 1996. "Trade and the Environment: Does Environmental Diversity Detract from the Case for Free Trade?" In *Fair Trade and Harmonization: Prerequisites for Free Trade*? vol. 1, edited by Jagdish Bhagwati and Robert Hudec. Cambridge: MIT Press.

Levinson, A. 1996. "Environmental Regulations and Industry Location: International and Domestic Evidence." In *Fair Trade and Harmonization: Prerequisites for Free Trade*? vol. 1, edited by Jagdish Bhagwati and Robert Hudec. Cambridge: MIT Press.

Wilson, J. 1996. "Capital Mobility and Environmental Standards: Is There a Theoretical Basis for a Race to the Bottom?" In *Fair Trade and Harmonization: Prerequisites for Free Trade*? vol. 1, edited by Jadish Bhagwati and Robert Hudec. Cambridge: MIT Press.

VII

Free Trade Areas Are Not Free Trade!

25   Let GATT Live

The decision to renew the steel quotas, and the earlier Super 301 actions against Japan, Brazil, and India, underline the pressures that the Bush administration faces from Congress to move trade policy away from the multilateralism embodied in the General Agreement on Tariffs and Trade.

The GATT trading system has achieved unprecedented trade expansion and world prosperity. What accounts then for Congress's hostility? The explanation lies in a host of fallacies.

Fallacy 1.   Multilateralism does not work: At best, the pace is too slow.

This is simply not true. Under GATT auspices, tariff barriers among the industrialized countries—including Japan—were successively lowered to negligible levels. It took more than two decades and seven negotiating rounds, but it worked.

Many Americans believe that the failure to get an eighth round started in 1982 proved multilateralism's failure. But only four years later, the desired round began. The subject matter is complex and tricky this time, covering difficult new sectors (agriculture and services) and issues (intellectual property) that cannot be rushed if wise solutions are to be negotiated.

Originally published in the *Wall Street Journal* (July 28, 1989).

Fallacy 2.   Unilateral threats of trade retaliation are necessary to prevent "unfair traders" from exploiting America's more open economy. The GATT would, at best, produce exchange of trade concessions whereas the United States is entitled to get something for nothing.

This is no more than self-serving rhetoric. The United States has more than its share of trade-restraining arrangements—"voluntary" restraints on steel, textiles, etc.—and the East Asian economies are often forced, as with automobiles, to exercise export restraint in the face of a hostile Congress even when there are no formal arrangements. The European Community has even released lists of American unfair trade practices, paying us back in our own coin.

Fallacy 3.   The U.S. trade deficit is unsustainable and requires immediate correction. Tough tactics must be used to open Japan fast.

The American trade deficit reflects America's own macroeconomic folly. If the United States does not bring its excess spending down by reducing the budget deficit, the removal of foreign trade barriers will not make any sustained difference to the trade deficit. Remember: The U.S. trade deficit became large in the mid-1980s—when Japan's trade barriers fell.

Fallacy 4.   Japan is different from the United States. Its market is inherently harder to penetrate. Therefore, we must scrap the "unrealistic" GATT system and shift to some form of managed trade.

There is nothing more silly than the assertion that trade imbalances necessarily follow because trading countries are different culturally or economically. Imbalances reflect macroeconomic factors. If this is hard to grasp, just ask yourself, Why did Japan's "inevitable" surplus wait so long to emerge when Japanese cultural impenetrability had been with us ever since Commodore Perry?

Fallacy 5.   Free trade can work only between culturally homogeneous nations.

In fact, the opposite is true: If we were all identical, there would be no profit from trade. Equally, we must dismiss the notion that Japan's cultural difference makes mutual trade, driven by prices, impossible. In the past two years, Japanese imports of manufactured goods increased by 33 percent annually, mostly because of the rise in the value of the yen. The Japanese *do* belong to the human race that Adam Smith wrote about.

Fallacy 6.   The GATT is dead because there are so many violations of its rules.

Some important GATT rules have indeed been sidetracked. Thus, countries seeking relief from unmanageable imports can, under Article 19 of the GATT, protect their economies from foreign competition so long as they treat all exporters equally. Instead, industrialized countries, the United States among them, have simply forced selected exporting countries to restrain export "voluntarily."

When the rule of law is breached, you do not turn automatically to the law of the jungle; instead you try to see where things went wrong and to improve law enforcement. The current Uruguay Round is accordingly concentrating on issues, like rejuvenating Article 19, that will strengthen the GATT.

Fallacy 7.   GATT is dead because the world is shifting to regional blocs and rejecting multilateralism.

This thesis is partly true and mostly false. The U.S-Canada Free Trade Agreement and Europe 1992 are at center stage for now. But so is the Uruguay Round of multilateral negotiations. Besides, both 1992 and the free trade agreement reflect a coincidence of events from which it is impossible to infer either a trend or a rejection of multilateralism. Nineteen-ninety-two merely intensifies an ongoing phenomenon, making the Common Market commoner. Its impulse was internal unification, political and economic. The free trade agreement, equally unprotectionist in intent, reflects altogether different forces. The United States, wanted to take the political momentum away from protectionists in Congress. Canada wanted to escape from the consequences of America's "unfair trade" mania.

Fallacy 8.   The GATT is dead because increasing trade conflicts will force bureaucrats and politicians to settle them bilaterally.

True, countries have turned to crying foul against their trading rivals. Dumping and foreign subsidization are often charged; failure to sell is translated into conspiratorial refusal to buy. Presently bilateral skirmishes follow because a mutually acceptable evaluation of the allegation is rare. Rather, when made by Americans, the allegations go before American commissions and agencies and are decided by Americans. More than ever, an impartial dispute settlement mechanism is needed. The GATT has experienced but little clout in playing this role. The need to enhance its authority to do so is now widely accepted.

The GATT has to be built afresh, filling in the gaps that have arisen as the world economy has evolved. Services and agriculture have to be brought within its ambit. Market disruption and dispute settlement mechanisms have to be overhauled. There is simply no alternative to making the effort needed to establish the GATT firmly at the center of the world's trading system in this way.

26   Why Ross Is Wrong

This book is vintage Ross Perot. Catchy phrases, damning quotes, simple charts and simplistic arguments are deployed brilliantly in a short, pithy frontal attack on the proposed North American Free Trade Agreement. Written with Pat Choate, an exponent of the Japanese threat to us, the book is filled with the passion that such fears prompt. Add an unabashed display of panic-fueled patriotism, and you will see why *Save Your Job, Save Our Country: Why NAFTA Must Be Stopped—Now!* promises to make money for the authors and trouble for Bill Clinton.

Messrs. Perot and Choate do not simply argue that those who support NAFTA are taken in by notions of gains that are illusory. No, they denounce NAFTA as "a drastic and unfair scheme" that "will pit American and Mexican workers in a race to the bottom," "give away American jobs," and "radically reduce the sovereignty of the United States." It will, besides, have been perpetrated on us by "the most expensive lobbying campaign [by a foreign government] in U.S. history."

To be fair, the authors have good reason, other than the compulsions of the political marketplace, to hype up their case. The

Originally published in the *Wall Street Journal* (September 2, 1993).

This chapter reviews Ross Perot and Pat Choate's *Save Your Job, Save Our Country: Why NAFTA Must Be Stopped—Now!* (Westport, Conn.: Hyperion 1993).

proponents of NAFTA have not exactly been sober in making their case either. To get a word in, it was probably necessary to yell, even to rant. But surely they err in their critique of Mexican lobbying.

In truth, Mexico's President Carlos Salinas de Gotari has played his cards well and paid his Washington lobbyists handsomely. But, frankly, why make such a fuss about it? We are a nation with a strong tradition of debate and dissent. Has the Mexican lobbying been able to silence NAFTA's opponents? Hardly. This book itself proves otherwise. America is resilient enough to take the foreign lobbying in stride. In fact, our willingness to permit such lobbying reflects the strength of our pluralism rather than the weakness of our institutions.

Worries over NAFTA's effect on jobs and wages are another matter altogether. The fear that freer trade with poor countries with abundant labor will eliminate jobs in the rich countries and pull down real wages is a genuine one. What trade will start, investment will reinforce. Capital will flow from the rich to the poor nations to take advantage of cheap labor: New factories will be built there rather than here, old ones relocated from San Jose to Tijuana.

Unfortunately, the response of NAFTA supporters to these fears has been dismissive instead of decisive. Again, specious arguments have been deployed, as when the fear of outflow of investment to Mexico has been dismissed as a fantasy because such investment outflows have "already" occurred without NAFTA, ignoring the fact that NAFTA provisions make investing in Mexico more attractive and less risky, and that Mr. Salinas himself has often cited this ability to attract more investment as a principal benefit of NAFTA for Mexico. It would be better to argue that just as European Community–induced Japanese investment has gone to Britain more than to (poorer) Spain, NAFTA-induced foreign investment could favor us rather than Mexico, putting us ahead.

An effective answer to the alleged threat to the wages of the unskilled must cite studies showing how trade and net outflows of investment during the 1980s had almost nothing to with the stagnation and fall of real wages during the same time. The emerging consensus is that the true culprits were technology and technical change, both of which (in the information age) militate against unskilled labor. In fact, during the 1980s, we experienced a net inflow of foreign equity and other capital, whereas in trade we became more protectionist instead, while the poor countries liberalized their trade.

The real problem with the current administration, I suspect, is that few in it believe in their gut that free trade can lift all economic boats. Especially when it comes to trading with the poorer countries, they seem to share, rather than reject, the fears of Perot and Choate.

When did this administration say unambiguously that gains from trade will accrue even when we trade with countries with different, albeit lower, environmental and labor standards? Instead, the administration, through its ambivalent accommodation on these questions, has legitimated the notion that free trade requires such harmonization. It is, of course, a short step to believing that lower wages also imply unfair trade, and bring with them predation rather than gain. Mr. Salinas has already agreed to action on minimum wages.

While Mr. Salinas, with his political fortunes tied to NAFTA's passage, and bargaining with asymmetric power in a one-on-one context with us, has been a patsy for these illogical demands as preconditions for freer trade, the many nations negotiating multilaterally at the Uruguay Round of the General Agreement on Tariffs and Trade will not be. So, administration negotiators schooled in the NAFTA experience could be forced by the environmental and labor lobbies to make similar demands at the GATT talks in Geneva. This posture could poison the talks and propel the conclusion of the GATT negotiations yet further beyond the "very final" December 15, 1993, deadline. That could be NAFTA's worst legacy: a Faustian bargain in which a preferential free trade area among only three countries would have succeeded at the expense of free trade for all.

27   Beyond NAFTA: Clinton's Trading Choices

Although the debate over the North American Free Trade Agreement (NAFTA) will be loud and distracting, its passage seems assured, albeit with some tougher environmental and labor standards. It is time, then, for President Bill Clinton to plan his next, critical step on trade. He must now decide whether to continue with a free trade area (FTA) approach, be it global or confined to the Americas, or to throw his weight exclusively behind a multilateral approach based on the General Agreement on Tariffs and Trade (GATT). Unfortunately, the president seems to be headed down the least attractive of those paths; the embrace of more regional FTAs in the Americas alone.

The president and U.S. Trade Representative (USTR) Mickey Kantor have occasionally remarked, without making a formal policy statement, that they would carry the NAFTA process southward. In a policy statement on March 30, 1993, Larry Summers, the Treasury Department's assistant secretary for international affairs, supported the trade component of the broader Enterprise for the Americas Initiative, which was launched in 1990. After Mexico, then, the Clinton administration is likely to embrace Chile and thus, wittingly or unwittingly, the regional FTA approach—without seriously examining the other options.

Originally published in *Foreign Policy* 91 (Summer 1993): 155–62. © Carnegie Endowment for International Peace. Reprinted with permission.

Inertia, however, is not a sound basis for policy. Analysis of the choices at hand and an appreciation of the history of such choices are essential if the administration is to make such a momentous decision with vision and wisdom. Indeed, history is most enlightening on this question. When the GATT was crafted at the end of World War II, the United States was wedded to the cause of open, multilateral trade. It resolutely fought the British, who favored discrimination in defense of Imperial Preference. Because of U.S. efforts, nondiscrimination became a central principle of the GATT: If trade barriers were lowered for one trading partner, they had to be lowered for all trading partners. Virtually the only exception to that rule is found under Article 24 of the GATT, which allows a group of countries to dismantle all trade barriers only among themselves.

That was the door through which the European Community (EC) passed in 1957, with U.S. approval. Though Americans were not at the time interested in Article 24 for themselves, the EC effort led to an outpouring of short-lived FTAs in the developing countries, with the 1960 Latin American Free Trade Association being the most prominent. But the time was not yet ripe for their success. Few developing countries were willing to adopt a regime under which free trade, not planning, would regulate economic activity.

In the 1960s, the use of Article 24 by the United States emerged as a real possibility in a manner that has immediate relevance today. Several influential economists, politicians, and intellectuals in Great Britain and North America came up with the proposal for a NAFTA. But NAFTA then stood for the North *Atlantic* Free Trade Area, which was nonregional at its inception and meant to push outward to the Pacific for new members—with the United States right in the middle of it all. Economist Harry Johnson and Senator Jacob Javits (R-New York) were among the first NAFTA proponents.

The 1960s NAFTA initiative, much like the early 1980s turn to FTAs by the United States, was essentially prompted by the fear that the GATT-based multilateral-negotiations route to lowering trade barriers worldwide had run its course. FTAs, open to new members on a nonregional basis, seemed to offer an alternative, indeed the only, route to free trade everywhere. Thus, at the time, there was a widespread feeling that the Kennedy Round would turn out to be the last opportunity under the GATT to lower trade barriers. NAFTA proponents also viewed the EC as an inward-looking customs union that would resist efforts to liberalize world trade under the GATT. At the same time, Atlanticists in Britain and the United States preferred to see Britain link its destiny with the United States rather than with the EC. As British efforts to join the EC met with French president Charles de Gaulle's continuing *non*, others felt that Britain might well have no option but to turn to other initiatives.

De Gaulle's opposition to British entry was, of course, driven wholly by the fear that Britain would act as the Americans' Trojan horse within the EC, bringing in the interests and influence of the United States and undermining the French policy of independence from U.S. hegemony. British prime minister Harold Wilson recalled a 1965 cartoon from the *Observer* where a diminutive Wilson says, in short, "I even wake up tired!" to which a towering de Gaulle, a stethoscope in his ear, responds: "Hm. It's all those late night telephone calls to Washington. What you need is an independent policy on Vietnam." Indeed, de Gaulle made no secret of his suspicions about the British. Thus, immediately before his resounding November 1967 rejection of British membership in the EC, de Gaulle had queried Wilson on precisely that issue. As Wilson put it: "The whole situation would be very different if France were genuinely convinced that Britain really was disengaging from the U.S. in all major matters such as defense

Figure 27.1
Britain's entry into the European Common Market was desired by the United States to contain France, a fact that was understood by President de Gaulle who regarded the British therefore as a Trojan Horse. In this cartoon, which appeared in *The Observer* (March 3, 1965), the Gaullist suspicions are illustrated in the context of Vietnam policy, with "Doctor" de Gaulle telling the tired patient, Prime Minister Harold Wilson, that his fatigue is due to the late-night calls from Washington. © .abu.

policy and in areas such as Asia, the Middle East, Africa and Europe.''

As it happened, it was precisely the flip side of de Gaulle's concerns that made the American government eager, for political reasons, that Britain join the EC and hence unenthusiastic about the NAFTA proposal. Britain would help moderate, it argued. Gaullist anti-Americanism. In fact, American leaders were also wary of a NAFTA on economic grounds because they were in no mood to give up on multilateralism and GATT. Both Secretary of State John Foster Dulles and Secretary of the Treasury Douglas Dillon had supported the European Community on political grounds. In 1950, the U.S. House of Representatives had amended the Economic Cooperation Act to include among its objectives the "economic unification of Europe" as part of the effort needed to restore Western Europe to prosperity, strengthening it against the Soviet menace. Both Dulles and Dillon opposed a Europe-wide free trade area, as distinct from the then six-member EC. Thus, any FTA that focused on free trade alone, as the first NAFTA was designed to do, the American government found unacceptable. It saw America's interests in multilateralism and nondiscrimination, as typified by the GATT: A trading regime embodying those principles would provide a predictable and orderly framework for trade among all countries and hence benefit the United States in turn. By contrast, the North Atlantic initiative, despite its ultimate objective of free trade worldwide, would have entailed preferences and discrimination at the outset.

The 1960s NAFTA initiative then came to naught: The U.S. government refused to play. But the conjunction of factors encouraging a U.S. policy shift to FTAs had returned in the early 1980s and, this time, the United States changed its mind and its course. Faced with European refusal to start multilateral trade negotiations in 1982, and with growing protectionism at home that required countervailing moves to expand trade, the Reagan administration initiated the talks culminating in the Canada-U.S. Free Trade Agreement now turning a decade later into NAFTA, the North *American* Free Trade Agreement, with Mexico.

The new NAFTA is clearly a regional FTA, and extending it to South America would undoubtedly stamp it as regionalism par excellence. Yet, it is noteworthy that, as with the aborted 1960s NAFTA initiative, the policy shift to Article 24–blessed FTAs by the United States in the 1980s was not conceived as being narrowly regional in scope. When the U.S.-Canadian agreement was first negotiated, its supporters could be roughly divided into two camps, both of them antiregionalist.

The first group, the GATT optimists, thought that the U.S.-Canadian agreement would push the EC and the developing countries into a new GATT round. Without the United States, all would realize, the GATT would have little future, and world trade would revert to the law of the jungle, which would be most painful to the weak. The strategy worked, and the American embrace of Article 24 through the Canada-U.S. FTA did indeed prompt countries to come to the table with the GATT Uruguay Round of multilateral trade negotiations. When completed, the Uruguay Round will radically transform the GATT, implementing many of the reforms for which the United States has been fighting over the past decade. According to that school of thought, the turn to FTAs was a tactical move designed to jumpstart the GATT multilateral negotiations. Having succeeded in doing so, it is now time for America to return to its original commitment to the GATT as the best means to liberalize world trade.

A second group, the GATT pessimists, also favored the Canada-U.S. FTA. But much like the earlier proponents of the North Atlantic initiative, they saw FTAs as part of a global strategy that sought to build FTAs that were open-ended, not regionally exclusive. Ambassador William Brock, the USTR in the early years of the Reagan administration, offered FTAs even to members of the Association of Southeast Asian Nations. He would have no doubt offered them to the moon if only he could have found life there and a government with whom to negotiate.

The GATT pessimists thought of the GATT process of trade negotiations as less effective and rapid than the FTA approach to worldwide trade liberalization. But that is a hasty and illconsidered view. A comparison of the two processes of trade liberalization is surprising. It turns out that the problems that plague the one also afflict the other. As economists Bernard Hoekman and Michael Leidy have pointed out, the holes (areas left out) and the loopholes (areas where the disciplines of free trade are avoided) are practically identical in either case. As for slowness, consider the European Community: The process began in 1957, with the

Treaty of Rome pledge to eliminate trade barriers as required by GATT Article 24. As of 1993, it still has not succeeded—not exactly a record of alacrity. The NAFTA talks, which aim to bring together only three countries, have taken nearly a decade, while the Uruguay Round, with 112 countries participating, has so far taken only seven years.

Nonetheless, the nonregional FTA approach embraced by Brock became the U.S. trade policy in the early 1980s, downgrading the option of sticking to multilateralism despite its revival at the Uruguay Round. Yet, down the road, that policy turned into the narrow regional FTA option that is the least attractive of those available. Some of the blame lies with the U.S. Treasury Department, which was able to capture the FTA idea for its own purposes, offering preferential trade to South America in lieu of debt relief. When the South Americans responded positively, the State Department muscled in, turning the trade initiative into a foreign policy initiative and making it an integral part of the Enterprise for the Americas Initiative. That program harked back to President John Kennedy's Alliance for Progress, except that the latter did not include an offer of regional FTAs because the United States was correctly devoted to multilateralism at the time.

The effect of that narrower vision has been to encourage the notion that the United States is interested in trade regionalism no matter how strong its professed commitment to multilateralism. Since the United States also recognizes its vital trade interests in the rapidly expanding markets of the Far East, it has found itself in an awkward position. George Bush's secretary of state, James Baker, was trying to convince the Asian countries not to form their own Japan-centered FTA even as he worked on the NAFTA and its exclusive extension to the south—an incoherent position that argues that what is good for me is not good for you.

Many have even tried to convince themselves that an Asian trade bloc is unlikely because the Asian countries will not soon forget Japan's wartime cruelties—conveniently forgetting that other countries have learned to live with and profit from Germany despite the unparalleled crimes of the Holocaust. The profit motive can help numb the gray cells of memory.

Indeed, few would have thought that anti-Yanqui sentiments would so quickly evaporate from the Mexican scene, allowing President Carlos Salinas de Gortari's splendid team to hitch Mexico's economic destiny to America's. Salinas turned on its head Porfirio Diaz's famous dictum: "Poor Mexico, so far from God and so near the United States."

But if the United Sates pushes FTAs only southward, it will certainly invite a defensive, if not retaliatory, bloc in Asia. Divisions will be sharpened and the world economy fragmented into four blocs: an expanded EC, a NAFTA extended to the Americas, a Japan-centered Asian bloc, and a marginalized group of developing countries, many with low incomes and only just turning to export-oriented strategies. We should not favor that scenario.

If the United Sates continues to pursue FTAs, the least it can do is to return to the Brock agenda, to the vision of the 1960s North Atlantic initiative. That would mean developing a new strategy of openness before adding any new members, especially from South America.

Such a policy would have to be unambiguously stated and diplomatically credible. Negotiations to add one or more non-hemispheric countries before adding hemispheric ones would help. Then again, if U.S. domestic politics drives America farther south, well beyond the Rio Grande, Canada could be explicitly encouraged to seek out new NAFTA members from the British Commonwealth, countries to which Canada surely has stronger economic and historical links. Indeed, instead of playing the complaisant junior partner in NAFTA, Canada could itself play a leadership role; prime ministers like Lester Pearson and Pierre Trudeau did not shy away from the world stage.

But all that is more readily urged than undertaken. Clayton Yeutter, the former USTR who negotiated the U.S.-Canadian agreement, has candidly described the enormous difficulties of such talks. Then again, the politics of pushing the next agreement through Congress could be quite a challenge. Imagine what would happen if Congress were considering an FTA with India—or with Japan.

Yet many analysts seem drawn to FTA blocs, to a power-political conception of trade that sees the world as a jigsaw puzzle. Some call for a U.S.-Japanese Pacific free trade area, with the two economic superpowers bringing along their respective regions to provide a counterweight to the enlarging EC. In turn, taking a cue from Margaret Thatcher—the irrepressible Atlanticist —and from the Japanophobes, columnist Charles Krauthammer recently argued that the three NAFTA countries should free up trade with the EC instead. "A transatlantic free-trade zone would signal Japan that if it had thoughts of creating a rival Asian bloc or did not modify its predatory drive for market dominance, it might find itself shut out of the new world economic order," he wrote in *Time*. And thus each of us will act out our own fantasies, seeking allies against imagined adversaries, lining up our pre-ferred blocs against the others, and vying for political attention and action.

The more deeply one thinks about the issue, and about the basic choice between multilateralism and FTAs as ways of bring-ing down trade barriers worldwide, the more disenchanted one is likely to be about the latter. Even the popular notion that the two processes and policies can coexist—the "GATT-plus" proposi-tion—and even be benignly symbiotic, is too simplistic. Lobbying support and political energies can readily be diverted to prefer-ential trading arrangements such as FTAs, where privileged access to markets is obtained at the expense of outside competitors (such as the EC and Japan in NAFTA). That deprives the multilateral system of the support it needs to survive, let alone be conducive to further trade liberalization.

The wisest option for the Clinton administration, therefore, is to move NAFTA with Mexico through Congress, conclude the Uruguay Round, and then focus exclusively on the multilateral trading regime of the GATT. Will the administration rise to that challenge or, in choosing the least attractive option of regional FTAs, continue the sorry spectacle of thoughtless trading choices?

28 Preferential Trade Agreements: The Wrong Road

In Blackpool, at the Conservative Party meeting its in 1995, Prime Minister John Major invoked the early George Orwell in his radical youth, when he went by his given name of Eric Blair, to tweak his Labour Party opponent, Tony Blair as having changed everything except his name. I would like to invoke the later George Orwell and begin by asserting that the widespread usage of the term *free trade agreements* (FTAs) to describe what are really preferential trade agreements (PTAs) is nothing but Orwellian newspeak.

For, FTAs are *not* the same as free trade, even though that is certainly what nearly all politicians and journalists believe because of the two magic words *free trade* that begin and dominate the phrase *free trade agreements*. In the nature of the case, FTAs offer free trade (eventually, when complete) only to their members but not to nonmembers. Thus, they are two-faced: implying free trade for members but (relative) protection against nonmembers. First-year students of international economics would be asked to shift to another field if they did not grasp this elementary and elemental distinction. But today, politicians believe they have become

Originally published (with minor editing) in *Law and Policy in International Business* 27, 4 (1996): 865–71. Reprinted with permission of the publisher, Georgetown University, and *Law and Policy in International Business*, © 1996. The text adheres to the original version, reflecting remarks made in Stockholm, Sweden, at Trade Minister Hellström's conference on WTO issues.

statesmen who have endorsed free trade when they embrace these inherently discriminatory PTAs that masquerade as free trade.

As these PTAs proliferate, the main problem that arises is the proliferation in turn of discriminatory access to markets, with a whole maze of trade duties and barriers that vary according to source. (In turn, as I argue below, this leads to increased transaction costs and inevitably invites protectionist capture of de facto rules of origin.) I have called this outcome the "spaghetti bowl" phenomenon—though I must confess that I once used this analogy at an afterdinner speech when the chairman on my right was an Italian who did not quite share my difficulty with handling spaghetti and seemed genuinely puzzled![1] Mr. David de Pury, a distinguished representative of the globalized private sector, has also been eloquent today on this point and on the advantage, even the necessity, of having uniform nondiscriminatory rules and barriers; and I only endorse this objective, which only multilateral WTO-sanctioned treaties make posible. In view of its importance, let me say a little more on this question.

The Spaghetti Bowl: Problems with Preferential Trading Arrangements

The spaghetti-bowl proliferation of preferential trading arrangements clutters up trade with discrimination depending on the "nationality" of a good, with inevitable costs that trade experts have long noted. In particular, consider the following points.

First, rules of origin, which are inherently arbitrary despite the codifications with which we must live, multiply under free trade areas because different members have different external tariffs. That makes the occupation of lobbyists (who seek to protect by fiddling with the adoption of those rules and then with the estimates that underlie the application of those rules, as in the Canadian Honda case) and of customs officers (who can make much money by assigning goods to different origins, as suggested by those fetching gifts) immensely profitable at our expense.

Second and more generally, it is increasingly arbitrary and nonsensical to operate trade policy of all kinds on the assumption that you can identify which product is whose. When I was a student at Oxford in the 1950s, there used to be a *Who's Whose*, designed to list the bondings (or"steady relationships" in our slang) among the undergraduates. Needless to say, the sexual revolution and the rise of uninhibited promiscuity put an end to it. Similarly, with the phenomenal globalization of investment and production, a *Who's Whose* in defining trade policy is an increasing anomaly, tying up trade policy in knots and absurdities and facilitating protectionist capture.

Take some telling examples. We in the United States have tried assiduously to tell the Japanese that exports from their transplants in the United States to Japan are not to be counted as U.S. exports. On the other hand, when the Europeans tried to include the cars exported from those very transplants in their VER quotas on Japanese cars, U.S. Trade Representative Carla Hills was up in arms! Again, just because imports from Japan are sought to be controlled, rather than imports from all sources without discrimination (as would be the case simply with a tariff or an auctioned VER), European Union is tied in knots about whether Japanese transplants in the United Kingdom are to be allowed freedom of access within the European Union and when a car produced in Oxfordshire would be British rather than Japanese.

Indeed, as the world economy increasingly muddies up the idealized picture of Japanese, American, British, Indian, and Mexican goods that drives much of trade policy, including particularly the pursuit of free trade areas, the more we trade economists can see the wisdom of the great trade theorists of the past —Jacob Viner, James Meade, Gottfried Haberler, and others— who were strongly wedded to nondiscrimination and hence to most-favored-nation status and multilateralism. As usual, a quotation from Keynes, who had renounced his earlier skepticism of nondicrimination during the British-American discussions of the design of the postwar Bretton Woods institutions, from his speech in the House of Lords in 1945, says it best:

[The proposed policies] aim, above all, at the restoration of multilateral trade.... [T]he bias of the policies before you is against bilateral barter and every kind of discriminatory practice. The separate blocs and all the friction and loss of friendship they must bring with them are expedients to which one may be driven in a hostile world where trade has ceased over wide areas to be cooperative and peaceful and where are forgotten the healthy rules of mutual advantage and of equal treatment. *But it is surely crazy to prefer that.*[2]

So the question does come before us: why *are* we crazy enough to go down the PTAs route, as indeed many trade ministers seem keen to do? Before I turn to that, let me make an important distinction.

Two Types of PTAs

I believe that we should distinguish between PTAs that are among nonhegemonic countries, chiefly the developing countries, as is Mercosur (among Argentina, Brazil, Uruguay, and Paraguay), and PTAs that involve also hegemonic countries of the Triad, such as the North Atlantic Free Trade Agreement and its proposed extensions, the proposed turning of the Asia Pacific Economic Cooperation council into a PTA as advocated occasionally by Mr. Fred Bergsten and the proposed Trans Atlantic Free Trade Agreement (which would both be interhegemonic) and the EU and its association agreements with others.

The nonhegemoic or, broadly speaking, developing country PTAs, I would say, are not of great concern. For one thing, they do not count for much: what Mercosur does or ASEAN does is of little consequence outside itself, certainly compared with what the big-ticket hegemonic PTAs would do.

But the main reason for going along with them is simply that, compared with the protectionist policies of many developing countries, a movement toward freeing of trade is good news. Also, compared with the undisciplined, freewheeling, and chaotic set of preferences that they granted to each other under the ECDC (Economic Cooperation among Developing Countries) regime, sanctioned as part of the special and differential treatment under the GATT, their acceptance of Article 24 discipline can only be seen as a progresive measure, even though the better and ideal thing would be for them to lower trade barriers in a nondiscriminatory fashion instead.

Those arguments, however, do not apply to the PTAs involving hegemonic powers within their membership. Their course of action affects the system for sure. Besides, they—especially the United States—have been wedded to multilateralism so that the move is from the optimal approach to a suboptimal one when they opt for PTAs. For those PTAs, therefore, we must impose more drastic standards for approval.

Two Criteria for Approving PTAs

What are those criteria? In essence, I would make exceptions for such PTAs on two grounds. First, we are building a common market with full factor mobility and a common external tariff, and with even political integration: that is the core EU, of course, and it offers the advantages that the United States enjoys, for example, as a federal country with deep integration among its states. Second, where such a building of a common market is not at issue, embracing PTAs is the only way to get to multilateral free trade among all nations because the multilateral trade negotiations process under GATT/WTO auspices is stalled; that is the option that the United States chose in 1983 when, at the November 1982 GATT ministerial, it found the EC in a denial mode when the demand was made to launch a new round for multilateral trade negotiations. In that instance, when the United States started the negotiations on the Canada-U.S. FTA, the United States was choosing an inferior (PTA) option simply because the preferred multilateral option was not available. I would say that the apt analogy is that the United States took the dirt road because it could not take the turnpike.

Unfortunately, the United States has since abandoned that rationale for choosing the PTA route: for, although the Uruguay Round was then launched in 1986, has been successfully concluded, and has led to a functioning WTO, and although the world's attention is focused on what the WTO's next agenda should be, the United States is poised to continue its pursuit of PTAs, through NAFTA exapansion and possible through turning APEC into a PTA eventually. In short, the United States is now committed to "walking on two legs," multilateral and preferential trade agreements; my fear is that it is destined to get itself and, through its unwitting example, us walking down the wrong path. As Mr. Larry Summers, the current deputy secretary of the Treasury, has once written, "Economists should maintain a strong, but rebuttable, presumption in favor of all lateral reductions in trade barriers, whether they be multi-, uni-, tri-, plurilateral." His, and others', presumption is also that the PTAs will exercise a benign, beneficial effect on the course of multilateral trade.

My own view of this presumption is that it is totally unpersuasive and that the effect of the PTA path on the multilateral trade path has been malign, if anything, not benign. I have written on that issue at length in two different places: in an essay entitled "Regionalism and Multilateralism: An Overview"[3] and in an essay entitled "U.S. Trade Policy: The Infatuation with Free Trade Areas."[4] I shall not repeat those arguments here but would urge you to read them in the original. But let me select from many the following two arguments to give you a flavor of the debate.

First, Mr. Bergsten, who likes the PTA approach, has argued recently that the Uruguay Round was closed successfully because the Seattle APEC meeting served notice to the Europeans that the United States would go that alternative route, which would cut the Europeans out instead. I consider that quite fanciful indeed. The notion that the Europeans would credibly feel that the Asian members of the APEC would play for the United States against the European Union, when they are in both markets in a big way and when Asia has for nearly two centuries been within Europe's sphere of influence and interest, is a little hard to swallow. Besides, it is clear that, in the end, the round was settled, pretty much—I would say, over 90 percent—along the lines of the Dunkel draft, because the U.S. administration decided to accept the advice of many, including mayself: settle the round for what you can get (basically from the French) and go on to build on that in the next set(s) of negotiations. But the desire to balloon up the claims on behalf of the PTAs is so strong on the Washington scene, especially now that the Clinton administration has firmly put itself on that side of the street, that it is hardly surprising to find that many who live close to that scene fall prey to it.

As for the malign impact of PTAs instead, it is not difficult to find examples either. I must say that the effect of the NAFTA debate was to create political salience in the United States for the issue of the effect of trade with the poor countries on jobs and wages in the rich countries. The fact that Mexico was a source of much illegal immigration of illiterate, ill-nourished, and impoverished millions across Rio Grande was enough to make many feel that free trade with Mexico was an indirect way in which Mexico's masses would have an adverse effect on jobs and wages as well. By contrast, the Uruguay Round did not create that issue despite India and China's having many more millions of poor in their midst, simply because those countries were too far away, whereas the round was also diffused over many issues and many countries. The legacy of NAFTA, a PTA, has therefore been to make all future liberalizations with poor countries that much more difficult than if there had been no NAFTA.

Caveats on NAFTA, APEC, and TAFTA

Let me then conclude by arguing against the extension of NAFTA to Chile and other countries and in favor of intensifiying NAFTA into a common market in North America itself, along the lines of the European Community.

Equally, the idea of turning APEC into an FTA is a bad one. Fortunately, the Asian members of APEC have shown little enthusiasm for such a prescription, opting instead for liberalization on an MFN basis, despite U.S. pressures to choose the FTA model and ambiguities on that behalf in some of the pronouncements on the subject.[5]

As for TAFTA, I am happy to see that Mr. Renato Ruggiero, Mr. Peter Sutherland, and Sir Leon Brittan have been widely reported as having insisted that TAFTA should be on an MFN basis; that, of course, is another way of saying that it should not really be an Article 24 type of PTA.[6]

I would hope, therefore, that the welcome initiatives in those regards continue to be prevented from being turned into PTAs. In fact, true statesmanship requires that, in full recognition of the advantages of nondiscriminatory multilateralism, those initiatives be folded instead into the next multilateral trade negotiation, the first WTO round, the modality of whose launching should be the first order of business in Singapore at the first WTO ministerial in December 1996. It would be good to see Sweden, which has often played an independent and leadership role in world politics and economics, take the lead among the developed countries on that critical issue and declare itself in favor of multilateralism and against the current, mindless infatuation with PTAs.[7]

Notes

1. See, for instance, Bhagwati (1995).

2. Quoted in Bhagwati (1991, 64, emphasis added).

3. Bhagwati (1993).

4. Bhagwati (1995).

5. Subsequent to the Stockholm meeting, the Osaka summit of APEC did not announce anything except MFN trade liberalization measures.

6. The subsequent Madrid meeting on U.S.-EC trade and investment cooperation has not endorsed TAFTA in the form of a PTA.

7. I might add that this support for multilateralism should extend to strengthening the WTO Secretariat, which currently has fewer economists than a respectable department in the United States or the United Kingdom. As I have suggested in a guest column that appeared in the *Far Eastern Economic Review* the week before the Osaka APEC summit, Mr. Ruggiero could do that by securing support for a special research facility from the Far East and Scandanavia, at a minimum, if the entire membership did not approve of the expansion from an abysmally small and inefficient size.

References

Bhagwati, Jagdish. 1991. *The World Trading System at Risk*. Princeton: Princeton University Press.

———. 1993. "Regionalism and Multilateralism: An Overview." In *New Dimensions in Regional Integration*, edited by Jaime de Melo and Arvind Panagariya. Cambridge: Cambridge University Press.

———. 1995. "U.S. Trade Policy: The Infatuation with Free Trade." In Jagdish Bhagwati and Anne O. Krueger, *The Dangerous Drift to Preferential Trade Agreements*. Washington, D.C.: AEI Press.

29   The Watering of Trade

Politicians love to discriminate in trade: they favor domestic producers, they want free trade with allies and friends rather than with foes. Free trade areas, (FTAs) which exclude the benefits of free trade from nonmembers, play particularly well for them: in the era of soundbites, when no one can grasp more than two words at one time, politicians can pretend they are statesmen favoring free trade by falsely equating free trade areas with free trade.

Membership of such FTAs, or what are more truthfully defined as preferential trade areas (PTAs), has reflected all kinds of politically salable criteria. The best known FTAs to date have been by common history: the European Free Trade Area (EFTA), NAFTA, the U.S.-Israel FTA, and the numerous overseas FTAs by the European Union with mostly former colonies are the prime examples.

But there is never any ceasing of the search for excuses to launch yet more PTAs. Having exhausted history, the politicians are now exploiting geography. Indeed, we are now witnessing the "watering of trade" as the sharing of common waters has become a politically salient way of launching PTAs. The oceans have provided the first act in this new play.

Originally published in the *Journal of International Economics* 42 (1997): 239–41. Reprinted with permission.

Common Oceans

The credit for that innovation belongs to the United States. Though the initiative for some kind of Pacific cooperation goes back some decades, and the APEC (the Asia Pacific Economic Cooperation forum) was initially designed to do just that, without turning it into an FTA, it is an open secret that the United States would like to see it turned into an FTA.

But with the Pacific Ocean now in the game, the other three oceans cannot be far behind. The Atlanticists have launched the Transatlantic initiative, the TAFTA, with the British foreign secretary, Michael Rifkind, a principal player, following in the footsteps of Minister Klaus Kinkel in Chancellor Kohl's cabinet. Again, the FTA issue is wide open; but the train has left the station and may well reach the FTA destination some day.

Trust India then to launch the Indian Ocean FTA initiative, with its own New Delhi meeting, attended enthusiastically by the potential members.

That leaves only one ocean now, the Arctic. Will the Arctic Ocean FTA, the AFTA, be launched by President Clinton, President Yeltsin, or Prime Minister Chertien?

Common Seas

But there is no reason why politicians and their think-tank allies should stop at oceans. After all, we have the seas, the gulfs, the bays: each provides a wealth of opportunities for the PTA fans to launch trade initiatives that can enable them to bask in the glory of "free trade" while leaving their little names behind for posterity to celebrate. And if we ran out of those, we could go on to basins (e.g., Peru, Brazil, Angola, and Southeast Pacific) and passages (Drake). And then to lakes (e.g., Tanganyika and Victoria, if you know your Discovery of the Nile).

Take the seas alone. Wow, what an opportunity for new PTAs they provide for the trade ministers who have missed out so far on the circus! Take your school map off the shelf, dust it, spread it out, and then you will see that the world is inundated by seas, several (though not all) still offering new FTA opportunities. Thus, the Beaufort Sea spans Canada and the United States: but those nations are taken already by NAFTA. Just think, however, of the Caribbean sea: there you have immediately Venezuela, Colombia, Panama, Costa Rica, Nicaragua, Honduras, Guatemala, Belize, Cuba, Mexico, Jamaica, Haiti, Dominican Republic, the United States (Puerto Rico), St. Kitts, Dominica, St. Lucia, Barbados, Grenada, and Trinidad and Tobago, no mean number!

Or travel east and find the Black Sea: and you get an FTA among Turkey, Bulgaria, Romania, Ukraine, Russia, and Georgia. Or take the Caspian Sea and you get an FTA among Russia, Azerbaijan, Kazakhastan, Turkmenistan, and Iran. A little further probing of the map and you get the Aral Sea, the Arabian Sea, the Sea of Okhotsk, the Sea of Japan, the South China Sea, the Tasman Sea (but the FTA around it is already in place between Australia and New Zealand) and the Barents Sea, the Mediterranean, the Norwegian Sea and ... one's mouth waters at the rich menu of FTA possibilities!

Common Gulfs and Bays

But then we get to the gulfs and the bays. How about the Persian Gulf: if only Iran could go with Saudi Arabia, Kuwait, and the United Arab Emirates on the one hand and Iraq on the other! Or take the Bay of Bengal: could we not get India into a Baybe FTA with Myanmar and Sri Lanka? Or the Baffin Bay: it would be just dandy to have Canada and Greenland in a Baba FTA!

And, since policy wonks cannot leave out the "corner solutions"—the end points of the spectrum here—how about an FTA of the nations without water? These are clearly the landlocked countries: Nepal, Niger, Hungary, and Paraguay could kick it off, cutting across continents in a cosmopolitan display of true solidarity in trade!

The WTO: The Largest Water of All

But then think of the other extreme. Is not the treaty constituting and enforced by the WTO the host to the largest water of all, combining countries with common oceans, common seas, common bays, and common gulfs?

Then again, we ought to remind the oceanic aficionados that the oceans are after all connected, as Ferdinand Magellan discovered when he set forth from San Lucar in 1519 and sailed from the Atlantic into the Pacific, an ocean unknown at the time.

So, even as we swim in our waterworld, we finally arrive at the wisdom of our multilateralist forebears: go for worldwide free trade, boldly seeking it at the WTO, and forego the petty pursuit of PTAs that now afflicts the politicians and their waterlogged advisers.

Threats to the World Trading System: Income Distribution and the Selfish Hegemon

The Uruguay Round is closing after a marathon of negotiations stretching well over seven years; so the timing of this panel is exquisite from my viewpoint. The ceremony, besides, is in Marrakesh, an exotic place that sets our minds racing with thoughts of Casablanca, Humphrey Bogart, and Ingrid Bergman. Indeed, one can imagine a movie being made of this historic occasion with Peter Ustinov cast as Peter Sutherland, the brilliant and portly new director general of the GATT who finally brought the round to successful conclusion, Dustin Hoffman playing our own inimitable Mickey Kantor, and perhaps Al Pacino as the elegant and suave Sir Leon Brittan of the European Union: the three principal players in the closing days of the round.

In any event, the closure of the round puts the GATT, or its new version the WTO, right at the center of the world trading system. This is a triumph that should not be underestimated. It was only a few years ago that my good friend Lester Thurow, reading the mood around him, had pronounced at Davos that the GATT was dead. His colleague at MIT, Rudiger Dornbusch, had urged that the GATT be killed. And their brilliant MIT colleague and my justly renowned pupil, Paul Krugman, before his celebrated recent return to the fold of free trade and multilateralism, had

Originally published, in slightly shorter form, in the *Journal of International Affairs* 48 (Summer 1994): 279–85. Reprinted by permission of the *Journal of International Affairs* and the Trustees of Columbia University in the City of New York.

flirted with both thoughts. Evidently, the company you keep affects you. Fortunately, this anti-GATT MIT School—christened by me as the Memorial Drive School since MIT's famous economics department is located on Memorial Drive in Cambridge, while the phrase also evokes aptly the funereal view of the GATT that the School epitomized—seems today to be more obviously silly than when some of us pronounced on its demerits some years ago.[1] That school's demise and GATT's success are a cause for celebration. So is President Clinton's belated but strong support for the round, though we must still see him take the agreement skillfully through Congress in the coming year.

All this is on the positive side of the ledger. But there are also problems that lie ahead, which threaten the world trading system in varying degrees, where careful examination is warranted. I shall touch on just two of the central problems confronting us today.

Income-Distribution Concerns and Reverse Special and Differential Treatment for Developing Countries

Among the danger points currently is the increasing preoccupation in the European Union and in the United States with the *distributional* effects of freer trade with the developing countries. A new North-South divide is opening up, in consequence. Traditionally, economists have had to fight the "pauper labor" argument against free trade by the North with the South. That argument asserts that trading with cheaper-labor countries will harm a country's overall economic welfare; in reality, the case for free trade is proof against that charge. But the new fear is not that trading with countries with paupers will harm oneself; rather it is that such trade will produce more paupers in one's own midst. In other words, the fear is that our proletariat, the unskilled, will be immiserized by freer trade with the poor countries of the South.

That fear comes from the experience of the 1980s, when in the EU unemployment increased and in the United Stated the real wages of the unskilled fell. While nearly all careful studies show that the cause was overwhelmingly the outbreak of technical change that was unskilled-labor-saving and that North-South trade had very little to do with that distressing reality, the fear that trade was the culprit has become widespread.

In fact, you will recall that the debate over NAFTA was particularly acrimonious precisely because the unions were petrified that it would lead to job losses and a decline in the real wages of U.S. workers. One could plausibly argue that, just because many Americans had that stark image of Mexico as a source of pauper labor that was illegally coming across in large numbers and depressing the wages of our unskilled workers, and because they intuitively felt that free trade with Mexico would simply be an *indirect* way in which that would happen via imports of goods made with cheap labor, a most unfortunate effect of NAFTA was to exacerbate those fears and to undermine the political case for free trade. That would not have happened with the Uruguay Round because freer trade with the developing countries would have been alongside the many other issues negotiated at the round.[3] Indeed, that debate has not surfaced in the same way, and with the same passion, in that context to date.

I suspect that the fear of freer trade with the South, no matter how exaggerated, will dominate trade policy through the rest of this millennium. The effect will be precisely what we observed in the case of NAFTA: attempts at somehow linking cost-raising issues with trade liberalization with the developing countries. Thus, attempts were made then, and conceded in spirit though without serious teeth, to raise Mexico's minimum wages, to raise her labor standards, and to improve her industry's environmental standards as well.

The GATT is similarly under pressure to adopt measures to harmonize up the environmental and labor standards in developing countries; and attempts have begun in earnest, with the United States teaming up with France (that great ally of ours on trade, as you will recall from the disputes we had over EU agriculture and audio-visual services at the Uruguay Round) to push a social clause onto the GATT. The case for such upward harmonization, and linkage thereof to trade as well, is exceptionally weak; and developing countries have raised objections to it.

But the capture of those issues by "green" and "blue" protectionists gives them great salience in the developed countries, while the ability to hide behind the umbrella of "social causes" in advancing those issues gives them the cachet of high moral ground. In short, one almost sees the white man's burden being used to advance the white man's interest; and one also sees, in the selection of issues and the precise shape being given to them, the other cynical reality: that stones are being (properly) thrown at other people's glass houses by people who (improperly) construct fortresses around their own.[4]

To put it yet another way, what one is beginning to see is demands from developed countries now to introduce special restrictions on trade of the developing countries. Ironically, just as special and differential treatment *in favor* of the developing countries has finally been greatly circumscribed as a GATT principle after years of intellectual battle, we are now getting into *reverse* special and differential treatment, designed to work *against* the developing countries.

It will be a major task for economists, and free-trade-oriented politicians, to confront those new problems. The main task will be to keep arguing (what I believe is true)[5] that the fears of immiseration of the proletariat from freer trade with the South are grossly exaggerated and therefore misplaced, that the real problem has to do with technical change, that the policy that can help address the issue is not protectionism but rather encouragement of widespread skill formation to diffuse the benefits of the technological revolution that favors skills, and that such encouragement of environmental and labor policies as we seek on other grounds should be done, not by linking them to trade rights and access—which will inevitably be captured by protectionists and those seeking to rip off the developing countries instead of really wanting to improve and help them—but by suasion as through subsidizing NGO activity and by concerted, multilateral efforts at securing consensus on core values and policies as desirable objectives to be aspired to.

The Selfish Hegemon and the Impact on Multilateralism

The other question of some importance today is our attitude to multilateralism, since we have recently come to embrace both regionalism (free trade areas, more strictly) and aggressive unilateralism (via 301 actions).

Historically, our embrace of NAFTA was largely inspired by the fact that the process of getting a multilateral negotiation at the GATT started had stalled in 1982 when the EC refused to go along.[6] In essence, we then served notice that we would try alternative ways of getting to worldwide freer trade, the chief one being the use of free trade areas (FTAs). The Canada-U.S. FTA did work in the end to jumpstart the GATT as the EC did turn around and agree in 1986 to the Uruguay Round and to including in the agenda several new issues, such as agriculture and services. But the dynamic of FTAs and their eventual packaging into regionalism has been such that we have pushed FTAs beyond Canada, and despite the success of the Uruguay Round and the GATT, to NAFTA and now seek to push them beyond, to other countries.[7]

Similarly, we have become familiar with the use of Section 301 of the 1974 and 1988 trade acts to issue trade threats to extract concessions from other countries concerning all sorts of issues where we unilaterally define and determine those countries to be indulging in "unreasonable" or "unfair" trading practices, quite ragardless of whether any treaty-defined obligation exists on their part to do so. That is what economists have come to call aggressive unilateralism.[8]

One might expect therefore, with the Uruguay Round almost concluded, and the GATT triumphantly turning into the WTO, and therefore there being no excuse to multiply inherently preferential FTAs as a necessary way to liberalize free trade further, that the United States would cease and desist from further FTAs, especially of the regional variety—with their potential for retaliatory Asian response and hence for fragmentation of the world economy into blocs. Similarly, since the strengthened Uruguay Round dispute settlement procedures make the use of 301 actions to extract unilaterally specified trade concessions by other contracting parties more risky and almost certainly GATT-illegal, especially in case of tariff retaliation, the use of aggressive unilateralism by the United States would also seem to be destined to become a relic of the past.

Yet, it would be a mistake to think that WTO-centered multilateralism, uncluttered by FTAs (and regionalism) and 301 actions for unilateral extractions of trade concessions, will now emerge triumphant. Instead, I fear that those new instrumentalities will continue somehow in place. Why?

The reason is that, no matter why those policy options were arrived at earlier, the United States cannot but see them now as useful instruments for advancing its self-interest. I think that we now confront a model of the *selfish hegemon*, just as my great teacher Charles P. Kindleberger advanced the influential thesis of the *altruistic hegemon*. Let me explain.

Kindleberger thought of the United States after the Second World War as backing the GATT and the liberal international trading regime as a "public good." Now, the United States has been for some time in what Douglas Irwin and I have called the "diminished giant syndrome," where it wants "finally" to "look after its own interest."[9] The architectural approach to building a socially productive, good-for-all world trading system is at a discount as the United States finds itself pursuing agendas defined more pointedly by domestic interests.

Thus, we have witnessed the United States seeking excessive intellectual property protection and exploiting environmental and labor issues to reduce competitive pressures. FTAs are then used as an *incentive strategy*[10] and 301 is used as a *punishment strategy* to bargain to advantage with individual, especially developing and smaller, countries,[11] to extract the best terms from the targeted countries on those matters that are strategically characterized by the interested lobbies as "linked" to trade.

While those favorable bargains are struck with specific countries with the aid of the incentive and the punishment strategies that I have identified, they are codified and enshrined eventually in the GATT in a multilateral agreement (like the Uruguay Round) with a divided, partially coopted, and weakened opposition. If the United States were to go directly to the GATT and bargain directly with all, on the other hand, she would extract a much inferior bargain. Thus, there exists a symbiotic—and, for the hegemon, diminished as it is, a productive—relationship between the new policies of FTAs and 301, and multilateralism at the GATT or WTO, that favors a continuation of the U.S. embrace of those new policies.[12]

I suspect, in fact, that most lobbies, with their own agendas, are now aware of these advantages of the FTA-*cum*-301 selfish hegemon strategy. Indeed, each domestic lobby now cites the previous one that prevailed as a sound reason for the U.S.

government to extract concessions also for itself by use of the incentive and punishment strategies that I have identified. Thus, the environmentalists cite success in securing (for business) intellectual property protection; the labor unions cite the progress by environmentalists when seeking to impose labor standards on others; and other lobbies will doubtless cite the labor unions efforts and prospective success, in turn.

I believe therefore that we are now likely to continue being saddled with the instrumentalities of FTAs and unilateralism, even though they violate the spirit of genuine multilateral negotiations, fair and square, and indeed constitute violations in themselves of the spirit (and, in case of unilateralism, also of the letter) of the multilateralism enshrined in the GATT. It will be interesting to see how the world trading system will evolve, as those new perceptions and political realities shape U.S. trade policy and intrude on the working of the multilateral trading regime at the WTO.

Notes

1. See Bhagwati (1991c, chap. 1 and app. I).

2. For a detailed analytical and empirical analysis of this question, see Bhagwati and Dehejia (1994).

3. The British debate at the time of the enactment of the 1905 Immigration quota legislation, the first national legislation of its kind, happened to divide the politicians and policy advocates into two camps: the free traders and free immigrationists on one side and protectionists and antiimmigrationists on the other, precisely because, as I argue in the text, free trade with the countries containing paupers was considered to be similar in effect to free immigration of the paupers themselves. In fact, free immigration was described as "free trade in paupers" in that debate! See the discussion in Bhagwati (1991a).

4. Thus, the United States itself has serious problems with its children: recent studies show that over four million children live in great hazard, and black children's infant mortality rates and life expectancy are a matter of embarrassment for a country of such relative affluence. Yet, the focus of our unions is on children in developing countries, since that is where they think their competition comes from.

5. See Bhagwati and Dehejia (1994).

6. See Bhagwati (1991b).

7. See Bhagwati (1993).

8. See, for instance, the essays in Bhagwati and Patrick (1991), and in Bhagwati (1991c).

9. See Bhagwati and Irwin (1987) and Bhagwati (1988).

10. I draw this idea from John Whalley, who has recently asked why a hegemonic power like the United States has created FTAs and found small countries like Canada and Mexico to go along with it. He talks of the United States' using market access to itself as a way of extracting what he calls "side payments" that presumably would not be possible to extract in multilateral negotiations right out.

11. Thus, facing the United States in a one-on-one bargain, President Salinas had to accept the worst possible terms on intellectual property protection, something which the United States could not extract at the GATT earlier. Then, the Mexican acceptance of these outrageous terms was touted by the United Stated as the "model" which others should follow, with Special 301 threats and actions leveled at particularly recalcitrant countries. In the end, the concessions so gained by the United States at the GATT on intellectual property protection were dramatically one-sided and certainly excessive from a worldwide efficiency viewpoint, thanks to the strategy that I have identified in the text.

12. Thus, the proponents in Washington of the "GATT-plus" concept and phrase, when they imply that regionalism, aggressive unilateralism, and multilateralism are simply different routes to freeing trade, each simply separable from and additive to the others, forget this symbiotic relationship among them. They are as naive as the proponents of the "marriage-plus" view turned out to be in Robert Redford and Demi Moore's film, *An Indecent Proposal*.

References

Bhagwati, Jagdish. 1988. *Protectionism*. Cambridge: MIT Press.

Bhagwati, Jagdish. 1991a. "Free Traders and Free Immigrationists: Strangers or Friends?" New York: Russell Sage Foundation, photocopy.

———. 1991b. "Jumpstarting the GATT." *Foreign Policy* 83 (Summer): 105–18.

———. 1991c. *The World Trading System at Risk*. Princeton: Princeton University Press.

———. 1993. "Beyond NAFTA: Clinton's Trading Choices." *Foreign Policy* 91 (Summer): 155–62; chapter 27.

Bhagwati, Jagdish, and Vivek Dehejia. 1994. "Freer Trade and Wages of the Unskilled-Is Marx Striking Again?" In *Trade and Wages: Leveling Wages Down?*, edited by Jagdish Bhagwati and Marvin H. Kosters. Washington, D.C.: AEI Press.

Bhagwati, Jagdish, and Douglas A. Irwin. 1987. "The Return of the Recioprocitarians: U.S. Trade Policy Today." *World Economy* 10 (2): 109–30.

Bhagwati, Jagdish, and Hugh Patrick. 1991. *Aggressive Unilateralism*. Ann Arbor: University of Michigan Press.

VIII

Coping with Immigration

31   A Champion for Migrating Peoples

The United Nations High Commission of Refugees celebrated its fortieth anniversary last November. The occasion symbolized both its contribution, recognized by two Nobel prizes, and the gap in the international infrastructure regarding the world's fleeing and moving multitudes.

The International Monetary Fund (IMF), the World Bank, and the General Agreement on Tariffs and Trade (GATT) address the world's financial and trade problems. The New World Order now needs a World Migration Organization to oversee solutions to the major challenges posed by international migrations of all kinds, legal and illegal, forced and voluntary.

Refugee flows have exploded. They are currently above 17 million, counting not merely refugees in the narrow sense of those having a well-founded fear of persecution because of race, religion, or political belief—the definition that countries have been comfortable with to date. Refugees also include vast new flows of humanity fleeing for their lives from famine, pestilence, and war.

Internal refugees, as opposed to those who move across borders, have also become a standard feature of the landscape in Central America, Africa, and the Middle East.

Originally published in the *Christian Science Monitor* (February 28, 1992). Reprinted with permission.

Illegal immigration is also substantial, and it's likely to grow as population expands in the third world.

The immediate worries are out-migration from the former Soviet Union and Eastern Europe. This movement of people was suppressed in times past by emigration restrictions, and it's likely to happen now even if these nations manage their affairs soundly and become functioning economies.

The probable results: an overhaul of immigration regimes and the surrender of liberal values. This change could include more Draconian enforcement, as foreshadowed by the U.S. return of Haitians picked up at sea and the forced repatriation of Vietnamese boat refugees from Hong Kong.

Other ominous signs: the sacrifice of asylum traditions in some countries, summary expulsion of aliens (as happened recently to Zaireans in the Congo and to Yemenis in Saudi Arabia), and the denial of basic rights to illegal immigrants in order to deter their entry.

A World Migration Organization (WMO) could influence these developments, which are now largely ad hoc and reflect diverse national responses to emerging immigration crises. The WMO could do this in three ways.

Periodic Country Reviews

The WMO's principal task would be to track and monitor the immigration policies of countries. Like the pope, the WMO would have no troops. But by issuing comprehensive reviews of national policies and actions, it might embarrass countries into more humane and liberal ways of dealing with influxes of aliens.

This, in fact, is what the GATT has been doing since 1989. Selecting a few member countries at a time, GATT officials had issued eighteen trade policy review reports by the end of 1991. The reports brought into focus the failings and achievements of countries in the matter of free trade. The WMO has a worthy model here.

Burden-Sharing Indices

Like the Development Assistance Committee of the Organization for Economic Cooperation and Development, the WMO could also move toward developing "burden-sharing" indices of immigration altruism.

In regard to refugees, for example, a country such as Japan, with its tradition of being an insular nation with a homogeneous population, may be unable to absorb large numbers of refugees. But to compensate it might undertake a larger share of the cost of resettling people.

Codes of Rights and Obligations for Migrants

The WMO should seek to develop codes for the rights and obligations of different types of immigrants. Among the issues that need to be addressed: access by illegal migrants to welfare safety nets; the rights of their children to free public education alongside native children; and the voting rights of legal immigrants.

We need to work toward humane codes, building on the experience of progressive nations like the United States. A precedent exists in the international agreements on the unacceptability of forced repatriation and other intolerable practices. It will be an arduous task. But it is an endeavor to which humanity itself draws us.

32   Behind the Green Card

We imported workers and got men instead: so said the Swiss novelist Max Frisch as he contemplated the inability of Western European governments, facing the economic crisis of the 1970s, to return foreign guestworkers to their homes, despite the explicit understanding that the *gastarbeiter* program gave none of them the right to linger. In directly confronting the fate of human beings, immigration policy raises questions that escape easy answers. Should we exclude? How many should we exclude? Whom should we exclude? These questions, about the design of legal immigration quotas, are complex enough and are typically resolved by compromises dictated by economics, ethics, and politics. Except that they aren't really resolved: legal immigration quotas are rarely effective.

Aliens fly, swim, row, and walk in past our patrols and into our underclass. What should we do with the illegals already in our midst? Pursue them with ferocity? Create a climate of fear that prevents their riskless access to our social entitlements, including even the denial of public school to their children, in the hope that this will dull America's glitter and reduce the fevered and furtive

Originally published in the *New Republic* (May 14, 1990): 31–39. Reprinted with permission.

   This chapter reviews Julian L. Simon's *The Economic Consequences of Immigration* (Cambridge: Basil Blackwell, 1989), and George J. Borjas's *Friends or Strangers: The Impact of Immigrants on the U.S. Economy* (New York: Basic Books, 1989).

inflow? Or should we seek to ease their life instead, no matter their illegal status, humanely looking the other way since they are already here?

Other aliens land right at our doorstep, to seek first-asylum refuge. They challenge our ethical sensibilities and strain our public purse to the breaking point. Our return of the asylum-seekers to El Salvador and Guatemala led to the sanctuary movement; and Hong Kong's British masters face international outrage as they seek to deny asylum and return the boat people to Vietnam.

For the United States, a country whose history and psyche were defined by the open door of the nineteenth century, the operation of the closed door in the twentieth century has been particularly difficult. Starting with the national embrace of immigration restrictions in 1921, when the first quota limits were established, we have been witness to successive attempts at rewriting legislation, always in anguish, trying to come to terms with changing circumstances and sensibilities as best the political process permits.

The 1980s have seen one more such effort, ambitious in scope and complex in architecture. The admission of refugees was settled in the 1980 Refugee Act, which allocated 50,000 visas for "normal flow" refugees and permitted the president, in consultation with Congress, to increase the allocation. Illegal immigrants were addressed in the 1986 Immigration Act; its key features included the amnesty program and the introduction of employer sanctions penalizing the hiring of illegals. Now we are in the process of legislating the admission of all others. This three-layered legislation is designed to define our immigration policy until at least the end of this century. For that reason, a scholarly look at this entire edifice is an urgent necessity, especially since there are excellent reasons to think that it is seriously flawed.

Julian Simon's book should have undertaken this task. It does not. The bulk of it is narrowly targeted, instead, at the critics of liberal immigration policies, seeking to establish that immigrants do us good and that added numbers would do even more. Simon certainly has a keen nose for rubbish. He demolishes many of the farcical, if popular and effective, claims of the anti-immigrationists. His scalpel is particularly sharp when he confronts, with cool logic and cold facts, those who claim that immigrants, whether legal or illegal, are a large net burden on the tax system, taking more in entitlements than they pay in revenues. Where Roger Conner of the Federation for American Immigration Reform argues that "taxpayers are hurt by having to pay more for social services," and Leonard Chapman, then commissioner of the Immigration and Naturalization Service (INS), adds that "we spend millions every month supporting people who are not supposed to be here," Simon argues that the data demonstrate otherwise. The immigrants are young and pay more into the Social Security system; they do not have significantly greater unemployment rates, and do not therefore claim differentially higher unemployment benefits; and in any event, the illegals tend to keep their heads in the sand and out of trouble, forgoing benefits that they can claim only at peril. On balance, they bring profit, not loss, to our tax system.

If you were a victim of the alarmist assertions that immigration today is at an all-time high or that illegal immigration is in excess of 10 million, Simon will assure you that you do not know your history, that patient research yields more comforting numbers. Simon can be a formidable foe of foolishness. But not always. Every now and then he buries the rubbish of others under his own. This is partly because economics is a hard taskmaster: you know it well or you pay the price. Simon's turgid technicalities and elementary algebra create an air of scientific rigor, but they do not save him from lapses in economic argument when the going gets tough.

Simon argues, for instance, that immigration will be beneficial because a greater population means that "more of everything is produced, which promotes learning by doing." But surely more population need not lead to more production of everything; more babies are born, more diapers are demanded and produced, and the economy then *reduces* the production of shirts for the adults who must care for the babies and cannot afford to buy new shirts as often as before. Then again, as resources get reallocated due to the newborn, production may expand in those activities where the pace of learning by doing is less than in the sectors in which production declines.

But if Simon's economics can be sloppy, his statistical evidence is often cited with disregard for conceptual clarity, to draw conclusions that it cannot support. Thus, in urging that more people mean more prosperity, Simon asserts that the evidence shows larger population leading to higher "productivity." In support of this proposition he cites Hollis Chenery's 1960 study of the manufacturing sector: "All else being equal, if one country is twice as populous as another, output per worker is 20 percent larger. This is a very large positive effect of population size no matter how you look at it." But increased productivity must be properly defined as getting more from the same resources. Such an increase cannot be inferred from an increase in output per worker, which can increase because workers have more equipment to work with. Chenery's findings cannot be used to infer that "true" productivity increases with population.

Similarly, Simon cites Colin Clark's 1967 studies showing that the productivity of American industries relative to Canadian industries rises as their relative production levels rise. For Simon, this means that more "learning by doing" follows from higher production levels; with production assumed in turn to increase with population, immigration is proved to be beneficial to our productivity and hence to us. Yet, disregarding the inadequacy of Clark's productivity indices to the task at hand, the economist will surely wonder whether the causality runs the other way, with greater relative efficiency leading to higher relative production. Econometricians have ways of getting around this "identification problem," but Simon fails to identify it at all. As a consequence, the case for liberal immigration that is based on the benign link between more population and more productivity remains unproven.

Part of the problem is that Simon is so offended by what he castigates as the "bunkum" produced by the anti-immigration lobbies during the long battles over the 1986 legislation, and is so partisan in favor of more immigration (a conviction that he acknowledges and that I share) that he falls prey to the well-known "ballooning up" process. Where analysis and evidence show that the anti-immigrants' claims are not necessarily correct, he tends to conclude that they are necessarily not correct. Or he will occasionally indulge in the logical fallacy of *ignoratio elenchi*, more popularly known as creating a straw man. Thus, to counter the valid claim that many of our immigrants are ill-educated and low-skilled, he argues that they are more educated than the natives on average. This is interesting, but it is not the issue.

Simon's excesses follow also from his politics and his economics. A conservative, he leans toward optimism about the world's failings and pessimism about our ability to fix them. Even when he admits to problems that immigration occasionally causes, such as crowding in the schools, he asserts that in the long run things will wind up being better than they would have been. This optimism may be a useful corrective to the doomsayers, but it badly mars Simon's claims to scientific superiority over his adversaries. To take a gross example, he invokes "overlapping empirical studies" to claim the "absence of causal influence of population growth upon economic development," and then goes even further to assert that "in the *very* long run more people [should] have a *positive* net effect" because of the (unproven) productivity effects of more numbers. But a National Research

Council expert group of demographers and economists, including those cited by Simon, came to this conclusion in 1986, in their report on "Population Growth and Economic Development": "On balance, we reach the qualitative conclusion that slower population growth would be beneficial to economic development for most developing countries."

If Simon's politics make him Panglossian, his economics makes him indifferent to the distributional consequences of immigration that bother others. Conservative economics tends to ignore distributional issues, concentrating instead on efficiency. Economists' conventional "welfare criterion" for approving a policy change is simply that it should be *possible* to compensate the losers while some gravy remains with the winners. Whether the compensation is actually made is not an issue normally raised by those who use this "potential compensation" criterion in a knee-jerk fashion. Sophisticated economists, by contrast, understand that there is a world of difference, for the losers, between potential compensation and actual compensation. Few would approve of immigration if Simon and I profited from the immigration of domestics, the wages of black domestics fell (or rose less), and we declared this a beneficial event simply because we could compensate the blacks but actually did not. Yet conservative economists are more likely in practice to settle for the potential-compensation approach, arguing that worrying about compensation will hold up efficiency-enhancing changes, and that things will work out well in the wash for everyone.

Simon's review of the empirical analyses of the wage and unemployment effects of immigration cannot really dispose of the argument that specific disadvantaged groups are adversely affected from time to time. Indeed, George Borjas, a prominent empirical researcher on immigration into the United States, concludes in his carefully argued and gracefully written book that a 10 percent increase in the number of immigrants will depress the wages of the foreign-born by at least 2 percent. But Simon's response is, again, optimism about the long run—and, in any event, "where the society responds with restrictive action to the request of every group—even every relatively poor group—which is threatened by imports or immigrants or technological change or change in public tastes, there will be no end to the claimants, and the economy will suffer from drag."

This view really won't do, and not only because of its ethical unattaactiveness. It is also politically naive. Pluralist politics is not merely about the size of the pie, but also, even more, about who gets the bigger slice. The adverse distributional impact caused by external phenomena such as immigration and imports cannot be equated with that resulting from internal sources of change; Simon ignores the fact that the revealed social contract suggests a considerably lower level of tolerance by most groups for uncompensated harm imposed on them by the former in the interest of efficiency.

Immigration is manifestly one area where retreat into the potential-compensation option won's work. Simon's failure to see this is also evident, and particularly crippling, in his discussion of the effects of immigration on revenues and expenditures. He barely focuses on the nature of the net gain: the federal government's gain exceeds the local governments' losses. That is precisely where the question of distribution arises again: local communities such as Lowell, Massachusetts, and Miami are worried about the costs of immigrant and refugee influx and the failure of the federal government (the winner, by Simon's calculations) to compensate them, the losers.

Simon's case for liberal immigration, a policy that is fundamentally sound, is thus underargued and overstated. The fearful stereotypes that are used against the immigrants—principally that they create unemployment among us—do not survive his (and Borjas's) scrutiny. Immigrants become productive members of our society, and they do not subtract from our income, leaving distributional effects aside. But the claim that they actually enhance our well-being is another matter altogether. It requires proof that the immigrants put more into the pie than they take for themselves, leaving us with extra icing. Unfortunately, Simon's assertion that there are beneficial productivity effects will carry no conviction except to those already converted. The surprising demonstration that we take more in revenues from the immigrants than they take in entitlements from us is all that firmly supports Simon's optimism; but the magnitudes involved are, at best, not staggeringly large.

Simon's brief, penultimate chapter on immigration reform is disappointing in other ways. Astonishingly, he fails to ground his views firmly in a critical appraisal of the key aspects of the important 1980 and 1986 legislation; the two acts of Congress are not even in the index. Nor does Simon adequately recognize the many important differences among legal, illegal, and refugee admissions. He does not recognize, for instance, that illegals raise unique economic, ethical, and social issues because many of them enter the underclass, whereas legally admitted aliens do not. As for refugees, Simon thinks of them essentially in terms of their productivity vis-à-vis other migrants. He recommends that they be treated identically, and that, when they are not productive, we take the productive ones and bribe other nations into accepting the unproductive ones; this, he thinks, would mean the accommodation of more refugees in the world.

This is bad economics. We must compare potential immigrants' productivity not just in the United States but also elsewhere, if an "optimal" economic allocation is to be made. But it is bad ethics, too. Can we really assign refugees this way, altogether regardless of their feelings and aspirations? Would we send the Vietnamese boat refugees in Hong Kong to China simply because China will accept them from us at a price? Would we really be able to take in no refugees at all, as Simon suggests, getting other countries to "buy" them from us, when we pride ourselves on having an immigration policy based more on refugee and familial criteria and not on the purely who-is-best-for-our-needs criterion that underlay the Western European *gastarbeiter* system?

The science of economic policy concerns the search for maximizing or satisficing solutions subject to constraints, but those constraints are provided not merely by resources and know-how, as the elementary economics textbooks teach, but also by ethics, culture, history, and politics. In fact, the truly difficult issues that we face in immigration policy are not narrowly economic at all. The questions raised by illegal immigration and by first-asylum refugees go to the heart of the matter, and to our hearts. The 1986 act, designed to deal with illegals, and the 1980 act, addressed to refugees, are not adequate to the problems we confront. The former was wrongly premised and has become an irrelevance; its fate was predictable. The latter has been overtaken by the sudden emergence of first-asylum refugees; its inadequacy could not have been readily anticipated. But it's worth starting with a look at the current state of debate about legal immigration, before turning to illegals and refugees.

Legal Immigration

How are any given quotas to be assigned among different claimants? This question has been debated in Congress. American policy since 1965 has overwhelmingly favored admissions on family criteria. Of the 270,000 numerically limited legal admissions in 1988, nearly 90 percent were assigned to the familial categories, First to Fifth Preference. Indeed, since 1978, 95 percent of all nonrefugee legal immigrants have been admitted under such criteria. Is such a policy "fair"? Is it economically the most rewarding for us?

Some think that the policy is unfair because it is "nepotistic." The ethnic groups that do not profit from it, such as the Irish, object strenuously (and effectively through the good offices of Senators Kennedy and Moynihan), especially to the Fifth Preference for "brothers and sisters" of U.S. citizens, with its quota of 64,800 in 1988. The defense of "nepotism" comes, on the other hand, from Italians and Indians, who evidently have an abundance of siblings at the gates of our consulates in Rome and New Delhi. Fairness, in sum, is in the mind of the beholder; and conflicting views of it are resolved by the relative strength of the different pressure groups that play the political game.

For economists such as Simon and Borjas, however, the key problem with the family-reunification system is that it does not maximize the attendant import of skills, and hence the benefit to the United States from immigration. Simon simply assumes this when he argues, oddly, that "independent persons selected on economic grounds would be preferable to relatives, were there to be no humanitarian considerations. This change is unlikely, however, so no further consideration will be given to the matter." Borjas, by contrast, makes this a central issue in his work, arguing that the skill level of immigration has actually declined with the massive shift in 1965 to the family-reunification system. Presumably, the familial system has shifted the source of immigration to developing countries that send immigrants with lower educational levels than the earlier immigrants from the Western developed nations.

Borjas's evidence is mainly indirect, based on the fact that earnings estimates of the entering "foreign born" from census data show a decline. But earnings and skills are not the same thing. Nor do the data permit an explicit linkage between the category of the immigrant visa and the earning profiles: the thesis does not necessarily hold, for instance, for spouses who enter under the Second Preference from India. The reason lies in economics. There is an active "market" in India for potential spouses for holders of American green cards and citizens of Indian origin. The latter, because of the potentially large pool of candidates, can choose spouses who are educated and skilled enough to yield high economic returns to the family.

Moreover, the criticism that the familial system produces significant deterioration in the skill levels of immigrants entering the United States, as opposed to a skills-based system of the kind that both Simon and Borjas seem to favor, is particularly doubtful if we consider also that such skills-based systems are hard to fine-tune successfully (as shown by the Canadian "points" system of immigration, which grades applicants on a scale of zero to 100, requiring a minimum of fifty, and awarding extra points for education, age, and initiative). But then, if a skills-based system will not necessarily produce a truly substantial increase in skills for the United States, and if family values are important to us, then should economists, worrying only about the economic efficiency of immigration, encourage all the current fuss in Congress against the familial system?

Illegal Immigration

A worldwide phenomenon today, illegal immigration is truly substantial for the United States. It comes largely from Mexico, though it now appears, based on the 1980 census and other evidence, that Mexican illegals amounted to not much more than half of the illegals here in the early 1980s. The influx from Mexico is the product of the economics of vast disparity in opportunity between the two countries, the fortuitous circumstance of a long border, and the morality that makes us unable to sustain drastic, Draconian measures to enforce sanctions. Many cross the Rio Grande firm in the belief that Porfirio Diaz got it exactly wrong when he said: "Poor Mexico, how far from God and how near the United States."

We intercept abundantly. But all we do is send the Mexicans back; and they cross the Rio Grande again, and again, until they strike pay dirt in getting past the INS. We do not construct Berlin Walls, we do not shoot gleefully at the people violating our borders. And we cannot expect that internal enforcement against those who get past the border can be successful in a civilized society. Attempts to cut off the demand for illegal labor by enacting employer sanctions to penalize those who hire illegal aliens, as in our 1986 Immigration Control and Reform Act, have been generally unsuccessful wherever they have been adopted, even in such "no-nonsense" societies as Germany and Switzerland. Judges have been lenient; it is hard to come down heavily when the crime is the employment of impoverished aliens and the punishment could mean their deprivation and their destitution. And in the United States, we have had yet another civil rights complication. Faced with the prospect of discrimination against lookalike citizens and legal aliens, our legislation has often emasculated employer sanctions, reducing their bite even before they could haul offending employers to lenient courts.

There are more constraints. We cannot contemplate making enough investment in Mexico, or granting it sufficient aid, to make enough of a dent in Mexican misery to roll back the numbers seeking entry to the north. If anything, limited improvements, which is all we can hope for, could enable more Mexicans to finance the journey, and may paradoxically increase the illegal influx and compound the problem.

Given the fetters on policymaking that derive from ethics, and the paradoxes that derive from economics, we have no option except to regard as infeasible the goal of reducing illegal immigration to negligible levels. Since illegals will remain in our midst, and more will keep coming, the only meaningful, and indeed compelling, question for us becomes a moral one: How do we treat these illegal aliens with decency, assuring them and their families the civil rights that would rescue them from the afflictions of their illegal status? In my view, the answer has to take us in the direction of less internal enforcement, more protected and effective access by the illegals to our welfare programs, and equal rights (for example, to education and health) for the children of illegals as for the children of legal aliens and citizens. These are solutions that contrast sharply with Simon's quick and conventional prescription to get tough on illegals' access to welfare services.

The 1986 legislation failed to get to this redefinition of our policy because it proceeded from the entirely false premise that illegal immigration could be eliminated. It offered amnesty to the backlog of aliens already here. To shut off new inflows, it created employer sanctions, while promising a mild increase in border enforcement. It was apparent, though not to many on the 1978 Select Commission on Immigration and Refugee Policy (which was split on the issue of employer sanctions as on many others) or to the architects of the 1986 act, that neither measure could succeed in its objectives. Now we know who was right. A few more than 2 million have benefited from the amnesty, while a quarter of a million are expected to get legalized under the SAW (Special Agricultural Workers) Program. Large numbers, in other words, almost certainly languish in their illegal status, if Borjas's cautious estimate of 3 million to 4 million in 1980 is accepted. The illegal flows continue. The INS apprehended 1.6 million illegals at the border in (fiscal year) 1986; in 1988 the numbers were still running close to a million.

First-Asylum Refugees

The drafters of the 1980 Refugee Act imagined that we would continue to enjoy the luxury of deciding mainly on the admission requests of refugees situated *elsewhere*, distributing our quotas to those we favored and denying them to others with little fuss, and even less guilt since they were distant, their sorrows beyond our consciousness and our conscience. The problems that countries of first asylum face—how to handle refugees already in their midst, how to make the morally unsettling decisions (to deport them, to offer them the protection of our international-legal obligations without opening the door to all claims), how to handle sudden and large inflows—were matters that we simply did not think through.

In fact, the 1980 act did not even specify how asylum claims were to be handled; the matter was left to the attorney general. All that we had done, starting with our accession to the 1967 Protocol, an international treaty adhered to by nearly a hundred countries, was to accept the procedure of *refoulement*, or return of a refugee, that a civilized nation should follow in treating first-asylum refugees. In particular, we would have to forgo the *refoulement* to territories where their life or freedom would be threatened. In the practice of those principles, however, problems soon arose.

We have now had three "crises" with first-asylum refugees. The Haitian "boat refugees," who started to arrive in late 1972 and increased in numbers in the late 1970s, were the first wave to attract retribution from the INS. Then, beginning in 1980, came the refugees from El Salvador and Guatemala. And in late 1988 a resurgence of Central American refugees occurred, principally from Nicaragua and El Salvador. Our response included such novel enforcements as taking aliens off domestic flights and joint combing operations with Mexicans (whose firm objections to collaboration directed at Mexican illegals crossing the Rio Grande contrast with their complicity in targeting the unfortunate Central Americans).

In each instance, the INS reacted with actions that offend our ethical traditions and violate the spirit, if not the letter, of the principles on asylum that we have embraced. In each instance, men and women of conscience objected, recalling us to our moral principles and providing much of the countervailing force that has constrained the INS from continued and further excesses. Our treatment of the Haitians illustrates this only too well. It was truly scandalous. James Silk of the U.S. Committee for Refugees records the existence of a 1978 INS "Haitian Program" under which "asylum claims were prejudged, various techniques were used to keep Haitians from gaining legal counsel, and hearings were speeded up and simultaneously scheduled, making it impossible for the few available lawyers to appear at all of them." (Judge James Lawrence King stopped this program in July 1980.)

Reversing the earlier policy of releasing most arriving aliens, the INS then started detaining all Haitian arrivals in South Florida, placing many in Camp Krome and others in federal detention facilities. This policy of detention was later extended to all arrivals, discrimination against Haitians being held legally untenable. The incarceration meant real hardship: separation of families (since men and women were typically divided), restraints put on contacts with relatives outside, obstacles to contacting lawyers who could help process asylum claims with an INS keen to see them denied—some of the many ways in which our procedures violated the spirit of Protocol 31, which bars any penalties on asylum-seekers and binds us not to restrict their movement unnecessarily.

And that is not the worst part of the treatment of the refugees by the INS. In the Haitian case, we went a step further. Knowing full well that incarcerations and the denial of due process to the Haitians (admittedly not their right under our Constitution, which nonetheless affords some protections to aliens not legally accepted by us) would lead to protests and undercut support for these methods, the Reagan administration proceeded to interdict the Haitian boats at sea. While official noises were made about ensuring *nonrefoulement*, and the agreement of President Duvalier was obtained that no returned Haitian would be prosecuted (though unauthorized exit from Haiti was legally a crime), one would have to be morally defective to pretend that *refoulement*, with retribution in Haiti, did not occur. The problem of dealing with Haitian first-asylum claimants was to be solved by inter-diction, away from our eyes and our outrage, by the return of the Haitians to the tender mercies of the Tontons Macoute.

We could persist in these policies for so long because there was no sizable Haitian community in the United Sates and no power-ful lobby to plead their cause, until public-interest groups began to agitate on their behalf. But why did we beat up on these defenseless boat people in the first place? The reason has to do with panic.

The American panic is owed partly to the large size of illegal immigration lately, and to the illusion, as Simon beautifully demonstrates, that it has been vastly larger than it actually is. Frustrated by the long and porous border to the south, the INS, with the administration not far behind, has tended to pick on anyone else they can, putting a finger in any hole they can find in the dike. Thus, we have been going after foreign students seeking admission here, getting our consuls to read their minds and to decide, arbitrarily and without due process, and without even bothering to justify their actions to the applicants, that a visa must be denied because the student is "likely to immigrate." Merito-rious but poor students have been denied entry, on the empiri-cally nonsensical and morally offensive assumption that they are more likely to stay on than dumb but rich students. Their mis-fortune is simply that we can seize on them and keep them out.

We poked our finger in the Haitians' eyes for much the same reason: they were within the reach of our power. And the American panic also reflects the fear that, if the Haitians, and now the Central Americans, were treated more humanely, we would be sending "the wrong message," and countless numbers would come. Fear has big eyes, goes the Russian proverb.

The panic must be met not by the methods of the INS, but by respect for our traditions and our obligations, by adhering to genuinely fairminded procedures to evaluate the asylum claims. Brutality and cutting corners are unworthy of a nation that lives by the rule of law and respect for human rights, both virtues that we properly urge on others. And the notion that toughness will deter substantial numbers from seeking entry into the United States is arguably false. Even if we were to intern them all, and then deny them all asylum applications, violating all canons of decency and some canons of international law, should we not expect many of these same people, fleeing war and devastation in Central America, simply to join the masses that cross the Rio Grande illegally? We would only have diverted the inflow into another channel.

If we cannot bring ourselves to offer asylum to many of these people, moreover, let us at least meet their needs by offering them temporary safe haven until normal conditions return to their homelands, as now in Nicaragua. Vastly poorer countries than us have done this for much larger numbers: India for nearly 10 million refugees from East Pakistan, Pakistan for almost half as many refugees from Afghanistan. An acknowledgment of our moral obligation, and its codification in legislation, are called for.

If our current policies toward illegals and refugees were thus recast, there surely would be some increase in the number of aliens who get in. And there would surely be some reduction in the net benefit to our revenues as we treat illegals better. But neither is a cause for alarm. The real problem is distributional. We need, in particular, more generous compensatory assistance to the communities that must bear the financial brunt of larger alien inflows. As Simon shows, Washington is the winner in revenues from immigration, and it should find the funds to finance the losers. This is not too much to ask, when the consonance of our policies with our values is at stake.

33   Control Immigration at the Border

Neither the problem of illegal immigration nor "solutions" like the Simpson-Mazzoli Bill—which narrowly failed to clear a congressional conference committee and become law this year—will go away. Attempts at reviving Simpson-Mazzoli are already under way, but the debate over immigration reform is being sidetracked by its wrongheaded approach. The bill focuses on internal solutions (employer sanctions and amnesty) when the simplest and more effective approach is an external solution, that is, *increased* border enforcement coupled with *reduced* immigration controls inside this country. The bill's policies are, in fact, counterproductive.

In its final conference-committee form, Simpson-Mazzoli— named after its sponsors Sen. Alan Simpson (R-Wyoming) and Rep. Romano L. Mazzoli (D-Kentucky)—had two widely shared popular objectives and two associated and less popular objectives.

One objective was to restrict illegal immigration, or what is picturesquely described as "regaining control of our borders." The other was to ameliorate the conditions that the "underclass" of illegal immigrants often face.

The first objective is primarily economic and political. It reflects alarmist judgments concerning the adverse effects of current

---

Originally published in the *Wall Street Journal* (February 1, 1985).

levels of immigration. It would be best if we learned to treat illegal immigration as a phenomenon rather than a problem, but it may be too late for that. The second objective, by contrast, is social. If Mexicans live at home, miserable and destitute, distance places them beyond our view and responsibility. But if they are in our midst, even though illegally, their exploitation offends our moral sensibility.

Employer Sanctions

Simpson-Mazzoli offered two policies to address these objectives. Employer sanctions were proposed. The conference-committee version would have imposed criminal penalties for persistent hiring of illegal aliens. By "cutting off jobs," the bill expected to eliminate the magnet that draws in the illegals. Coupled with the sanctions was the amnesty provision. Its principal rationale was the rescue of enormous numbers of illegals from the underclass.

Between the sanctions and the amnesty provisions the bill's proponents believed the two objectives would be achieved. But ironically, we may expect such measures to produce precisely the opposite results: The influx of illegals would increase and their status in the underclass could worsen.

Simply put, sanctions will be ineffective for several reasons rooted in our social, political, and juridical traditions. At the same time, the sanctions will draw resources away from patrolling the borders, where the numbers of people who get past are affected somewhat by the level of enforcement. Thus, the net result could well be an increase in illegal immigration. At the same time, by increasing the disruption—and hence harassment—at work that attempts at enforcing them would cause, the sanctions will only increase the sense of vulnerability that leads to the immigrants' underclass status.

The ineffectiveness of the sanctions can be safely predicted. Self-interest alone can be expected to lead employers to lobby and litigate against the Immigration and Naturalization Service, draining its budget and weakening effective enforcement. The lobbying groups of ethnic Americans who have strenuously opposed the sanctions will use similar tactics. But morality is the more critical factor and, in this instance, only weakens further the enforceability of the sanctions.

The principal problem is that we are dealing with human beings. As the Swiss novelist Max Frisch has remarked, reflecting on the European difficulties with guest workers: "We imported workers and got men." Our natural instincts make it hard to collaborate in efforts to seize and deport people, no matter what we think of illegal immigration in the abstract. Indeed, it is remarkable that when the administration incarcerated the Haitian boat people, who had no organized ethnic group here to lobby on their behalf, it did not take long for civil liberties groups to take up the boat people's cause with eventual success.

Our courts also have repeatedly struck down discrimination against resident legal aliens. Recent Supreme Court rulings affirmed the rights of the children of illegal aliens to a public education and the right of illegal aliens to the protection of federal labor laws. More remarkable is last month's acquittal by a Corpus Christi, Texas, jury of Jack Elder on charges of illegally transporting aliens into the United States Mr. Elder's defense was simply a moral one, that is, that he and his associate Roman Catholic lay workers were offering sanctuary to Salvadorans fleeing political persecution.

Employer sanctions have a poor record of results. The General Accounting Office found that the sanctions have not been particularly effective elsewhere, even though some countries such as France and Canada have subsequently chosen to increase their reliance on them.

By contrast, enhanced border enforcement has resulted in increased interceptions. Between 1965 and 1970, the number of seized illegal aliens tripled to more than 300,000 a year. In recent years, the seizures have reached as high as one million a year. Doubtless, this reflects increased attempts at entry. But stepped-up enforcement by the Border Patrol, now with more than 2,500 officers, has evidently played a major role too. Even if every intercepted alien attempts to get back in again, the higher rate of seizure as a result of increased enforcement must cut back the total number that eventually get through.

As for the amnesty program, the other pillar of the Simpson-Mazzoli architecture, it is also flawed. One can plausibly maintain that it could accelerate the influx, magnifying the total size of the illegal immigrants in the foreseeable future, while increasing their underclass status.

An amnesty implies that an illegal status with associated low wages will be transformed into legal status at significantly higher wages. Since in economics and public policy bygones are rarely bygones, an amnesty now may lead to the expectation of amnesty later, encouraging more people to attempt illegal entry-especially if they believe wages will be higher under an amnesty than before.

If Rep. Robert Garcia (D-New York) is right, as I think he is, then the most liberal amnesty program we can adopt will legalize only 25 percent of those already here illegally. We will thus, over time, probably have *more* illegal immigrants here than we do now. It is also likely that the INS may well feel compelled, once the amnesty has been offered and implemented, to "go after" and harass more intensely those who remain illegal: Those not "re-born" may appear more damnable! This would only make them more insecure, accentuating their underclass psychology and status.

Border Enforcement

I would therefore propose an altogether different approach. In essence, we should greatly diminish internal enforcement and correspondingly increase external enforcement, that is, at the border. Border enforcement cannot eliminate, or even significantly reduce, the influx as long as we seek to control the border consistent with our traditions (which should rightly preclude Soviet-bloc-style techniques). But it does have an impact; and the measure would be sufficiently visible to satisfy those who feel that we should be "doing something" to control our border. The "price" counterpart of border enforcement could be to encourage creation of an "economic fence" at the border, by promoting investments and economic activity near the border that could act as an incentive for aliens to stop there and step off the road to the U.S. hinterland.

The downgrading of internal enforcement would mean dropping the employer sanctions. It would also mean going easy on INS enforcement, much as we did during the last census count in 1980. A de facto policy posture of this kind, which preserves the important distinction between legality and illegality, would substantially reduce the fear and consequent exploitation that the illegals suffer.

This mix of policies, which puts the focus of immigration control and reform back at the border, offers the prospect of getting as close to our shared central objectives as possible. It requires legislative action for major increases in the border-enforcement budget, and action from the White House to reduce INS enforcement at home.

34   Sanctuary

This is the story of the Sanctuary movement that captured the headlines in 1986.

Faced with indisputable evidence that U.S. authorities, in violation even of the limited safeguards built into our laws, were returning to certain death the desperate refugees that were arriving from El Salvador and Guatemala, a number of men and women took a searing look at their conscience and then the law into their own hands.

They turned to a higher law, risking the wrath of an administration that had sacrificed our moral impulses and traditions in refugee policy to the passionate pursuit of anticommunism in Central America. The risk was real; the retribution came swiftly with federal indictments and conviction.

Ann Crittenden tells us, blow by blow, how the underground railroad was organized, with the aid of hundreds of church groups, several activists, and widespread outpouring of support across the country, to assist border crossings and to provide safe haven to those refugees. In the end, as the Sanctuary movement gained national and international attention, the administration moved and a grand jury in Pheonix, Arizona, indicted a targeted few on January 10, 1985, for a conspiracy to smuggle aliens into

This chapter reviews Ann Crittenden's *Sanctuary: A Story of American Conscience and the Law in Collision* (New York: Weidenfeld & Nicolson, 1988). It was commissioned by the *New Leader* but remained unpublished.

the country. Eighteen months later, U.S. District Court Judge Earl H. Carroll, whose anti-Sanctuary bias and judicial conduct are described by Ms. Crittenden sufficiently candidly to make the reader sit up in consternation, predictably sentenced five members of the Sanctuary movement to three to five years in detention. But, reflecting extensive sympathy for the defendants and, more compelling for sure, an appeal from Senator Dennis DeConcini, to whom he owed his judicial elevation, the judge immediately put them on probation.

Ann Crittenden's narrative is immensely moving. She writes with passion and compassion, sketching events and portraying people with an artist's eye and a writer's pen, building up the narrative to a climax and shattering our complacency on the way. The book is worth reading for the Sanctuary movement's account alone. But its value lies yet more in focusing our attention on the tangled mess that our immigration policy has gotten into.

The problems that our present immigration policy confronts, and the failure of our 1986 legislation to address them meaningfully, can only be understood by grasping one single fact. It is that immigration is par excellence an issue that is at the crossroads of economics and ethics. And, as Ann Crittenden's book amply underlines, moral sensibilities and traditions can limit, indeed cripple, the economic efficacy of restrictive immigration policies, requiring one to reexamine one's entire approach to the problem from the ground up. Indeed, this is precisely what we need to do in the matter of illegal immigration, which has been an overriding issue for at least a decade.

Max Weber wrote of the paradox of unanticipated consequences. With illegal immigration, the problem rather is one of consequences that are totally predictable. Restrictions inevitably generate evasion; they are porous therefore in varying degrees. Since nation-states everywhere have embraced exclusionary legislation in the twentieth century, illegal immigration is a worldwide phenomenon today.

But our illegal immigration is truly substantial. Arising chiefly from Mexico, it is a product of the economics of vast disparity in opportunity between the two countries, the fortuitous circumstance of a long border, and the ethics that makes us unwilling and unable to take drastic, Draconian measures to enforce sanctions.

Millions cross our borders, firm in the belief that, one way or another, if not immediately then later, they will make their way into the United States. We intercept abundantly: more than a million annual apprehensions have occured recently. But we simply send them back; they cross again, and then again, until they strike pay dirt in getting past the INS. We do not put up walls or barbed wires, nor do we shoot freely and gleefully at those violating our borders: neither our people nor the Mexican people and president would tolerate incarcerations and worse.

Nor can we expect that internal enforcement against those who penetrate past the border can be successful in civilized societies. Attempts to cut off the demand for illegal labor by enacting "employer sanctions" to penalize those who hire illegal aliens, as in our 1986 Immigration Control and Reform Act, have been generally unsuccessful wherever adopted, indeed even in the law-and-order societies such as Germany and Switzerland. Judges have proven too lenient: it is hard to come down heavily when the crime is the employment of destitute aliens and the punishment could mean their total devastation. At home, we have had yet another civil rights complication. Faced with the prospect of discrimination against look-alike citizens and legal aliens, our legislation has effectively emasculated employer sanctions, turning them into a paper tiger, reducing their bite even before offending employers were taken by INS to court.

Nor can we contemplate making enough investment in Mexico, or granting it sufficient aid, to make a dramatic enough dent on Mexican misery to roll back the numbers seeking illegal entry to the north.

Given these constraints on policymaking from the direction of ethics and the paradoxes that afflict policies from the direction of economics, we have no option except to regard as infeasible the goal of reducing illegal immigration to negligible levels. Since illegals are therefore here to stay, and to keep coming, the only meaningful, and indeed compelling, question for us becomes an ethical one: how do we treat these illegal aliens with decency, assuring them and their families the civil rights that would rescue them from the afflictions of their illegal status? In my view, the answer has to take us in the direction of less internal enforcement, more protected and effective access by the illegals to our welfare programs, and equal rights (for example, to education and health) for the children of illegals as for the children of legal aliens and citizens.

The 1986 legislation failed to get to this redefinition of our policy because it proceeded from the entirely false premise that illegal immigration could be eliminated. It offered amnesty to the backlog of aliens already here. To shut off new inflows, it created employer sanctions, while promising a mild increase in border enforcement. It was apparent, though not to many including the Select Commision on Immigration and Refugee Policy (established in 1978 under the chairmanship of Father Hesburgh) and the architects of the 1986 act, that neither measure could succeed in its objectives. Now, we know for sure who was right. Not more than 1.5 million appear to have benefited from the amnesty: greater numbers are estimated to languish in their illegal status. The illegal inflows continue. The 1986 legislation has become irrelevant at best.

The ethical questions raised by the presence of illegals in our midst remain and must be faced. Alongside the related question of how we treat the refugees who stream across our borders, whose inflow we are able to control no more effectively, these evidently constitute the most critical agenda in immigration policy today.

35 Student Visas Drop Anchor

Governments' efforts to control people typically lead to un-anticipated consequences as the authorities try to cope with the evasions and avoidance always prompted by the controls. Immigration controls are no exception. A particularly important and offensive but little-noticed consequence for the American immigration system relates to foreign students.

The American system permits foreign students to convert their student vises to immigrant status, and student "stay-ons" make up a sizable share of the total number of what the immigration authorities call "professional, technical, and kindred" immigrants into the United States. Running close to 20,000 annually in recent years, on average they accounted for more than 65 percent of the professional and technical immigrants who entered the country each year from 1970 to 1978.

A number of these young people do indeed come here for higher education and then return to their own countries with new "human capital." Many others, however, are using their American education as an instrument of migration—a way through the heavily guarded door. Paradoxically, some of these young people who are determined to migrate have had excellent educations in their home countries but have decided to enter inferior American universities and acquire educationally un-rewarding American degrees simply because it may enable them eventually to exchange their student visas for immigrant status.

Clearly, those who seek an education in the United States only to immigrate are violating the spirit and letter of their student visas, which are issued on the declared presumption that the applicant does not intend to immigrate.

American consuls abroad, who are required to satisfy them-selves that applicants for temporary visas do not intend to stay in the United States, have in consequence been tougher recently in denying visas to students who, in their judgment, are more likely to immigrate as stay-ons. Consuls are not required to disclose and justify their reasoning to the foreign students who are denied visas, but it seems clear enough that in these cases their judg-ments often have little to do with "due process" or "fairness"—no matter how well-in-tentioned the consular officers may be.

What is particularly disturbing is that the toughness in re-stricting entry to foreign students has begun to weigh heavily against students with limited economic means. Why? Consuls assume that poor students are likely to immigrate because of "need" whereas rich students are not. Certainly, the official visa requirements—applicants are asked to produce certificates from Americans with huge bank balances who promise to be responsi-ble for the students and from people who indicate that a job waits for them at home—often work against poorer applicants.

In fact, however, there is no evidence to support the pre-sumption that the poor migrate while the rich do not. And even if it did—even if that were the general statistical trend—that would hardly mean that every rich or poor individual was going to act according to the statistical trends. Morever, the effect is to bias immigration toward the rich rather than the meritorious—an outcome that is surely at odds with the fundamental values that underlie American public policy.

What should be done about the foreign students using their educational status as a way to get around immigration controls? One more equitable and efficient response would be to tighten up the procedures for converting student visas to immigrant status. But better still would be to do nothing. Why? Because, in fact, the student stay-ons often bring great assets to the United States. They bring skilled labor into the country. They are also more readily assimilated than many less educated immigrants into the mainstream of American cultural and social life. Their numbers are small and, even if the consuls are instructed to reverse their present procedures, can fully be expected to remain manageable.

We are only shooting ourselves in the foot by raising inequitable restrictions on student entry into the country.

36   The U.S. Brain Gain—At the Expense of Blacks?

On April 29, 1992, Congress began hearings on a bill (H.R. 4595: American Math and Science Support Act) that recognized the preponderance of foreigners in American science and engineering graduate schools. The bill's premise was that this is inherently bad for the United States. It proposed, therefore, a drastic reduction in the number of foreigners in these programs. The sponsor of the bill (Paul Henry, R-Michigan) died and, therefore, so did the bill. But the nativist sentiments it reflected have survived. They continue to surface in different ways.

Indeed, some educators now claim that foreign students are responsible for the dearth of black Ph.D.s. In a recent front-page story in the *New York Times*,[1] Frank Morris, Dean of Graduate Studies at Morgan State University—historically a black university—and president of the Council of Historically Black Graduate Schools, argues: "There clearly seems to be a move afoot to freeze out American minorities, especially black males, from future faculty positions.... At the heart of it is a fundamental aspect of American culture that really does value some immigrants over some American minority groups—university departments just don't believe many minorities can be successful."

Originally published in *Challenge* (March–April 1996): 50–54, with Milind Rao. Reprinted with permission.

He goes on to claim that the image of the "aggressive black male in the laboratories is unnerving [to the faculty]," while that of "the model Asian immigrant scholar is attractive."

While reflecting the natural frustration and anguish about the slow pace at which blacks are moving up the educational ladder, such sentiments are misplaced. Foreign students are not the cause of the problem. Reducing their numbers would not be its solution either. In fact, such a pseudosolution will do certain harm, adversely affecting American supremacy in science and technology and harming foreign students to no advantage for us.

The Facts

The facts on foreign students are truly dramatic. In 1990, 62 percent of engineering doctorates in the United States were given to foreignborn students, mainly Asian. The figures are almost as high in mathematics, computer science, and the physical sciences. In economics (which, at graduate level, is a fairly technical subject requiring familiarity with college-level mathematics), the Committee on Graduate Education of the American Economics Association (COGEE) similarly found that in 1990 54 percent of the Ph.D.s awarded in economics went to foreign students. In the past two decades, graduate programs in these fields have witnessed an upward trend in foreign admissions, chiefly from Asian countries, such as India, South Korea, and China.[2]

Most of these students are among the best in their own countries. India, for instance, produces about 25,000 engineers (at the bachelor level) every year, only 2,000 (or about 8 percent) of whom graduate from the Indian Institutes of Technology (IITs), which are modeled on MIT and Caltech. (Every year 100,000 of India's top students take a competitive examination for the 2,000 places at the IITs, in contrast to about 10,000 applicants for the 1,000 places at MIT.) Seventy-eight percent of the U.S. engineering Ph.D.s awarded to Indians went to graduates of the IITs. Almost half (48 percent) of all Taiwanese students who received Ph.D.s in the United States attended either the National Taiwan University or Cheng Kung University. Even more telling, 65 percent of the Korean students who received science and engineering Ph.D.s in the United States were graduates of one university—Seoul National University. The numbers were almost as high for the elite schools of the PRC: Beijing University and Tsinghua University.[3]

These top students of Asia come to our graduate programs for several reasons. Our graduate programs are among the best in the world. But, equally, success in them opens up the strong possibility of becoming what immigration experts call a "student stay-on" in the United States. Indeed, over 70 percent of foreign-born Ph.D.s remain in the United States, many eventually becoming citizens.

Although the attraction of U.S. graduate schools for foreign students is high, it is the science, engineering, and economics graduate programs that profit most from it, rather than our professional schools such as business, law, and medicine. That is in part because our top students opt to go to these professional schools rather than into science and engineering (S&E). The average returns on investments made in higher education are not substantially higher in the former; if you succeed, however, you succeed wildly, and that gamble often dominates the choice of careers. For most of the gifted foreign-born students, however, the choice is dictated by the fact that they simply do not have the cash or the credit to enter the expensive professional schools, whereas the graduate programs in engineering, science, and economics offer a more abundant supply of talent-seeking scholarships.[4]

Consequences of Efficiency: A Brain Gain

The advantages of the current situation are manifest. Our investment in foreign graduate students in the sciences and engineering taps into the exceptionally talented—doubly screened by foreign institutions and our own. Because of the extremely high rate of immigration among these students (despite the current road blocks facing those who wish to stay on), this investment produces an augmented supply of high-level scientists and engineers for the United States itself and enables it to maintain its scientific and technological leadership.

A significant proportion of university faculty in science and engineering are foreign-born: 50 percent of the assistant professors in science and engineering hired in 1992 were foreign-born. In the postwar period, 50 percent of the Nobel Prizes in physics won by the United States went to naturalized Americans. Foreign-born Ph.D.s are most heavily employed by R&D labs and by computer, electronics, chemical, and pharmaceutical firms, contributing from 30 to 40 percent of the scientific and engineering work force in these internationally oriented industries in which the United States has long held a competitive edge.[5]

That these students are foreign-born, and not native, should be the matter of least concern in a country that is built on immigration and where the distinctions between greencard holders, naturalized Americans, and native-born Americans are, by constitutional provisions as interpreted in several Supreme Court judgments, still miniscule (as compared with almost any other country).

Distributional Consequences: Foreign versus Black Students?

Our arguments thus suggest a policy that would encourage rather than discourage the inflow of foreign students. But then what are we to say when Frank Morris argues that universities are turning to foreign students as an alternative to reaching out to black students and that blacks are being "crowded out" by foreign students?[6] Our reaction is unambiguous: this argument is incorrect.

The facts on black students are, of course, alarming.[7] Of the 36,027 Ph.D.s in all subjects awarded in 1990, only 320—less than 1 percent—were awarded to black men, and 508, or just over 1 percent, were given to black women. Even more ominous is that the number of blacks getting Ph.D.s in all subjects has dropped since 1977. This contrasts strikingly with the experience of foreign students, which we just highlighted. But Morris's inference from this contrast is unwarranted.

To begin with, we reject the notion that there are a fixed number of places in graduate programs and, therefore, that an increase in the numbers of foreign students must be at the expense of the native-born—black or otherwise. The facts show that the supply of places in graduate S&E programs, which attract the greatest concern, is quite elastic: Over the past two decades, the number of Americans in these Ph.D. Programs has remained constant (at about 13,000); the Ph.D. programs have simply expanded to accommodate the increased foreign demand.[8] Thus, the increase in the number of foreign students in these Ph.D. programs has not been at the expense of the native-born.

Could we then argue instead that black students are crowded out in a financial sense, that the competition for the limited financial support available for Ph.D. programs, which would otherwise be available to the black students, is being won by better-trained foreign students?

This would prima facie appear plausible since, unlike most foreign students, most black graduates do not receive extensive financial assistance from the universities. In 1990, for example, 69 percent of all foreign graduate students were supported by universities; by contrast, only 25 percent of black graduate students received grants and assistantships.[9]

But this contrast is explained by the fields of study of the two groups.[10] Thus, 81 percent of foreign graduate students are in S&E Ph.D. programs. Only 14 percent of black graduate students are in these programs. Most black graduate students are in humanities and, especially, in education Ph.D. programs (over 50 percent of black graduate students are in education graduate programs). At the same time, graduate programs in the United States have different financial aid policies.[11] S&E graduate students are almost all wholly supported by their universities: over 70 percent of the students in S&E Ph.D. programs list the university as the primary source of financial assistance. By contrast, only 25 percent of the students in Ph.D. programs in the humanities, and a mere 13 percent of the students in education Ph.D. programs, receive financial assistance from the university.

Hold the field of study constant, and the disparities in financial assistance awarded by universities disappear. Black American students in S&E Ph.D. programs do receive primary financial support from the university; for instance, over 70 percent of black graduate students in the physical sciences receive primary support from universities.[12]

Besides, much of the financial support in S&E (about 40 percent) comes in the shape of research assistance in federally supported projects: their share in the support is over 75 percent of the total research assistance support.[13] These projects are funded by the Defense Department, Energy Department, NASA, and the National Science Foundation. The awards here go generally to those who are best prepared to undertake the research; this includes, of course, black students.

On the other hand, federal funding for "affirmative action," for which foreign students are ineligible, is based on different criteria and awarded and administered by different government agencies —the U.S. Department of Education, in particular, as well as the Higher Education Opportunity Progam (HEOP), funded by the states. The budget for this type of aid is distinct from, and not in the least affected by, the federal "projects-oriented" grants. The latter, where the foreign students predominate, does not cut into the former, where the black students do.

Most telling, the number of black Americans securing S&E Ph.D.s—precisely the fields to which foreign graduate students flock—has actually increased over the past two decades.[14] Hence, while the total Ph.D.s awarded to blacks did, indeed, fall from 999 in 1975 to 828 in 1990, in engineering they increased from 11 in 1975 to 28 in 1990, in life sciences from 56 in 1975 to 63 in 1990, and in social sciences from 153 in 1975 to 172 in 1990.

The real problem appears to be that the pool of black students from which the Ph.D. programs draw upon is small and, worse, getting smaller. The number of blacks securing baccalaureate degrees in S&E actually fell from 18,700 in 1975 to 18,400 in 1990 (so that the fraction of black S&E baccalaureates who secured Ph.D.s actually *increased*). This occurred, moreover, during a period when the total number of baccalaureate degrees in S&E awarded in the United States *increased*; so the proportion of blacks in these areas decreased significantly.

Conclusion and a Proposal

Our analysis therefore suggests that the real problem facing the black community lies in the educational hurdles before the Ph.D. programs rather than in the influx of foreign students. Equally, our analysis suggests that we ought to treat foreign students as an important source of brain gain for us and that we ought to facilitate, rather than impede, their arrival and their entry into our work force. How could this be done?

There is a long-standing provision in our immigration laws under which those who bring in a certain amount of financial capital (which will "create jobs") are allowed to immigrate: A foreigner who invests one million dollars in a commercial enterprise established in a high-unemployment area, which creates jobs for at least ten Americans, is automatically given immigrant status (that is, a green card). We suggest extending the idea from financial to human capital.

Currently, graduate students who wish to stay on in the United States after their Ph.D.s must be sponsored by their employers, a process that imposes substantial hardship both on the students and on smaller employers.

The standard procedure is in two stages. First, the U.S. Department of Labor must, on the basis of a U.S. employer's sponsorship, certify that "no American can do this job." Then, the would-be immigrant must apply for immigrant status at the Immigration and Naturalization Service (INS). If all goes right, the entire process takes about two years (considerably more for citizens of certain countries). But things may not go right: there could be hitches at either stage. Thus, the employer or the "alien" must hire an immigration lawyer. The current process, then, is costly both to the would-be immigrant and to the employer (and hence, it unfairly penalizes smaller firms that cannot afford this expensive process and so cannot recruit this foreign talent).

The Immigration and Naturalization Act of 1990 introduced an alternative route for professors and researchers to secure immigrant status. Essentially, it eliminates the labor certification stage. While this reduces the average processing time to about one year, it does not eliminate any of the uncertainty or the need for expensive legal counsel.

We suggest that automatic green cards be given to all those who obtain a Ph.D. in the science and engineering programs at our universities. In adopting such a "guaranteed green card" proposal, we would be recognizing the important contribution that these students make to our scientific eminence by placing human capital on a par with financial capital.

Notes

1. Anthony DePalma, "As Black Ph.D.'s Taper Off, Aid for Foreigners Is Assailed," *New York Times*, April 12, 1992.

2. Figures provided by the National Research Council.

3. See Ries and Thurgood (1983).

4. See, for instance, National Science Foundation (1987, 1991a, 1991c).

5. See, for instance, Morris (1993).

6. See National Science Foundation (1990, 1991b, 1993).

7. See National Science Foundation (1990, 1991b).

8. See National Science Foundation (1994).

9. See National Science Foundation (1990, 1991b).

10. See National Science Foundation (1993, 1994).

11. See Thurgood and Weinman (1991).

12. See National Science Foundation (1994).

13. See National Science Foundation (1990, 1991b).

14. See National Science Foundation (1991c).

References

Morris, F. 1993. "Doctoral Opportunities in the U.S.: Denial of Equal Treatment for African American Students." *Urban League Review* 16 (Winter).

National Science Foundation. 1987. *Foreign Citizens in U.S. Science and Engineering: History, Status, and Outlook.* Washington, D.C.: Government Printing Office.

———. 1990. *Selected Data on Science and Engineering Doctorate Awards: 1990.* Washington, D.C.: Government Printing Office.

———. 1991a. *International Science and Technology Data Update.* Washington, D.C.: Government Printing Office.

———. 1991b. *Science and Engineering Doctorates: 1960–90.* Washington, D.C.: Government Printing Office.

———. 1991c. *Science and Engineering Indicators—1991.* Washington, D.C.: Government Printing Office.

———. 1993. *Selected Data on Science and Engineering Doctorate Awards: 1993 Special Survey of Race and Ethnicity.* Washington, D.C.: Government Printing Office.

————. 1994. *Selected Data on Graduate Students and Post Doctorates in Science and Engineering: Fall 1992*. Arlington, Va.

Ries, P. and D. H. Thurgood. 1993. *Summary Report 1991: Doctorate Recipients from United States Universities*. Washington, D.C.: National Academy Press.

Thurgood, D. H. and J. M. Weinman. 1991. *Summary Report 1990: Doctorate Recipients from United States Universities*. Washington, D.C.: National Academy Press.

37   The False Alarm of "Too Many Scientists"

What a difference a few years makes. Until very recently, voices filled the air with complaints that the United States lacked adequate science talent. Now, suddenly, a widely reported Stanford-RAND study has drawn an alarming picture of a *glut* of science and engineering Ph.D.s. Current S&E graduates, the study claims, have low prospects of getting suitable jobs, with perhaps one in four having to accept a position below the expected rung of university instructor or corporate researcher. Calls for reductions in science education have begun to be heard in the land. There are demands even to reduce foreign student admissions and to restrict the entry of foreign scientists to the United States.

But these demands are badly flawed. A benign, even beneficial, situation has been misportrayed by alarmists as something harmful. A "glut" of scientists and engineers is something we should welcome rather than deplore. Abundance makes talent available to increasing numbers of universities, research labs, and corporations that otherwise could not access it.

Foreign students are in fact at the heart of both the "glut" and its beneficial effects for the United States. Large proportions of the students coming out of American science and engineering graduate schools today are foreign students. The cause of this is

Originally published in the *American Enterprise* (January/February 1996): 71–72, with Milind Rao. Reprinted with permission.

a sharp increase in superbly trained and screened foreign appli-cants. These students study. They make valuable contributions in university labs. And because they generally end up as immi-grants, they add to the supply of talented scientific manpower in the country, which can only benefit the United States.

And the foreigners themselves also benefit, even in an over-supplied professional market. For the fact is, even a secondary position in the United States is usually going to be more stim-ulating and lucrative than working in their home country for many of the young scientists in question. Even deflated by the Stanford-RAND estimates of only a three-in-four chance of getting a "suitable" job, the returns to individual students and to the United States from graduate science education are quite attractive.

First, the facts: In 1990, over 50 percent of the engineering Ph.D.s in the United States were awarded to foreign students. The figures are almost as high in mathematics, physics, chemistry, and computer science. More than eight out of every ten foreign graduate students in the United States is in an S&E program, with over half of these students coming from just four countries: Taiwan, China, Korea, and India.

The vast majority of these students are tremendously talented. From among the large populations in their home countries, they are handpicked through mandarin-style entrance examinations for undergraduate study at their leading national universities and institutes. Their supply has increased substantially as the four countries named above have built up first-rate scientific and engineering programs, often with the help of America's best universities. Thus, for instance, about three-fourths of the U.S. engineering Ph.D.s recently awarded to Indians went to gradu-ates of the prestigious institutes of technology there, while two-thirds of those going to South Koreans went to graduates of the famous Seoul National University. These gifted and splendidly trained students apply to our S&E programs and win a growing share of our admissions, which are based overwhelmingly on merit.

The explosion of superb foreign applicants to science and engineering programs has not been accompanied by similar increases among native-born Americans. In fact, there is some evidence that science and engineering programs have recently become slightly less attractive to our best native-born students. The "professional" schools of law, medicine, and business have substantially better starting salaries at present, and a small edge also in average rates of return. S&E graduate programs, on the other hand, are vastly more attractive to talented foreign students because most of them are cash-strapped, and professional schools, unlike S&E programs, offer little financial aid or paid research employment for graduate students.

The preponderance of foreign students in S&E programs has an important consequence in the technical job market—certain "gluts" are likely to persist. The traditional way in which such "gluts" are removed is simply by market forces: students walk away from education that yields low rates of return. But when foreign students are in the game, the market returns must fall more drastically before this happens. Even the currently diminished rates of return are unlikely to turn away foreign S&E students, because even these reduced rates of return will be favorable compared with the compensation in their home countries. Thus, even if they must wind their way down to second-tier jobs at smaller colleges instead of MIT or Caltech, or less lucrative corporate positions, they will still do substantially better than had they stayed at or returned home. This means that scientist and engineer gluts, and consequent gripes against universities, can be expected to continue.

But why should we take this as a problem? As these Ph.D.s eventually take jobs downstream, their expertise becomes available to institutions and firms that can benefit from superior talent and education at unexpectedly affordable prices. Economists have documented how such downstreaming improves national medical care, for instance, as doctors crowded into urban areas find their earnings falling and then begin to settle in rural areas. This should be a matter for satisfaction, not lament.

Should we be concerned that so many students are not native-born? Many, such as Phillip Griffiths of the Institute for Advanced Study at Princeton, have been quoted as worrying about the preponderance of foreigners in graduate science and engineering programs. This concern is misplaced. Foreign graduate students typically stay on in this country. Indeed, the possibility of eventual immigration is often the reason why entering our graduate programs and working hard to acquire the education necessary for America's highly competitive labor market is attractive to talented foreigners in the first place.

Recent estimates suggest that nearly three-quarters of those trained in America remain in America. The final figure may be even higher, for some returnees initially go home only to return later to a rewarding professional life in the United States when circumstances permit. This immigration of brainpower is a great bonus to our country. Consider that fully 50 percent of the assistant professors hired in engineering in the United States in 1992 were foreign-born.

Yet even if it is clear that the arrival of foreign science and engineering students is a boon to the United States as a whole, one might worry that particular subgroups of the population could be hurt by the competition. Some black educators have made the specific argument that foreign students in Ph.D. programs are crowding out blacks. An example would be Frank Morris. Since total black Ph.D.s have tapered off while those awarded to foreign students have shot up, advocates seek restraints on foreign acceptances.

The facts on black higher education, particularly in the sciences, are indeed disappointing. The remedy of excluding foreign applicants, however, is unwarranted. For one thing, the number of native-born Americans in S&E Ph.D. programs has not declined. As increasing numbers of foreign students have arrived, native enrollments have held constant over the past thirty years at around 13,000 annually.

As for financial "crowding out," it is true that 60 percent of all foreign graduate students in the United States are aided financially by their university—much higher than the 25 percent of black graduate students so helped. But the reason for this differential is the very different fields of study chosen, on average, by the two groups. Fully 81 percent of foreign graduate students are in science and engineering programs—where almost all students are wholly supported by their university (mainly through assistantships in funded research projects). On the other hand, black graduate students are overwhelmingly enrolled in the field of education and in humanities programs where there is much less aid. Eliminate the field of study difference and blacks do immensely better. Over 70 percent of the black graduate students in the physical sciences, for instance, receive substantial aid from their universities.

A final reason for caution is that the number of blacks within science and engineering graduate programs has actually increased in the past two decades, both in total and as a fraction of all black Ph.D.s. The main problem facing blacks in the field of science and engineering today is the small and shrinking pool of the blacks with bachelors degrees in science. The number of blacks securing bachelors in science and engineering fell from 18,700 in 1975 to 18,400 in 1990, even as the total number of these degrees awarded was on the increase. The gnawing problem of too few blacks in scientific graduate programs has causes and solutions quite unrelated to the arrival of foreign students.

The intelligent and highly motivated foreign students who come to this country for scientific education and then "stay on" in large numbers assimilate readily, becoming indistinguishable from native-born Americans, who are themselves ethnically diverse. The scientific eminence of the United States thus reflects a virtuous circle: the best and the brightest from around the world are attracted to our universities, and they in turn help make our universities world class.

This heavy influx of talent is a sign of our strength, not of a problem or weakness. To dam the scientific inflow instead of removing the debris that clogs the streams would be folly.

38

Free Trade Can Cut Health Costs

While the experts working on Hillary Rodham Clinton's task force on health care have now been identified, the ideas they are exploring have not. But if leaks and informed guesses are any guide, an obvious and significant way of containing explosive health care costs is being ignored. International trade in goods and services often lowers prices substantially. It will do the same for medical services.

Both doctors and patients increasingly move across borders. Most Americans and nearly all Britons have been treated by foreign-born doctors at some time. Foreign patients often seek out top-level specialists at the Mayo Clinic and Sloan Kettering here and in Harley Street in London. India has set up hospitals that work overwhelmingly with patients from the Middle East. The influx of Soviet doctors and the abundance of local ones has led Israel to attract foreign patients as well. Affordable prices and attractive facilities thus seduce patients today across nations, taking them to foreign providers of choice.

If only the necessary institutional changes are made, there is clearly tremendous potential to lower medical costs by importing more foreign doctors and exporting more patients.

Originally published in the *Journal of Commerce* (April 8, 1993).

The entry of more foreign doctors wouldn't require anything as formidable as easing immigration restrictions. Temporary visas for providers of professional services can be made available readily to qualified doctors from abroad; indeed, that's already happening for most services and for many professionals who work with multinational corporations.

After a decade of trying to open foreign markets for other professional services—legal, advertising and accounting among others—we know that professional organizations in some countries impose restrictions on the export of other nations' services. These restrictions, ostensibly in defense of certain "standards," are a real restraint on the export of professional services. Appropriately, these certification requirements have been the subject of scrutiny by trade negotiators and the targets of market-opening efforts.

The same must be done if we are to open our medical markets to imports. The effective restraint on the entry of foreign doctors comes from an examination conducted by the American Medical Association to certify foreign medical graduates.

Economic research strongly suggests that the AMA makes this examination tougher when doctors' earnings are under pressure, thereby reducing the pool of eligible applicants for visas. Limiting entry eases competition among doctors and keeps their earnings—and the cost of health care—higher than it might otherwise be.

If the administration is interested in importing more doctors, the foreign medical exam must be reviewed by an agency that is not a creature of the AMA. Moreover, international agreements to encourage mutual recognition of medical qualifications—as now exist for many professions within the European Community—will have to be seriously considered if importing medical services is to become an effective means of cost containment.

A less obvious way of using trade in medical services to lower costs is to take patients where the inexpensive doctors are. The current differences in surgeons' fees between the United States and English-speaking India, for instance, are enormous. Open-heart and neurosurgeries by the best Indian surgeons (many with advanced training abroad and vast experience at home), cost about one-tenth of what the average American surgeon charges. Similar differences occur across the entire range of surgical procedures.

If the patient can travel, there is much to be gained by the United States and by countries that produce excellent doctors—such as India and the Philippines—from encouraging the new U.S. health care program to exploit this "trade-in-service" opportunity fully.

Wouldn't patients worry about the quality of care? No, not if a convincing comparison could be made with facilities here. Then again, the hospitals abroad into which our insurance and HMO programs would be tied under this proposal could be operated under maintenance contracts with our own health management service organizations which, in fact, were major earners in the Middle East.

Air fare would be only a minor cost if such a program were launched; bulk buying of travel would be at bargain prices. Imagine what this also could do for airlines tied into the program.

The expansion of medical facilities under such a plan, especially in countries like India and the Philippines, also would do wonders for local people by providing spillover public-health effects. That's important since so much of our bilateral foreign aid is now dominated by security concerns. Even the International Monetary Fund and the World Bank are under pressure to turn on the spigot for the former Soviet Union instead of for developing countries. So any policy that assists developing countries, even if inadvertently, is an extra dividend.

Exploiting trade in medical services in this fashion is so appealing that it is a puzzle why the White House appears to have missed it. The explanation lies perhaps in the administration's obvious fixation with manufacturing, high-tech generally and automobiles, and its obvious distaste for services, which often seem associated with the easy amassing of fortunes by Wall Street's takeover tycoons during the 1980s. The resulting "commodity fetishism" is a folly we cannot afford.

You do not have to be a member of "the strange union of business interests, naive libertarians, and misguided left-wing urban advocates" to disagree with Orlando Patterson's advice to the president to tighten the screws on unskilled legal and illegal immigration in the interest of the earnings of our "low-class workers."[1] While the evidence that the unskilled component of our current immigration hurts the wages of our workers is problematic, at best, Patterson's demand for an enhanced enforcement of sanctions on the hire of illegals (who are manifestly among the unskilled) to make their entry unprofitable is nothing less than misguided.

Patterson makes a fatal mistake, shared by economist George Borjas, by both political parties, and by even well-meaning liberals such as Father Hesburgh and the late Barbara Jordan. He assumes that the inflow of illegals can be virtually eliminated by domestic (and, for that matter, border) punishment strategies. The wage and opportunity differentials are so immense, as between us and the poor countries from which the illegals mainly come, that efforts at reducing incentives, whether by taking the illegals off the welfare rolls or ejecting their children from the schools or by imposing ever greater penalties on their employers, will yield

Originally published as a letter to the editor in the *New Republic* (December 9, 1996): 4. Reprinted with permission.

little response. To my knowledge, no serious scholar has ever demonstrated otherwise.

While they do little therefore to reduce the illegals in our midst, these efforts only serve to drive more of them, unable to rear their heads in protest and able only to extend their hands in supplication, into the underground economy of sweatshops and exploitative work conditions that a well-meaning but ineffective Secretary Robert Reich seeks to fix with bandaid gestures such as marching into New York's garment district with the hapless Kathie Lee Gifford! Few unions here have traditionally come to their aid, as did some empathetic German unions in support of the foreign guest workers in the 1970s when they demonstrated with placards saying: *"Ihr kampf ist unser kampf"* (their battle is our battle). Instead, the demonization of the illegals has only prompted a general cry of *Mein kampf.*

Surely it is time to come to terms with this reality. Domestic enforcement has been tried without success before: that was in fact the principal aim of the 1986 Immigration Act that introduced employer sanctions despite objections that they could not work.

The only policy that combines decency with sense is then to remove the illegals from the political radar screen, freezing domestic enforcement instead of expanding it. Once the illegals get past the border, we ought to rein in, rather than enhance, the harassment and penalties that produce misery and no results.

But I believe that this must go hand in hand in hand with stricter enforcement at the border itself. Not that even the border enforcement can be particularly effective. The Rio Grande could be fenced up, a ditch dug, the army deployed, all at great cost along the huge border, and we may optimistically hope to dent the flow from Mexico. But how do we effectively stop the illegals who arrive on legal short-term visas and then get lost in our land? They already number close to 60 percent of the estimated illegal inflow.

The best defense of border enforcement (which Patterson dismisses as ineffective while accepting uncritically the assumption that domestic measures will work instead) is simply that the government must show, despite the stark reality that immigration is increasingly beyond control, that it is doing *something* to control it. And that something has to be a policy that creates the maximum such illusion at least cost in terms of our traditions of liberty, justice, and fairness. Domestic enforcement measures, whether directed at illegals or at employers, do worst in this regard; border enforcement measures do best. The policy choice is both obvious and the opposite of what Patterson wants.

Note

1. See Patterson (1996).

Reference

Patterson, Orlando. 1996. "An Agenda for a Second Term." *New Republic,* November 11.

IX

Democracy and Its Contents

40   Democracy and Development: New Thinking on an Old Question

The occasion of Prime Minister Rajiv Gandhi's fiftieth anniversary is an apt time to recall India's long-standing democracy: a phenomenon almost unique at one time among the developing countries and a source of legitimate pride to our leaders and our people.

New versus Old Thinking

It is also a fitting occasion to affirm the new thinking on the relationship between democracy and development, more sanguine and optimistic now, that has replaced the old thinking, more despondent and pessimistic then. Many subscribed to the view then (for reasons that I shall presently discuss) that democracy definitely came at the expense of development, so that one had to choose between doing good and doing well. The new thinking is that this tradeoff, or the "cruel dilemma" as I called it nearly thirty years ago,[1] is by no means a compelling necessity, that one may be able to eat one's cake and have it: either democracy does not handicap development or, in the best of circumstances, it even promotes it.

Originally presented as the Rajiv Gandhi Golden Jubilee Memorial Lecture in New Delhi, India, on October 22, 1994.

Thus, the pursuit of political and civil virtue, as the embrace of democracy implies, need not be at the expense of the drive for economic development. All good things may sometimes go together, just as we have discovered that literacy is good in itself and for development, and that female education emancipates women while restraining the growth of population and enhancing the possibility of greater economic prosperity for smaller numbers.

Echoes of Old Thinking

The new view represents a nuanced change, of course. Few claim that democracy is necessarily, or even overwhelmingly, better for development, but only that democracy can be consonant with, even promoting, development. In doing so, they keep in mind the witticism, attributed to the Oxford social anthropologist Evans-Pritchard, that the only generalization in social sciences is that there is no generalization, or the Cambridge economist Joan Robinson's mischievous remark that, in economics, everything and its opposite are true (for you can almost always find evidence somewhere, for some historical period, in support of almost anything).

Indeed, if one eyeballs the postwar performance on growth rates and the prevalence of democracy in the developing countries, it is hard to find a strong relationship between democracy or its absence in a country and its growth rate. Democracy has broken out only in recent years across the developing world: in the past two decades, nearly forty countries have turned to democracy.[2] For the bulk of the postwar period, therefore, we had only India, Costa Rica, and Sri Lanka as democracies over a sustained period. True, their growth rates were far from compelling. But then the nondemocratic countries had also an immense variety of performances, ranging from the spectacular in the Far

East to disastrous in many nations of Africa. Looking only at the developing countries in the postwar period, therefore, it would be hard to conclude that democracies have had less rapid developmental performance. In fact, if the developed countries are considered instead, the democracies have done immensely better than the socialist dictatorships that have now happily vanished, at least for the present, from our midst.

To maintain therefore, as did the old view, that democracy necessarily handicaps development whereas authoritarianism aids it, is to argue a case that must explain away these facts by citing other factors and cross-country differences that overwhelm the outcomes.[3] Indeed, democracy and authoritarianism are only one dimension on which countries and their developmental performances differ: and, to develop the more nuanced and new view that is favorable to democracy as compatible with, even conducive at times to, development, I shall address qualitatively and directly the ways in which, and the reasons why, such a happy symbiosis is the likely reality.

But it would be wrong for me to suggest that the old, dismal, and deterministic view is necessarily dead. Echoes, amplified by nondemocratic governments with successful developmental performance, can often be heard. It is not uncommon, for instance, to find Prime Minister Lee Kuan Yew talking continually on the theme of democracy's "undisciplined" ways that his "soft" authoritarian rule has prevented from debilitating Singapore and crippling her development. Thus, he has argued: "I believe what a country needs to develop is discipline more than democracy. The exuberance of democracy leads to indiscipline and disorderly conduct which are inimical to development."[4]

And indeed the phenomenal success of the Far Eastern economies—South Korea, Taiwan, Singapore, and Hong Kong—none of them democracies in a substantive sense,[5] has created for some a sense that the old thinking was right after all, especially when these economic miracles are contrasted with India's poor economic performance over more than three decades within a democratic framework.

Those who think thus, believing that authoritarianism facilitates more rapid growth (with other suitable policies such as market reforms in place, of course) have also argued that the optimal policy *sequencing* of markets and democracy in the developing countries, as also in the former socialist countries, must be to get markets first and democracy next. This conclusion is reinforced in their minds by the recent Russian descent from a superpower to a supine status when the sequence she chose was to put *glasnost* before *perestroika* while the Chinese, who clearly introduced markets before democracy, evidently did immensely better. Does this not imply that *perestroika* must precede, not follow, *glasnost*? If so, this prescription rests on two legs.

First, it reflects the old view on democracy and development— that the two are at odds and authoritarianism must be tolerated to facilitate rapid growth. Second, It invokes the notion, based both on historical experience and the recent evidence that democratic demands have arisen in South Korea and other economically successful countries, that growth will ultimately create an effective push for democracy. The historical experience is substantial and persuasive, starting from Ralf Dahrendorf's illuminating analysis of Germany[6] and Barrington Moore's classic demonstration that the rise of the bourgeoisie led to democracy.[7]

Yet, these proponents of the old view are now outnumbered by those who take the new view. The reason is not necessarily ideological: indeed, social scientists are not proof from the blinkers that blind us to facts that fail to support our beliefs, and it is indeed true that the new view has triumphed when democracy has become both a widespread value and reality, and dictatorship a devalued mode of governance, so that we may be seeing virtues in democracy the way a nomad in the desert finds water in a mirage. The fact rather is that the old view is now seen as having rested on premises that were false, and our thinking on the question has become more nuanced and acute.

The Old View: The "Cruel Dilemma" Thesis

The old view reflected a particular way of looking at the developmental process, fashionable during the 1950s and 1960s. It was also grounded in a specific historical context that defined the constricting assumptions under which the old view gained credence.

The historical context was, of course, the contest between the two "sleeping giants": China and India. China was totalitarian and India a democracy then; nothing has changed in that regard! In the intellectual eye, trained politically on the cold war and the arena of the Third World, the developmental succes of India, rather than of China, would set the correct example for the Third World nations: if democracy did better and totalitarianism worse, this would put more nations in the Third World on a course that would favor the Western democracies in their struggle with the Soviet bloc.

The race was, in turn, between two nations that had committed themselves to economic development. This, of course, removed from the intellectual context the question that must be faced if democracy and authoritarian rule are to be contrasted fully: which system is more likely to seek development? The question rather was, Once you are committed to development, which political regime, democracy or authoritarian rule, is likely to facilitate the fulfillment of that goal?

To answer that question, one must have a "model" of the developmental process. In fact, one always does, whether explicitly if one is an economist or implicitly if one is not. The model that nearly everyone actively planning for development in the early postwar decades happened to use was attributed to the British economist Sir Roy Harrod and the American economist Evsey Domar. It is called, quite properly, the Harrod-Domar model, even though Domar wrote independently about it only several years after Harrod, in contrast to the fiercely cruel practice in the natural sciences where, as James Watson reminded us in his vivid account of the contest for the Nobel Prize in *The Double Helix*, if you beat your rival to a discovery by an epsilon moment, you have reduced her to the disappointment of oblivion. Contrary to their subject matter that builds on man's basest, not his noblest, instincts to show how the pursuit of private interest can be harnessed to produce public good, economists can be quite generous indeed!

The Harrod-Domar model, much used then,[8] analyzed development in terms of two parameters: the rate of investment and the productivity of capital.[9] As it happened, for policymaking purposes, the latter parameter was largely treated as "given" as a datum, so that the policy freedom was assigned only to the former parameter, the investment rate.[10] The debate therefore centered only on the question of how to promote investment. That approach, favored by mainstream economists, coincided with the Marxist focus on "primitive accumulation" as the mainspring of industrialization and also with the cumbersome quasi-Marxist models elaborated in the investment-allocation literature that grew up around the Cambridge economist, Maurice Dobb.

But if the focus was on accumulation, with its productivity considered a datum, it was evident that democracies would be handicapped vis-à-vis authoritarian regimes, when both were similarly wedded to accelerating development. For, it seemed natural to assume that the authoritarian regimes would be able to extract a greater surplus from their populations through taxation and "takings" and be able therefore to raise domestic savings and investment to higher levels than would democracies that had to woo voters to pay the necessary taxes and accept the sacrifices more willingly. Economist Richard Cooper of Harvard University has an amusing but telling analysis of the remarkable association between the fall of finance ministers and the fact that they had devalued their currencies: I have little doubt that the finance ministers who have wittingly or unwittingly crossed the line through tough taxation have fared no better, being scapegoated and sacrificed by their prime ministers or dumped by irate voters at the polls soon after. Hence, I wrote in the mid-1960s of "the cruel choice between rapid (self-sustained) expansion and democratic processes."[11]

But that thesis was to be proven false for three reasons that have a bearing on the new view. First, the argument that the state would generate the necessary savings through tax effort, to accelerate development, has simply not held true: public sector savings have not been one of the engines of growth since public sector profligacy and deficits, rather than fiscal prudence and budget surpluses, have been the norm. Second, savings rates have risen substantially in the private sector instead, when many thought that they would be relatively unimportant, suggesting that where *incentives* to invest have increased dramatically, so has the necessary savings to exploit those opportunities, in a virtuous circle that has taken savings and investments to higher levels in both democracies (including India) and authoritarian countries (such as the Far Eastern superperformers, whose savings rates are higher than those of India). Third, the differential performance among different countries seems to have reflected, not so much differences in their investment rates as the productivity of these investments, and that in turn surely has reflected the efficiency of the policy framework within which those investments have been undertaken.

I would say that, by the 1980s, it was manifest that the policy framework, in its broadest sense, determining the productivity of investment (and possibly even increasing saving and investment themselves through incentive effects) was absolutely critical, and that winners and losers would be sorted out by the choices they made in that regard and indeed quite differently from the way we thought in the 1950s.[12]

Incentives promoting development, not the ability to force the pace through Draconian state action, became the objects of a key shift in focus. And here democracy was far from being the obvious loser; in fact, it seemed, at least at first blush, to be at an advantage instead. For who could doubt that democracy would relate development to people and build on incentives rather than compulsions? Yet, this can only be the starting point for a fresh inquiry into the relationship between democracy and development, a question that is now seen to be more complex and difficult and yielding an answer that is arguably more favorable to democracy than we thought earlier.

Indeed, reflection on the problem suggests three plausible and profound propositions that I shall presently address. First, for ideological and structural reasons, democracy may well dominate authoritarianism as a political system that produces economic development. Second, the quality of development also can be expected generally to be better under democracy; and the better the quality of the democracy itself, yet greater is likely to be the quality of development. Third, the dividends from political democracy are likely to be greater if it is combined with economic markets: the combination of democracy and markets is likely to be a powerful engine of development.

These propositions are stated in terms of likelihoods rather than certainties because the argument must proceed at times in terms of the balance of contrary forces and a judgment of their relative importance. The apparent contradiction nonetheless between them and reality must also be resolved by observing that, in the real world, one cannot expect the factors that suggest the plausibility of these propositions to be proof from the invasion of other countervailing events. Thus, for instance, even if democracy were expected to generate more development, initial conditions conducive to growth may be more favorable in an authoritarian country than in a democracy, leading to more development in the former: as indeed may have been the case with the authoritarian superperforming Far Eastern economies that inherited both egalitarian land reforms and remarkably high rates of literacy: two factors that are widely considered by economists today to stimulate development.

Democracy and Development: Bedfellows?

Democracy, considered to consist of a troika—the right to vote and turn out governments, an independent judiciary, and a free press—defines both an ideology and a structure. The ideology is that of the process of governance—by consent. The structure consists of the institutions by which that ideology is implemented. Both the ideology and the institutions of a democracy can be argued to contribute to development, though there are some downsides as well.[13]

Ideology

The most plausible arguments in favor of democracy as being conducive to development on grounds of its ideological or process-of-consent content are twofold. One, for which there is now substantial evidence, is that democracies rarely go to war against each other. The other, which is speculative, is that authoritarian regimes "bottle up" problems while democracies permit catharsis, the apparent chaos of democracy in fact constituting a safety valve that strengthens, instead of undermining, the state and provides the ultimate stability that is conducive to development.

Democracies at Peace among Themselves

If democracies do not fight wars with one another, and they fight only with nondemocratic nations that fight each other in turn, the probability of entering a war if a nation is democratic could well be less than if it was nondemocratic.[14] That, in turn, could mean that democracies are more likely both to provide governance that is conducive to peace and hence prosperity and to spend less on fighting wars and preparing for them.

As it happens, political scientists have now established that, in nearly two centuries, democracies "have rarely clashed with one another in violent or potentially violent conflict and (by some reasonable criteria) have virtually never fought one another in a full-scale international war."[15]

In his "Perpetual Peace," published in 1795, philosopher Immanuel Kant argued why democratic "republics" would naturally pursue peace. The ingrained habit of "respect" for others that such a republic would foster, as also the interests of the citizens whose welfare rather than that of absolute monarchs would be at stake, would both serve to promote peace rather than war.

Thus, Kant thought that the *ideology* of democracy, embodied in the idea of rule by consent, would mean that democracies, used to domestic governace by such consent, would naturally extend to other republics, similarly governed, accommodation by mutual discourse, dialogue, and the resolution of disputes without war.[16]

But he also argued that the *structure* of democracy, or what we might call *interests*, would also inhibit wars because democratic leaders would find it more difficult to mobilize their citizens to fight wars. To quote him:

If the consent of the citizens is required in order to decide that war should be declared (and in this constitution it cannot but be the case), nothing is more natural than that they would be very cautious in commencing such a poor game, decreeing for themselves all the calamities of war. Among the latter would be having to fight, having to pay the costs of war from their own resources, having painfully to repair the devastation war leaves behind, and, to fill up the measure of evils, load themselves with a heavy national debt that would embitter peace itself and that can never be liquidated on account of constant wars in the future. But, on the other hand, in a constitution which is not republican, and under which the subjects are not citizens, a declaration of war is the easiest thing in the world to decide upon, because war does not require of the ruler, who is the proprietor and not a member of the state, the least sacrifice of the pleasure of his table, the chase, his country houses, his court functions, and the like. He may, therefore, resolve on war as on a pleasure party for the most trivial reasons, and with perfect indifference leave the justification which decency requires to the diplomatic corps who are ever ready to provide it.[17]

It is not altogether clear whether the ideological or the structural argument should predominate as the explanation of democratic peace, even as both contribute to the outcome;[18] recent empirical tests suggest that the ideological one does.[19] That is perhaps what one should expect: the habits of mind, and patterns of practice and procedure, set by the "norms" that a society works with domestically, will surely constrain and shape behavior toward others beyond the nation-state.

Thus, it is entirely in keeping with the Kantian argument that the liberal states in the Western world, which maintain the rights of their own citizens to exit, which, despite the social and political strains posed by rising refugee flows and illegal immigration, have by and large worried about providing rights to such immigrants, not the states that have denied their own citizens the right to move away.[20]

"Safety Valve" versus "Bottling Up"

The "respect" for others that Kant observed as the mark of republics as against monarchies, of democracies as against authoritarian rulers, also leads to dialogue and debate, at times vociferous and impassioned. This is often mistaken for crippling chaos: it is merely the robust noise of a functioning democracy.

Its chief virtue is that where different groups, whether classes, tribes, or castes, jostle for voice and representation, it provides a platform for the contest and an airing of the demands, yielding a catharsis if not the satisfaction that success brings and thus acting as a safety valve.

The instinct and the practice of authoritarian regimes, on the other hand, is to repress, to bottle up, those conflicts, building toward eventual eruption when the pressures have built up to an explosive level. I suspect that the success in some of the Far Eastern countries in maintaining an authoritarian structure over a long period owed in part to their initial equality of incomes, which made class conflicts less compelling, to the racial homogeneity of their populations (except for Singapore), which ruled out interethnic tensions, and to the absence of religious divisions. It is unlikely that they would have managed so well if these favorable conditions had been absent: the disadvantages of authoritarianism would probably have shown up in those regimes.

Structure

The structure of democracy, with its institutions of voting rights, an independent judiciary that often requires judicial review and leads to judicial restraint on legislative and executive power, and a free press, also sets it apart from authoritarian rule. The restraint of arbitrary power can be a powerful source of development: but a functioning democracy can also lead to what Jonathan Rauch has called demosclerosis: the paralysis of gridlock afflicting a lobbying-infested democracy.

One could argue that authoritarian governments may be prone to extravagance and waste, inhibiting development, because there is no restraining hand among the citizenry to hold them back and also because, as the late Nobel-laureate economist from St. Lucia,

Arthur Lewis, who had advised many governments in single-party authoritarian governments in Africa, remarked to me, the leaders in such governments manage to delude themselves that the monuments they build for themselves are really a gift to posterity, equating personal indulgence with social glory. And, reflecting on how the authoritarian governments of Latin America and the socialist bloc ran up impossibly large debts during the mid-1970s and much of 1980s, just before and after the debt crisis arrived on the world scene, one may well conclude that, by and large, autocrats are likely to argue, with Keynes, that "in the long run we are all dead," and then ignore posterity for immediate gain, whereas the democracies are likely to be characterized by leaders who see continuity of national interests beyond their own rule more naturally.

Economist Mancur Olson has produced a rather different argument that also militates in favor of democracy as an institution likely to produce development.[21] He argues that dictators are more likely to overshoot in the direction of "takings" from their subjects than Kantian republicans, since they will attach less weight to their citizens' welfare than to their own. The effect will correspondingly be to leave citizens less secure in their property rights and hence to reduce their incentive to produce more income.[22] In effect, Olson suggests that the incentive to save and invest, and hence the growth of the economy, will be adversely affected under a dictatorship.

Not merely are authoritarian rulers likely to be more self-regarding than democratic leaders. They will also be able to be more self-regarding. This follows from the structure of democracy, for democracy will lead to restraints on "takings" from the citizens, in particular via the possibility of appeal to an independent judiciary that may well reverse such "takings" as unconstitutional or unjustified and the availability of a free press that can document and thus restrain the state's extravagance.

But the structure of democracy, in other ways, can also create waste, even paralysis of useful state action, through the lobbying activities of special interests. To see how lobbying can indirectly lead to waste as surely as directly wasting resources, conduct a mental experiment. Imagine that some revenue is to be spent. That may lead to conventional waste: the government may build tunnels that lead nowhere. But suppose now that the minister for trade is restricting imports and allocating licenses for scarce imports that then fetch a hefty premium to those who are able to get the licenses: economists call those premiums "windfall profits" or, more technically, "rents" to scarcity. You and I will lobby to get those licenses, of course, for we can get rich by getting them. Economist Anne Krueger, who highlighted that phenomenon, described the situation of people seeking to get those licenses as "rent-seeking," whereas I have called it unproductive profit-seeking.[23] Its effect is to have us spend resources trying to make money by lobbying to persuade politicians and bureaucrats to give those licenses to us rather than to others, instead of using those resources to produce useful goods and services and make profits that way. Such rent-seeking wastes resources then as swiftly and surely as if our governments were directly wasting them by building white elephants.

The reality is that lobbies that inevitably indulge in rent-seeking, even in rent-creation where governments are persuaded to create by policy the scarcities that lead to the rents that are then collected by the lobbies, are an endemic and indeed a growing presence in democratic societies. The good that they produce, in creating for instance the different perspectives on policy that alone can lead to informed policy, can be outweighed by such costs. Economists are busy debating how large those costs are; but that they do obtain under democracies is indisputable. And that such costs would be less under dictatorships is equally plausible, even though there would be rent-seeking in the form of trying to become the brother-in-law of the dictator so that the licenses come to oneself (as they do in fact accrue to the families of most dictators in reality)!

On the other hand, the other possible defect of democratic governance, the paralysis of government that a proliferation of lobbying can cause, is an outcome of lesser likelihood. It has, however, occurred to many shrewd observers who have contemplated the recent gridlock in the U.S. Congress. Of course, the United States has a form of democratic governance where the president must deal with a Congress whose members are not subject to the party whip and instead regard themselves as autonomous agents with whom the president must bargain on each issue. David Broder, the perceptive political columnist of the *Washington Post* has remarked that the United States has virtually 536 presidents. In turn, those members of Congress are responsive to their constituents, hence to lobbies, to a degree that is unparalleled in other forms of democratic governance. As a wit has remarked, a U.S. congressman is virtually required to supply a missionary for breakfast if a cannibal constituent demands it!

But "demosclerosis," the arteriosclerosis or clogging of arteries that afflicts the U.S. democracy, is an acute product of a certain institutional structure of democracy, surely "off the curve" and off the wall as far as other institutional forms of democracy (such as the British Parliamentary model) are concerned. It does not seem to me to be an affliction that democracy must inherently accept.

But if you do, then a benign or "soft" authoritarianism sounds attractive as an alternative until you ask, as I did already, whether the authoritarian rulers will in fact have the incentives to deliver development to their subjects by making the "right" choices. That a few did, as seems to have been the case in the Far East in the postwar period, when in fact countless others in the socialist world and in many nations in Africa and South America did not, is hardly proof that this would be the central tendency of authoritarian rulers. In fact, the foregoing analysis and evidence strongly suggest otherwise.

The Quality of Democracy and the Quality of Development

The analysis of democracy's impact on development must reflect, as I have already remarked, the fact that the institutional struc-ture that democracy provides is critical. In fact, Adam Smith's profound case for laissez faire in economic matters[24] must be un-derstood in light of the fact that democracy in his time was based on suffrage that was not universal but was confined to those with property, so that both he and philosopher David Hume, two of the greatest minds of their century, could not vote. The govern-ment that such a democracy produced led to governance that, in economic matters, was one that Adam Smith castigated as inefficient and socially undesirable because it reflected oligarchic interests. Laissez faire, if only adopted somehow in place of the economic governance produced by this form of democracy, would provide a superior organizing principle: but, to my knowledge, Adam Smith did not indicate how one could get that done![25]

So, what might be called the *quality of democracy* matters greatly. A defective oligarchic democracy may well distort eco-nomic choices in the inefficient direction, imperiling prosperity. But then it may also affect what might be called the *quality of development*.

Development is many-sided; it is not just the growth rates of income. True social needs, such as public health, protection of the environment, and the elimination or relief of extreme poverty, cannot be provided unless governments have the resources that only growth can generate. But the use of those resources for such public needs will not automatically follow unless the political system permits and provides the incentives to mobilize and translate those needs into effective demands. I would say that democratic regimes that are characterized by structures and pro-cesses that provide effective access by the groups, often on the economic periphery, who are to profit most from those social

Figure 40.1
This South American picture of men struggling with, and distracted by, babies at a meeting carries the legend: "If child care were men's responsibility, they would already have found the solution." It dramatically illustrates the maxim that effective participation by minorities in the democratic process is necessary for social progress; the "quality of democracy" is an important issue.

programs, are more likely to have such social needs translated into effective demands (see figure 40.1).

The central nature of this observation about the ability and the incentive to vote and to mobilize under democracy is seen best by examining the contention of economists such as Amartya Sen that democracy has promoted the control of famines in India because India's democracy implies a free press so that we get informed about famines such as the Bihar famine, whereas the big Chinese famine under Mao was hidden from view by his iron rule.[26]

I believe that this contrast is a trifle too simplistic about the advantage of democracy in such matters. For one thing, information about the occurrence of a serious famine tends to diffuse and become widely available in one way or another within most countries, even authoritarian ones. There are several ways in which such information has traditionally spread among the people in even the most traditional societies: Indian sociologists have shown conclusively for example that the notion of the "self-sufficient village" is a myth.[27] I have little doubt that this is true of China as well, and that serious research, which may become possible with the political opening up of China, will reveal that information on the Chinese famine was not confined wholly to where it occurred and must have diffused horizontally in traditional ways.

Of course, I can think of ways in which such horizontal diffusion of the information on the famine could have been handicapped in Mao's China. Thus, the extreme totalitarianism under Mao may have reduced such traditional diffusion of knowledge among his subjects because of severe restrictions on travel within China at the time.

Again, the horizontal diffusion of knowledge of the famine may have been crippled owing to "denial." Thus, we know from Nadezhda Mandelstam's poignant observation in her memoirs that the potential victims of Stalin's terror wished to assume that those who had been seized and destroyed were truly guilty of the crimes they were being charged with because, if they were not, then the fact of one's guiltlessness would not protect one from a similar arbitrary fate at the hands of Stalin's police. Equally, China's peasantry may well have discounted reports of a catastrophic famine in China, unmet by corrective relief, so as to protect themselves psychologically from the propsects of a similar, cruel fate.

True, "hard" authoritarian regimes make it easy for the rulers (as distinct from citizens) to be shielded from unpleasant news: the messenger is not protected in such regimes from the retribution that his disturbing message may provoke in an arbitrary regime. Thus, vertical diffusion of information could be impaired under totalitarian regimes simply because the incentive structure of such regimes makes it costly to those below.

But, whether the information on a serious famine is widely diffused horizontally or vertically, the key fact we must confront is that it *is* available for sure at the level where the famine occurs. The key question then is whether that information will translate better under democracy into pressures for a change in the regime's policies in the required direction.

And here we come to the real reasons why democracy would fare better than a dictatorship in addressing serious famines. Surely, a democratic regime is able to provide the *ability*, and the *incentive*, to translate the information on the famine on the ground into pressure on the government to change its policies as required. Mobilization by the citizens through meetings, marches, representations, and petitions is surely difficult, if not impossible, in dictatorships. The incentive to do so would also be less because the probability of affecting a dictator's policies through such means is surely less—and the risks of retribution for one's labors substantially greater[28]—than in a democracy.

Both the incentive and the ability to vote, to mobilize, and to be heard are thus the key ways in which the quality of one's democracy matters to the quality of development. A governance where the poor or the minorities (such as women until only recently in Switzerland) are effectively unable to vote, for example, then is simply not good enough. A judiciary that protects habeas corpus is not so good as one that also provides effective standing for the poor through public interest litigation (as in India). A free press is important but not so good as one that reflects broader interests than those of the elites.

Improving Democracy: Technology and NGOs

As it happens, not merely has democracy spread around the world; its quality has also improved. The diffusion of ideas and better democratic practices is swift today: public interest litigation is spreading from India; judicial review, originating in the United States, is coming to the European nations.[29]

The contributory factor of central importance in this steady progress of democracy and the quality of development in consequence is the revolutionary information technology today that makes the willful rejection or suppression of the interests of the peripheral groups more difficult and equally makes the growth of nongovernmental organizations that represent those interests more effective in the political domain.

Ironically, the celebrated pessimists George Orwell and Aldous Huxley, the authors of *1984* and *The Brave New World*, imagined modern technology as the enemy of freedom and the unwitting tool of totalitarianism: things, however, have turned out for the better, not worse. Modern technology was supposed to make Big Brother omnipotent, watching you into submission; instead, it has enabled us to watch Big Brother into impotence. Faxes, video cassettes, and CNN have plagued and paralyzed dictators and tyrants, accelerating the disintegration of their rule.[30] As a wit has remarked, the PC (the personal computer) has been the death-knell of the CP (the communist party).[31]

Equally, modern technology has illuminated the obscure face of poverty and pestilence, propelling us in the direction of better development. Modern information technology thus produces the extended empathy that can inform a democracy into better democracy. On the other hand, it also increasingly takes work into homes where we work in isolation at our computer terminals, linked only long-distance to others living and working elsewhere, so that the economies from working under one roof—which the Industrial Revolution ushered in, which Adam Smith theorized about, and which led to factories in place of the earlier "putting out" system of production—are now receding. That can produce less bonding and hence more alienation that can coexist with the increase in extended empathy. Thus, we may well see both weakened bonds within communities and strengthened bonds between them. [32]

The recent rise of NGOs, cutting across countries but built around societal issues such as the protection of the environment and of labor rights, may be explained partly in terms of such extended empathy that produces common international causes and movements.[33] Those organizations certainly constitute a powerful new institutional phenomenon that serves to make the voice of the periphery within each nation more audible since it is exercised with other similar voices in unison.

It is also a remarkable fact that the hostility of governments in the developing countries to the activities of foreign institutions, among them NGOs, has reduced sharply today. That is a sea change from the early postwar years when the developing countries jealously guarded their sovereignty and worried about neocolonialism, embraced the West warily, and, in place of the notion that such embrace would lead to mutual gain, feared instead a malign impact and even malign intent. Again, it is in keeping with Kantian reasoning that it is the democracies that have opened their doors wider in this way, not the authoritarian governments: witness the contrast between India and China again.

Democracy and Markets

Evidently then the "cruel dilemma" thesis, forcing us to choose between democracy and development, was too simple-minded; the relationship between the two is far more textured, and less unfavorable to democracy, than we thought then.

But we can say something more. Think of well-functioning markets as leading, *ceteris paribus*, to development: that seems to be quite plausible, in light of both theory and empirical evidence.[34]

Since democracy and authoritarian rule are in reality combined with absence or prevalence of well-functioning markets, we may well ask whether experience suggests anything interesting in regard to the interaction among those two sets of institutions.

The postwar reality seems to divide into four typologies on those two dimensions. The first, *democracy with markets*, are by and large, the Western democracies; they had strong performance until the OPEC crisis; they also have generally good social indicators. The second, *democracy without markets*, has India as its prime example; she had a sorry economic performance and her social indicators are also unsatisfactory. The third, *authoritarian rule with markets*, includes China in the last decade, and the Far Eastern countries since the 1960s; such regimes had a rapid impact on poverty, and their social indicators are not bad. The fourth, *authoritarian rule without markets* includes the former socialist countries; they are abysmal failures, both in terms of growth and social indicators.

What do we learn, if anything, from that typology? Perhaps not much that is firm and compelling in itself, since any typology on just the two dimensions of "democracy" and "markets," each in turn concealing variations in the "quality" of democracy and of markets, leaves out too many complicating factors that affect specific outcomes. Nonetheless, the typology does suggest three broad propositions that a reasonable analyst should be able to defend without being summarily routed. First, where neither democracy nor markets function, the incentive structure for production and innovation will have been weakened so much as to impair productivity and growth. Second, markets can deliver growth, with or without democracy. Third, democracy without markets is unlikely to deliver significant growth. The last proposition, which speaks naturally to India's experience in the postwar period until the current reforms, is perhaps the most interesting to contemplate further.[35] Why should the lack of well-functioning markets subtract from democracy's possibly favorable effects on development?

The answer seems to cry out from Indian experience. Democracy, with its civil and political rights including the ability to travel,[36] work, and be able to learn and invent abroad, has made the elite Indians, who had the advantage of access to modern education over a century, extremely capable of absorbing, even building intellectually on, innovative ideas and technologies from everywhere. But the *ability* to translate those ideas and know-how into effective innovation and productive efficiency was seriously handicapped by the restrictions that straitjacketed economic decisions at all levels. Thus, for instance, even while Indian surgeons were right at the frontier in open-heart surgery, following the Massachussetts General Hospital's feat shortly thereafter in Bombay, the inability to import medical equipment without surmounting strict exchange controls, even when gifts were at issue, prevented the effective diffusion of technology to India on a scale commensurate with her abilities. Equally, the *incentive* to produce and to innovate was seriously compromised because the returns to such activity could not be substantial when there were extensive restrictions on production, imports, and investment.[37]

By contrast, the Far Eastern economies, countries with markets despite authoritarianism, profited immensely from the far freer inward diffusion of technology that their substantially freer domestic and international markets permitted and facilitated. The economic interventions of the Indian government, after the early years of more satisfactory growth and promotional rather than restrictive interventions that jump-started the economy from its low pre-Independence growth rates, degenerated quickly into a series of *don'ts*, straitjacketing the economic decisions of the citizens. On the other hand, the Far Eastern economies worked with a series of *dos* that left open considerable room for freedom to produce and innovate (in shape, especially, of importing new-vintage and economically productive technologies).[38]

The chief lesson may then well be that democracy and markets are the twin pillars on which to build prosperity.[39]

Notes

1. See Bhagwati, (1966). Princeton political scientist, Atul Kohli, has thus christened this the "cruel dilemma" thesis; see Kohli (1986).

2. At the same time, Samuel Huntington (1993, 35) has noted, since the early 1970s, only four or five of the new democracies have returned to authoritarian rule.

3. A number of statistical and quasi-statistical studies, by economists such as John Helliwell and political scientists such as Atul Kohli, have argued that the evidence does not support the view that the relationship between democracy and growth rates is negative, nor does it support the contrary view. These results are therefore more eclectic and enable us to raise the qualitative questions that are considered in the lecture. Sec Kohli (1986) and Helliwell, 1993.

4. Cited in the *Economist*, August 27, 1994, p. 15. Also, see Prime Minister Yew's nuanced and fascinating interview with Fareed Zakaria in *Foreign Affairs*, March/April 1994, pp. 109–26.

5. Hong Kong, while not a democracy, has had more of its attributes than the other three countries.

6. See Dahrendorf (1966).

7. See Moore (1966). For those who work with regressions, one must then also caution that a strong association between democracy and development may mean, not that democracy promotes development, but that development leads to democracy.

8. Perhaps the only other influential idea, to be formally modeled only forty years later, was that of Paul Rosenstein-Rodan, who, just at the end of the Second World War, argued that several investments would have to be coordinated and simultaneously undertaken in a big push with the aid of state intervention to rescue a developing country from a stagnant equilibrium. This idea provided the theoretical impetus for the planning approach to development and to the widespread practice of five-year plans in several countries, even though the actual practice went back to the Soviets.

9. The idea is perfectly simple. The increment in income, which naturally determines the growth rate of income, must obviously depend on how much you invest and how much you get out of it. The two parameters in the text are precisely what will tell you the magnitudes of these determinants of the growth rate.

10. Interestingly, some economists such as Gunnar Myrdal thought at the time that the socialist countries would be able to grow faster than capitalist countries also because they would be able to increase the productivity of investment, reducing the capital required to produce output (and thus reducing the marginal capital-output ratio in the denominator of the Harrod-Domar growth equation, which can be written to equate the growth rate of income with the average savings ratio divided by the marginal capital-output ratio), by technological innovation in things like prefab housing. How wrong they were: for, as discussed in the text, they failed altogether to consider the question of the incentives to innovate and to produce efficiently in these regimes that had neither markets nor democracy.

11. Bhagwati (1966, 204). Also see Kohli (1986, 156).

12. See Bhagwati (1993, 31–38).

13. I consider democracy broadly here, in contrast to authoritarianism, without entering the added nuances that come from considering the quality of democracy, an issue taken up later in the Lecture.

14. Take three countries. If there are one democracy and two dictatorships, each country can fight the two others. But, if there are two democracies and one dictatorship, each of the former can fight only with the dictatorship while the latter can fight with each democracy. Relying only on the data on *actual* wars to make the foregoing argument is not correct, however. There may be many dictatorships that have not gone to war while every democracy has, so that the average tendency of a dictatorship to get into a war may be less than that of a democracy.

15. See Maoz and Russett (1993, 624). As always, there is extended debate among political scientists whether this observation is robust. Some have contended that the proposition is exaggerated by some fairly fast and loose characterization of selected countries in the data set, whereas others (for example, Farber and Gowa (1995) have argued that the evidence for this relationship between democracy and peace is less compelling before World War II and that, after World War II, the peace among democracies was due to shared political interests expressed in political alliances (a contention that itself may be rejected as a qualification since the alliances in turn may simply be reflecting a shared peaceability among the democracies).

16. The most striking and original revival of Kant's argument is due to Doyle (1983).

17. Kant (1974, 790–92).

18. My former student, Manmohan Agarwal of Jawaharlal Nehru University, has suggested a quasi-Kantian reason that may prompt democracies at times to be peaceful in their disputes with other democracies. Consider cases where one needs to demonizse the enemy before one can carry one's citizens into a war. This may then be a lot more difficult if the enemy is a democracy that is open and

accessible and hence hard to paint in stark colors as a rogue nation than if the enemy were authoritarian and contacts with its subjects made it difficult to sustain the necessary propaganda. Of course, this is also a principal reason why totalitarian countries such as the Soviet Union have gone to great lengths to prevent contachs by their subjects with the citizens of the democracies such as the United states that they were pitted against.

19. See Maoz and Russett (1993). Again, my political science colleague Ed Mansfield has reminded me that some political scientists have reservations about the Maoz-Russett tests and about the specific proxies used by them. Among the recent reexaminations of the issue, see in particular Layne (1994) and Spiro (1994).

20. I should also add that the Kantian argument, and the Russett-Moax evidence in support of it, relate to democracy, not to the process of democratization. The latter raises the question as to how warlike the transition to democracy is likely to be. Comparing no-change to such transition, Ed Mansfield and Jack Snyder (1995) have contended that the former is shown by some empirical evidence to be more peaceable.

21. Olson (1993).

22. Theoretically, this argument can be invalidated if the dictator saves more than the citizens, implying that the dictator is future-regarding rather than simply self-indulgent. Olson must therefore be implicitly assuming that the dictator is extravagant rather than frugal, an assumption that must in turn be justified as I did earlier.

23. See Krueger (1974) and Bhagwati (1982).

24. Most economists are fully aware that Adam Smith did allow for governmental intervention, indeed asked for it, in matters such as education, where he thought that, while the division of labor produced economic benefits, it would produce automatons turning the secrew to the left or to the right every day, all the time, like Charlie Chaplin in Modern Times, so that education would have to be provided to restore them as human beings with texture and sensitivity. To regard Adam Smith as a strict proponent of abolition of all intervention by the state, as is often done by extreme conservatives and libertarians, is to understand Adam Smith improperly.

25. Adam Smith would thus have been an inadequate guide to economic reforms!

26. See, for example, Dreze and Sen (1989).

27. Srinivas and Shah (1960).

28. Thus, it is well known that fear among the rural party-government cadres was one of the most critical factors in the Chinese famine. The information cer-

tainly existed about the famine at the ground level, but the incentive to act on it by seeking immediate relief and action was missing because of the totalitarian structure of the Maoist government. Local officials in some of the famine-stricken areas assumed that Beijing would react to the famine by retribution against them because of failure to fulfill outlandish production targets, instead of reacting by procuring necessary food from, say, foreign countries via commercial or aid-financed imports, as the Indian government did during the Bihar famine.

Hence, we must also ask whether totalitarian regimes will react to information, even when available, in a way that would address it meaningfully. The incentive for such regimes to address a serious famine is itself likely to be less compelling than for democracies.

On the Chinese famine, see Bernstein (1984).

29. See Ackerman (1994). Paper presented to the Nobel Symposium on *Democracy's Victory and Crisis*.

30. This observation also provides yet another critique of the emphasis on information within the country as the key difference that makes famine prevention more likely under a democracy. It is not the information within the country that is likely to be much different; it is the information that percolates out of the country. Is there any doubt that even Mao would have found it difficult to ignore the big famine in China if only the outside world had been able to see, through CNN or other access to China, the deaths and pestilence?

31. One may well conjecture what would have been the outcome of Mao's big famine if only the *outside* world had had even a glimpse of it. As it happens, Joseph Alsop was the only journalist who wrote about it at the time, and no one quite believed it.

32. The former phenomenon seems to have arisen in the United States, for this and other reasons, as documented startlingly by political scientist Robert Putnam.

33. Salomon (1994) has documented the rise of national and international NGOs, calling it the global "associational revolution" and analyzing several cultural and political aspects of that phenomenon.

34. Economist Alice Amsden likes to say, in regard to the Korean experience, that they did well by "getting prices wrong," because the state used credit allocations to affect resource allocation. But surely this is conceptually confused and misleading: if they did the right things, they were getting the social or "shadow" prices right, and these were different from the market prices. In other words, market prices and social costs were unequal, requiring state taxes, subsidies, or both to fix the market failure. So, the "right prices" were different from the market prices, and the Korean authorities did well by using the "right" prices rather than the inappropriate or "wrong" market prices to guide allocation. Whether these interventions were in fact sensible is a different and difficult question, on which there is division of opinion.

35. Of course, India was not without markets altogether. But the vast overreach of bureaucratic intervention in the economy meant that India came pretty close to having few well-functioning markets in trade and in the modern economy.

36. The Indian Supreme Court has arguably upheld this right more broadly than even the U.S. Supreme Court, which has upheld restrictions on travel to Cuba, for instance. Thus, in the well-known case, Mrs. Maneka Gandhi *versus* Union of India and Another, decided on January 25, 1978, the leading judgment by Justice P.N. Bhagwati treated the right to travel abroad as part of "personal liberty," and the impounding by the government of the passport of Mrs. Maneka Gandhi under Section 10 of the Passports Act of 1967 was struck down as an infringement of Article 21 of the Constitution.

37. The deleterious effects of such restrictions on the Soviet economy's dismal performance have been extensively documented by Sovietologists such as Joseph Berliner, Abram Bergson, and Padma Desai.

38. The contrast between interventions in the shape of *don't*s and *do*'s was made by me earlier in (Bhagwati, 1988).

39. In this regard, I must also cite an ambitious statistical study by economist Bhalla (1994). Bhalla works with ninety countries for 1973–1990. His conclusions are broadly supportive of the propositions I have outlined in the lecture, while he concludes more strongly that the statistical evidence shows a favorable impact of "political freedom" (that is, democracy), when treated in a way that enables us to differentiate among different democracies in terms of how democractic they are on different relevant dimensions. His definition of development also extends beyond growth rates to include a couple of social variables: secondary school enrollment and decline in infant mortality. I might add that Bhalla's work is unique among several recent statistical studies in looking at both economic and political "freedom" in exploring the connection between democracy and development.

References

Ackerman, Bruce. 1994. "What Kind of Democracy?: The Political Case for Constitutional Courts." Yale Law School, photocopy.

Bernstein, Thomas. 1984. "Stalinism, Famine, and Chinese Peasants: Grain Procurements During the Great Leap Forward." *Theory and Society* 13 (May): 339–77.

Bhagwati, Jagdish. 1966. *The Economics of Underdeveloped Countries*. London: Weidenfeld & Nicholson.

———. 1982. "Directly Unproductive Profit-Seeking (DUP) Activities." *Journal of Political Economy* 90 (October): 988–1002.

———. 1993. "Democracy and Development." In *Capitalism, Socialism, and Democracy Revisited*, edited by Larry Diamond and Marc Plattner. Baltimore: Johns Hopkins University Press.

Bhalla, Surjit. 1994. "Freedom and Economic Growth: A Virtuous Cycle?" Paper Presented to the Nobel Symposium "Democracy's Victory and Crisis," Uppsala University, August 27–30.

Dahrendorf, Ralf. 1966. *Society and Democracy in Germany* New York: Doubleday.

Doyle, Michael. 1983. "Kant, Liberal Legacies, and Foreign Affairs, Part I." *Philosophy and Public Affairs* 2 (Summer).

Dreze, Jean, and Amartya Sen. 1989. *Hunger and Public Action*. Oxford: Clarendon Press.

Farber, Henry, and Joanne Gowa. 1995. "Politics and Peace." *International Security* 20 (Fall).

Helliwell, John. 1993. "Empirical Linkages between Democracy and Growth." Cambridge: National Bureau of Economic Recearch Working Paper No. 4066.

Huntington, Samuel. 1993. "The Ungovernability of Democracy." *American Enterprise* (November/December): 35.

Kant, Immanuel. 1974. "Perceptual Peace." In *The Enlightenment*, edited by Peter Gay. New York: Simon and Schuster.

Kohli, Atul. 1986. "Democracy and Development. London: Weidenfeld & Nicolson." In *Development Strategies Reconsidered*, edited by John Lewis and Valeriana Kallab. Washington, D.C.: Overseas Development Council.

Krueger, Anne O. 1974. "The Political Economy of the Rent-Seeking Society." *American Economic Review* 64 (June).

Layne, Christopher. 1994. "Kant or Cant: The Myth of the Democratic Peace." *International Security* 19 (Fall): 5–49.

Mansfield, Edward, and Jack Snyder. 1995. "Democratization and War." *Foreign Affairs* (May/June): 79–97.

Maoz, Zeev, and Bruce Russett. 1993. "Normative and Structural Causes of Democratic Peace, 1946–1986." *American Political Science Review* 87 (September).

Moore, Barrington. *1966. Social Origins of Dictatorship and Democracy.* Boston: Beacon Press.

Olson, Mancur. 1993. "Dictatorship, Democracy, and Development." *American Political Science Review* (September).

Salomon, Lester. 1994. "The Rise of the Nonprofit Sector." *Foreign Affairs* (July/August).

Spiro, David. 1994. "The Insignificance of the Liberal Peace." *International Security* 19 (Fall): 50–86.

Srinivas, M. N., and Arvind Shah. 1960. "The Myth of the Self-Sufficiency of the Indian Village." *Economic Weekly* 12: 1375–78.

41

Better than Bloomsbury?

In *A Mathematician's Apology*, G. H. Hardy writes of the excitement that overtook him and Littlewood as they scrutinised the "theorems, most of them wild or fantastic looking," that the unknown Ramanujan had mailed to Cambridge. The discovery of this mathematical genius, an obscure and untutored clerk in Madras, was the one romantic episode in Hardy's life.

Martin Weitzman's work on the share economy plunges us into similar excitement. He is already famous as a technical theorist of considerable originality and power, working at MIT in one of the world's leading economics departments. He has also written extensively on the Soviet economy; indeed he is recognised as the most notable figure in Soviet economics since Abram Bergson. That he should have emerged from this unlikely flank and produced arguably the most profound work in macroeconomics since Keynes certainly makes the publication of this slender volume a romantic episode if not a major event.

Weitzman's argument is audacious. The two recent crises of capitalism, the prewar plunges into deep recessions and massive unemployment epitomised by the Great Crash of 1929, and the

---

Originally published in *Mainstream* (November 30, 1985). Reprinted with permission.

This chapter reviews Martin L. Weitzman's *The Share Economy* (Cambridge: Harvard University Press, 1984).

postwar emergence of stagflation where unemployment accompanies inflation instead of reducing it, are fundamentally a result of the capitalist wage system. Hiring of labour by firms for a fixed wage is the root of these macroeconomic evils. Replacement of it by some form of "sharing" arrangement (for instance, profit sharing) will alter the capitalist system in an essential way. Involuntary unemployment will not endure; inflation will be moderated.

Weitzman promises that the share-economy firms, unlike the fixed-wage-system firms, will be "ever hungry for labour ... crawling around like vacuum cleaners on wheels, searching in nooks and crannies for extra workers to pull in." At the same time, the share-economy firms will be less prone to raise prices and create inflation since sharing translates increased prices automatically into higher costs.

Weitzman's central argument can only be appreciated by putting it into an economic-philosophical and ideological perspective, as he himself invites the reader to do. Indeed, we must go back to Keynes.

Keynes certainly recognised that the malfunctioning of the labour market was critical. The classical economists before him had argued that wage rigidity was the culprit, sustaining massive unemployment. Keynes protested that even wage cutting would run into an insuperable difficulty. Economywide wage cuts would tend to increase employment immediately. But they would simultaneously reduce purchasing power. The consequent fall in "aggregate demand" would cut into employment. The direct micro and the indirect macro effects of wage cuts on employment were therefore at cross purposes. The classical faith in the eventual restoration of full employment through wage reductions was therefore misplaced. At best, successive wage cuts would be a painful and impossibly slow antidote to unemployment. Capitalism was thus in a Catch-22 situation: wage rigidity was a curse but wage cuts held no promise either.

Was capitalism then doomed by this inherent flaw? Keynes's genius lay in a brilliant tactical manouever. He turned to discretionary fiscal policy as a tool with which the government would offset any deficiency in aggregate demand. The malfunctioning of the labour market was in effect treated as unavoidable. Instead, its consequences were to be subjected to a policy quick-fix that no economist of repute had included in his tool kit in thinking of the unemployment malaise (though Gunnar Myrdal and the Swedish School had come close to doing so).

With the world ravaged by the Great Depression and hungry for solutions, and armed by a new paradigm eloquently set forth in his *General Theory*, Keynes had everything going for him. Governments eagerly embraced his activist prescriptions; intellectual opponents capitulated or were swept away.

But this masterly shift of focus that Keynes managed, from worrying about a direct solution (to the labour market problem he had so beautifully diagnosed) to proposing an indirect strategy of fiscal-policy intervention, had within it the seeds of discord. Ultimately, the strengthened role of the state in the Keynesian solution would invite ideological counterattack.

Expectedly, the reaction came from the influential Chicago School, led by the formidable Milton Friedman. The intellectual successor to the Manchester School, wedded to the virtues of the invisible hand, the Chicago School was faced since the late 1990s by two serious crises.

The *microeconomic* threat had come from notable economists led by Joan Robinson and John Kenneth Galbraith, the latter providing the fresh insights and the former also the necessary paradigm without which a science will not change course. In their view, the capitalist world was dominated by large firms, producing differentiated products. The case for the unassisted invisible hand, however, was founded in essence on the altogether different conception of a competitive economy of atomistic firms. It had therefore elegance but no relevance. Chicago responded vigorously by arguing that the imperfectly competitive large firms that Galbraith's naked eye had perceived from the editorial offices of *Fortune* magazine were in reality in competition because of threats of entry by other large firms. The world was "as if" fully competitive. For years, Chicago students would work away, testing econometrically the implications of the hypothesis that industries with large firms were in fact competitive, seeking to destroy the seditious casual empiricism of Galbraith and therewith the empirical rationale for the new paradigm.

The *macroeconomic* threat from Keynes was evidently more serious. But the very success of Keynesianism in banishing major slumps of the 1929 variety in the postwar period cleared the ground eventually for revisionism that would win battles obfuscating the fact that the war was lost.

In particular, Friedman came up in 1951 with the subtle argument that countercyclical intervention to achieve full employment could result in more instability than would less intervention or inaction. "In this field, as in all others, the 'will' is too often mistaken for the 'deed'." Much later, his successor at Chicago, Robert Lucas, Jr, would head the new "rational expectations" school, which would claim that, when policy was anticipated, it would be allowed for and become wholly ineffective. Between Friedman and Lucas, therefore, policy intervention was nailed to the wall: either it might worsen things or it was simply impotent! Faced with this, liberal and Left-wing economists cannot but recall the Graham Greene story where two Englishwomen, on returning from a European holiday, give vent to their disappointments. One complains that the food was terrible; the other responds that there was not enough of it either.

In the end, Friedman's passionate resurrection of monetary policy (which Keynes had virtually dismissed as ineffective) as the key and only control instrument for macroeconomic management can also be understood in an ideological perspective. If fiscal policy was dethroned as a necessary macromanagement tool, state activism at the heart of the polity would have been snuffed out. As one tries to understand what motivated the Reagan administration faithful to ignore the macro implications of the budget deficit, reducing fiscal policy therefore to a micro tool oriented simply to incentives and efficiency while letting Paul Volcker address macromanagement, one sees unmistakeably the shadow cast by the ideological response to Keynes.

The Keynesian magic, conjuring macro policy out of the hat when a malfunctioning wage system had gone into it instead, thus invited fractious ideological debates that then took the center stage. Keynesianism's ultimate irony however was that, as its success reduced the scourge of massive unemployment and helpless governments to a neolithic memory, capitalism was catapulted into the new malaise of stagflation.

Rising prices had traditionally been associated with near-full employment. No longer so. As Weitzman emphasises, wage-push inflation, presumably underwritten by vanished fears of resulting unemployment in a Keynesian world, began to coexist with substantial unemployment. Keynesianism had simply no answer to this new crisis. Nor did Friedman's monetarism: sitting tightly on the money supply would cure inflation only by creating massive unemployment. It was as if the vet had cured dysentery by plugging up the beast: the dysentery would vanish but the beast would be dead!

Economists have been baffled, scorned, frantic, as they have desperately looked for a solution to this new crisis. The air is thick with proposals such as wage and price controls and tax-based incomes policy (designed to tax wage increases beyond a norm). They are clever gimmicks, no doubt. At best, however, they are palliatives of varying efficacy and appeal. None gets to the heart of the matter.

Weitzman does. He puts the solution back where Keynes had found the problem. If the wage system is at fault, why not fix *that* directly? Weitzman's dramatic breakthrough owes, I suspect, precisely to his familiarity with the centrally planned economies. China's erstwhile communes, for instance, were long considered to be ways of increasing employment in a surplus-labour economy. A capitalist farmer would hire labour only up to the point at which the marginal (that is, incremental) product from an extra hand would equal the marginal cost of the wage paid to him. But a commune would increase employment further until an extra hand could produce no more. By delinking the payment to the worker from the hiring decision, the commune would maximise employment and output. The form of wage payment is thus a critical issue.

Weitzman's share economy performs the same sort of trick. If workers are paid by a formula that ensures that the marginal cost of hiring an extra hand is always below the marginal revenue that the firm earns from selling the added output, clearly there will always be an incentive to hire more labour. A variety of compensation contracts will fit this bill, chief of them being profit-sharing arrangements. The capitalist system will then be transformed into one where there is a "kind of 'suction' equilibrium, in which all firms are actively seeking to employ more workers at existing compensation parameter rates," whereas the fixed-wage system has "zero demand for unemployed labour" instead. With most firms on such share arrangements, the economic system will work inexorably to cut into unemployment, as firms chase the unemployed like Pac-men on the prowl.

Weitzman, who has backed up this simple and profound insight with technical work in the professional journals, writes of its nuances and ramifications in the pungent prose of Brooklyn, where he grew up, rather than with the cultivated elegance of Keynes's Bloomsbury. Here we have possibly the first authentic American voice since Adam Smith founded the dismal science.

Weitzman has cleverly outlined the Promised Land. But how do we get there? The real problem is that the share economy's splendid virtues arise from the ability of the firm to hire more labour, and the attendant ability to reduce the *average* compensation to labour (and thus meet the key Weitzman requirement that the marginal cost of extra employment be always less than the marginal revenue from selling the output produced by the extra hand). This is essentially what transforms the hackneyed idea of profit sharing, endlessly and tepidly discussed in the Gaitskellite faction of Left-wing parties such as British Labour and strangely enough embraced by David Steel's Liberal Party in England as well, into the potent tool that Weitzman has shown it to be.

This does create a central difficulty. Will the unions, who may well approve of profit-sharing contracts, agree simultaneously to their being designed such that more labour can be hired freely and average wages fall within the firm in consequence? If the social dynamics of profit sharing turns out to be such that unions and firms on such contracts wind up acting as "closed shops" instead, Weitzman's share-economy firms will transform into a surrogate for the worker-owned firms under Yugoslav *socialism* without the magic macro properties of the share economy. Weitzman is fixing *capitalism*, while preserving it; the firm must continue to control the hiring decision.

The attitude of the unions is therefore critical to Weitzman's game plan. Weitzman urges unions to recognize that the share economy will substantially reduce unemployment, consequently improving labour income over what it would be under the fixed-wage system. A "labour-hungry" system should also, simply through the powerful profit motive, lead to improved treatment of labour on the job just as, in product markets, "buyer-hungry" firms woo and pamper buyers in the capitalist system (while, as Weitzman donning his Sovietlogical hat notes wryly, the miserable Soviet buyer chases sellers instead).

The working *class* ought therefore to improve its lot under a share-economy capitalism. Will the unions take this long view?

42

America Grows Roots Outside the Old Testament

Our little daughter Anuradha came home from school recently and asked: Daddy, are we Jewish? Tickled down to our Hindu toes, we jested: No, darling, we are the next best.

But our curiosity was aroused. The question, it turned out, was prompted by her school, liberal and progressive, deciding that Rosh Hashana and Yom Kippur would now be holidays. We were delighted. Surely Diwali, and perhaps even Holi if every religion was allocated two holidays, could not be far behind. Nina and Natalia would learn about our religion and culture just as Anuradha would bone up on theirs. Alas, we should have known better!

The unwitting neglect of our sensibilities, while hard to take, is easy to explain. Significant religious and ethnic diversity, outside of Judeo-Christianity and the European stock, is a quite recent phenomenon in America. It reflects our changed immigration laws and procedures.

The 1965 Immigration Act eliminated the national origin quotas that biased professional immigration heavily in favor of Europe. Entry was now by queue, common to all. Aspiring immigrants of all races, colors, and religions competed on equal terms. Immigration has since gone up greatly from non-Christian developing countries, including India and Pakistan.

Originally published in the *Wall Street Journal* (December 2, 1985), with Padma Desai.

The composition of the refugee influx remains more subject to the vagaries of domestic politics. Here too, however, the fall of Vietnam and the tragic refugee exodus by boat have led to a large recent inflow of non-Christian Asians.

The Census statistics, while treacherous to compare over time, broadly underline this changed reality. Between 1890 and 1950, the "nonwhite, other races" in the U.S. population increased only twofold to a paltry 711,070, while the total population grew faster by 2.5 times to 150 million. The 1980 Census, on the other hand, shows just the Chinese, Korean, Asian Indian, Vietnamese and Japanese to number 2.5 million, well over a threefold increase since 1950. By contrast the total population has grown less than 50 percent to 226 million.

These immigrant groups are now reaching a significant size. They are also exceptionally accomplished in the sciences, the arts, the universities, the professions, and increasingly in business. They have been a quick study, observing that these precise preconditions assisted the Jewish immigrants once despised and the target of exclusionary national legislation, to organize effectively and to obtain their civil rights. They have therefore started organizing as pressure groups.

But should their rights and sensitivities be left merely to their lobbying within our pluralistic system? Surely, we need here also the enlightened efforts of intellectuals, academics, and common-cause groups to raise the issue above self-seeking politicking to the arena of principle.

In particular, these efforts should be directed at reviewing the appropriateness of our customary modes of manifesting religiosity in public rituals. We are not a religious state like Saudi Arabia and Iran. Nor are we populated any longer by adherents of one religion, Christianity. Is it not thoughtless then to have, for instance, at commencement exercises of secular nonreligious universities or at national conventions such as the Republican Party's at the last presidential election, benediction being pronounced exclusively by Christian priests and ministers, with an occasional rabbi breaking the monotony?

Mahatma Gandhi, who borrowed civil disobedience from Thoreau, can offer us an idea in turn. During his public meetings, he often had prayers. But, devout Hindu though he was in a pre-ponderantly Hindu country, he insisted on using snippets from the holy books of India's other religions. This public evenhandedness, consistent with private preferences, in religiosity is the model we should adopt as we come to terms with the new social realities of America's ethnicity.

As it happens, Gandhi and Massachusetts are of one mind again on this. In Cambridge, our first destination as immigrants from India, the Massachusetts Institute of Technology has a non-denominational chapel. The altar changes to suit your faith, prompting the gag that you can change your religion at MIT by pushing a button. But seriously, it points the way.

43

Learning from the
Religions of Others

You report on the Transfiguration parochial school in New York City's Chinatown, with 95 percent Chinese students, 80 percent of them Buddhists (news article, February 16, 1991).

What Transfiguration does, despite possible impressions to the contrary, is to combine the cross and the dragon, not Christ and Buddha. The encouragement of Chinese culture is not synonymous with the elevation of the Buddhist faith of these pupils to parity in the school's curriculum with Roman Catholic instruction.

Indeed, the wonderfully tolerant, syncretic, and inclusive sentiments of the largely working-class Buddhist parents that you record ("I am a Buddhist," says one, "and when I open my son's religion books, I see the same human values I believe in") puts into embarrassing perspective the school's insistence that "[a]ll children, regardless of their faith, attend all Masses and religious ceremonies"—meaning Catholic ceremonies.

There are other, better models for the spirit of toleration. In St. Xavier's, the splendid Catholic mission school that I attended in Bombay in the 1950s, the Catholics and other Christians had Bible classes; the rest of us were instructed in morals, altogether free from Christianity's theology and rituals. The good deed of providing an excellent education was its own reward, here and in

Originally published as a letter to the editor in the *New York Times* (March 17, 1991). Copyright © 1991 by the New York Times Co. Reprinted by permission.

heaven. Perhaps the hope was that the very example of a religion that would evenhandedly dispense benefits to all, while denying itself the advantage of insidious indoctrination, would attract others to its fold.

This is the wiser, and the more appropriate, path for our increasingly multireligious society. Respect for other religions, even while one is wedded to one's own, has to be genuine and strong; it is a sine qua non for harmony and pluralism, values that make our society less fractious.

We should therefore pray for the day when Transfiguration makes the transition from the dragon to the Buddha.

44

Crisis Helps Advance Ideological Positions on Population Growth

Edward Mortimer's article[1] on the Cairo conference on population misses the point in arguing that the delegates miss the point by focusing on ideology rather than on population growth which, in any case, can be expected to become "nearly stationary" on current trends.

As it happens, the complacent and comforting population projections that Mortimer accepts are as fragile as the alarmist ones, if past projections are any guide, which is why it has become customary to work with alternative scenarios. Nor is Mortimer well advised to rely on economists who dissociate hunger and destitution from population explosion. These scourges occur despite the per capita availability of enough food to avoid them since need and demand are two different things, but it is a non sequitur to conclude that therefore they cannot occur due to pressure of population: in a raft at sea with the last bottle of fresh water, Robinson Crusoe would do well without Man Friday, you bet.

Even if you do not believe the alarmist estimates, however, it may be prudent to rely on the precautionary principle. But many go with the estimates for a different reason. They seek to create and then use a sense of crisis to advance ideological positions,

Originally published as a letter to the editor in the *Financial Times* (September 13, 1994).

exaggerating in turn the impact of their preferred policies to advance them as cures to the crisis. Just as John Stuart Mill shrewdly observed that "a good cause seldom triumphs unless someone's interest is tied up in it," the women's groups that properly seek empowerment and abortion rights see political value in a sense of crisis (no matter how weak its intellectual underpinnings) that creates ferment, fuels urgency, and fertilises the ground for their causes to take root.

In fact, even the suggestion that female education—and Mortimer may well have added female participation in the workforce—rather than ideology aids population control draws a false contrast. Female education has generally advanced because of ideology, not because of a cost-benefit calculation by us economists of its value for population control or growth rates. That we can simultaneously argue, thanks to the research of economists such as Robert Repetto, that it advances these other causes, while being a good in itself, is splendid: it enables us to do well while doing good.

But we must not forget that a good society will address precisely these ideological questions at every opportunity, seeking progress in the well-being of women that, astonishingly, still eludes them in every part of the world.

Note

1. Edward Mortimer, "False Alarm in Cairo," *Financial Times*, September 7, 1994.

45

Panic, Petulance, and Paranoia about Japan

The designer of this book's jacket has beautifully captured Pat Choate's panic and petulance about Japan and his paranoia about its *Agents of Influence* in our midst.

An arresting circle in red represents the rising sun; it also suggests a spreading stain. Lest the subliminal message not suffice, the jacket crassly adds: "How Japan's Lobbyists in the United States Manipulate America's Political and Economic System." Equally, political economist Choate supplements innuendo by naming names.

Indeed, the book is replete with explicit accounts and implicit criticisms of the writings and other activities of specific individuals who are "excessively" pro-Japan and see little virtue and much embarrassment in the rise of Japan-fixation and Japan-bashing. Among the targets are the renowned Japan experts, Dean George Packard of John Hopkins and Professor Gary Saxonhouse of the University of Michigan, and Hobart Rowen of the *Washington Post* (the doyen of our economics columnists, along with Leonard Silk of the *New York Times*).

Originally published in the *Detroit News* (November 14, 1990). Reprinted with permission of The Detroit News.

This chapter reviews Pat Choate's *Agents of Influence: How Japan's Lobbyists in the United States Manipulate America's Political and Economic System* (New York: Knopf, 1990).

Among their many sins are relationships with Japanese research institutions (Saxonhouse); writing in support of moderation in U.S. demands on Japan (Packard); and accepting Japanese corporations as clients in trade talks or disputes and nonetheless having the gall to write articles on U.S.-Japan conflicts as well as on U.S. trade and foreign investment policy as if they had independent views (former government officials, now businessmen, Elliott Richardson and Peter Petersen).

What infuriates Choate most is that these men treat the energetic Japan-worriers in the United States with such scant respect. James Fallows of the *Atlantic Monthly* is described as having been "outraged" by economist John Makin's characterization of his several critical articles on Japan as having been prompted by Fallows' stay there and his resulting dislike of the Japanese. Admittedly, Makin got it wrong; but Fallows certainly helped him get it wrong by indulging in fearful cultural stereotypes such as "The lack of [Japanese] interest in principle makes sheer power the main test of what is 'fair'" and urging us to "contain" Japan.

Seeing Japan's invisible hand everywhere, strangulating us steadily and surely, Choate fancies himself as a plucky David standing up to the colossal Goliath in kimono. In his passionate conviction that Japan can do no right, Choate comes across instead as the "bad guy" in free-style wrestling, who breaks every rule in the game to win and enjoys every moment of it.

The tragedy is that, in place of the false alarms and finger-pointing, often based on shoddy research and a failure to investigate alternative viewpoints, Choate could have provoked a more focused and informed debate by arguing (from the perspective of Japan-worriers) that:

• Japan is rising economically at our expense and will continue to do so.

• This is happening because of a peculiar, and damaging, constellation of ideology, interests, and institutions in the United States.

• The ideology is that free trade and investments are good for us, no matter what. This keeps our economy open and vulnerable to Japan, which closes its economy and prospers.

• The interests that do harm are the lobbyists who accept Japanese clients and academics who receive financial support for their institutions. They consequently take Japan's side in its feuds and struggles with us for economic supremacy.

• The institutions that permit these interests to function include the "revolving door" in Washington (in which former government officials use their expertise to represent foreign countries in trade matters) and the acceptance of foreign monies by our universities and think tanks.

These are at least reasonable arguments, though they are incorrect. For instance, empirical researchers, not just "ideologues," have argued that open markets build stronger industries than closed markets.

But the basic problem with Choate is that he views Japan as infiltrating our open system with extensive lobbying and purchase of people. This is wrong on two counts.

First, much of the lobbying is a result of the extensive Japan-bashing that goes on these days, in both action and talk. Is it surprising that the Japanese corporations, institutions, and government feel constrained to spend outrageous sums of money to explain, defend, and negotiate their way out of this adverse, selective trade treatment by us?

Second, while the fast-revolving door is an ugly blot on the U.S. scene, it is also a rush to judgment to imply that those who take Japanese clients are serving an alien regime and therefore cannot serve our interests. Thus, Choate is worried that Carla Hills, before her appointment as the U.S. trade representative, had Japanese clients.

Leaving aside the fact that multiple clients may lead to loyalty to none, it is revealing that Choate is unaware that she also served on the board of directors of major U.S. corporations. Among the chief executive officers of these corporations, we find the leading advocates of "managed trade"—a popular euphemism for securing privileged access to Japan's markets through intimidation and at the expense of our multilateral trading obligations. Our national interest surely lies in resisting such damaging and self-serving pressures from corporate interests. Is Hills, who has bravely defied such pressures, not serving out national interest even though it happens to coincide with Japan's interest in resisting the breakdown of its rules-based trade with us?

Indeed, the truly insidious effect of Japan on us has been not in the fanciful ways that Choate's fevered imagination concocts. It has been in the growing coziness of our intellectual and corporate interests that Japan's success has prompted.

Traumatized by our sense of decline and blaming it on our divisiveness, while attributing Japan's rise to the symbiotic relationship imagined among its many interests, the Democrats and their intellectuals (among them, quite prominently, Choate) have increasingly come to confuse corporate (or producer) interests with our national interest. Even were we to break down the revolving door, this loss of the old, fierce independence from narrowly sectional interests that marked the great liberal intellectuals in our country would remain. What a pity.

46

"Agents of Influence":
An Exchange

The exchange between Fred Bergsten and James Fallows[1] over the latter's review of Pat Choate's *Agents of Influence*[2] is a superficial skirmish that provides entertainment. But it fails to illuminate why scholars, not just of Japan, find the book reprehensible.

Among the Japan-in-America-focused allegations contained in Choate's charge-sheet, two are prominent: First, that American scholars essentially produce apologetics or propaganda on behalf of Japan because their institutions and projects are financed by Japanese funds (the very prospect of losing them being enough to produce compliance). Second, in the more benign version favored by Fallows, that by financing those whose research findings are "pro-Japan" the Japanese funds put at disadvantage in the policy debate those who find Japan different or wicked and therefore inimical to American interests.

The "facts" on which these judgments are based are themselves dubious. It is untrue that the scholarly critiques of the endless litany of complaints by the Japan-worriers of Japan's uniqueness and perfidy are overwhelmingly, even largely, financed by Japan. The error arises from the vulgar assumption, readily made by those inside the beltway and hence outside the universities, that research requires, not reflection and scholarship, but that wonder-

Originally published as a letter to the editor in the *New York Review of Books* (May 16, 1991): 64. Reprinted with permission.

ful American invention: "financial support." Many of us are still content to do research on our academic salaries: after all, that is what professors, who are a public good, are traditionally *supposed* to do. Many economists whom I know, and not just I, write on Japan just as Maynard Keynes wrote on India and Joan Robinson on China without financial support beyond our university stipends!

If anything, many more get funds from *American* sources, including predominantly our corporate sector, whose economic (self-)interests are not necessarily congruent with our *national* interest, as the older Democrats should remind the younger ones. Indeed, many of these corporate interests are engaged in intense competition with Japanese firms. Surely, Messrs Choate and Fallows, whose worries about such matters are destructive of the delicate fabric of our civil society (as I argue blow), must know that the academics who support the semiconductors agreement imposed by us on Japan include those who serve on the boards of directors of Silicon Valley firms. Also, the economists who ask for aggressive strikes against Japan to "open her markets" include those who accept moneys to lend their distinguished names to pamphlets published by corporations with a stake in the Japanese market. All this is possibly imprudent, and certainly (by my book) even in bad taste; but none of it is venal, wicked, or proof that these economists speak, not for themselves, but for these corporations.

And *that* is the heart of the matter. What Choate wounds more than the facts is the shared belief, uniquely American, that we can transcend the constraints imposed by the special circumstances and interests that define our social and economic situation. Thus, when Henry Kissinger and Congressman Stephen Solarz (both Jews) support the congressional resolution on the Gulf War, or when Congressman Robert Matsui (a nisei) advocates restraint in trade disputes with Japan, or Zbigniew Brzezinski (a Pole) advocates militancy toward the Soviet Union, we correctly do not insist on their identifying their ethnicity, for we presume that they speak as Americans. So do we permit our universities and think tanks to accept funds from foundations and from corporate and labor groups, whether domestic or foreign: we trust the good sense of our citizens to protect their integrity and of our institutions to preserve their independence (as they, in fact, generally do through appropriate procedures and restraints).

These values make our civil society less fractious and more harmonious; they also tend to be self-validating. They would surely begin to erode if we were to surrender to the hysterical reaction to Japan's economic success that Choate represents and recommends.

Lest anyone doubt this, may I note that both Fallows, and Karel van Wolferen in his equally sympathetic review in the *New Republic*,[3] feel constrained to identify themselves as Choate's acquaintances and the beneficiaries of his attention? If "full disclosure" (van Wolferen's phrase) were required each time Mr. Silvers published a review, and whenever each of us expressed views other than bland banalities, we would surely have turned into an uncivil society of humourless, suspicious, finger-pointing, and conspiracy-minded citizens.

Notes

1. See Fallows (1991).

2. See Fallows (1990).

3. See van Wolferen (1991).

References

Fallows, James M. 1990. "The Great Japanese Misunderstanding." *New York Review of Books* 37, November 8: 33–39.

———. 1991. "'The Japanese Power Game': An Exchange." *New York Review of Books* 38, January 17: 57.

Van Wolferen, Karel. 1991. "America's Illusions." *New Republic*, February 11: 35–41.

47   Exclude the Exclusionary Rule

The relaxation of the exclusionary rule in the House of Representatives crime bill, which would allow evidence seized illegally but in good faith to be admitted in court, has outraged liberals. They rely on the conventional argument that this will violate our fundamental right to be protected from unconstitutional searches. Conservatives justify the revision on the equally tired ground that criminals should not get off simply on "technicalities" (a question that arose in the O. J. Simpson trial when critical evidence, allegedly collected without proper warrant, was nearly excluded).

In truth, however, our current exclusionary rule and the revision proposed by the House are both inadequate. The first regularly derails justice by placing crucial evidence out of reach, while the latter excuses police violations of fundamental rights so long as they are made accidentally rather than maliciously.

A better approach emerges from economic theory—which holds that efficient achievement of multiple objectives generally requires multiple problem-solving instruments. (This is the insight that won Jan Tinbergen the first Nobel Prize in economics.) Or as our forefathers put is so well: you cannot kill two birds with one stone.

Originally published under the title "... Or Get Rid of It Altogether" in *American Enterprise* (May/June 1995): 44–45. Reprinted with permission.

Currently, in cases where evidence has been seized in some constitutionally indefensible way, the courts must struggle to reconcile two very different objectives: the guilty must be punished, and at the same time citizens must be protected from overzealous police. In rejecting any use of "tainted" evidence (as was standard until the limited exemption for "good faith" behavior whose extension is now being contemplated), we force the courts to use a single policy instrument to pursue these different, sometimes contradictory, goals.

It would surely be more effective to use two instruments to address the two problems at hand. This could be done by admitting all solid evidence in court, no matter how obtained, so that judicial determination of guilt is as accurate as possible, while simultaneously providing separate mechanisms that hold police accountable for their searches, punishing them when constitutional improprieties are legally established.

Such a solution would improve the efficiency of the criminal justice system in punishing the truly guilty, and it would also be a more effective protection of our constitutional rights. Simply excluding improperly gathered evidence deters the police from future repetitions of their violations only indirectly, via the hope that failing to bring criminals to justice will so frustrate them that they correct their ways. Direct punishment of rogue police would be a better deterrent, and it would do so without the side effect of penalizing the public by freeing known criminals into their midst.

As it happens, Judiciary Committee Chairman Orrin Hatch has introduced in the Senate a reform that fits right into the approach just outlined. Sen. Hatch's provision would kill the eighty-year-old exclusionary rule, and in its place allow victims of illegal searchers to sue police and collect judgments for actual and punitive damages (with the punitive damages capped at $10,000).

Alternative, and perhaps better, ways to punish and deter rogue cops could also be devised. Trigger mechanisms could be installed for the state itself to initiate the judicial action, instead of relying on individual tort action. If that were done, the state would obviously require some prima facie evidence that an illegal search had occurred. But this can only materialize during the trial, and with the defendant having lost the right to exclude tainted evidence, his lawyers have no incentive to establish the constitutional impropriety of the search. To get around this "incentive" problem, the reform could include a fractional mitigation of the punishment that ensues on conviction with tainted evidence.

No matter how we get at the rogue police, it is evident that a two-track solution is needed if we are to efficiently pursue the dual objectives of just punishment for crime and robust protection for our rights. Establishing police accountability is one rail. Ending our unproductive experiment in evidence exclusion is the other.

48   Recalling Orwell

The multilateral trading system centered on the General Agreement on Tariffs and Trade (GATT) and supported by the United States since World War II is being challenged on many fronts today. Protectionists claim legitimacy from new trade theories. Aggressive unilateralists, seeking to take trade laws into their own hands, dispute the rule of trade law at the GATT. Proponents of regionalism mock the multilateral route of trade liberalization, some claiming that the GATT is dead, others that it should be killed, and yet others asserting both simultaneously.

As always in economic debate, there is room for disagreement. Economists divide on policy issues because they view the world differently (for example, Keynesians versus monetarists), or they disagree on the facts to be fed into the framework they share. For the politicians whom economists seek to advise and the lay public whom they seek to influence, sorting through the myriad conflicting opinions that accompany this debate becomes enormously difficult.

It is worth recalling British Prime Minister Robert Peel's lament as he searched for counsel in the writings of the important economists of the time before the repeal of the protectionist Corn Laws in 1846. (That repeal, by the way, signaled the triumph of

Originally published under the title "Revealing Talk on Trade" in the *American Enterprise* (November/December 1991): 72–76. Reprinted with permission.

free-trade doctrine in Britain.) A classic article by Douglas Irwin recounts that Peel "found only confusion and dissension" among the economists about the laws' effects on wages, profits, and rents. Peel found that David Ricardo thought Adam Smith was wrong on the question of the laws' impact on rents, that John McCulloch thought that both Ricardo and Smith were wrong, and that Robert Torrens in turn disagreed with all of the others.

Peel described a book of Torrens's on the subject as "enough to fill with dismay the bewildered inquirer after truth." He quoted in Parliament chapter headings that do indeed strain credulity: "Erroneous views of Adam Smith respecting the value of corn," "Errors of Mr. Ricardo and his followers on the subject of rent," "Errors of Mr. Malthus respecting the nature of rent," "Refutation of the doctrines of Mr. Malthus respecting the usage of labor."

The trade policy debate in the United States today certainly reflects similar unavoidable problems stemming from differing scholarly opinions. But it suffers also from the avoidable proliferation of conceptual confusions, fallacies, and newspeak. This gratuitous prostitution of an important debate comes from the entry into the debating arena of amateurs unencumbered by sufficient knowledge of economics. But, sadly, even more damage is done by the influx of errant economists who divide into two classes: trade scholars, the specialists, writing none too carefully, and nontrade generalists, writing outside their area of competence. The former need only to be reminded of the consequences of sloppiness. The latter are harder to deter.

Should we tell them that while generalists have a useful role to play in the analysis of simpler questions, trade policy issues today are so complex that generalists are doomed to demonstrate that comparative advantage needs to be practiced as well as preached? Or should we hope to dissuade them from their folly with humor? We can tell Nobel-laureate Robert Solow's story of his experience with his economist colleague Charles Kindleberger. Solow had briefly ventured into talking about the dollar in the course of his presentation in a panel discussion; Kindleberger then began his remarks by saying, "First, I would like you to remember that MIT does not pay Professor Solow his salary to think about international economics."

Perhaps the best antidote to the fallacies and confusions is the application of what I call the Dracula principle: Expose evil to sunlight to kill it. In that spirit, I will discuss the prevailing conceptual and terminological confusions, then digress on selected fallacies regarding the GATT and what trade theory says about trade policy, and finally demonstrate how the debate over granting fast-track authority to negotiate the Mexican Free Trade Agreement (FTA) was turned by newspeak into obfuscation and evasion of the key issues it raised.

Conceptual Confusions

Since the 1960s, international economists have held to certain usages that were developed in the context of commercial policy theory in the 1960s and 1970s. In scholarly circles, these usages have provided necessary clarity and consistency to exchanges on economic subjects. But the current public debate on trade policy, by not adhering to the standard definitions, has become confused and confusing. The following, which I call a Guide to Straight Talk on Trade Policy, will outline this terminology and then point out the conflicting uses that have become commonplace.

• *Domestic policy instruments* include taxes on production, consumption, sales, and factor-use, subsidies, and quantitative restraints. By contrast, *foreign policy instruments* (also called *trade policy instruments*) comprise trade taxes, trade subsidies, import and export quotas, voluntary export restraints (VERs) and other export limitations, and voluntary import expansions (VIEs) that set targets for imports by foreign countries.

• *Selective policy* means the use of domestic and/or foreign policy instruments for a subset of sectors of the economy (or for specific firms), while *generalized policy* would apply to all sectors without discrimination among them.

• *Quantitative instruments* set specific limits, as VERs do, whereas *price instruments* use price incentives such as tariffs.

• *Managed trade* means using quantitative instruments, setting targets and constraints in trade. It is also called *results-oriented trade. Rules-oriented trade*, in which quantities traded are not pre-determined but emerge from the markets operating under given rules, is its opposite. The contrast is equally acute in the economists' terminology *fix-quantity* (versus *fix-rule*) *trading regime.*

Managed trade, or a *fix-quantity regime*, is confused with *trade management*, which refers to rulemaking trade negotiations and enforcement of negotiated trade rights and obligations, all of which complement, sustain, and expand the scope of a *fix-rule regime.*

It is then easy to recognize the hopeless confusions in the debate today.

Managed trade is a term that is now widely used to mean all kinds of interventions in trade and in domestic policy, not just quantitative target-setting in trade. The few new, and the many old, arguments in trade theory for tariffs and export subsidies are routinely cited as proof that managed trade is triumphing over free trade when in fact these are arguments for appropriate trade policy intervention, *not* for managed trade.

Advocates of managed trade among the intelligentsia are relatively rare: they include the Japan-bashers, who ask that we assault the Japanese with massive tariffs unless they increase their imports of manufactured goods at a targeted rate (macro-economist Rudiger Dornbusch); the proponents of the 1991 semiconductor pact that imposes an import target on the Japanese; and the advocates of the voluntary export restraints on Japanese autos and of the Multifiber Agreement assigning quotas to foreign suppliers (economic journalist Robert Kuttner). Those who exhort Japan to reduce her trade balance (Henry Kissinger and Cyrus Vance come to mind) are not managed-traders.

We must also condemn the sloppy way in which *trade management* is often used synonymously with *managed trade*. Trade management is essential for maintaining and expanding the fix-rule trading system, which is the antithesis of managed trade! The practice of seeming to find support for managed trade everywhere when in fact support is thin is a surefire recipe to condition unsuspecting public opinion into accepting it.

• *Industrial policy* is a term that is often used, but in different senses. One equates it with selective policy, which favors one or more sectors of the economy or some specific firms but not all firms. Another utilizes the term to convey instead the use of domestic policy, not foreign policy, instruments: for example, the domestic policy instrument could be an R&D subsidy to favor a particular industry, or it could be a generalized R&D subsidy used for all sectors of the economy that wish to take advantage of it.

Because of these two wholly different ways in which the term industrial policy is used, it would be ideal to banish it. But Gresham's law will again apply: Bad usage will drive out the good. Thus, what one should urge upon those who use the term is to make clear to themselves and then to their audience which usage they have in mind.

• In *strategic trade policy* the world *strategic* is thrown, like sand into a fuel tank, at those who favor open markets. Strategic trade policy proponents gain the high rhetorical ground by the very use of the term *strategic*. Yet once again, the term is used in altogether different ways. In discussions of trade policy, it refers to the recent theoretical analysis of international competition among oligopolistic firms that enjoy abnormal (excess) profits and "strategically interact" with one another (that is, the pricing and production decisions of one must consider the reactive behavior of others, so the game played is like chess, not solitaire). In these cases, trade or domestic intervention by the government may shift some of the excess profits and activity to one's own nation and may improve economic welfare.

The term *strategic trade policy* is also used frequently, however, to characterize a governments's use of trade policy—as in a poker game—in the form of threats, confrontations, deliberate exit from negotiations, and other ploys to extract further gains from other nations and even to drive hard bargains that leave others impoverished.

But usages such as these of the word *strategic* in the context of trade policy must be separated from conventional uses as applied to industries or activities that politically or economically are considered to be significant for our economy.

There is no reason for specific industries to be "strategic" in more than one of these many senses. Yet the different meanings are often thrown together deliberately or unwittingly by lobbyists seeking protection for their clients.

Fallacies about the GATT

If the terminological confusions threaten the case for open markets and multilateralism, misconceptions about the GATT, harbored and spread by some ill-informed economists, undermine it further. Surprisingly, even well-known MIT economists Rudiger

Dornbusch and Paul Krugman have committed some egregious mistakes, including:

(1) *"The GATT forbids permanent import quotas but says nothing about export restrictions."*
This is simply wrong. Article II of the GATT begins: "No prohibitions or restrictions other than the duties, taxes, or other charges, whether made effective through quotas, import or export licenses, or other measures, shall be instituted or maintained ... on the importation ... or on the exportation or sale for re-export of any product."

(2) *"Countries are free to violate the spirit as long as they adhere to the letter [of the GATT],"* and *"the GATT polices what nations claim de jure to be doing, not what they may be up to de facto."*

This is also wrong. Economist Michael Finger (1989, 379) has demolished these assertions:

The GATT's negotiating history demonstrates that the persons who negotiated the agreement were aware that, with a bit of imagination, a country could find ways to restrict trade that would not be covered by GATT's stated limits however the limits on policy actions were worded.

It would not do, then, to limit the "policing" or "dispute settlement" provisions of the GATT to instances in which a country had imposed a policy or taken an action that the GATT specifically prohibited. Instead the GATT bases its dispute-settlement procedures on the concept of *nullification* or *impairment* of any *benefit* the complaining country might expect under the agreement.

(3) *"GATT regulates policies that occur at the border. ... The underlying assumption is that ... [border] policies can be clearly distinguished from domestic policies that may also have effects on trade."* In the same spirit, *"Because [Japan's fifth-generation computer program] does not tax, subsidize, or restrict at the border, it does not fall under GATT rules."*

But Article 3 of the GATT explicitly recognizes that "internal taxes ... laws, regulations, and requirements" can afford protection to domestic production. The nullification or impairment of negotiated trade concessions through such internal measures can be brought up before the GATT "court." These economists also ignore the efforts at the GATT that have succeeded in bringing several nonborder practices more formally into the GATT. Evidently, familiarity breeds contempt, but contempt does not breed familiarity.

Regrettably, few know the facts, and these fallacies undercut the multilateral trading system, encourage GATT-bashing, and fuel the drift toward aggressive unilateralism and regionalism.

Fallacies about Trade Theory

The developments in trade theory during the 1980s have been carelessly presented to the public by enthusiastic pioneers as if they had finally overturned the theoretical case for free trade. Such erroneous claims have been eagerly taken up by the media and by lobbies to legitimate their protectionist demands.

Paul Krugman is fairly typical of the proponents of the new theory of trade under imperfect competition in product markets. He argues: "In the last ten years, the traditional constant-returns, perfect-competition models of international trade have been supplemented and to some extent supplanted by models that emphasize increasing returns and imperfect competition. These new models ... open the possibility that government intervention in trade via import restrictions, export subsidies, and so on may under some circumstances be in the national interest after all.... [Thanks to these theoretical developments in the 1980s], there is still a case for free trade as a good policy, and as a useful target in the world of politics, but [free trade] can never be asserted as the policy that economic theory tells us is always right."

But it is simply not true that before the 1980s trade theorists did not produce any theoretical arguments for trade protection and trade subsidies or that as a consequence they thought that free trade was "always right" in economic theory.

In fact, the earliest and most influential theoretical exceptions to the case for free trade were proposed more than a century ago: John Stuart Mill argued for infant-industry protection, and Robert Torrens showed that a country that was able to improve its terms of trade with a tariff should do so. The postwar developments in the theory of commercial policy also analyzed a great number of market imperfections, particularly in factor markets, and analyzed whether trade or domestic policy interventions were appropriate to deal with them. The 1980s simply extended this scientific edifice to product market imperfections; this was important, but from the viewpoint of the theory of commercial policy, it was hardly revolutionary in conception.

The choice of free trade has therefore *always* depended on its being judged an empirically useful and appropriate policy. Some have considered the myriad exceptions to the case for free trade resulting from the presence of market failures to be empirically unimportant. Others have argued that in practice intervention would make matters worse. These are also the time-honored twin routes by which the pioneering trade theorists of the 1980s have returned to the fold of free trade.

The Mexico-U.S. Free Trade Agreement

If confusions and fallacies were the only obstacles we had to contend with in debating trade policy, life would be relatively simple. But the debate over the Mexico-U.S. Free Trade Agreement shows that Orwellian newspeak may also compound our difficulties.

Even a cursory familiarity with international economics would make an economist begin an analysis of free trade agreements

(FTAs) by distinguishing them sharply from free trade: FTAs are inherently preferential and discriminatory (since they remove trade barriers only for members), whereas free trade is not. Since the noted economist Jacob Viner taught us the distinction in *The Customs Union Issue*, we have emphasized that FTAs are two-faced: they liberalize trade (among members), but they protect (against outsiders). A key question therefore is, Which aspect of an FTA is dominant? Or, to put it in economists' jargon: Is a particular FTA trade-diverting (that is, taking trade away from efficient outside suppliers and giving it to inefficient member countries) or trade-creating (that is, generating trade from one more efficient member at the expense of another less efficient member)?

Yet, one may scan the op-ed articles, the editorials, and the congressional testimony when the renewal of fast-track authority for the FTA was being debated, looking for references to trade diversion—and find scarcely any. Astonishingly, it was not just the politicians and lawyers for Mexico's lobby who equated the FTA with free trade; reputable economists (admittedly writing outside of their competence but still not absolved from elementary knowledge of international economic principles) did so, too. The newspeak was: Call the FTA "free trade," and then every sophisticated economist who expresses reservations about the FTA becomes a "protectionist," an alchemy that would turn me into one, too!

This issue of trade diversion is not negligible. The trouble is that trade creation can quickly be replaced by trade diversion today because countries typically use selective and elastic instruments of protection (such as VERs and antidumping actions). This is important to understand and easy to illustrate.

Imagine that the United States begins to eliminate—by out-competing—an inefficient Mexican industry once the FTA goes into effect. Even though the most-efficient producer is Taiwan, if the next-efficient United States outcompetes the least-efficient Mexico, that would be desirable trade creation (though the best course would be free trade so that Taiwan would take more of the Mexican market instead).

But what do you suppose the Mexicans would be likely to do? They would probably start antidumping actions against Taiwan, which would lead to reduced imports from Taiwan as the imports from the United States increased, leaving the Mexican production relatively unaffected. Trade diversion from Taiwan to the United States would have occurred. Similarly, the effect of Mexican competition against the United States could well be that the United States would start antidumping actions and even VERs against Taiwan.

My belief that FTAs will lead to considerable trade diversion (because of modern methods of protection, which are inherently selective and can be "captured" readily for protectionist purposes) is one that may have been borne out in the EC. It is well known that the EC used antidumping actions and VERs profusely to erect Fortress Europe against the Far East. Cannot much of this be a trade-diverting policy in response to the intensification of internal competition among the member states of the EC?

The economist activists among the proponents of the Mexico-U.S. FTA did not distinguish themselves by appropriately analyzing the question of *investment diversion* from more efficient locations abroad to Mexico, either. Such investment diversion could lead to inefficient allocation of the world's capital supply. It can thus be a source of harm to cosmopolitan efficiency and to the world trading system. It may be understandable for a small country like Mexico to ignore this danger and concentrate instead on benefits to itself: President Salinas is not on center stage, and Mexico sets no example even approaching that of the United

States as the linchpin of the world trading system. Lobbying for Mexico is a role that suits firms hired by the Mexican government. The economist should have a higher calling, however: an architect's ambition to look at the whole.

Reference

Finger, J. M. 1989. "Picturing America's Future: Kodak's Solution to Trade Exposure." *World Economy* 12 (September): 377–80.

X

In the Ring: With Soros, Wriston, Sachs, and Valenti

49   Wheel of Fortune

George Soros is an investment manager. But he is not your run-of-the-mill Wall Street gnome. He has made it like no one has. For those of us who wince when the Dow Jones average interrupts our daily television news, the jacket blurb describes Soros's spectacular success. The Quantum Fund, over which he presides, has grown from $4 million in 1969 to over $2 billion today; it has yielded a dizzying annual compound growth rate of 45 percent over nearly two decades. *New York* magazine, in an unaccustomed lapse into cultivated penmanship, was moved to describe Soros as the "Michelangelo, Renoir, and Beethoven of Wall Street all wrapped into one."

Now that Soros has made his fortune, he is eager to tell all. But his aspirations as a writer soar above a simple narrative of his financial dealings. He wants to think big, to speculate about the differences between scientific method in economics and in the natural sciences. He wishes to develop a theory that would embrace equally his mundane financial activities and grander themes such as the reform of the international economic system. It is tempting to treat Soros's analytic ambition as a manifestation of

Originally published in the *New Republic* (October 5, 1987): 40–41. Reprinted with permission.

This chapter reviews George Soros's *The Alchemy of Finance: Reading the Mind of the Market* (New York: Simon and Schuster, 1987).

what sociologists call the Sanskritization process: wealth seeks status by acquiring the attributes of the higher classes—in this instance, their intellectual pursuits. But for Soros, the sequence has been exactly reversed.

A Hungarian émigré to the United States, Soros claims to have acquired his thirst for intellectual accomplishment en route, at the London School of Economics. He credits the influence of Karl Popper, but surely an economics undergraduate in England cannot have failed to note that financial and philosophical speculation have been combined in some of the great masters of the discipline. David Ricardo—to whom we owe the theory of gains from trade through specialization, a theory that Adam Smith sketched and Richard Gephardt foolishly (if unwittingly) rejects—was a successful stockbroker. Even John Maynard Keynes, as first bursar of King's College at Cambridge from 1924 to 1946, managed two investment funds to great advantage. Indeed, of these, the Chest Fund, where Keynes had a free hand, considerably outperformed the *Banker's Magazine* Ordinary Share Index. Here was the stuff of which dreams are made. Success on Wall Street has given Soros the sangfroid, and wealth the wherewithal, to pursue his dream. This book is the consequence. Alas, it prompts the question: Money talks, but can it write?

The core of Soros's book is concerned with what he wrongly (indeed, astonishingly) considers to be a major new discovery: the Theory of Reflexivity. If you wish to be bamboozled, consider his algebraic formulation. Let $x = f(y)$ and $y = g(x)$—that is, x is a function of y, and the other way around, too. In classrooms we call this a system characterized by simultaneity. I have successfully conveyed what it means to my students by recalling the country where men are bad lovers and women yet worse cooks. Reflexivity arises because poor lovers are penalized by bad food, and bad food is rewarded with indifferent love.

Soros uses reflexivity, however, with an important but familiar twist, central to his argument. Economic analysis must reckon, he thinks, with the fact that agents or "participants" understand and act in light of the economic situation. This defines a "cognitive" relationship. But their perceptions, in turn, can affect the situation itself. This defines a "participating" relationship. And these cognitive and participating functions (which correspond to Soros's algebraic equations), acting recursively (in sequence, that is), define "the theoretical foundation" of Soros's approach. "The two recursive functions do not produce an equilibrium but a never-ending process of change." Hence, "the outcome tends to diverge from expectations, leading to constantly changing expectations and constantly changing outcomes."

Of course this is not really a "theory" but a way of thinking, an analytical framework that draws attention to the critical role of feedback from subjective expectations to objective events. Economists have been considering such feedback for decades. The precise way in which the objective reality can be affected depends naturally on the nature of the feedback. Consider the classic case of a self-fulfilling prophecy: the analysis of exchange rates dating back to the 1960s. Let the objective reality initially be that the dollar will not depreciate. But suppose that speculators expect the opposite, and move out of the dollar, depreciating it. If the reality were independent of the actions of the speculators, the dollar would go up again, and the market would have chastised and ruined the speculators. But it may well be that as the dollar falls initially with the speculation, wages and hence prices rise in sympathy. If so, the objective reality would itself have changed, legitimating the devaluation of the dollar in view of the speculation-induced rise of prices. Such self-justifying speculation shapes its own reality.

Soros regards the stock market as an ideal place for such feedback effects. Stock prices can influence "underlying values," or "fundamentals" in Soros's language, in important ways. An un-justifiably high stock valuation, for example, can reinforce a firm's ability to raise finance and validate in turn the valuation. As the research of Lawrence Summers and Robert Shiller on asset pricing suggests, an unduly low valuation may lead to managerial shake-outs aimed at short-run profits and causing long-run neglect, which once again legitimates the initially inappropriate valuation. Evidently, booms and busts also can follow, for a vicious circle can arise in which one mistake, duly rewarded, leads to another until some overriding, unshakable constraint interrupts the pro-cess. Such reversals can come easily in financial markets, where confidence can evaporate as rapidly as it arises.

I have no quarrel with Soros when he reminds us that the analysis of the stock market must occasionally reckon with such reflexivity. I find it difficult to follow him completely, however, in his different, and far more debatable, view that his superior grasp of reflexivity is what gives him the edge over his rivals. Yes, he made a great deal of money during the conglomerate boom of the 1960s when reflexivity was working, with indiscriminately high stock valuations feeding the ballooning acquisition process. But so did many others.

Or take the fascinating case of Soros's "killing of a lifetime." After the Plaza Hotel meeting of the Group of Five in September 1985, Soros expected the yen to rise; he bought into yen and earned in one fell swoop more than enough to offset handsomely his accumulated losses on currency trading in the previous four years. Was this the result of reflexivity? Surely Soros owed this good fortune to guessing right about what these governments would do rather than to the reflexive effects of that deed in the market, or his better grasp thereof.

Perhaps Soros has just been plain lucky rather than smart. Having made money, he is in no mood to attribute his success to luck. But luck could well be what made Soros's fortune, if we are to believe the academic proponents of the so-called random walk or efficient markets theory of the stock market. That theory holds that the market fully discounts all future developments, and hence the individual's chances of over- or underperforming the market are even. Soros asserts that this theory "is manifestly false—I have disproved it by consistently outperforming the averages over a period of 12 years." Indeed, Warren Buffett, who managed Berkshire Hathaway Inc., has outperformed the Standard & Poor 500 for each of 29 years.

As it happens, however, the random walk theory permits Buffett and Soros to have an impressive string of successes without being in possession of better gray cells. To understand this theory, consider the analogy of tossing a coin: over a large number of trials, heads will come up as often as tails. But this does not rule out the possibility that Soros has had an unmitigated succession of heads in *all* trials. From the scientific point of view, it is simply impossible to decide between Soros's self-congratulatory "I-am-smart-because-I-understand-reflexivity" explanation and the rival "random walk" explanations of his success just by reading his accounts of his successes and failures. The issue remains as open and contentious among professors as it is among investors.

In *The Alchemy of Finance*, Soros goes beyond the stock market to larger issues. Though he offers an abundance of views, on matters ranging from currency reform to the American budget and trade deficits, he reminds me of another distinguished Hungarian émigré, Lord Balogh, of whom his foes said that his conclusions were more obvious than his arguments. Financial specialists, though, will be intrigued by the conclusion that Soros draws concerning the need to regulate financial markets, ever susceptible (thanks to reflexivity) to "excesses, which sooner or later become unsustainable." In his view, "after nearly half a century of what now appears as excessive regulation, we have been moving towards excessive deregulation. The sooner we recognize that some kind of regulation is necessary in order to maintain stability, the better are our chances of preserving the benefits of a nearly free market system." Here he parts company with Walter Wriston, who cheerfully led us into the Third World debt crisis, and walks over to Henry Kaufman's and Felix Rohatyn's corner. I believe rightly so.

Bankers who can write are as rare as economics professors who can make money. If you thought that bankers simply transacted in cash and debt and muttered the more profane four-letter words as they confronted failing clients, you could be forgiven for expecting Mr. Wriston to do no better. You would be dead wrong.

The CEO of Citicorp for seventeen years, Mr. Wriston evidently enjoys turning from the world of high finance to sit at his fancy word processor and his laser printer, symbols of the new technologies that fascinate him.

In this, he reminds you really of Felix Rohatyn. Both share the same wide grin that success breeds; and both write gloriously, with wit and erudition. But the contrasts are more compelling. Where Mr. Rohatyn is "our man on Wall Street" for the liberals, Mr. Wriston is a conservative with the right ear of Ronald Reagan. As Mr. Rohatyn profits hugely from masterminding mergers, he laments the risk they pose for the economy. As Mr. Wriston has recycled the OPEC-created petrodollars to South America from the top of his skyscraper in New York, creating the

Originally published, in slightly shorter form, in the *New Leader* (April 7–21, 1986): 15–16. © American Labor Conference on International Affairs, Inc. Reprinted with permission.

This chapter reviews Walter B. Wriston's *Risk and Other Four-Letter Words* (New York: Harper & Row, 1986).

debts that now invade our newspapers incessantly, he has been nothing short of euphoric.

Indeed, Mr. Wriston writes of Third World debts only to congratulate the bankers for having adroitly facilitated the investment of OPEC surpluses when few thought this could happen without active supranational intervention such as the creation of a "safety net" to prod bankers into lending to poor countries strapped for funds. This comforting posture could be mistaken as self-serving: after all, Mr. Wriston led the financial troops into the Third World during the 1970s. It reflects however a deeper, philosophical strain in Mr. Wriston.

For, the central theme that runs through most of his essays is that "crisis" and doomsday scenarios are just so much alarmist hype circulated worldwide by modern information technology, that they often trigger governmental action that has unanticipated and untoward consequences, that governments typically build themselves in Kafkaesque image, and that unfettered markets and individuals are the necessary guarantors of economic progress and liberty.

In short, Mr. Wriston has little patience for the view that economic efficiency or survival requires what the classical economists called "prudence," that is, design. He trusts rather the apparently anarchic but actually efficient workings of the marketplace, which, guided as it were by an invisible hand, magically produces social good from the pursuit of private greed.

His heroes thus include Adam Smith, John Locke, Edmund Burke, George Orwell, and Milton Friedman. But he can recall apt quotes also from less likely sources. You probably would not have guessed that Justice Brandeis had written: "Experience should teach us to be most on our guard to protect liberty when the government's purposes are beneficent.... The greatest dangers to liberty lurk in insidious encroachment by men of zeal, well-meaning but without understanding." I am surprised however that, for one who delights in quotemanship, Mr. Wriston misses out on Herbert Spencer's famous remark (in his *Essays*) on the virtues of competition and the vices of regulation: "The ultimate result of shielding men from the effects of folly is to fill the world with fools."

Mr. Wriston's theses are thus always grand and mostly familiar. Governments can indeed do worse rather than better: they say that there are two things you do not want to see made, laws and sausage. Mr. Wriston certainly regales us in his essay on Banking in Wonderland (pp. 63–83) with accounts of the deleterious banking legislation he has suffered from. He is also at his biting best when he writes: "At a closed hearing on a tax bill once, several senators complained that they did not understand what they were being asked to approve. The chairman of the Senate Finance Committee is reported to have replied: 'If every man insists on knowing what he's voting for before he votes, we're not going to get a bill reported out by Monday.' Monday clearly had priority over clarity" (p. 85).

Again, in this year of tax reform, he is compelling when he recalls the history of the 1968 Truth-in-Lending Act: "By 1977, the fifty-three sections of that law had been interpreted forty-three times by the Board of Governors of the Federal Reserve, no doubt practicing law without a license. Their pronouncements have been revised in the light of some twelve hundred staff letters of further interpretation. The result is six thousand pages of regulations.... There is no way the small banks can read these six thousand pages.... Consequently, at one point there were ten thousand lawsuits in courts throughout the United States based on Truth-in-Lending laws. You don't have ten thousand lawsuits if everyone agrees on what the law is" (pp. 42–43).

Now, if you were a knee-jerk liberal who believed that governments are necessarily benign and efficient instruments for fixing the failures of the market and pursuing the social interest, you

do need the salutary corrective that Mr. Wriston provides. But
you must part company from him when he implies gloomily (or
perhaps cheerfully as he celebrates his conservatism?) that governments are *doomed* to be incompetent victims of a senseless
ballooning-out process or (as his eminent friends would argue)
that they will be captured by special interests or that they will
pursue their own rather than your happiness (as with Milovan
Djilas's "new class").

In fact, the debt crisis, arguably Mr. Wriston's gift to mankind,
illustrates well how dangerous it is to view governments as necessarily malign, in impact if not intent, and the market forces as
deserving of free play. The creation of these immense debts were
doubtless due to extravagant borrowings by imprudent governments. But can anyone deny that the blandishments offered by
our banks' jet-setting emissaries, flush with cash, also played a
major role? If the world were always on an exponential path,
there would have been no problem. But, as Professor Charles
Kindleberger has emphasised, financial markets are notoriously
subject to panics and manias. They fail as soon as confidence
does. The Reaganomics-administered deflation, with its double
whammy of high interest rates and falling world income and
trade, delivered the *coup de grâce* to Mr. Wriston's optimism by
breaking confidence in the ability of the debtors to repay. Repay-
ments would now have to be made, rather than financed by new
borrowings on an ever-rising escalator. Suddenly, therefore, we
had a modern equivalent of the German "reparations problem"
that Keynes made his reputation on.

Is Mr. Wriston not aware that, had not the creditor banks
piggybacked on the government-created, IMF-centered "adjustment" efforts, and now the World Bank–centered Baker Plan
supplements to the market-determined capital flows to the debtor
countries, Citicorp might have faced bankruptcy and Mr. Wriston

might have been on the dole, not to cite the disruptions that these events might have caused in our lives as well?

Indeed, these governmental rescue efforts, so vital to out well-being given the excesses of the banks and their debtors, could hardly have been mounted were it not for the alarm bells that the "crisis mongers" had sounded through the past few years. Mr. Wriston is indeed right when he deplores the tendency to cry wolf, especially when the fatted calf is at the door. But, at times the wolf is indeed out there! Moreover, public policy cannot be prudently made on the assumption of the best-case scenarios without "betting the company" as they say on Wall Street. And, again, Mr. Wriston is simply too pessimistic about the creative role that is played by the debate that follows the strained voices that overstate to grab our attention.

But then these essays could not have survived moderation. Their interest derives from the clarity of the author's vision. They yield pleasure also because they are crisp, like bank notes fresh from the mint. I, for one, would like to encourage him to embrace the risk, take the plunge, and write more.

51 Shock Treatments

It is ironic that Jeffrey Sachs's celebratory account of economic "shock therapy" in Poland arrives just as the same therapy seems to have foundered on the legendary shoals of Russia. After all, if Russia's failure was inspired by Poland's success, it may be that Poland has finally managed to repay Russia for all the trouble that Russia has visited upon Poland in the past. Now that the virtues of shock therapy are no longer taken for granted by all reasonable men and women, a real debate over its wisdom can begin. The stakes of this discussion are high: only a dispassionate analysis of what went wrong in Russia yesterday can illuminate the problems that await us there today.

As is often the case when great issues and articulate protagonists are involved, the analysis of shock therapy has been bedeviled by language. The proponents of shock therapy are masters of rhetoric; and they have often relied on attractive phrases and misleading analogies to advance their argument. The phrase itself suggests a drastic but necessary corrective to unmanageable disorder; and "big bang"—another term in the shock therapists' lexicon—suggests nothing less than the creation of the

Originally published in the *New Republic* (March 28, 1994): 39–43. Reprinted with permission.

This chapter reviews Jeffrey Sachs's *Poland's Jump to the Market Economy* (Cambridge: MIT Press, 1994).

universe. Both imply that we must push ahead at full speed: when there is chaos, and everything is a mess, surely that is the right thing to do. Gradualism, by contrast, suggests procrastination, a theory of lameness.

The debate over economic reform often becomes an angry exchange of analogies. One side claims that you can only cross a chasm in a single leap. The other side retorts that unless you are Indiana Jones, you drop a bridge. Then again, the shock therapists argue, if you want to cut a dog's tail, you do it with one slash of the knife, not bit by bit. And the gradualists reply that you train a dog by setting incrementally escalating heights for him to jump.

The shock therapists, who strike rather romantic figures on a dreary policy landscape, have succeeded in suggesting that economists who advocate gradualism are knaves or worse. But the truth is that the optimal speed of any reform is an issue of much controversy in theoretical research today, and there is no basis for the sweeping presumption that the more speed, the better. Indeed, gradualist thinking has a distinguished past in economics. Adam Smith, whose credentials on the subject of markets are naturally indisputable, wrote in *The Wealth of Nations*:

It may sometimes be a matter of deliberation, how far, or in what manner it is proper to restore the free importation of foreign goods ... when particular manufacturers, by means of high duties or prohibitions upon all foreign goods which come into competition with them, have been so far extended as to employ a great multitude of hands. Humanity may in this case require that freedom of trade should be restored only by slow graduations, and with a good deal of reserve and circumspection.

And in a similar spirit, Keynes wrote in 1933 of the danger of haste, citing, ironically enough, the example of Russia moving toward socialism:

Paul Valery's aphorism is worth quoting—"Political conflicts distort and disturb the people's sense of distinction between matters of importance and matters of urgency." The economic transition of a society is a thing to be accomplished slowly.... We have a fearful example in Russia today of the evils of insane and unnecessary haste. The sacrifices and losses of transition will be vastly greater if the pace is forced.... For it is of the nature of economic processes to be rooted in time. A rapid transition will involve so much pure destruction of wealth that the new state of affairs will be, at first, far worse than the old, and the grand experiment will be discredited.

One thing is clear: the debate over shock therapy cannot be conducted with catch phrases and sound bites. It is only when these distractions are dismissed that the important issues come into view. The actual content of the reform strategy in Poland and Russia, and its contrasting fortunes in the two countries, are subjects that require serious investigation. Sachs has advised both the Polish and Russian governments, and so he is an invaluable guide through these dense thickets. His little book presents a protagonist's view with admirable clarity and conviction. The main subject of his analysis is Poland, but he draws parallels between the "failed" policies of Russia and Poland before shock therapy and argues for the method's promise in Russia after its success in Poland.

Of course, Sachs's confident prescription for Russia contrasts sharply with Russia's sorry condition today. John Kenneth Galbraith once said wittily of an economist foe that his misfortune was to have his theories tried (and to have them fail); and Sachs's misfortune may be that his theories were so successful in Poland that they were tried again in Russia. What was bold in Poland turned out to be rash in Russia. Poland earned Sachs a place in history. But Russia overwhelmed him, laying waste, not for the first time, to a great ambition.

To understand what happened, it is necessary to trace the decline and disintegration of the Polish and Soviet economies before the introduction of shock therapy. Indeed, modern economic history would do well to distinguish among four historical phases: (1) the decline under socialism; (2) the deepening crisis as foreign borrowing without reforms led to excessive debt burdens; (3) the disintegration under "market socialism," when market reforms were attempted within the Socialist framework; and (4) shock therapy, with its benign consequences in Poland and malign outcomes in Russia.

The economic decline under socialism has been well-documented. Scholars have long noted that the Eastern bloc's high rates of investment unfailingly produced few results. The blood, sweat, and tears were to no avail: growth rates plummeted; and efficiency and technical innovation, the twin sources of increased productivity from investment, were incompatible with a regime that decried initiative and ignored incentives.

Faced with the chilling prospect of economic decline, the Socialist regimes of Gorbachev in Moscow and Gierek in Warsaw passed through two phases of "reform." Initially, both leaders tried to preserve the inherited economic system. They urged workers to work harder, and they sought to improve technology and productivity with high levels of foreign borrowing. But the results were exactly what economists had earlier witnessed in the developing countries: huge foreign debts were contracted with little economic payoff. The influx of capital bought a little time, but it burdened the economy with interest and repayment bills that simply could not be met. Consider an impoverished peasant who borrows and invests with little return and then finds himself hopelessly indebted. For Poland and the Soviet Union, the results were much the same.

Thus began the phase of "market socialism": market reforms carried out within the confines of continued state ownership. State-owned firms were now allowed to "set wages, inputs and outputs (but typically, not prices)." Sachs contends that these reforms were not merely incomplete and inadequate; because they were undertaken without privatization, he believes they contained the seeds of disaster.

Both Poland and Russia did indeed take nosedives under market socialism. But was the lack of privatization really to blame? Common sense suggests that privatization should yield greater gains by allowing more play to the profit motive as market incentives are introduced. But losing these incremental gains is not the same thing as losing your shirt. Are we truly faced with the option of going all the way or going down the tubes? Not really.

Regardless of privatization, Poland's and Russia's reforms could not have been expected to produce significant results. A key problem, Sachs notes, was that the born-again reformers were still prisoners of the assumption that competition (which, in principle, is compatible with state-owned enterprises acting under new rules) did not matter. Restrictions on new enterprises, import controls, and a host of other interferences continued, and nipped competition in the bud. Reforms reinforce each other: one, without others, will not work.

But this does not explain the collapse of market socialism. To do so, Sachs follows a different line of argument, proposing that the liabilities of state ownership were exacerbated by the growth of democracy. In other words, glasnost helped to kill perestroika. This is a counterintuitive and interesting thesis, because the normal presumption at the time was that democracy would bring immediate and palpable benefits to a people that had been starved of freedoms for too long. These benefits, it was thought, would buy Gorbachev the time to bring the economic reforms along in a gradual, measured way. But the general consensus today seems to be that Gorbachev's reforms and Gierek's economic reforms failed because the terror had died. Reforms freed gigantic state-owned enterprises from the "command" system that communism worked with an iron fist. At the same time, the full play of the market and the invisible hand were not in place. Hence, discipline broke down and so did the economy.

This view is not original with Sachs, but he states it well:

Under the old "command economy," before the Gorbachev reforms, enterprise policies were controlled by central fiat, backed up by threat of force against workers and managers who tried to evade the commands. When the commands, and the threat of force, were (mercifully) removed in the enterprise reforms in the second half of the 1980s, managers and workers attempted, not surprisingly, to increase their incomes at the expense of the state by absorbing whatever income flow and whatever assets they could from state enterprises. They demanded higher wages and stripped assets through various means—either overt or covert.

This argument does not persuade me, at least in its general form. Sachs seems to think that wage explosions and asset stripping happened because "when there are no capitalists, there is nobody to represent the interests of capital." If state-owned enterprises had been replaced with private enterprise, he believes, these rude occurrences would have been avoided. But asset stripping, or "looting," is also a fact of life in capitalist systems with private ownership. Thus, economists George Akerlof and Paul Romer have argued quite persuasively that our own S&L crisis was in no small measure the result of straightforward villainy, and not simply due to unwise financial deregulation. Nor are excessive wage demands a rare problem for capitalist societies.

Sachs also overlooks an important aspect of market socialism. Once economic decision-making was shifted to the state-owned enterprises, and there was less retribution from the state, it became a lot easier to direct supplies and outputs to more profitable uses. Indeed, as the Sovietologist Padma Desai noted several years ago, the breakdown of the command system did lead Soviet farms to ignore the state's procurement demands and to sell their products instead in open rural markets that fetched higher prices. As farmers' incomes rose, agricultural production increased. Meanwhile, state-supplied urban shops began to run out of food as procurement flagged. One solution to this problem would have been to direct domestic effort and foreign financial and technical assistance to building a better transportation system so that profit-seeking entrepreneurs could shift their rural supplies to more profitable urban markets.

It's important to recognize that the ills of market socialism might have occurred even with privatization; and that some good did occur even without it. In short, it was not the absence of privatization that led to the implosion of Poland and Russia. And that is a good thing. If market reforms could not be pursued without privatization in place, we would be in deep and unmanageable trouble. Privatization takes time, just as building an effective population control policy or extending agricultural assistance programs takes time. The critical problem was, rather, that neither Gierek nor Gorbachev had the instruments of social policy and of monetary and fiscal control in place as they experimented with market reforms.

If you shift to markets, you deserve to get micro-efficiency. But to reap the rewards in good measure, you have to use the social instruments that go with markets. A social safety net and adjustment assistance are necessary to reform, especially if you expect enterprises to respond to price signals and lay off workers when required. The shift from a society of entitlement to a society of opportunity, and hence from total security to total insecurity in one's working life, creates the kind of fear that Americans witnessed in their own country during the NAFTA debate. American workers, coming off a decade when real wages fell, were extraordinarily resistant to the administration's appeal for their support, because they knew that freer trade means greater flux and adds to insecurity.

A successful shift to a market economy requires the social instruments that capitalism has evolved over the past century. Unfortunately, these instruments were not readily available in Moscow and Warsaw for the simple reason that they had been unnecessary in a Socialist society. Ironically, monetary policy also slipped from government hands even though the monetarists were as much in charge under communism in its heyday as they were in Milton Friedman's utopias. The market Socialists might have tried to halt the wage explosion with tough monetary policies; but they failed to do so. In place of monetary restraint, Poland and Russia practiced an accommodating monetary policy that indulged the wage explosion by printing the money necessary to pay for it.

This failure of macroeconomic policy had different causes in Poland and Russia. Gierek simply did not have the political legitimacy to enforce strict discipline on the workers. Under Gorbachev this legitimacy existed, at least for a time, but it did not help. When Yeltsin took control of Russian revenues, Gorbachev had to print money to pay for Soviet expenditures, and a profligate monetary policy inevitably resulted. Gorbachev had little choice in the matter.

Contrary to Sachs's conclusion, the absence of privatization was not the "fatal flaw" that undermined Gorbachev's and Gierek's reforms. If there was a fatal flaw, it was the absence of the social and macroeconomic policy instruments that are essential to the effective functioning of market capitalism. In any case, market socialism did not work, and it became clear that a change of course was in order.

It may be that Sachs's apocalyptic view of market socialism predisposed him to drastic measures when he arrived in Poland in June 1989 at the invitation of Solidarity. It is also possible that Sachs was simply following orders; he writes that Solidarity instructed him to draw up "a program of rapid and comprehensive change." In August 1989, the Mazowiecki government appointed as its deputy prime minister for the economy the now celebrated Leszek Balcerowicz to spearhead such a program. It is hard to decide who led whom by the hand. It is certain, however, that they walked hand in hand.

The Balcerowicz plan that resulted must be clearly understood, for it is the essence of shock therapy. Sachs emphasizes the plan's dramatic and "holistic" features:

[Poland had] to break decisively with the Communist system, *to end halfway reform*, and ... *to jump to the market economy* [my italics]. The goal was to create an economy "in the style of Western Europe," based on private ownership, free markets and integration into world markets. The plan also combined long-term market reform with a short-run emergency stabilization program to end the incipient hyperinflation.

Like other economists, Sachs defines hyperinflation as a monthly rise in prices of 50 percent or more. The phenomenon is a familiar one in South America, where it calls to mind the magical realist fiction of Garcia Marquez. But it is virtually unknown here or in India, where rates of inflation reaching even two digits lead to corrective action—an approach to macroeconomics more consonant with the tranquility of the village of Malgudi in the fiction of R. K. Narayan. Americans can get a better feel for the phenomenon from the advice to take a taxi instead of a bus under hyperinflation, since you pay for a bus ride when it starts and for a taxi ride when it ends.

No macroeconomist will quarrel with the proposition that hyperinflation has to be attacked swiftly and surely. This requires a ruthless assault on the budget deficit, and on the printing of money that finances it. Fiscal and monetary policies must be geared toward the task of macroeconomic stabilization. And so in 1990 Poland initiated a drastic plan of action: food and other household subsidies were slashed or eliminated entirely; cheap credits to industry disappeared; and ceilings on borrowing were set.

The novelty of Sachs's plan, however, lay elsewhere. He insisted that reforms in the incentive structure of the Polish economy must be carried out with equal speed. Consider the convertibility of the zloty. The introduction of effective international competition is impossible, economists agree, without a convertible currency that enables traders to import cheaper foreign goods whenever domestic goods are particularly expensive. But Sachs rejected the conventional wisdom which held that a quick transition to convertibility for Poland was impossible since Western Europe had taken a decade after the Second World War to reach convertibility and most developing countries were still afflicted with inconvertible currencies. Instead, Sachs persuaded Poland to introduce convertibility practically overnight, setting the exchange rate at an attractively low level and backing it up with a stabilization fund that guarded against speculation. As a result, Poland maintained a stable exchange rate throughout 1990, even as its currency became convertible.

Shock therapy also mandated a full liberalization of prices. It was expected that prices would rise steeply once, and then they would stabilize as tough monetary and fiscal policies emptied the fuel tanks driving hyperinflation. At the same time, wage discipline was imposed through a tax on wage increases that exceeded a norm: the so-called popiwek tax. It was expected that this curb on raises would limit unemployment and reduce the need for monetary restraint, since the government would not have to combat wage increases by refusing to print more money.

Sachs argues persuasively that this therapy produced dramatic results. Prices rose initially by 77 percent in January, by 16 percent in February, and then by less than 4 percent a month in the two years afterward. The exchange rate was stable. Foreign exchange reserves actually increased. Confidence in the currency rose, and Poles began exchanging dollars for zlotys. But the bad news, as feared by opponents of shock therapy, was that unemployment rose dramatically. It increased from an average of 3.5 percent in 1990 to an average of 9.2 percent in 1991 and to an average of 12.8 percent in 1992. I suspect that the true rate of unemployment in Poland was even higher, since firms probably kept mostly idle workers on their rolls who shared work with each other in a makeshift way. The old gag from the years of communism was still good: asked where the unemployed had gone, a local wit replied that they were working.

Of course, unemployment rates were high in Western Europe as well. And they were high in Eastern European countries that did not undergo shock therapy. But the increase in unemployment in Poland was surely not unrelated to shock therapy. And the increase was dramatic despite the "popiwek" tax that a Solidarity-backed government had succeeded in imposing on Poland's workers. It is not surprising, then, that the social contract began to fray. In the parliamentary elections of September 1993, Polish voters gave less than 12 percent of the vote to the pro-reform Suchoka government, while returning to the legislature former Communists and future fascists who added up to more than a third of the new Parliament. The many successes of the Balcerowicz reforms were overshadowed in the political market-place by the pain attributed to the therapy.

This unfortunate turn of events should give us the clues we need as to why shock therapy failed in Russia. In Poland the political preconditions existed for shock therapy to be given a fair chance. In Russia the political preconditions appear not to have existed at all. In January 1992 Yegor Gaidar, Russia's deputy prime minister, announced a program of reform that paralleled Poland's. Gaidar's plan, devised with Sachs's assistance, was to cut Russia's budget deficit from an officially estimated 17 percent of gross domestic product all the way to zero in just four months. There was no consensus in support of this bold proposal. The Russian economist Yasin Yevgeni has said that the plan was conceived and announced "Soviet-style": no efforts were made to consult with Parliament or with the regional governments or with the people. At the same time, as in Poland, nearly all price controls were lifted, with the result that prices immediately rose by 300 percent.

The price increases cut deeply into the population's cash savings, which were widely treasured because most other productive assets could not be legally held. Meanwhile the link between wages and prices was severed by the removal of wage indexation for state employees. These developments magnified the widespread, and understandable, fear that a rise in unemployment would follow from the proposed budget cuts.

In a country accustomed to full employment, in which full employment was not only a principle of economics but also a principle of culture, the fear of joblessness went very deep. For a Russian worker, the loss of employment raised a specter of personal disaster that went beyond the loss of wages. Just as health insurance in the United States is linked to employment by a strange quirk of wartime history, so much else is linked to one's employment in Russia. Of course, no social safety net was yet in place: unemployment insurance was still being worked at. But even with a safety net, workers had little reason to assume that new jobs would become available to them. Meanwhile, a long tradition of paternalism toward workers possibly reinforced the hostility of factory managers to economic change.

To be sure, many converts to shock therapy were aware of the pain that their policies would cause. But it was their expectation that large doses of foreign aid would ease that pain. Sachs himself was a party to the so-called "Grand Bargain" or "Harvard Plan," which proposed that foreign countries deliver as much as $30 billion per annum for five years. Though he later withdrew from its sponsorship, he did not abandon the numbers. A funny story made the rounds at the time among Russian experts who were disconcerted by the fact that the Harvard plan had been put together by Americans who had little knowledge of Russia's history, institutions, or language. Someone asks an American reformer, "How did you become an expert on Russia?" He says, "I have been there five times." And the Russian replies, "And if you have been to the bathroom five times, are you qualified to be a urologist?" But the real problem was not that the authors of the grandiose plan knew little about Russia; it was that they did not know enough about their own habitat. Numbers such as $30 billion were simply out of bounds. How could so much aid possibly have been mobilized?

The supporters of shock therapy in Russia were sadly miscalculating the aid they could get, confusing exhortations with expectations. Indeed, when shock therapy was announced in January 1992. Russia was not even a member of the IMF, and George Bush had not yet committed himself firmly to any aid at all. The complaint that the IMF did not deliver what it eventually promised is factually correct. But it is incorrect to imply, as Sachs has implied, that this was why the plan did not succeed. For shock therapy was already failing, and the system was returning to fiscal and monetary chaos, and so the IMF held up the release of funds until some fiscal discipline was restored. This is standard IMF policy everywhere in the world, and it surely has merit.

In the end, the Russian system simply could not accommodate the demands that shock therapy made upon it. And so shock therapy was reversed, returning the regime to large budget deficits and high rates of inflation. Political and economic realities on the ground drove the moderates in Parliament to join hands with the extremists. Meanwhile, the technocrats who were wedded to shock therapy branded all who opposed it as Communists, reactionaries, rejectionists, and worse. The eventual confrontation between the Russian Parliament and the Yeltsin government was a tragedy whose script had been written unwittingly by the shock therapists. The self-deluding world in which they lived was further in evidence when Anders Aslund, a former Swedish diplomat doubling with Sachs as an adviser to Gaidar, wrote in the *New York Times*, just before the disastrous election of December 12, of the certain victory that awaited the reformers.

Would more modest efforts to cut the budget deficit and slow the inflation have been more acceptable to the country and more readily supported by foreign assistance? Such a course was feasible. Most analysts agree that Russia faced high inflation, not hyperinflation, at the time of the shift to shock therapy, and that this problem allowed a gradual assault. The gradualists contend that the shock therapists achieved too little in attempting too much. Of course, the gradualists have the advantage of having a theory that is only a counterfactual. The shock therapists, for their part, tried and failed.

52   Free Trade at the Movies Puts U.S. in New Role

In "High Noon at Uruguay Gulch"[1] Karl E. Meyer defends French foot-dragging on the demands in the General Agreement on Tariffs and Trade concerning United States access to Europe's audiovisual market and France's insistence on a cultural exception. The question has, at any rate, now been deferred (front page, Dec. 15).

Mr. Meyer is right that France is "not alone in fearing for the survival of its national culture." Even the United States does not leave culture entirely to markets. At year end, the rich remember tax writeoffs for gifts to museums. The real question is: How do we best protect national culture? The answer appears to be: Subsidize your movies, but permit free access (without quotas) to ours.

But the French-American dispute has other ironies that only economists will recognize. Jack Valenti, head of the motion picture association, and Mickey Kantor, the United States trade representative, have claimed that, since 57 percent of the movies shown in French theaters are American, the 11 percent surcharge levied on all movies (and spent on subsidizing French film production) must be shared with Hollywood.

I suggest that this remarkable new principle of taxation be adopted symmetrically by the United States. Our toll receipts (often earmarked for our highway spending) should be shared with Japan pro rata to the number of Japanese cars that pay road and bridge tolls in this country.

For those who have tracked and fought the Clinton administration's shift to a tough, managed-trade, "results-oriented" trade policy toward Japan, based mainly on industry complaints that our shares in Japan's markets are low while Japan's shares in our markets are high, the irony is that the French are accusing us in the same way on movies.

Since Hollywood takes 80 percent of the European market, while European films take only 2 percent of ours, France accuses us of invisible protectionism, of structural impediments, much like those of which our industries accuse Japan!

Perhaps this role reversal might help to restore sanity to a Japan-fixated administration that has allowed itself to become a handmaiden of Japan-bashers and special interests.

Note

1. Karl E. Mayer, "High Noon at Uruguay Gulch," Editorial Notebook, *New York Times*, December 13, 1993.

XI

Economists and Economics

53   Remembering Harry G. Johnson

Harry Johnson passed away, at the age of 53, in Geneva, Switzerland, on May 9, 1977. He had been in indifferent health since February, having suffered from a second stroke, but had seemed to be recovering with his usual tenacity so that the final coma and death came as a great shock to his many friends.

Harry Johnson's premature death merits special attention in the *Journal of International Economics*, not merely because of his lasting impact on international economics, but also because he was co-founder of the journal. When Bart van Tongeren of North-Holland, at the instance of Jan Tinbergen and Robert Solow, approached me in 1969 with the idea of starting a journal exclusively addressed to international economics, this was the very first "specialized" economic journal that North-Holland was initiating, though there were to be many successful Schumpeterian imitators later from both North-Holland and the Academic Press. I was therefore extremely cautious and contacted Harry Johnson for cooperation. Unless he was willing to join as coeditor, along with John Chipman, I would not be willing to launch this enterprise. Harry Johnson was most enthusiastic and urged me to go ahead, offering his support as coeditor but requesting that, in

Originally published in the *Journal of International Economics Supplement* (January 1982): 3–13. Reprinted with permission.

view of his many other editorial responsibilities, he should be used minimally. During the formative years of the *JIE*, Johnson nonetheless provided invaluable advice on all sorts of editorial matters, including the organization of special symposia, writing invited papers, and even pitching in promptly with technical reports on manuscripts that I ventured to send to him despite his caveats in 1969. When, finally, in 1976, the phenomenal success of the *JIE* had led to such a serious overload for the editors that it had become critical for us to have coeditors with substantial refereeing obligations, Chipman and I were loath to have Harry Johnson leave altogether and were delighted that he agreed to stay on at least as an associate editor and to continue offering to the *JIE* his support.

I first met Harry, as he was known to all, when I went to Cambridge for the Economics Tripos in 1954. Cambridge then was coming to the end of a long period of glory, the thread running from Marshall through Pigou and Keynes. Pigou was in fact still alive and could occasionally be seen if you strolled through the main court of King's College at the right time; and Lal Jayawardene from Ceylon, Harry's student and now a leading light in the deliberations of the Group of 77, had even the strange fortune of having Pigou watch over him as he took his Tripos examination in the sick room at King's! The superstars who epitomised Cambridge then and even now, especially Nicky Kaldor and Joan Robinson, were still in their full prime. Kaldor would soon be lecturing to us on his celebrated *Alternative Theories of Distribution* while Mrs. Robinson, eagerly taking on all of the bright pupils who wished special tutorials from her, would presently be plotting our conversion to her revolutionary notions on capital theory by immersing us summarily, and often with the bewilderment that spread to her readers at large, in the page proofs of her *Accumulation of Capital*. Piero Sraffa was carefully hidden through my two years and little did we know that he would be surfacing

after three decades' labour with his second pearl of wisdom.
[Many years later, I heard Kalecki being credited with the witticism that the only two perfect gentlemen that he had encountered
in England had been Piero Sraffa, an Italian, and Maurice Dobb, a
card-carrying communist. If Kalecki had been an English gentle-
man and had therefore the celebrated wit that goes with it, he
would have probably added a third to his list: Joan Robinson.]
Richard Kahn was almost equally invisible, though we caught a
glimpse of him at lectures late in 1955–56: fastidious, weighing
each word carefully as he slowly worked his way through the
theory of interest rates, clearly an intellectual force but also suggesting a certain impatience, inherited from the wild successes of
the Keynesian era, with the obtuseness of those who would not
see the light. And we still had Sir Dennis Robertson, a real dividend; scarred from the battles with the Keynesians, he remained a
charming, soft-spoken, distinguished figure whose lectures on
Principles to the Tripos students were a model blend of humour,
wit, irony, and insights.

It would have required great gifts to capture the Cambridge
undergraduate's arrogant imagination against this competition;
and Harry seemed to the best and the brightest to have these in
ample measure.

Harry was very much in his prime then: many of his classic
papers on trade theory had already been written and had established him as a trade theorist of considerable accomplishment and
importance. His *Optimum Tariffs and Retaliation* piece had qualified Tibor Scitovsky's earlier classic on the possibility of gaining
with an optimum tariff despite Cournot-type retaliation. The
superb *Transfer Problem and Exchange Stability* paper had brilliantly
synthesised and extended the classical and Keynesian analyses of
the two problems and revealed the essential link between them.
And his pioneering papers on trade and growth, especially those
published eventually in the *Manchester School*, were to transform

the ideas of Balogh and John Williams, and Hicks's theoretical thoughts thereon in his *Inaugural* as the Drummond Professor of Political Economy at All Souls, into extremely influential theoretical constructs that would stimulate the leading trade theorists of his students' generation.

A lucky few had Harry as their College Tutor at King's. But none of us really needed to be Harry's tutees to profit from his immense presence. His lectures on the theory of international trade attracted a large audience of undergraduates, graduate students, and visiting scholars—I remember being introduced, after a class, to Lorie Tarshis. Harry spoke rapidly from a text and handed out sheets of mathematical derivations and diagrams mimeographed in two tones of red and blue on a machine reputedly at the Department of Applied Economics. In virtually eight, tightly crammed lectures, we were treated to a remarkably succinct review of the principal dimensions of trade theory. It was fascinating, and in fact seduced me into trade theory permanently, but it left us all somewhat breathless. I recall venturing up to Harry, just after he had finished stating extremely tersely the algebra on the Metzler paradox, and seeking illumination: he was kind but it did not help much. It will amuse those who knew the later Harry, who insisted on avoiding tedious mathematics and at times carried this aversion to excess, that when I ran to my own tutor, a perfectly English Cambridge don, as my lender of last resort, he took one long look at Harry's handout of tightly packed mathematics and sighed: "Johnson is a *glutton* for algebra, isn't he?"

We took most, however, to Harry's warmth and generosity of spirit. He read carefully, and often improved, our efforts. My piece on immiserizing growth was written, with Harry's aid and encouragement, after I took the basic ideas to him at the end of one of his lectures; and when the *Quarterly Journal of Economics* turned it down, he encouraged me to submit it to the *Review of*

Economic Studies and probably helped to get it published. The theory class that he ran for the Tripos students was again a model of enlightened encouragement: Harry would reword, rephrase, and make sense out of our ill-formulated remarks.

But his generosity was most evident at the Political Economy Club over which Sir Dennis Robertson presided and which was modeled after Keynes' earlier version of that Club. Here, the undergraduates who had secured Firsts and Upper Seconds in the examinations would be invited to Sir Dennis's rooms in Trinity for periodic meetings after supper. A brief paper would be read, usually by an undergraduate, and the meeting would break for tea while, in the winter sessions, Sir Dennis stoked the fire and circulated. The crunch came when lots had to be drawn and those who drew a number (up to six) had to speak their hasty thoughts when we had reassembled. It was a marvellous education, once you got over the terrors of drawing a number and performing as best you could. I recall seeing Harry often at these meetings, seeking us out for conversation during the break and generally being genial and charming. But his presence itself, we came to notice, was an act of kindness. Cambridge then was dominated by the Keynesians, who had still not forgiven Sir Dennis for his recalcitrance: one could feel the bitterness with which he was still regarded by the victors of the battles among Pigou, Robertson, and Keynes. Interestingly, in the year that I was a member of the Political Economy Club, I hardly ever saw Kaldor or Kahn or Joan Robinson, to name the most eminent, there. Harry, himself a Keynesian, deliberately exposed himself to the risk of their wrath by coming to the Political Economy Club sessions, thus lessening the intellectual and psychological isolation of Sir Dennis in his later years. This fundamental sense of decency was the essential core of Harry's personality; and it is remarkable that he was willing to stake a great deal for it.

When he left for Manchester in 1956 to take their Chair in economic theory, his reputation in internation trade was unassailable. During the three years that he spent there, Harry primarily wrote, and published in the *Manchester School*, the two well-known papers on Income Distribution, both masterpieces of geometrical theorising: the demand and supply sides in the standard 2×2 model of trade theory were elegantly tied together for all future trade theorists. For some reason, these were somewhat quiet years by Harry's creative standards; and I recall, during a trip to Manchester to talk to him about my own work on the Stolper-Samuelson theorem (later published in the *Economic Journal*), Harry's being full of sparkle and enthusiasm as he had just conceived the essence of his two income-distribution papers while reading my paper. With his customary generosity, he would go on to make a gracious reference to that effect in his published papers as well: a show of hand that would help along a student! We were then also to collaborate on a long paper on historical controversies in the theory of international trade (in the 1960 *Economic Journal*) and our last joint effort was to be on the theory of tariffs (in the 1961 *Oxford Economic Papers*), this latter paper having been written mostly when I spent a term with him in Chicago (to which he had moved in 1960) and then finished when he took me with him to Queen's University at Kingston in Canada for the following summer.

Harry's transition to Chicago was to be marred by our joint paper in the 1960 *Economic Journal*. In the last section of the paper, which was almost wholly Harry's contribution, there was a rather strong footnote of the kind that Harry was so good at: it suggested that the enthusiasm for flexible exchange rates had led Egon Sohmen (whose death the *JIE* notes also in this issue) to miss a substantive point against flexible exchange rates; unfortunately for us, we had used the word *propaganda* where we meant *advocacy*. Sohmen, according to Roy Harrod, wished to reply; but what astonished Harry and me was that, at Chicago, Milton Friedman was up in arms. Oddly, Friedman considered the footnote to be an unprofessional piece of writing and also to constitute unwarranted bullying by Harry of a lesser economist. Harry seemed to have transited from a combative Cambridge to a Chicago that seemed no less pugnacious when ideologically aroused. Harry was left embarrassed and uncomfortable; quite conceivably, it may have added some vigour to Harry's early anti-Monetarist writings at Chicago. In time, of course, Harry's own writings acquired the grit and cutting edge of his environment, and he seemed to learn quickly to treat with unconcealed disdain any piece of writing that offended his strict standards of excellence and his notions of integrity. But, during his first months at Chicago, as the Sohmen episode unravelled, he would content himself with a dignified, scientific response. Thus, when Friedman proceeded to write a short comment. Harry drafted a reply: the point at issue being whether a finite equilibrium would *necessarily* exist if there was an unstable equilibrium (a point of issue in the debate, as then couched, on fixed *versus* flexible rates). We argued that we would be perfectly happy to assert the existence of a stable equilibrium if the analyst made it clear that the proposition included infinite (zero) exchange rates. Friedman presumably did not send his note to Harrod, and the exchange was not published; we took it to mean that Friedman had accepted our contention, and, to our satisfaction, John Chipman, in his later magisterial *Econometrica* survey carefully reviewed the controversy between Sohmen and us, to come out on our side.

But it was clear to me, and to Harry, that if Friedman had been right scientifically, we would have readily changed our minds. And here paradoxically may be the secret of what happened to Harry's views as he stayed on at Chicago for the rest of his magnificent career. If you are pragmatic and argue with an ideologue as bright as yourself, you will win some and lose some. Every

time you lose, you will change your views because you are pragmatic. But every time the ideologue loses, he is shielded from
perceiving this and will hold on to his assertions. Over time,
therefore, you will move closer to the ideologue. Harry, the
pragmatic scientist, who appeared to us to be mildly centrist
during his years at Cambridge, moved increasingly closer therefore to a Friedmanesque worldview: this was inevitable.

Chicago, in fact, was very Friedmanesque at the time. The
seminars seemed to oscillate between proving that elasticities
were large with markets therefore stable, and formulating competitive hypotheses for apparently imperfectly-competitive industries and coming up with high enough R^2s. Econometrics was
the handmaiden of ideology: things looked imperfect to the naked
eye, especially to that of Chamberlin and Joan Robinson, but they
were "really" not so and the world was "as if" competitive. At
the same time, rather strangely, Chicago seemed to loathe mathematical economics which, everywhere else, went hand in hand
with econometrics and theory. Again ideology explained this
paradox: most mathematical economics seemed to undermine the
case for laissez faire by producing esoteric constraints on existence and stability of competitive equilibrium and by facilitating
the construction of the influential economic case for intervention
—so it was reprehensible. Harry, in fact, had emigrated from a
Cambridge which focused on the theoretical failures of the market mechanism and its apparent imperfections to the Chicago
where the market imperfections were "demonstrated" to be negligible and the imperfections rather of governmental intervention
were the subject of active research. A breath of this different air
would have done any English-trained economist a great deal of
good; but Harry was to inhale it for nearly fifteen years. Harry's
later writings on the developing countries, his impatience with
UNCTAD (which he treated with undisguised and undeserved
contempt), and his *Encounter* piece on Peter Bauer and his critics
were the most overt indications of his shift in the political spec-

trum. However, Harry, who was scintillatingly successful in uncovering the political biases and value judgments in other economists' writings, especially when they were on his left, seemed strangely unaware of his own. I recall a recent letter of his to me, apropos of a piece of mine on multinationals, where he chided me for my (declared) value judgments and contrasted them with his own "scientific" writings, and my replying to him that when we were in Cambridge we both tended to be perhaps model examples of Lionel Robbins's ideal of the "neutral" economist but that, in the years since, the ideological company that we had kept had undoubtedly affected us both, albeit in different directions.

The other remarkable thing that was to happen to Harry on his shift to Chicago, and unrelated to it doubtless, was the extraordinary explosion of his creative and writing energies. Articles and books, edited and written, would flow from his ever-scribbling pen for the rest of his life at an accelerating pace, until he averaged at the end something like three books a year and, at the time of his death, had eighteen articles in proof! Alan Prest notes, in the *Economist*, how Harry was reputed to have finished two articles on one transatlantic flight; I myself saw him start and complete one (an algebraic note, with a literary appendix, on commodity schemes) on a flight back from Geneva where we had been attending an UNCTAD Expert Group session several years ago. Harry often wrote on the same topic for different journals and audiences, much like Keynes, and his papers turned up in exotic journals.

Tradition has it that an American journalist, characteristically hooked on numbers, had gone around Chicago asking the economists how many papers they had published; that, on coming to Stigler, and finding that he had only 70 to his credit, he exclaimed: "How come? There is a much younger professor, just across the corridor, who has published 365!" to which Stigler replied: "Ah, but mine are all different." Funny as this story is, it misses the essence of Harry's approach to publishing. Harry rarely, if ever, published in different places without adding new insights, however small. His mind was ceaselessly active, turning things around endlessly: there was always a new wrinkle. This also reflected the seriousness with which he undertook any professional responsibilities: he was not the one to placate a request for a contribution with a xeroxed version of what he had already written. The same, fundamental sense of professional obligation underlay his willingness to write for obscure journals in the professionally peripheral areas of the world. And, paradoxically, the enormous output of papers and books was to be explained in the same way: Harry thought it a professional obligation to publish rather than to communicate orally to the select few. Long ago, before his creative explosion, Harry explained to me that the Oxbridge tradition of communicating only to one another at High Table was elitist and wrong: that, if one had ideas, it was a professional obligation to put them down in print where the under-privileged, who were not born so well as to get to Oxbridge, would also have access. Few realised the democratic and scholarly instincts that moved Harry to his unique publishing performance.

Harry's range of contributions was equally remarkable. Within the theory of international trade, he straddled both the pure theory and international monetary economics with equal distinction. He made numerous original contributions, in which one must include the papers that he reprinted in his first major book, *International Trade and Economic Growth*, often picking up small ideas and turning them into big constructs. In fact, there was practically no important turn that international economics took in the past two decades where Harry was not in practically at the start. He had a fantastic sense of the novel and the important and rarely missed a good scent. And when he did, as with Linder and Hymer, he zeroed in very quickly afterwards with insightful extensions of his own. Thus, his classic papers on the transfer problem, on tariffs and retaliation, on the effects of tariffs on the terms of trade, on measuring the cost of protection, on customs union theory, on trade and growth, on domestic distortions and optimal policy intervention, on immiserizing growth, on smuggling and illegal trade theory, and on effective protection are on all our reading lists; one is practically embarrassed at the amount of Johnsonia to which one must treat the serious student of trade theory.

In the international monetary field, his classic paper, *Towards a General Theory of the Balance of Payments*, was a model of creative and insightful treatment of the monetary impact of payments deficits, anticipating the later focus on it by a whole generation of his and Mundell's students; he also introduced there the distinction between stock and flow deficits and between expenditure-switching and expenditure-reducing policies. And, more than in pure theory, his powers of creative synthesis were displayed to tremendous advantage in this field. In an area overcrowded with academic entrepreneurs organising conferences on the "latest" issues in international monetary policies, Harry was to come into his own: jet-setting from one conference to another, reviewing and tying together all that he had learned on this circuit, writing with clarity and rigour, helping the physically inactive to catch up with "what was going on."

His last scientific love was also in international monetary theory. He was very much taken up with what he called the monetary approach to balance of payments analysis, considering this (in a letter to Charles Furth of Allen & Unwin) to be the most important piece of work that he had been doing in the past few years. Recognizing the importance that the subject held in the eyes of perhaps the most influential international economist of his generation, John Chipman and I decided to invite a paper from Harry, addressing the issue of how the monetary approach led one to analyse important *policy* problems differently from the earlier absorption and elasticity approaches; and also to invite a major *theoretical* review article of the Frenkel-Johnson book that drew together the principal monetary contributions. The resulting papers of Harry and Frank Hahn appear, by a strange irony of fate, in this very *JIE* issue. But perhaps it is quite appropriate that these contributions on Harry's latest work should appear with this reminiscence: Harry, the professional scientist, could have himself thought of no more fitting tribute to the lasting importance of his work.

The most striking aspect of Harry's later years, however, was his remarkably successful emergence as an insightful and stimulating "thinker," in the vein of John Williams. His Wicksell Lectures are a superb example of this transition: they are not theory in the usual, technical sense, but they are skilfully written and cry out for new ways of thinking about comparative advantage. At the Nobel Institute's Symposium on the Allocation of Economic Activity in Stockholm in June 1976, I saw Harry divesting himself on the role of technology in international trade, not as the distinguished author of the trade-theoretic papers of his youth, but in the grand manner of an intellectual, reflecting on the transition from the nomadic society to the present interdependent world where people earned income in one country, spent it in another, and retired in a third, and on what that could imply for the study of the allocation of economic activity. Harry could think big *and* well; it was not what you would have expected from an economist of his immense technical accomplishments.

In fact, it was this streak of originality and freshness that attracted many of us to him, and not merely his technical mastery. He combined it with a command of style that enabled him to write with distinction in intellectual magazines such as *Encounter* and the London *Spectator*. The blend of historical insights, political and sociological sense, total grasp of the economics of an issue, and his writing skills also made him the favourite choice of the organisers of nearly all the distinguished Lecture series in Economics: he gave, among several others, the Wicksell Lectures, the de Vries Lectures, and the Stamp Lecture.

Harry's enormous interaction with the young international economists since the mid-1950s must also be recorded if one is to assess fully his unique impact on economic science. By the pedestrian criterion, sometimes fashionable among the illiterate, of how many Ph.D. students he guided during his career, Harry was a loser: one searches with difficulty for very many terribly distinguished pupils who were Harry's students in this narrow sense. Harry himself was sometimes fooled by this apparent inadequacy. I recall his theorising, at my Boston apartment, during one of his visits when Harvard was unsuccessfully trying to seduce him, that perhaps it was his tendency to work things out himself very quickly that inhibited students from pursuing leads provided by him. Harry need not have worried. He was, in reality, a truly exciting teacher who, by his example and encouragement, stimulated your interest and raised your sights: even his terseness and rapid pace in the classroom were not a barrier to your perception that here was a uniquely gifted economist, at the frontier of his field, giving you a rare and unified view of its essential structure. But it was everyone, everywhere, who had access to his critical and creative abilities. Countless numbers of manuscripts would reach him, from aspiring students of international economics, and somehow Harry found the energy and the time to read them carefully and to write back to the authors promptly. He continued doing this long after he had started publishing furiously and the opportunity cost of his time had risen astronomically: it was again a telling example of the responsibility that invariably animated his professional behaviour. He once remarked, with dry humour, when he was staying with us and my wife asked him what he had been doing in the early hours of the morning when we had been still asleep: " I read two manuscripts, one indifferent and the other bad; what is worse, I could have written one good paper during that time."

The last time that I saw Harry was at a conference in Tokyo, at the Centennial of the Nihon Keizai Shimbun, in November 1976. He was to lecture in Tokyo right after the conference, fly off to Chicago where he would change planes at the airport for Martinique for another conference and then he was to fly to yet another conference on the sociological role of conferences! The next I heard of him was from T. N. Srinivasan in India who wrote about the V. K. Ramaswami Lecture that Harry had given in New Delhi in January 1977. The second stroke cut him off, not in the infirmity of a once glorious mind, but in the midst of his vital and radiant creativity. He would not have wished to settle for anything less.

On Learned Journals in
Economics

The founding in 1891 of the *Economic Journal* of the Royal Economic Society as a learned journal, where economists write primarily for their peers, was a novel development that marked a break with the nineteenth century tradition, where economists such as Colonel Torrens, James and John Stuart Mill, David Ricardo, and the Reverend Malthus wrote serious economics only in an accessible form in pamphlets and volumes and in letters and essays in newspapers such as the *Traveller* and in magazines such as the *Edinburgh Review*. Their writings were read and even discussed with animation during legislative debates in the British Parliament.

Today's scene is yet further, and vastly, changed. When professional journals began to multiply early, with major university departments putting out their own (for instance, Chicago started the *Journal of Political Economy*, the London School of Economics founded *Economica*), they were all in the "generalist" tradition that was epitomized by the *Economic Journal* (of the Royal Economic Society), edited by John Maynard Keynes and then Roy Harrod.

By the late 1960s, however, there began a dramatic trend toward yet further specialization by fields within economics.

Originally published, in slightly shorter form and titled "The Economic Journal," in the *Times Literary Supplement* (March 7, 1997): 27–28. Reprinted with permission.

North-Holland of Rotterdam played a major pioneering role in the vast proliferation of these specialized journals, with its launching of the *Journal of International Economics* (with myself as the editor) in 1971 and the *Journal of Public Economics* (with Antony Atkinson, Warden of Nuffield College, Oxford, as the editor) almost simultaneously, to be followed by several other publishing firms such as Academic Press with their own journals.

The "narrowing" trend has been now complemented by a "broadening" movement, with new learned journals on the interface of economics with other disciplines now coming more into vogue. The classic journal in this regard used to be Chicago's *Journal of Law and Economics*, where the Chicago brand of economics was used to great effect in analyzing legal issues. But now we have *Economics and Politics* a recent venture from Basil Blackwell, and *Economics and Philosophy*, among others.

The economist today therefore has an immensely rich menu to choose from; and the resource-strapped libraries have their work cut out for them to select from an ever-enlarging number of journals put out by prestigious presses and distinguished editors. The proliferation has to do with both commercial and academic reasons.

In the United States, scholars are used to being bombarded by an army of traveling salesmen whose job it is to seduce them into writing ever more textbooks. While Paul Samuelson's celebrated *Principles* was a breakthrough in teaching and owed little to the profit motive (an amusing but fictional story is that he wrote the text when surprised with triplets), it is impossible to argue anything but the opposite for virtually all the textbooks written in recent years. Now, the presses pursue profits by pursuing us to start journals. The reason is twofold. Often, the younger, promising and upwardly mobile economists will work for nothing, giving their services to the journal because they get exposure and recognition, which they regard as adequate recompense. By contrast, few of them will settle for no royalties on books. But a chief advantage of journals over books is simply that, with journals, you get the (subscription) money ahead of the publication costs; with books, you incur the production and distribution costs ahead of sales. When interest rates are high, this becomes a decisive advantage for journals.

This commercial demand to create new journals is matched by the academic supply. Academics see profit in editing them: it can be seen as a way of setting your stamp on a discipline, influencing the research agenda, and making it in your own image. And, provided you play prudently, resisting the incessant profit-driven demands from the publishers to print more issues, and you do not move until you have the commitment from first-rate people to route some of their work to your new journal, there is really no shortage of good manuscripts to surmount the teething difficulties: good economics has broken out all over. I might remark, in fact, that Robert Frank gets it wrong when he argues in his winner-take-all thesis that the stars now have access to markets everywhere and so will command big premiums; by the same token, there can be also more stars from everywhere, reducing the stars' rewards.

But has this huge outbreak of the learned journals now turned serious economists away from the public policy arena? Will there be no more John Stuart Mill or Keynes, economists at the scientific frontier who communicate with the public and the policy elites instead of being shrouded, as many critics of economics today allege, in mathematics and jargon?

As it happens, serious economists have been attracted into the public arena by the proliferation of the Business sections in virtually every major newspaper, such as the *New York Times* and the *Washington Post* in the United States, and indeed in newspapers in many European countries, as well as by the growth of business and financial magazines. Some of today's best economists therefore walk on two legs: the scientific in the learned journals and the public in the media. And economists have turned again to writing shorter volumes, often of pamphlet length, much like novellas, even aspiring to a nineteenth century persona by entitling their efforts as "An Essay on ..."!

But, as the March 1996 issue of the *Economic Journal* illustrates very well, high theory can be married most successfully to public policy. The issue is an invaluable guide to some of the most compelling concerns of the day, casting scholarly light on issues ranging from why and when privatisation of state enterprises produces efficiency to whether empirical data show that "tenure" in the United Kingdom has diminished recently, an issue that bears directly on the question uppermost in our minds today: whether we are justified in fearing that technical change and the onset of the Global Age have ended "jobs for life." Simon Burgess and Hedley Rees of Bristol, the authors of the latter study, examine British data over 1975–1992 and show that, while there has been a reduction in the average tenure of jobs, by which economists mean the length over which a job is held (a phenomenon measured by the response to the General Household Survey question: how long have you been with your present employer), this is really rather small. For men, having remained around 10.5 years but reached 10.8 in 1982, the average tenure fell to about 9.4 years by 1991. And the picture does not change much if the data are broken down by age groups, though the slight decline is more apparent in the young and the old rather than among the group aged thirty-one to forty-five.

This is more or less the finding of economists for the United States as well in recent years: the length of time over which jobs have been held has not shown a precipitous decline in the past two decades. These studies show that the picture, drawn in the journalistic accounts, of downsizing's having led to the end of the era of long-held jobs is seriously exaggerated. Of course, this is only one, if important, element of the bleak scenario that many buy today; but other studies show that fears that changes in jobs now typically reduce executives to bagging groceries at the supermarkets and that the average search time between jobs has increased dramatically are equally exaggerated, at least for the United States. On the other hand, there is stronger evidence of displacement rates' having increased, especially for senior workers in the United States, so that the overall situation today in the labor markets, while not apocalyptic as many believe, is not comforting either. And we owe this important knowledge to work, using the most sophisticated economic analysis and econometric techniques, mostly carried in learned journals such as the *Economic Journal*.

But perhaps the best illustration today of the fact that it is foolish to draw a firm line between "esoteric" science carried in the learned journals and the needs of public policy in economics is provided by Paul Samuelson's Factor Price Equalization articles, again in the *Economic Journal*, in June 1948 and 1949. Samuelson's work, a piece of high theory in the most learned journal at the time, showed that trade between rich and poor countries would, under certain conditions, equalize wages worldwide. The 1948 article was widely considered to be absurd and wrong, leading Samuelson to write the 1949 article arguing its truth again. With its logical truth then conceded, this Factor Price Equalization theorem was still regarded by economists as a theoretical curiosum. Today, however, it is at the very heart of popular discourse! Ironically, John Cassidy, the engaging economics writer for the *New Yorker*, cited it in a recent column reviewing the arguments on the adverse effect of trade with poor countries on the real wages of workers in the rich countries, while decrying only a few weeks later (December 22, 1996) the capture of economics by mathematics—which discipline is not characterized by ever-more use of mathematics where useful?—and the presumed irrelevance in consequence of theoretical economics to thinking about the economy.

The End of All Our Exploring

Everything for Sale is the reaction of Robert Kuttner, a passionate and prominent American journalist on the Democratic Left, to what he considers to be the wrongheaded and dangerous ascendancy of antigovernment, "markets-only" views as they are expressed in American intellectual and political circles.

The problem with his spirited attack on this position, however, is that the libertarians who would make Adam Smith and Mikhail Bakunin bedfellows are only a small, fringe, group of little political consequence. Tilting against them is no contest. The real and difficult debate is rather between the likes of Kuttner and the many today who think that markets and government matter, but whose enthusiasm for the former is a great deal more impassioned and for the latter a little more cautious than Kuttner's. Indeed, since governments are elected to govern, the practical question again is, not whether there should be governance, but what its scope and content should be.

It cannot be answered without understanding the sharply differing reasons why the enthusiasm for markets, which we owe to Adam Smith (whose own embrace, over two centuries ago, was

---

Originally published under the title "What's Wrong with the Visible Hand" in the *Times Literary Supplement* (November 21, 1997): 28. Reprinted with permission.

This chapter reviews Robert Kuttner's *Everything for Sale: The Virtues and Limits of Markets* (New York: Knopf, 1997).

qualified) has ever since been challenged not merely by its opponents but also by its sophisticated supporters. Kuttner's account, while excellent in many ways, as when he reviews the American debate over airline deregulation, does not quite provide the architecture of the critique of markets that has come from disciplines as diverse as economics, philosophy, and political science. The market's critics can be divided into those who reject markets altogether, those who would limit their scope, and those who would fix them.

From the outset, there have been ideological nihilists, who simply rejected markets. Perhaps the most biting and brilliant attack can be found in Rosa Luxemburg's classic essay on "What Is Economics," the first chapter of a proposed ten-chapter work, only six of which were found in her apartment after her murder. She viewed the "new science of economics," with its legitimation of the "anarchy of capitalist production," as essentially "one of the most important ideological weapons of the bourgeoisie as it struggles with the medieval state and for a modern capitalist state." The "invisible hand," with its rationalization of markets, had a hidden agenda, hence it lacked veracity: a *non sequitur*, of course.

But there have also been mainstream nihilists, within the discipline of economics itself. The most numerous are those who have lost faith in markets because they have discovered that they are often imperfect in practice, and the invisible hand is therefore crippled. The late Nobel laureate, Sir John Hicks of Oxford, observed how the case for free trade had been subtly undermined "in a negative sort of way" by the extension of economic theory in the 1930s from perfect to imperfect competition. The case for free trade had been, by conventional reasoning, based on the assumption that perfect markets, which free trade exploited fully, would guarantee the best economic outcomes; but "if competition hardly ever is perfect, the bottom seems to drop out of the free trade argument. This is in fact a fair description of the state of mind which quite a number of economic students seem to have reached."

There are also those for whom the case for markets is simply not part of their intellectual equipment. Economist Albert Hirschman falls into this category, famously substituting historical experience, narrative, and political discourse for the conventional economic analysis of efficient resource allocation and growth that best allows for a role for markets.

Then again, there are the rejectionists, who lean toward dirigisme because the tastes that markets translate into resource allocation are themselves considered illegitimate. The urge to impose their "meta preferences" on others' preferences comes readily to the intellectual classes that reject authoritarianism and paternalism, but this position comes uncomfortably close to sharing these presumptions. Starting with John Stuart Mill's impassioned assault on the subjection of women, and with the modern trend towards enlarging the rights of children while enhancing parental obligations to them instead, the respect and scope for the autonomy of one's being and one's preferences have increased, however; and the "Aristotelian" assertions of virtue by those who would intrude into those domains are properly treated today with scepticism and scrutiny, if not cynicism.

A more compelling qualification to the rule of markets falls, however, within the domain of what Roy Harrod called "process utilitarianism." In every society, markets in certain matters are considered to be beyond the pale; the process they constitute is morally repugnant. Richard A. Posner, the leading light of the conservative Chicago Law School and a federal judge, is regarded by some as having blown his chance of getting appointed to the U.S. Supreme Court by having argued that a market in adopting babies would be more efficient in its outcomes. Again, there is the British sociologist Richard Titmuss's classic exhortation in *The*

Gift Relationship to retain the traditional donation of blood as an act of altruism and to discard the new selling and buying of it in the marketplace. Titmuss, unlike Posner, argued unpersuasively that the market would also produce an inefficient outcome; but his distaste for a market in blood was evident.

Kuttner is right to remind the libertarians of these limits imposed by every group. But it is equally necessary to recognize that the boundaries we set are continually shifting; and that the space for markets typically tends to enlarge. The economists studying development have long recognized this as the process of "commercialization"; Marxist sociologists recognize it as "commodification"; modern economists and sociologists have seen it as an attribute of "modernization." Inevitably punctuated by the setting of new limits as new technologies and perceptions emerge—as with the separation of sex from procreation which is now raising, with cloning, fundamental ethical questions about the appropriateness of unfettered private choice and markets in babymaking—the historical trend has been relentless in stretching the limits societies put on markets.

But, in the end, once the role for markets is accepted, the classic case against leaving them unfettered comes from economists themselves: if they do not work, they must be fixed. In the terminology that we owe to the Cambridge economist A. C. Pigou, market prices may not reflect social costs, thus fooling the invisible hand into pointing us in the wrong direction. The case for state action then follows as one of intervention designed to change the market prices, typically through taxes and subsidies, to better reflect the true costs. The theory of (activist) economic policy is then built around the exploration of different market failures and appropriate interventions to remedy them.

The conservative response to this corpus of economic analysis has been to advocate a return to a "leave markets alone" philosophy by invoking one or both of two powerful arguments, each of which is multilayered. The first argues that, if markets fail and intervention by the state is deemed to be warranted, the failure is not substantial enough to warrant intervention. This can be done by empirical, econometric analysis. Thus, recently, several international economists, often politically liberal, have dismissed the arguments against free trade that emerged in the 1980s from the forceful revival of the 1930s argument (noted by Hicks) that markets were imperfect. They argue that even smart protectionism would produce negligible improvements.

The conservatives of the remarkable Chicago School in economics worked the same argument in rejecting the assault on markets from the imperfect competition after the 1930s: even if the world looked imperfect to the naked eye, especially of left-leaning economists such as John Kenneth Galbraith, who talked of the small number and the big clout of the large corporations, in truth there was "as if" perfect competition. Econometrics showing this became the conservative instrument for a persuasive assault on the urge to intervene because the lack of perfect competition seemed "obvious."

Assisting in this response was the theoretical notion that market failure could (with the ideologues arguing that it would) be self-correcting: so, it was reasonable to find that such failure would be negligible in scope. The seminal contribution here is that of the British-born Ronald Coase, who settled in Chicago. The Coase theorem, which won him the Noble Prize, was brilliant in the simplicity of his demonstration of how negotiations between disputing parties with property rights clearly assigned would be sufficient, under carefully defined conditions, to create economic efficiency in situations where markets were generally regarded earlier as inadequate.

The second line of attack on those who would fix market failure is served, like Indian curry, in varying ferocities. The mild version simply argues that trying to fix what is broken will likely lead to no improvement because governments cannot have the necessary information or do not have the correct incentives. Friedrich Hayek stressed the former in a classic essay on the uses of knowledge; others, such as James Buchanan and Gordon Tullock, have underlined the latter.

The stronger version, however, is that intervention will make matters worse. The invisible hand may be weak; but the visible hand is yet weaker. But, while it is easy to produce examples where state intervention has made matters worse, it is a different thing to say that intervention is certain to, or even likely to, make matters worse. In specific contexts, such as the making of trade policy in the United States, one could argue this; as a general proposition, one cannot.

Kuttner is right to challenge the exaggerated versions of these assaults on intervention. But he misses the profound role that they have played in thinking about public policy. Coming from the libertarian perspective, Kuttner sees the weaknesses of these arguments. But seen from the interventionism on which we economists have been brought up in the mainstream schools, their strengths are more apparent. There is little doubt that these conservative responses have been intellectually the most rewarding, and for public policy the most productive, set of ideas to arrive on the economic scene since Keynes's General Theory. They have stirred the stagnant waters into which we had fallen, disturbed our shared presuppositions in favor of state action, and forced us to think more rigorously about the role of the state.

In virtually reacting to the arguments against interventionism as if we have reached the conservative conclusions as well, Robert Kuttner makes a common mistake among the ideological liberals. By enriching the debate, conservative economists have instead deepened and therefore strengthened our appreciation of why and when state action matters. As T. S. Eliot put it, "the end of all our exploring / Will be to arrive where we started / And know the place for the first time."

56   A Machine for Going Backwards

India at fifty remains an enigma. Its huge incoherences invite the witticism that, in India, anything and its opposite are true, in consonance with the ancient metaphysics of India: what is, is not. V. S. Naipaul's conversion from an exasperated critic in *An Area of Darkness* to an admiring celebrant in *A Multitude of Mutinies* is thus to be seen, not merely as a personal journey from the shock of first recognition to the fuller understanding that time brings, but also as his confrontation of the diversity that India maddeningly presents.

India's politics and economics underline these contrasts, showing India to be both a success and a failure. The politics, for all its shortcomings, has been an extraordinary success. Now that democracy has spread so widely, it is all too easy to forget that, almost uniquely among the newly liberated nations that entered the second half of this century, India managed to remain democratic despite its multitude of religions and languages and the tragic and inflammatory legacy of the turbulent partition. The brief and misguided descent into emergency rule by Prime Minister Indira Gandhi and its resounding rejection soon thereafter at the polls left Indians even more wedded to the institutions that define the democratic process. The politics of democracy is rarely

Originally published in the *Times Literary Supplement* (August 8, 1997): 11–12. Reprinted with permission.

as neat as that of authoritarian regimes. But the noise of democracy that bothers the rulers further East is wrongly mistaken for chaos. Instead it has been the safety valve of articulated dissent that has held the country together.

But if India's democratic success has made her the unique example for the theorists of democracy today to understand, her economics has been a disappointment. To put it plainly, it has been a disaster. More than a generation has been lost to policies that produced low growth rates, leaving the economy in a state of technological backwardness, low per capita income, high illiteracy, and massive poverty.

India had been marked out in the 1950s as the developing country most likely to succeed economically, with its uncommon assets in entrepreneurship (that, at its apex, boasted the Tatas, who gave India its first steel plant at Jamshedpur, a commercial success without the subventions that would corrupt the economy after independence), political leadership (whose pride was Jawaharlal Nehru), and bureaucracy (with its legendary Indian Civil Service). By the 1980s, however, India's failure had made it the classic case to study to learn what not to do. The success stories turned out to be the small nations in the Far East, characterized by sustained two-digit growth rates (compared with India's average around 3.5 percent over three decades), high levels of literacy that grew in turn with the economy, rising wages, and phenomenally low levels of poverty.

If we celebrate India's economy today, the cause is not India's achievements: for there are too few. Rather, it is India's recent reforms, demanded unsuccessfully by some of us over a quarter century ago, that have begun to undo the policies that crippled her performance. India has regressed to the early 1950s when her promise, not her performance, earned plaudits; the difference is that where India then was in the lead, now it is catching up.

At the moment, we do not know whether the reforms will succeed, or whether India will lapse into its old, sluggish pattern of reforms begun but stalled. If this question is to be answered plausibly, then we must understand why India failed in the first place. The most dramatic source of change, much as in Tony Blair's Labour Party, has been the final discrediting of the failed ideas. India's economic strategy rested on four principal errors: that the external environment for increased exports was bleak, this "export pessimism" justifying an inward-looking import substitution strategy; that, even if greater exploitation of the global economy were possible, it was a peril, not an opportunity: that massive state intervention was necessary, using an extensive licensing system, to guide and monitor production, trade, and investment decisions throughout the economy; and that, while nationalizations were to be generally avoided, investments in public enterprises should steadily expand in successive Five-Year Plans, eventually yielding the millennium of dominant state ownership of the means of production in a Fabian crawl.

Each of these premises turned out to be wrongheaded and fatal to Indian's economic health. As the East Asia experience would prove beyond doubt, export pessimism was a badly mistaken view. The fear of the world economy, moreover, leading to a hostile view of inward foreign investment, reduced it in the end to a trickle, blocking off this route to absorption of new technology, even as the stagnant export earnings, a result of India's import substitution strategy, blocked the absorption of new technologies embodied in imported capital equipment. While India, like the Soviet Union, could produce concentrated attacks on specific technological tasks of immense intricacy, such as picking up nodules from the ocean floor and going into space, the overall state of her technology in economic activity remained abysmal, again like the Soviet Union's.

The licensing system also rapidly degenerated into a "permit Raj," which, by creating a complex web of bureaucratic permissions and sanctions, killed off the possibility of entrepreneurial efficiency and innovation and produced irresistible incentives for the corruption that would become a new but endemic feature of the political scene.

Public enterprises also became an albatross. Soon, they were making losses, reflecting the inefficiency in operation that we have come to understand as a likely outcome because of the incentive structures under which they often operate. But the deleterious effects went far beyond their immediate losses. These enterprises became so dominant, as indeed was planned, that their inefficiency spilled over into other industries: often, they produced essential inputs such as steel, electricity, and transportation. The losses also meant that, instead of contributing to governmental revenues and savings, they became a drain on the budget, adding fuel to the deficit that would grow in the 1980s to the point where it led to the balance-of-payments crisis that threatened bankruptcy in early 1991 and led India finally to begin the reforms.

What led India down this road? Some of the ideas came, as many have remarked, from the politics of Harold Laski at the London School of Economics, and from the economics of Joan Robinson et al. at Cambridge. But it must also be said that, if the seeds were planted in England, much pruning was done in India itself. There was substantial, homegrown culpability on the part of India's economists, no matter that many had studied in England. Faced by the mounting evidence of the bankruptcy of India's policies, the economists generally dug in their heels, often exercising their theoretical talents to rationalize what was non-sensical. It has been well said that any elementary mistake in economics can be turned into a profound truth by ingeniously making the right assumptions to deduce what you want. So India suffered the tyranny of anticpated consequences from the wrong premises.

Thus, when the losses made by public enterprises became obvious, economist Amartya Sen, then at the Delhi School of Economics, wrote saying how economic theory showed that losses could be socially profitable. Indeed, that is true. But the problem was that social profit had little to do with why the losses were being made. Capital-intensive white elephants in the public sector were supported on the basis of models that deduced that this choice of techniques would yield a higher savings rate and hence higher growth: a conclusion that sounds now laughable, were it not so tragic in its consequences. When export pessimism was being successfully challenged already in the 1960s by perceptive economists such as Manmohan Singh, who would usher in the reforms in 1991, creating the possibility that India could have escaped its self-imposed straitjacket of bad policies a lot sooner, the development economists in India were busy building variants of models prescribing "optimal" choice of industries and techniques on the assumption that the economy was closed or had an insuperable export constraint. Economists drawing attention to the absurdities of the licensing system, and its costs, were dismissed by invoking the *non sequitur* that since markets were not perfect, they did not matter, and claiming that a reduced role for industrial policy was therefore reactionary rubbish.

This is now well understood. The reforms have dismantled much, but by no means all, of this remarkable machine for producing backwardness. Industrial and trade controls are greatly diminished, foreign investment is being wooed and even attracted, and the growth rate has picked up. Privatization remains on the shelf, though many sectors, reserved earlier for the public sector, have been opened up to private entry and competition, even from foreign investors.

The enthusiasm for reforms, even impatience with their slow course, are often manifest on the ground. Naipaul's mutineers are keen to enjoy their new economic freedoms and to expand them. No political party can expect to gain votes on a platform that promises to reverse the reforms; at least, they act as if this were so. This should translate into some forward momentum. But the prospects for a complete transition remain problematic, for several reasons.

Indian politics has become, more than ever, coalitional at the centre. The current United Front government has managed better than expected, but there is no doubt that the reform process has slowed down. The new finance minister, Palaniappan Chidambaram, an impassioned reformer in the earlier government of P. V. Narasimha Rao, has been reduced to offering popular tax cuts as a way of demonstrating his commitment to reforms, when in fact the taxes had already been substantially reduced earlier, and new reductions are likely to exacerbate the budget deficits that pose a danger to the economy's macroeconomic stability, and hence to the entire reform process.

Among economists, the old supporters of India's mistaken policies have been largely reduced to prudent silence on the reforms. But their dissent now takes the form of indirection: the obsession with the economic reforms is to be deplored, the economists Jean Dreze and Amartya Sen have recently written, because it "crowds out the time that is left to discuss the abysmal situation of basic education and elementary health care... (and) other issues that have a crucial bearing on the well-being and freedom of the population." The implied notion that reforms are only tangential to the provision of social opportunity of India's masses is a strange throwback to the obscurantism that shielded the inefficient policies from the brunt of early criticisms.

Growth, which reforms would enhance, is not a passive "trickle-down" strategy; rather, it is a radical "pull-up" strategy for removing India's poverty. There is enough evidence now that it works; India's problem has been that there has not been enough growth. Then again, the financing of schools and health programmes requires money which only an expanding economy and revenues can provide. In seeking to undercut the reforms, in the name of poverty and social opportunity, these economists can be justly charged with defeating the very social purposes that they espouse.

Illustration Credits

Chapter 1: A New Epoch

1. Reprinted, by permission, from Ross Garnaut, *Open Regionalism and Trade Liberalization* (Singapore: Institute for Southeast Asian Studies, and Sydney: Allen & Unwin, 1996), 112.

Chapter 4: The Diminished Giant Syndrome

1. Illustration by E. T. Reed, *Punch*, reproduced in Henry W. Lucy, *A Diary of the Unionist Parliament, 1895–1900*, London, 1901, p. 42.

2. Reprinted, by permission of AP/Wide World Photos.

Chapter 10: Super 301's Big Bite Flouts the Rules

1. Reprinted, by permission, from Jagdish Bhagwati and Hugh T. Patrick, eds., *Aggressive Unilateralism: America's 301 Trade Policy and the World Trading System* (Ann Arbor: University of Michigan Press, 1990). © by the University of Michigan Press.

Chapter 18: Samurais No More

1. Courtesy of the Tamba Collection, Kanagawa Prefectural Museum, Yokohama. Anonymous, *View of Yokohama*, ca. 1860. Ink and color on paper, $22\frac{7}{8} \times 52''$.

2. Reprinted, by permission of *Foreign Affairs*.

Chapter 20: Is This Showdown Necessary?

1. Reprinted, by permission of *Newsday*.

Chapter 22: The Case for Free Trade

1. Reprinted, by permission of Robert C. Feenstra, University of California, Davis.

Chapter 27: Beyond NAFTA: Clinton's Trading Choices

1. © .abu.

Chapter 40

1. "Congreso," part of the Tarjetas Cumbre series. Reprinted, by permission of the Movimiento Manuela Ramos. From a postcard supplied by Katie Roberts Hite, Vassar College.

Index